JUSTITIE

Drejtësisë

Giustizia

Pravda

정의

Hustisya

Tieslietu

正義

Second Edition

THEORIES ON **JUSTICE**

John M. Johnson • Sarah Prior
Katherine R. Abbott • Edward Z. Ableser

Arizona State University

Kendall Hunt
publishing company

Cover and interior images © Shutterstock, Inc.

Kendall Hunt
publishing company

www.kendallhunt.com
Send all inquiries to:
4050 Westmark Drive
Dubuque, IA 52004-1840

Printed in the United States of America
10 9 8 7 6 5 4 3 2

Contents

Introduction

Daily global events and the 2012 United States Presidential election raise important justice issues. The U.S. began 2011 by bombing Libya, the 23rd country the U.S. has bombed since last declaring war in 1941, even though the U.S. Constitution requires such a declaration. This raises questions about the legal foundations of American society, about what constitutes a threat to national security, and who should make that decision. Similar issues have been raised with our war efforts in Iraq and Afghanistan, which additionally confronted us with the justice (and Constitutional) issues of torture, using secret prisons outside the U.S., and other "black ops" (secret or clandestine operations). The "War on Terrorism" has led to the highest level of surveillance of our citizens. The recent economic crisis has raised many issues of social and economic justice, about the principles for the distribution of wealth, equal access to education and employment, individual vs. corporate freedom, and how to resolve competing claims for access to material goods. The globalization trends promoted by the Western powers continue some of the worst aspects of the earlier colonial period. Experts and pundits debate the causes of the economic collapse, and meaningful political resolutions depend on these discussions. The 2011 earthquake and tsunami in Japan, which led to the disasters at the nuclear power plants, raise issues of environmental justice, potential life-threatening issues concerning our relationship to the planet and our physical environment. What are the short term and long term consequences of our current practices, and who should make these determinations? How much power should they have? Should all countries have an equal voice? An equal vote? Who should make and enforce the rules?

The U.S. is one of the world leaders in disturbing statistics; rates of incarceration, rates of mass murder, serial murder, homicide and violent crimes, rates of divorce, child maltreatment and sexual exploitation, rates of death by state executions, auto accidents, gun accidents, diabetes, heart problems, and number of people killed by medical interventions. We spend more of our money on defense than all of the rest of the nations of the world combined, and we have more guns and more handguns than anyone else, and yet research since 1956 shows a consistent decline in our sense of security. The U.S. leads the world in rates of mental disorder, mental illness, and chronic diseases, while at the same time seeing educational performance plummet over several decades. Behind each one of these statistics is a justice issue, a question about the fairness of our legal and cultural institutions, a question about how the relative wealth and poverty is distributed. Age-old questions of racial justice, economic justice, and gender justice are still with us today.

Questions about justice originate from our religions. Experts estimate that there may have been as many as 2,000–4,000 religions in the past, but almost all of these were primal, tribal, and confined to small areas. Today we tend to think of religions as the so-called "World Religions," those local and tribal perspectives which expanded beyond their native tribes and local areas, and in the more recent 6,000 years left some kind of historical record. Western civilization has been greatly influenced by the monotheistic religions of the Abrahamic traditions, those that trace their worldly history back to the prophet Abraham: Judaism, Christianity, Islam. Their holy and sacred texts (the Talmud, Bible, and Koran) contain many commentaries about morality and justice, about how individuals should treat each other, and how rulers should act. These ancient texts have much to say about retribution and revenge, but relatively little to say about the complex social issues of our contemporary everyday life and globalized world.

In the Western philosophical tradition it is common to trace the concerns with justice back to Plato's *Republic,* one of the classic texts on this matter. For Plato and those who followed him, justice was a complex virtue, not only a virtue cultivated and developed by individuals, but also a virtue of the social order. This has remained one of the attractions of Plato's *Republic,* as it addresses the questions about the relations of individuals to others and to the larger social order. Plato stresses the potential harmony of a social order where there is a good "fit" between the cultivated virtues of its citizens (especially the leaders, or *guardians*) and the larger social order, or a city-state in Plato's time (about 2,400 years ago). While ancient Greece is considered a "democracy," citizenship was restricted to those who owned property, and excluded women and slaves, similar to the original 1789 U.S. Constitution. Athens was stratified by great racial, class, power, and gender inequalities, yet Plato had little to say about how these patterns emerged, how they served dominant interests, and how the structure could be changed to produce a greater sense of justice among those who lived under Athenian rule. Still, Plato should be credited with raising a fundamental question which is still debated today, should a society be in the business of promoting or developing the virtues of its citizens, or is this the business of other institutions such as the family, neighborhood, and church?

In the Old Testament of the Bible, the meaning of justice is closely related to ideas about punishment. By the time of Plato's *Republic,* however, revenge and retribution were seen as vices rather than virtues, and the idea of justice was associated with concepts of the ideal community. Plato thought that an ideal society would be a peaceful and harmonious social order, where the diverse interests and social classes would do their best to achieve a certain kind of functional interdependence, based upon their respective skills and roles. All institutions and all practices would be based on "Reason," which meant, for Plato, a studied deliberation of the right thing to do in order to achieve the overarching goal of social harmony. The guardians, or leaders, would be selected, at a very early age, from among the aristocracy, separated from their parents, and trained for many years at the best schools, with the best teachers, before undergoing a lengthy apprenticeship of military and then political leadership. The guardians would be motivated by the highest ideals, and would not take any pay or compensation for their leadership. The political unit in Plato's time was the relatively small city-state, much less complex than contemporary nation-states throughout our world. Still, Plato is commonly credited with asking fundamental questions about justice, especially those concerning the correct or appropriate relationship between individual citizens, and between rulers and citizens.

Plato's *Republic* develops a comprehensive theory about justice, but it is only one of many such theories. *What is a theory?* Perhaps it is best to view a theory or a theoretical perspective as a kind of search light or spotlight, a beam that shines on and illuminates some portion of the everyday world in which we live. Theories can then be seen as more or less comprehensive, meaning that they can illuminate more or less of empirical reality. While this metaphor is initially useful, it neglects the starting point or beginning point of justice, our values and our ideas about God or human nature. Many theories are built upon a foundation, certain key ideas about "human nature" which are asserted by the theorist. When we use the phrase "human nature" we commonly refer to assertions about what is universal or invariant among all peoples. Some theorists have a very dismal or negative view of human nature. Perhaps British philosopher Thomas Hobbes is the best exemplar of this negative view. Hobbes thought that human beings were very competitive, aggressive, and potentially violent with all of their fellow human beings, and with this "reading" of human nature he proposed a strong central state to control the potentially aggressive and unruly behaviors of its citizens. The eighteenth-century French philosopher Jean-Jacques Rousseau expresses a much different view of human nature, one founded on self-love and thus potential love for others, so he envisioned a more cooperative and less repressive state power to regulate the activities of citizens. So these highly abstract, or philosophical, ideas about human nature are embedded in the theorist's concepts of the ideal, or just, society. This is why we address this topic in the first section of this book. We present readings by important philosophers and theorists to represent some of these ideas about human nature. Do human beings have a nature? Is it a loving and cooperative nature or a selfish, aggressive, and potentially violent one? Do men and women share the same "human nature"? Do people from different cultures have the same human nature? Do individuals have the same nature through the life cycle, or does one's nature change from infancy to childhood to adolescence to young adulthood to parenthood to old age? What are the implications of human nature? Does it mean that a society or culture should be founded upon these ideas in such a manner so as to be consistent with them? Or does it mean that human nature is something to be changed by the society (as was tried in Russia's Soviet regime, China's regime under Mao Zedong, or Pol Pot's regime in Cambodia)? Can all or part of human nature be changed by education? Plato assigned a very important role to education and political leadership; he thought these institutions could lead all citizens to accept their proper role in a peaceful and harmonious social order.

In the second section of this book we present readings about social relationships and intersections; such concerns of justice also involve human nature. What do we owe other persons in our life, including friends, siblings, spouses, children, other family members, strangers, foreign visitors, and other community members? How are we to act toward these other individuals, and how should we regard them? Do we have an obligation to accept the values and moral norms of our own family-of-origin, which in some cultures might include killing a family member who challenged the "honor" of the family? Are we obligated to follow our own cultural laws and norms, even when these differ from more universal ideas about human rights? Should our behavior be different in public settings (where people of different values, cultures, sexual preferences, religions, ethnicities come to do their common business) as opposed to private settings or situations? How should men act toward other men, women, and vice versa? How should we act toward individuals who are members of historically oppressed or stigmatized groups, such as African Americans, women, the disabled, or indigenous people? How should we express or regulate our emotions and the complex personhood with so many diverse and cross-cutting boundaries? These issues may not involve the larger issues of state and legal institutions, but they influence how we will experience our daily lives, and thus how we routinely experience justice or its opposite.

The third section of this book raises questions about governance. What is the best type of government? Is democracy the best? Why? Should citizens have absolute rights which have to be legally protected by the state? If so, what rights? If not, what are the prerogatives and limitations of government? What should be the laws, and how should these be decided? How should they be protected? How can they be changed? Who should be the leaders, and what should be their qualifications? What should be the appropriate span of government for the national, state, regional, and local levels? Should the state protect the rights of minorities, or should there be rule by the majority? How much power should be given to regulatory authorities? How should the government be involved in the promotion or regulation of private business activities? These are only a few of the many important questions and issues about governance, and we can see many others raised in the run-up to the 2012 national elections.

The fourth section of this book addresses questions about the law and legal institutions, and how these are related to justice. What should be the powers of the state to punish? Who should decide this, and what are the limitations or restrictions on these powers? Who decides the criminal laws, and what are the procedural rules and safeguards for citizens? Should the government, or its elected officials, try to regulate the moral preferences of citizens? What should the punishments be? What kind of legal standing should business corporations have? What activities (nuclear power generation, meat processing, food production, operation of hospitals and schools) should be regulated and how?

The fifth section of this book raises questions about the economy. What kind of economy is the most just? Is it an economy (like socialism) which tries to minimize economic differences among individuals or groups, or one that tries (like communism) to eliminate them altogether? Is it an economy (like most mixed economies of today) which values economic incentives for individuals or corporations, and thus tolerates a great degree of economic difference? What should be the regulations or limitations of financial or other markets? Who should enforce these? How should wages or salaries or incomes be decided? How are we to regard the poor among us? Should there be entitlement programs to "even the playing field" for historically disadvantaged groups? How should these groups be treated in the economic sphere of society? Who should be taxed? How much? Who should decide the taxation procedures, and what should be the limitations or restrictions on these? What should be the role of the national state in the economic sphere? Should workers have the right to organize into labor unions? How should conflicts be resolved between labor and business leaders? Who should have ownership rights of businesses? Do the disabled have equal rights to work? These are just some of the many important issues concerning the economy, and most of these are subject to continuing conflicts, debates, and struggles. There are competing theories on all these issues, and these theories have competing ideas about a just society or global system. Our readings here only touch the surface of these complicated issues.

The readings in all of the sections of this book raise questions about justice, and these questions involve abstract or theoretical understandings of how societies do, in fact, operate, and/or how they should operate. If one seeks to produce a lasting or meaningful social change, then it is imperative to have a good theory, a theory which accurately portrays how society or some part of it actually operates.

Human Nature

This section is dedicated to laying the foundation for the differing views in which human nature informs the different theories of justice. Starting out by understanding the various views of human nature, it is easier to understand how theories of justice are constructed in other societal structures, such as relationships, family, gender, race, economy, governance, and law. The ability to deconstruct these and many other societal structures to the origins of human nature will enable and empower a more successful dialogue for opposing ideologies to understand each other.

Human Nature

One question some philosophers wrestle with is, "What is human nature?" How can the origins of human nature be deconstructed in order to make sense of the world we live in? The most common debate around human nature is structured between two principles: first, that human nature is equal and neutral, without moral judgment; and second, that human nature is inherently self-interested. Here is what various philosophers would say about human nature:

- John Locke states that human nature is a state "of equality, wherein all the power and jurisdiction is reciprocal" and each human has the "liberty to dispose of his person or possessions"; however, all of humankind is "equal and independent, no one ought to harm his life, health, liberty or possession" because we are all the property of God.
- Mencius promotes that "men have these four innate feelings", stating that the "feeling of distress (at the suffering of others) is the first sign of Humanity. This feeling of shame and disgrace is the first sign of Justice. This feeling of deference to others is the first sign of propriety. This sense of right and wrong is the first sign of wisdom."
- Jean-Jacques Rousseau states that there is a "common liberty (which) results from the nature of man . . . and all, being born free and equal, alienate their liberty only for their own advantage".
- Thomas Hobbes has a more sullen view of human nature, stating, "For such is the nature of men, that howsoever they may acknowledge many others to be more witty, or more eloquent, or more learned; yet they will hardly believe there be many so wise as themselves: for they see their own wit at hand, and other men's at a distance."
- St. Thomas Aquinas writes about human nature as humankind's soul and states, "Whereas the intellect apprehends existence absolutely, and for all time; so that everything that has an intellect naturally desires always to exist. But a natural desire cannot be in vain. Therefore, every intellectual substance is incorruptible."

Theories on Justice

One popular view of human nature stems from a religious perspective. This view of human nature uses the terms *good* and *evil* as representations of a religious philosophy. The idea that human nature can be inherently *good* assumes, essentially, that an individual's action, based on an instinctual, inherent nature from a God, is appropriate and correct. In contrast, the idea that human nature can be inherently *evil* entails the belief that an individual's actions, rooted in instinct and one's human nature, will be self-serving, inappropriate, and outside the will of God. The idea that one's inherent actions can be *evil* is a religious perspective and is rooted in the idea that humankind, apart from the direction of a higher power, acts within its *evil* nature. As stated in the Bible, in Romans 8:7, the "mind that is set on the flesh is hostile to God, and those who are in the flesh cannot please God".

As seen in this section, a libertarian theory of justice is based in the understanding that human nature is inherently *neutral* and *equal*. Libertarian justice maintains that individuals should be free of constraint over their life, liberty, and property, all of which are equally essential to a system of justice. As John Locke states, "All men are naturally in a state of perfect freedom to order their actions, and dispose of their possessions and persons, as they think fit, within the bounds of the law of nature".

Likewise, a contractarian theory of justice has some notions that human nature is inherently *neutral*. Contractarian theories hold that the primary principles in society are built upon the common will of the people in constructing a social contract, which promotes humankind's equality, independence, and freedom. Mencius states that "it is a feeling common to all mankind that they cannot bear to see others suffer". Along the same line, Jean-Jacques Rousseau states, "man is born free; and everywhere he is in chains", and that the first law in the nature of humankind "is to provide for his own preservation, he is the sole judge of the proper means of preserving himself".

This section will also explore an egalitarian theory of justice, in which the notion of human nature is inherently *self-interested*. Egalitarianism holds that as human nature acts in its own self-preserving way, regulations are essential in guiding individuals and society. Egalitarianism views justice as common restrictions and investments in order to produce fairness and equity amongst the citizenry. It is the hope that shared responsibility and regulation will yield not only material liberty (as with the libertarians), but will also create psychological and spiritual liberty, because of the shared moral code that the community follows. In *Summa Theologica*, St. Thomas Aquinas, discusses human nature, in that though "man and animals have a like beginning in generation is true of the body", however, "the human soul is produced by God". He is saying that the self-interested person in nature is that of the "brutes and is produced by some power of the body". In the same way, Thomas Hobbes wrote in the *Leviathan* that human nature is "solitary, poor, nasty, brutish and short" and the "condition of man is a condition of war of everyone against everyone". This view that human nature is inherently self-interested sets the foundation for a collective will to order and control the selfish behavior of humans to protect the good of all.

Historical Context

In this section there is a selection from *The Second Treatise of Government* by John Locke. Locke wrote this philosophical manuscript in 1690, as a defense for the overthrow of King James II, so that King William III could gain control of the United Kingdom. This is known as the *Glorious Revolution*. Locke objected to the religious controls that King James II was instituting and, with the help of the Whigs, the wealthy noblemen party, he helped defend this Glorious Revolution in which King William III took control. John Locke advocated for the liberty and sovereignty of all individuals acting in accordance with the rightness of their own nature. According to Locke, the monarchy of the United Kingdom limited humankind's liberty and freedom, thus *The Second Treatise of Government* challenged the monarchy to endow each human "the right to punish the offender, and be executioner of the law of nature" and claim liberty.

The Chinese philosopher Mencius wrote on human nature around the time of Plato (371–298 B.C.E.), in his work titled *On the Mind*. Mencius emphasized the idea of "humaneness" and "humanity" as traits inherent in all and guiding all. Mencius states, "The abilities men have which are not acquired by study are part of their endowment of good". Mencius also paints a strong social critique of society growing selfish and cutthroat; he asks, "Can it be that man's mind naturally lacks Humanity and Justice? If he loses his sense of good, then he loses it as the mountain lost its trees. It has been hacked away at—day after day—what of its beauty then?" His philosophical writings were intended to be a curriculum for the kings of China as a contract to live by, but he was unsuccessful in having any government adopt them. As a student of China's greatest philosopher, Confucius, Mencius gained recognition and respect for his ideals regarding justice. Yet, throughout Chinese history, the writings of Mencius have been banned because of his revolutionary idea that all are bound by a social contract, and if the King does not act in a humane fashion, the people can rebel.

Another reading in this section comes from the philosopher Jean-Jacques Rousseau, and is found in his 1762 book, *The Social Contract*. Rousseau, a French Enlightenment thinker, had his foot in both the philosophical camps of Locke and of Hobbes. In his writings, Rousseau asserts that humankind must be granted their freedoms and liberties in order to act appropriately without certain constraints; however, he also interjects that society must be governed by a social contract, where humans may lose their "natural liberty" but will instead gain their "civil liberty". This new sense of liberty, one that is embedded in a strong civility and citizenship, is influenced by Aristotle. This reading provides a helpful bridge to absolute controls of a government, for which thinkers like Hobbes and Aquinas lobby.

The next reading that will be examined is a portion of the 1651 book *Leviathan*, by Thomas Hobbes. In this reading, Hobbes has a strong belief that the nature of humanity is inherently and originally self-interested. This nature that is so selfish must be regulated and controlled so as to not destroy humanity. Hobbes, who sought to maintain the royal Monarchy in the United Kingdom during a time in which the republicanism of the people's Parliament was advancing, was fearful of the "brutish" and "warring" nature of man. Hobbes' writings are pivotal in understanding the arguments for "absolutism" in governance as a means to regulate society for its optimal success.

St. Thomas Aquinas provides a final reading on human nature, which is part of his 1274 completed book, *Summa Theologica*. Aquinas' writings were intended to be a primer on Christianity, for new Christians, about the theology of the faith. He writes that the human body is of the world, and if led by the world is corruptible; however, the human soul is of God and is based in the actions of love. In this selection, Aquinas posits that the nature of humanity as flesh and body is in opposition to God, thus humankind must be led by their soul, which is not corruptible. Aquinas' works creates a justification for "absolute" rule by the church in society to protect and empower individuals into Godly actions of their soul.

As you read in this section, there are various perspectives of human nature, which critique diverse notions of justice. By beginning with human nature we can see how theories on justice are constructed in other institutions of society such as social relations.

References

McGrath, A.E. (Ed) 1992. *The Holy Bible: New international version.* Grand Rapids, MI: Zondervan Publishing House.

SECOND TREATISE OF GOVERNMENT

JOHN LOCKE

Sect. 4. To understand political power right, and derive it from its original, we must consider, what state all men are naturally in, and that is, a state of perfect freedom to order their actions, and dispose of their possessions and persons, as they think fit, within the bounds of the law of nature, without asking leave, or depending upon the will of any other man.

A state also of equality, wherein all the power and jurisdiction is reciprocal, no one having more than another; there being nothing more evident, than that creatures of the same species and rank, promiscuously born to all the same advantages of nature, and the use of the same faculties, should also be equal one amongst another without subordination or subjection, unless the lord and master of them all should, by any manifest declaration of his will, set one above another, and confer on him, by an evident and clear appointment, an undoubted right to dominion and sovereignty.

Sect. 5. This equality of men by nature, the judicious Hooker looks upon as so evident in itself, and beyond all question, that he makes it the foundation of that obligation to mutual love amongst men, on which he builds the duties they owe one another, and from whence he derives the great maxims of justice and charity. His words are,

> The like natural inducement hath brought men to know that it is no less their duty, to love others than themselves; for seeing those things which are equal, must needs all have one measure; if I cannot but wish to receive good, even as much at every man's hands, as any man can wish unto his own soul, how should I look to have any part of my desire herein satisfied, unless myself be careful to satisfy the like desire, which is undoubtedly in other men, being of one and the same nature? To have any thing offered them repugnant to this desire, must needs in all respects grieve them as much as me; so that if I do harm, I must look to suffer, there being no reason that others should shew greater measure of love to me, than they have by me shewed unto them: my desire therefore to be loved of my equals in nature as much as possible may be, imposeth upon me a natural duty of bearing to them-ward fully the like affection; from which relation of equality between ourselves and them that are as ourselves, what several rules and canons natural reason hath drawn, for direction of life, no man is ignorant, Eccl. Pol. Lib. 1.

Sect. 6. But though this be a state of liberty, yet it is not a state of licence: though man in that state have an uncontroulable liberty to dispose of his person or possessions, yet he has not liberty to destroy himself, or so much as any creature in his possession, but where some nobler use than its bare preservation calls for it. The state of nature has a law of nature to govern it, which obliges every one: and reason, which is that law, teaches all mankind, who will but consult it, that being all equal and independent, no one ought to harm another in his life, health, liberty, or possessions: for men being all the workmanship of one omnipotent, and infinitely wise maker; all the servants of one sovereign master, sent into the world by his order, and about his business; they are his property, whose workmanship they are, made to last during his, not one another's pleasure: and being furnished with like faculties, sharing all in one community of nature, there cannot be supposed any such subordination among us, that may authorize us to destroy one another, as if we were made for one another's uses, as the inferior ranks of creatures are for our's. Every one, as he is bound to preserve himself, and not to quit his station wilfully, so by the like reason, when his own preservation comes not in competition, ought he, as much as he can, to preserve the rest of mankind, and may not, unless it be to do justice on an offender, take away, or impair the life, or what tends to the preservation of the life, the liberty, health, limb, or goods of another.

Sect. 7. And that all men may be restrained from invading others rights, and from doing hurt to one another, and the law of nature be observed, which willeth the peace and preservation of all mankind, the execution of the law of nature is, in that state, put into every man's hands, whereby every one has a right to punish the transgressors of that law to such a degree, as may hinder its violation: for the law of nature would, as all other laws that concern men in this world 'be in vain, if there were no body that in the state of nature had a power to execute that law, and thereby preserve the innocent and restrain offenders. And if any one in the state of nature may punish another for any evil he has done, every one may do so: for in that state of perfect equality, where naturally there is no superiority or jurisdiction of one over another, what any may do in prosecution of that law, every one must needs have a right to do.

Sect. 8. And thus, in the state of nature, one man comes by a power over another; but yet no absolute or arbitrary power, to use a criminal, when he has got him in his hands, according to the passionate heats, or boundless extravagancy of his own will; but only to retribute to him, so far as calm reason and conscience dictate, what is proportionate to his transgression, which is so much as may serve for reparation and restraint: for these two are the only reasons, why one man may lawfully do harm to another, which is that we call punishment. In transgressing the law of nature, the offender declares himself to live by another rule than that of reason and common equity, which is that measure God has set to the actions of men, for their mutual security; and so he becomes dangerous to mankind, the tye, which is to secure them from injury and violence, being slighted and broken by him. Which being a trespass against the whole species, and the peace and safety of it, provided for by the law of nature, every man upon this score, by the right he hath to preserve mankind in general, may restrain, or where it is necessary, destroy things noxious to them, and so may bring such evil on any one, who hath transgressed that law, as may make him repent the doing of it, and thereby deter him, and by his example others, from doing the like mischief. And in the case, and upon this ground, EVERY MAN HATH A RIGHT TO PUNISH THE OFFENDER, AND BE EXECUTIONER OF THE LAW OF NATURE.

Sect. 9. I doubt not but this will seem a very strange doctrine to some men: but before they condemn it, I desire them to resolve me, by what right any prince or state can put to death, or punish an alien, for any crime he commits in their country. It is certain their laws, by virtue of any sanction they receive from the promulgated will of the legislative, reach not a stranger: they speak not to him, nor, if they did, is he bound to hearken to them. The legislative authority, by which they are in force over the subjects of that commonwealth, hath no power over him. Those who have the supreme power of making laws in England, France or Holland, are to an Indian, but like the rest of the world, men without authority: and therefore, if by the law of nature every man hath not a power to punish offences against it, as he soberly judges the case to require, I see not how the magistrates of any community can punish an alien of another country; since, in reference to him, they can have no more power than what every man naturally may have over another.

Sect, 10. Besides the crime which consists in violating the law, and varying from the right rule of reason, whereby a man so far becomes degenerate, and declares himself to quit the principles of human nature, and to be a noxious creature, there is commonly injury done to some person or other, and some other man receives damage by his transgression: in which case he who hath received any damage, has, besides the right of punishment common to him with other men, a particular right to seek reparation from him that has done it: and any other person, who finds it just, may also join with him that is injured, and assist him in recovering from the offender so much as may make satisfaction for the harm he has suffered.

Sect. 11. From these two distinct rights, the one of punishing the crime for restraint, and preventing the like offence, which right of punishing is in every body; the other of taking reparation, which belongs only to the injured party, comes it to pass that the magistrate, who by being magistrate hath the common right of punishing put into his hands, can often, where the public good demands not the execution of the law, remit the punishment of criminal offences by his own authority, but yet cannot remit the satisfaction due to any private man for the damage he has received. That, he who has suffered the damage has a right to demand in his own name, and he alone can remit: the damnified person has this power of appropriating to himself the goods or service of the offender, by right of self-preservation, as every man has a power to punish the crime, to prevent its being committed again, by the right he has of preserving all mankind, and doing all reasonable things he can in order to that end: and thus it is, that every man, in the state of nature, has a power to kill a murderer, both to deter others from doing the like injury, which no reparation can compensate, by the example of the punishment that attends it from every body, and also to secure men from the attempts of a criminal, who having renounced reason, the common rule and measure God hath given to mankind, hath, by the unjust violence and slaughter he hath committed upon one, declared war against all mankind, and therefore may be destroyed as a lion or a tyger, one of those wild savage beasts, with whom men can have no society nor security: and upon this is grounded that great law of nature, Whoso sheddeth man's blood, by man shall his blood be shed. And Cain was so fully convinced, that every one had a right to destroy such a criminal, that after the murder of his brother, he cries out, Every one that findeth me, shall slay me; so plain was it writ in the hearts of all mankind.

Sect. 12. By the same reason may a man in the state of nature punish the lesser breaches of that law. It will perhaps be demanded, with death? I answer, each transgression may be punished to that degree, and with so much severity, as will suffice to make it an ill bargain to the offender, give him cause to repent, and terrify others from doing the like. Every offence, that can be committed in the state of nature, may in the state of nature be also punished equally, and as far forth as it may, in a commonwealth: for though it would be besides my present purpose, to enter here into the particulars of the law of nature, or its measures of punishment; yet, it is certain there is such a law, and that too, as intelligible and plain to a rational creature, and a studier of that law, as the positive laws of commonwealths; nay, possibly plainer; as much as reason is easier to be understood, than the fancies and intricate contrivances of men, following contrary and hidden interests put into words; for so truly are a great part of the municipal laws of countries, which are only so far right, as they are founded on the law of nature, by which they are to be regulated and interpreted.

Sect. 13. To this strange doctrine, viz. That in the state of nature every one has the executive power of the law of nature, I doubt not but it will be objected, that it is unreasonable for men to be judges in their own cases, that self-love will make men partial to themselves and their friends: and on the other side, that ill nature, passion and revenge will carry them too far in punishing others; and hence nothing but confusion and disorder will follow, and that therefore God hath certainly appointed government to restrain the partiality and violence of men. I easily grant, that civil government is the proper remedy for the inconveniencies of the state of nature, which must certainly be great, where men may be judges in their own case, since it is easy to be imagined, that he who was so unjust as to do his brother an injury, will scarce be so just as to condemn himself for it: but I shall desire those who make this objection, to remember, that absolute monarchs are but men; and if government is to be the remedy of those evils, which necessarily follow from men's being judges in their own cases, and the state of nature is therefore not to how much better it is than the state of nature, where one man, commanding a multitude, has the liberty to be judge in his own case, and may do to all his subjects whatever he pleases, without the least liberty to any one to question or controul those who execute his pleasure? and in whatsoever he cloth, whether led by reason, mistake or passion, must be submitted to? much better it is in the state of nature, wherein men are not bound to submit to the unjust will of another: and if he that judges, judges amiss in his own, or any other case, he is answerable for it to the rest of mankind.

Sect. 14. It is often asked as a mighty objection, where are, or ever were there any men in such a state of nature? To which it may suffice as an answer at present, that since all princes and rulers of independent governments all through the world, are in a state of nature, it is plain the world never was, nor ever will be, without numbers of men in that state. I have named all governors of independent communities, whether they are, or are not, in league with others: for it is not every compact that puts an end to the state of nature between men, but only this one of agreeing together mutually to enter into one community, and make one body politic; other promises, and compacts, men may make one with another, and yet still be in the state of nature. The promises and bargains for truck, &c. between the two men in the desert island, mentioned by Garcilasso de la Vega, in his history of Peru; or between a Swiss and an Indian, in the woods of America, are binding to them, though they are perfectly in a state of nature, in reference to one another: for truth and keeping of faith belongs to men, as men, and not as members of society.

Sect. 15. To those that say, there were never any men in the state of nature, I will not only oppose the authority of the judicious Hooker, Eccl. Pol. lib. i. sect. 10, where he says,

> The laws which have been hitherto mentioned, i.e. the laws of nature, do bind men absolutely, even as they are men, although they have never any settled fellowship, never any solemn agreement amongst themselves what to do, or not to do: but forasmuch as we are not by ourselves sufficient to furnish ourselves with competent store of things, needful for such a life as our nature doth desire, a life fit for the dignity of man; therefore to supply those defects and imperfections which are in us, as living single and solely by ourselves, we are naturally induced to seek communion and fellowship with others: this was the cause of men's uniting themselves at first in politic societies.

But I moreover affirm, that all men are naturally in that state, and remain so, till by their own consents they make themselves members of some politic society; and I doubt not in the sequel of this discourse, to make it very clear.

MENCIUS, "JUSTICE AND HUMANITY," FROM *ON THE MIND*

6.1

Mencius said, "It is a feeling common to all mankind that they cannot bear to see others suffer. The Former Kings had such feelings, and it was this that dictated their policies. One could govern the entire world with policies dictated by such feelings, as easily as though one turned it in the palm of the hand.

"I say that all men have such feelings because, on seeing a child about to fall into a well, everyone has a feeling of horror and distress. They do not have this feeling out of sympathy for the parents, or to be thought well of by friends and neighbours, or from a sense of dislike at not being thought a feeling person. Not so feel distress would be contrary to all human feeling. Just as not to feel shame and disgrace and not to defer to others and not to have a sense of right and wrong are contrary to all human feeling. This feeling of distress (at the suffering of others) is the first sign of Humanity. This feeling of shame and disgrace is the first sign of Justicé. This feeling of deference to others is the first sign of propriety. This sense of right and wrong is the first sign of wisdom. Men have these four innate feelings just as they have four limbs. To possess these four things, and to protest that one is incapable of fulfilling them, is to deprive oneself. To protest that the ruler is incapable of doing so is to deprive him since all have these four capacities within themselves, they should know how to develop and to fulfil them. They are like a fire about to burst into flame, or a spring about to gush forth from the ground. If, in fact, a ruler can fully realize them, he has all that is needed to protect the entire world. But if he does not realize them fully, he lacks what is needed to serve even his own parents."

6.2

Mencius said, "All men have things they cannot tolerate, and if what makes this so can be fully developed in the things they can tolerate, the result is Humanity. All men have things they will not do, and if what makes this so can be fully developed in the things they will do, then Justice results. If a man can fully exploit the thing in his mind which makes him not wish to harm others, then Humanity will result in overwhelming measure. If a man can fully exploit the thing in his mind which makes him reluctant to break through or jump over (other people's) walls, Justice will ensue in overwhelming measure." . . .

6.9

If the prince is a man of Humanity then nothing in his state but will be Humane. If the prince is a man of Justice, then nothing in his state but will be Just.

6.19

The difference between a man and an animal is slight. The common man disregards it altogether, but the True Gentleman guards the distinction most carefully. Shun understood all living things, but saw clearly the relationships that exist uniquely among human beings. These relationships proceed from Humanity and Justice, it is not because of these relationships that we proceed towards Humanity and Justice.

6.20

Mencius said, "Bull Mountain was once beautifully wooded. But, because it was close to a large city, its trees all fell to the axe. What of its beauty then? However, as the days passed things grew, and with the rains and the dews it was not without greenery. Then came the cattle and goats to graze. That is why, today, it has that scoured-like appearance. On seeing it now, people imagine that nothing ever grew there. But this is surely not the true nature of a mountain? And so, too, with human beings. Can it be that any man's mind naturally lacks Humanity and Justice? If he loses his sense of the good, then he loses it as the mountain lost its trees. It has been hacked away at—day after day—what of its beauty then?

"However, as the days pass he grows, and, as with all men, in the still air of the early hours his sense of right and wrong is at work. If it is barely perceptible, it is because his actions during the day have disturbed or destroyed it. Being disturbed and turned upside down the 'night airs' can barely sustain it. If this happens he is not far removed from the animals. Seeing a man so close to an animal, people cannot imagine that once his nature was different—but this is surely not the true nature of the man? Indeed, if nurtured aright, anything will grow, but if not nurtured aright anything will wither away. Confucius said, 'Hold fast to it, and you preserve it; let it go and you destroy it; it may come and go at any time no one knows its whereabouts.' Confucius was speaking of nothing less than the mind."

6.21

Mencius said, "I am fond of fish, but, too, I am fond of bear's paws. If I cannot have both, then I prefer bear's paws. I care about life, but, too, I care about Justice. If I cannot have both, then I choose Justice. I care about life, but then there are things I care about more than life. For that reason I will not seek life improperly. I do not like death, but then there are things I dislike more than death. For that reason there are some contingencies from which I will not escape.

"If men are taught to desire life above all else, then they will seize it by all means in their power. If they are taught to hate death above all else, then they will avoid all contingencies by which they might meet it. There are times when one might save one's life, but only by means that are wrong. There are times when death can be avoided, but only by means that are improper. Having desires above life itself and having dislikes greater than death itself is a type of mind that all men possess—it is not only confined to the worthy. What distinguishes the worthy is that he ensures that he does not lose it.

"Even though it be a matter of life or death to him, a traveller will refuse a basket of rice or a dish of soup if offered in an insulting manner. But food that has been trampled upon, not even a beggar will think fit to eat. And yet a man will accept emoluments of ten thousand *chung* regardless of the claims of propriety and Justice. And what does he gain by that? Elegant palaces and houses, wives and concubines to wait on him, and the allegiance of the poor among his acquaintance! I was previously speaking of matters affecting life and death, where even there under certain conditions one will not accept relief, but this is a matter of palaces and houses, of wives and concubines, and of time-serving friends. Should we not stop such things? This is what I mean by 'losing the mind with which we originally were endowed.'"

6.42

Mencius said, "The abilities men have which are not acquired by study are part of their endowment of good. The knowledge men have which is not acquired by deep thought is part of their endowment of good. Every baby in his mother's arms knows about love for his parents. When they grow up, they know about the respect they must pay to their elder brothers. The love for parents is Humanity. The respect for elders is Justice. It is nothing more than this, and it is so all over the world."

THE SOCIAL CONTRACT

JEAN-JACQUES ROUSSEAU

Book I

I mean to inquire if, in the civil order, there can be any sure and legitimate rule of administration, men being taken as they are and laws as they might be. In this inquiry I shall endeavour always to unite what right sanctions with what is prescribed by interest, in order that justice and utility may in no case be divided.

I enter upon my task without proving the importance of the subject. I shall be asked if I am a prince or a legislator, to write on politics. I answer that I am neither, and that is why I do so. If I were a prince or a legislator, I should not waste time in saying what wants doing; I should do it, or hold my peace.

As I was born a citizen of a free State, and a member of the Sovereign, I feel that, however feeble the influence my voice can have on public affairs, the right of voting on them makes it my duty to study them: and I am happy, when I reflect upon governments, to find my inquiries always furnish me with new reasons for loving that of my own country.

Chapter I

Subject of the First Book

Man is born free; and everywhere he is in chains. One thinks himself the master of others, and still remains a greater slave than they. How did this change come about? I do not know. What can make it legitimate? That question I think I can answer.

If I took into account only force, and the effects derived from it, I should say: "As long as a people is compelled to obey, and obeys, it does well; as soon as it can shake off the yoke, and shakes it off, it does still better; for, regaining its liberty by the same right as took it away, either it is justified in resuming it, or there was no justification for those who took it away." But the social order is a sacred right which is the basis of all other rights. Nevertheless, this right does not come from nature, and must therefore be founded on conventions. Before coming to that, I have to prove what I have just asserted.

Chapter II

The First Societies

The most ancient of all societies, and the only one that is natural is the family: and even so the children remain attached to the father only so long as they need him for their preservation. As soon as this need ceases, the natural bond is dissolved. The children, released from the obedience they owed to the father, and the father, released from the care he owed his children, return equally to independence. If they remain united, they continue so no longer naturally, but voluntarily; and the family itself is then maintained only by convention.

This common liberty results from the nature of man. His first law is to provide for his own preservation, his first cares are those which he owes to himself; and, as soon as he reaches years of discretion, he is the sole judge of the proper means of preserving himself, and consequently becomes his own master.

The family then may be called the first model of political societies: the ruler corresponds to the father, and the people to the children; and all, being born free and equal, alienate their liberty only for their own advantage. The whole difference is that, in the family, the love of the father for his children repays him for the care he takes of them, while, in the State, the pleasure of commanding takes the place of the love which the chief cannot have for the peoples under him.

Grotius denies that all human power is established in favour of the governed, and quotes slavery as an example. His usual method of reasoning is constantly to establish right by fact.[1] It would be possible to employ a more logical method, but none could be more favourable to tyrants.

It is then, according to Grotius, doubtful whether the human race belongs to a hundred men, or that hundred men to the human race: and, throughout his book, he seems to incline to the former alternative, which is also the view of Hobbes. On this showing, the human species is divided into so many herds of cattle, each with its ruler, who keeps guard over them for the purpose of devouring them.

As a shepherd is of a nature superior to that of his flock, the shepherds of men, *i. e.* their rulers, are of a nature superior to that of the peoples under them. Thus, Philo tells us, the Emperor Caligula reasoned, concluding equally well either that kings were gods, or that men were beasts.

The reasoning of Caligula agrees with that of Hobbes and Grotius. Aristotle, before any of them, had said that men are by no means equal naturally, but that some are born for slavery, and others for dominion.

Aristotle was right; but he took the effect for the cause. Nothing can be more certain than that every man born in slavery is born for slavery. Slaves lose everything in their chains, even the desire of escaping from them: they love their servitude, as the comrades of Ulysses loved their brutish condition.[2] If then there are slaves by nature, it is because there have been slaves against nature. Force made the first slaves, and their cowardice perpetuated the condition.

I have said nothing of King Adam, or Emperor Noah, father of the three great monarchs who shared out the universe, like the children of Saturn, whom some scholars have recognised in them. I trust to getting due thanks for my moderation; for, being a direct descendant of one of these princes, perhaps of the eldest branch, how do I know that a verification of titles might not leave me the legitimate king of the human race? In any case, there can be no doubt that Adam was sovereign of the world, as Robinson Crusoe was of his island, as long as he was its only inhabitant; and this empire had the advantage that the monarch, safe on his throne, had no rebellions, wars, or conspirators to fear.

Chapter III

The Right of the Strongest

The strongest is never strong enough to be always the master, unless he transforms strength into right, and obedience into duty. Hence the right of the strongest, which, though to all seeming meant ironically, is really laid down as a fundamental principle. But are we never to have an explanation of this phrase? Force is a physical power, and I fail to see what moral effect it can have. To yield to force is an act of necessity, not of will—at the most, an act of prudence. In what sense can it be a duty?

---

[1] "Learned inquiries into public right are often only the history of past abuses; and troubling to study them too deeply is a profitless infatuation" (*Essay on the Interests of France in Relation to its Neighbours*, by the Marquis d'Argenson). This is exactly what Grotius has done.

[2] See a short treatise of Plutarch's entitled "That Animals Reason."

Suppose for a moment that this so-called "right" exists. I maintain that the sole result is a mass of inexplicable nonsense. For, if force creates right, the effect changes with the cause: every force that is greater than the first succeeds to its right. As soon as it is possible to disobey with impunity, disobedience is legitimate; and, the strongest being always in the right, the only thing that matters is to act so as to become the strongest. But what kind of right is that which perishes when force fails? If we must obey perforce, there is no need to obey because we ought; and if we are not forced to obey, we are under no obligation to do so. Clearly, the word "right" adds nothing to force: in this connection, it means absolutely nothing.

Obey the powers that be. If this means yield to force, it is a good precept, but superfluous: I can answer for its never being violated. All power comes from God, I admit; but so does all sickness: does that mean that we are forbidden to call in the doctor? A brigand surprises me at the edge of a wood: must I not merely surrender my purse on compulsion; but, even if I could withhold it, am I in conscience bound to give it up? For certainly the pistol he holds is also a power.

Let us then admit that force does not create right, and that we are obliged to obey only legitimate powers. In that case, my original question recurs.

Chapter IV

Slavery

Since no man has a natural authority over his fellow, and force creates no right, we must conclude that conventions form the basis of all legitimate authority among men.

If an individual, says Grotius, can alienate his liberty and make himself the slave of a master, why could not a whole people do the same and make itself subject to a king? There are in this passage plenty of ambiguous words which would need explaining; but let us confine ourselves to the word *alienate*. To alienate is to give or to sell. Now, a man who becomes the slave of another does not give himself; he sells himself, at the least for his subsistence: but for what does a people sell itself? A king is so far from furnishing his subjects with their subsistence that he gets his own only from them; and, according to Rabelais, kings do not live on nothing. Do subjects then give their persons on condition that the king takes their goods also? I fail to see what they have left to preserve.

It will be said that the despot assures his subjects civil tranquillity. Granted; but what do they gain, if the wars his ambition brings down upon them, his insatiable avidity, and the vexatious conduct of his ministers press harder on them than their own dissensions would have done? What do they gain, if the very tranquillity they enjoy is one of their miseries? Tranquillity is found also in dungeons; but is that enough to make them desirable places to live in? The Greeks imprisoned in the cave of the Cyclops lived there very tranquilly, while they were awaiting their turn to be devoured.

To say that a man gives himself gratuitously, is to say what is absurd and inconceivable; such an act is null and illegitimate, from the mere fact that he who does it is out of his mind. To say the same of a whole people is to suppose a people of madmen; and madness creates no right.

Even if each man could alienate himself, he could not alienate his children: they are born men and free; their liberty belongs to them, and no one but they has the right to dispose of it. Before they come to years of discretion, the father can, in their name, lay down conditions for their preservation and well-being, but he cannot give them irrevocably and without conditions: such a gift is contrary to the ends of nature, and exceeds the rights of paternity. It would therefore be necessary, in order to legitimise an arbitrary government, that in every generation the people should be in a position to accept or reject it; but, were this so, the government would be no longer arbitrary.

To renounce liberty is to renounce being a man, to surrender the rights of humanity and even its duties. For him who renounces everything no indemnity is possible. Such a renunciation is incompatible with man's nature; to remove all liberty from his will is to remove all morality from his acts. Finally, it is an empty and contradictory convention that sets up, on the one side, absolute authority, and, on the other, unlimited obedience. Is it not clear that we can be under no obligation to a person from whom we have the right to exact everything? Does not this condition alone, in the absence of equivalence or exchange, in itself involve the nullity of the act? For what right can my slave have against me, when all that he has belongs to me, and, his right being mine, this right of mine against myself is a phrase devoid of meaning?

Grotius and the rest find in war another origin for the so-called right of slavery. The victor having, as they hold, the right of killing the vanquished, the latter can buy back his life at the price of his liberty; and this convention is the more legitimate because it is to the advantage of both parties.

But it is clear that this supposed right to kill the conquered is by no means deducible from the state of war. Men, from the mere fact that, while they are living in their primitive independence, they have no mutual relations stable enough to constitute either the state of peace or the state of war, cannot be naturally enemies. War is constituted by a relation between things, and not between persons; and, as the state of war cannot arise out of simple personal relations, but only out of real relations, private war, or war of man with man, can exist neither in the state of nature, where there is no constant property, nor in the social state, where everything is under the authority of the laws.

Individual combats, duels and encounters, are acts which cannot constitute a state; while the private wars, authorised by the Establishments of Louis IX, King of France, and suspended by the Peace of God, are abuses of feudalism, in itself an absurd system if ever there was one, and contrary to the principles of natural right and to all good polity.

War then is a relation, not between man and man, but between State and State, and individuals are enemies only accidentally, not as men, nor even as citizens,[1] but as soldiers; not as members of their country, but as its defenders. Finally, each State can have for enemies only other States, and not men; for between things disparate in nature there can be no real relation.

Furthermore, this principle is in conformity with the established rules of all times and the constant practice of all civilised peoples. Declarations of war are intimations less to powers than to their subjects. The foreigner, whether king, individual, or people, who robs, kills or detains the subjects, without declaring war on the prince, is not an enemy, but a brigand. Even in real war, a just prince, while laying hands, in the enemy's country, on all that belongs to the public, respects the lives and goods of individuals: he respects rights on which his own are founded. The object of the war being the destruction of the hostile State, the other side has a right to kill its defenders, while they are bearing arms; but as soon as they lay them down and surrender, they cease to be enemies or instruments of the enemy, and become once more merely men, whose life no one has any right

---

[1] The Romans, who understood and respected the right of war more than any other nation on earth, carried their scruples on this head so far that a citizen was not allowed to serve as a volunteer without engaging himself expressly against the enemy, and against such and such an enemy by name. A legion in which the younger Cato was seeing his first service under Popilius having been reconstructed, the elder Cato wrote to Popilius that, if he wished his son to continue serving under him, he must administer to him a new military oath, because, the first having been annulled, he was no longer able to bear arms against the enemy. The same Cato wrote to his son telling him to take great care not to go into battle before taking this new oath. I know that the siege of Clusium and other isolated events can be quoted against me; but I am citing laws and customs. The Romans are the people that least often transgressed its laws; and no other people has had such good ones.

to take. Sometimes it is possible to kill the State without killing a single one of its members; and war gives no right which is not necessary to the gaining of its object. These principles are not those of Grotius: they are not based on the authority of poets, but derived from the nature of reality and based on reason.

The right of conquest has no foundation other than the right of the strongest. If war does not give the conqueror the right to massacre the conquered peoples, the right to enslave them cannot be based upon a right which does not exist. No one has a right to kill an enemy except when he cannot make him a slave, and the right to enslave him cannot therefore be derived from the right to kill him. It is accordingly an unfair exchange to make him buy at the price of his liberty his life, over which the victor holds no right. Is it not clear that there is a vicious circle in founding the right of life and death on the right of slavery, and the right of slavery on the right of life and death?

Even if we assume this terrible right to kill everybody, I maintain that a slave made in war, or a conquered people, is under no obligation to a master, except to obey him as far as he is compelled to do so. By taking an equivalent for his life, the victor has not done him a favour; instead of killing him without profit, he has killed him usefully. So far then is he from acquiring over him any authority in addition to that of force, that the state of war continues to subsist between them: their mutual relation is the effect of it, and the usage of the right of war does not imply a treaty of peace. A convention has indeed been made; but this convention, so far from destroying the state of war, presupposes its continuance.

So, from whatever aspect we regard the question, the right of slavery is null and void, not only as being illegitimate, but also because it is absurd and meaningless. The words *slave* and *right* contradict each other, and are mutually exclusive. It will always be equally foolish for a man to say to a man or to a people: "I make with you a convention wholly at your expense and wholly to my advantage; I shall keep it as long as I like, and you will keep it as long as I like."

Chapter V

That We Must Always Go Back to a First Convention

Even if I granted all that I have been refuting, the friends of despotism would be no better off. There will always be a great difference between subduing a multitude and ruling a society. Even if scattered individuals were successively enslaved by one man, however numerous they might be, I still see no more than a master and his slaves, and certainly not a people and its ruler; I see what may be termed an aggregation, but not an association; there is as yet neither public good nor body politic. The man in question, even if he has enslaved half the world, is still only an individual; his interest, apart from that of others, is still a purely private interest. If this same man comes to die, his empire, after him, remains scattered and without unity, as an oak falls and dissolves into a heap of ashes when the fire has consumed it.

A people, says Grotius, can give itself to a king. Then, according to Grotius, a people is a people before it gives itself. The gift is itself a civil act, and implies public deliberation. It would be better, before examining the act by which a people gives itself to a king, to examine that by which it has become a people; for this act, being necessarily prior to the other, is the true foundation of society.

Indeed, if there were no prior convention, where, unless the election were unanimous, would be the obligation on the minority to submit to the choice of the majority? How have a hundred men who wish for a master the right to vote on behalf of ten who do not? The law of majority voting is itself something established by convention, and presupposes unanimity, on one occasion at least.

Chapter VI

The Social Compact

I suppose men to have reached the point at which the obstacles in the way of their preservation in the state of nature show their power of resistance to be greater than the resources at the disposal of each individual for his maintenance in that state. That primitive condition can then subsist no longer; and the human race would perish unless it changed its manner of existence.

But, as men cannot engender new forces, but only unite and direct existing ones, they have no other means of preserving themselves than the formation, by aggregation, of a sum of forces great enough to overcome the resistance. These they have to bring into play by means of a single motive power, and cause to act in concert.

This sum of forces can arise only where several persons come together: but, as the force and liberty of each man are the chief instruments of his self-preservation, how can he pledge them without harming his own interests, and neglecting the care he owes to himself? This difficulty, in its bearing on my present subject, may be stated in the following terms—

"The problem is to find a form of association which will defend and protect with the whole common force the person and goods of each associate, and in which each, while uniting himself with all, may still obey himself alone, and remain as free as before." This is the fundamental problem of which the *Social Contract* provides the solution.

The clauses of this contract are so determined by the nature of the act that the slightest modification would make them vain and ineffective; so that, although they have perhaps never been formally set forth, they are everywhere the same and everywhere tacitly admitted and recognised, until, on the violation of the social compact, each regains his original rights and resumes his natural liberty, while losing the conventional liberty in favour of which he renounced it.

These clauses, properly understood, may be reduced to one—the total alienation of each associate, together with all his rights, to the whole community; for, in the first place, as each gives himself absolutely, the conditions are the same for all; and, this being so, no one has any interest in making them burdensome to others.

Moreover, the alienation being without reserve, the union is as perfect as it can be, and no associate has anything more to demand: for, if the individuals retained certain rights, as there would be no common superior to decide between them and the public, each, being on one point his own judge, would ask to be so on all; the state of nature would thus continue, and the association would necessarily become inoperative or tyrannical.

Finally, each man, in giving himself to all, gives himself to nobody; and as there is no associate over whom he does not acquire the same right as he yields others over himself, he gains an equivalent for everything he loses, and an increase of force for the preservation of what he has.

---

[1] The real meaning of this word has been almost wholly lost in modern times; most people mistake a town for a city, and a townsman for a citizen. They do not know that houses make a town, but citizens a city. The same mistake long ago cost the Carthaginians dear. I have never read of the title of citizens being given to the subjects of any prince, not even the ancient Macedonians or the English of to-day, though they are nearer liberty than any one else. The French alone everywhere familiarly adopt the name of citizens, because, as can be seen from their dictionaries, they have no idea of its meaning; otherwise they would be guilty in usurping it, of the crime of *lèse-majesté:* among them, the name expresses a virtue, and not a right. When Bodin spoke of our citizens and townsmen, he fell into a bad blunder in taking the one class for the other. M. d'Alembert has avoided the error, and, in his article on Geneva, has clearly distinguished the four orders of men (or even five, counting mere foreigners) who dwell in our town, of which two only compose the Republic. No other French writer, to my knowledge, has understood the real meaning of the word citizen.

If then we discard from the social compact what is not of its essence, we shall find that it reduces itself to the following terms—

"*Each of us puts his person and all his power in common under the supreme direction of the general will, and, in our corporate capacity, we receive each member as an indivisible part of the whole.*"

At once, in place of the individual personality of each contracting party, this act of association creates a moral and collective body, composed of as many members as the assembly contains votes, and receiving from this act its unity, its common identity, its life and its will. This public person, so formed by the union of all other persons, formerly took the name of *city*,[1] and now takes that of *Republic* or *body politic*; it is called by its members *State* when passive, *Sovereign* when active, and *Power* when compared with others like itself. Those who are associated in it take collectively the name of *people*, and severally are called *citizens*, as sharing in the sovereign power, and *subjects*, as being under the laws of the State. But these terms are often confused and taken one for another: it is enough to know how to distinguish them when they are being used with precision.

Chapter VII

The Sovereign

This formula shows us that the act of association comprises a mutual undertaking between the public and the individuals, and that each individual, in making a contract, as we may say, with himself, is bound in a double capacity; as a member of the Sovereign he is bound to the individuals, and as a member of the State to the Sovereign. But the maxim of civil right, that no one is bound by undertakings made to himself, does not apply in this case; for there is a great difference between incurring an obligation to yourself and incurring one to a whole of which you form a part.

Attention must further be called to the fact that public deliberation, while competent to bind all the subjects to the Sovereign, because of the two different capacities in which each of them may be regarded, cannot, for the opposite reason, bind the Sovereign to itself; and that it is consequently against the nature of the body politic for the Sovereign to impose on itself a law which it cannot infringe. Being able to regard itself in only one capacity, it is in the position of an individual who makes a contract with himself; and this makes it clear that there neither is nor can be any kind of fundamental law binding on the body of the people—not even the social contract itself. This does not mean that the body politic cannot enter into undertakings with others, provided the contract is not infringed by them; for in relation to what is external to it, it becomes a simple being, an individual.

But the body politic or the Sovereign, drawing its being wholly from the sanctity of the contract, can never bind itself, even to an outsider, to do anything derogatory to the original act, for instance, to alienate any part of itself, or to submit to another Sovereign. Violation of the act by which it exists would be self-annihilation; and that which is itself nothing can create nothing.

As soon as this multitude is so united in one body, it is impossible to offend against one of the members without attacking the body, and still more to offend against the body without the members resenting it. Duty and interest therefore equally oblige the two contracting parties to give each other help; and the same men should seek to combine, in their double capacity, all the advantages dependent upon that capacity.

Again, the Sovereign, being formed wholly of the individuals who compose it, neither has nor can have any interest contrary to theirs; and consequently the sovereign power need give no guarantee to its subjects, because it is impossible for the body to wish to hurt all its members. We shall also see later on that it cannot hurt any in particular. The Sovereign, merely by virtue of what it is, is always what it should be.

This, however, is not the case with the relation of the subjects to the Sovereign, which, despite the common interest, would have no security that they would fulfil their undertakings, unless it found means to assure itself of their fidelity.

In fact, each individual, as a man, may have a particular will contrary or dissimilar to the general will which he has as a citizen. His particular interest may speak to him quite differently from the common interest: his absolute and naturally independent existence may make him look upon what he owes to the common cause as a gratuitous contribution, the loss of which will do less harm to others than the payment of it is burdensome to himself; and, regarding the moral person which constitutes the State as a *persona ficta*, because not a man, he may wish to enjoy the rights of citizenship without being ready to fulfil the duties of a subject. The continuance of such an injustice could not but prove the undoing of the body politic.

In order then that the social compact may not be an empty formula, it tacitly includes the undertaking, which alone can give force to the rest, that whoever refuses to obey the general will shall be compelled to do so by the whole body. This means nothing less than that he will be forced to be free for this is the condition which, by giving each citizen to his country, secures him against all personal dependence. In this lies the key to the working of the political machine; this alone legitimises civil undertakings, which, without it, would be absurd, tyrannical, and liable to the most frightful abuses.

Chapter VIII

The Civil State

The passage from the state of nature to the civil state produces a very remarkable change in man, by substituting justice for instinct in his conduct, and giving his actions the morality they had formerly lacked. Then only, when the voice of duty takes the place of physical impulses and right of appetite, does man, who so far had considered only himself, find that he is forced to act on different principles, and to consult his reason before listening to his inclinations. Although, in this state, he deprives himself of some advantages which he got from nature, he gains in return others so great, his faculties are so stimulated and developed, his ideas so extended, his feelings so ennobled, and his whole soul so uplifted, that, did not the abuses of this new condition often degrade him below that which he left, he would be bound to bless continually the happy moment which took him from it for ever, and, instead of a stupid and unimaginative animal, made him an intelligent being and a man.

Let us draw up the whole account in terms easily commensurable. What man loses by the social contract is his natural liberty and an unlimited right to everything he tries to get and succeeds in getting; what he gains is civil liberty and the proprietorship of all he possesses. If we are to avoid mistake in weighing one against the other, we must clearly distinguish natural liberty, which is bounded only by the strength of the individual, from civil liberty, which is limited by the general will; and possession, which is merely the effect of force or the right of the first occupier, from property, which can be founded only on a positive title.

We might, over and above all this, add, to what man acquires in the civil state, moral liberty, which alone makes him truly master of himself; for the mere impulse of appetite is slavery, while obedience to a law which we prescribe to ourselves is liberty. But I have already said too much on this head, and the philosophical meaning of the word liberty does not now concern us.

Chapter IX

Real Property

Each member of the community gives himself to it, at the moment of its foundation, just as he is, with all the resources at his command, including the goods he possesses. This act does not make possession, in changing hands, change its nature, and become property in the hands of the Sovereign; but, as the forces of the city are incomparably greater than those of an individual, public possession is also, in fact, stronger and more irrevocable, without being any more legitimate, at any rate from the point of view of foreigners. For the State, in relation to its members, is master of all their goods by the social contract, which, within the State, is the basis of all rights; but, in relation to other powers, it is so only by the right of the first occupier, which it holds from its members.

The right of the first occupier, though more real than the right of the strongest, becomes a real right only when the right of property has already been established. Every man has naturally a right to everything he needs; but the positive act which makes him proprietor of one thing excludes him from everything else. Having his share, he ought to keep to it, and can have no further right against the community. This is why the right of the first occupier, which in the state of nature is so weak, claims the respect of every man in civil society. In this right we are respecting not so much what belongs to another as what does not belong to ourselves.

In general, to establish the right of the first occupier over a plot of ground, the following conditions are necessary: first, the land must not yet be inhabited; secondly, a man must occupy only the amount he needs for his subsistence; and, in the third place, possession must be taken, not by an empty ceremony, but by labour and cultivation, the only sign of proprietorship that should be respected by others, in default of a legal title.

In granting the right of first occupancy to necessity and labour, are we not really stretching it as far as it can go? Is it possible to leave such a right unlimited? Is it to be enough to set foot on a plot of common ground, in order to be able to call yourself at once the master of it? Is it to be enough that a man has the strength to expel others for a moment, in order to establish his right to prevent them from ever returning? How can a man or a people seize an immense territory and keep it from the rest of the world except by a punishable usurpation, since all others are being robbed, by such an act, of the place of habitation and the means of subsistence which nature gave them in common? When Nuñez Balboa, standing on the sea-shore, took possession of the South Seas and the whole of South America in the name of the crown of Castille, was that enough to dispossess all their actual inhabitants, and to shut out from them all the princes of the world? On such a showing, these ceremonies are idly multiplied, and the Catholic King need only take possession all at once, from his apartment, of the whole universe, merely making a subsequent reservation about what was already in the possession of other princes.

We can imagine how the lands of individuals, where they were contiguous and came to be united, became the public territory, and how the right of Sovereignty, extending from the subjects over the lands they held, became at once real and personal. The possessors were thus made more dependent, and the forces at their command used to guarantee their fidelity. The advantage of this does not seem to have been felt by ancient monarchs, who called themselves King of the Persians, Scythians, or Macedonians, and seemed to regard themselves more as rulers of men than as masters of a country. Those of the present day more cleverly call themselves Kings of France, Spain, England, etc.: thus holding the land, they are quite confident of holding the inhabitants.

The peculiar fact about this alienation is that, in taking over the goods of individuals, the community, so far from despoiling them, only assures them legitimate possession, and changes usurpation into a true right and enjoyment into proprietorship. Thus the possessors, being regarded as depositaries of the public good, and having their rights respected by all the members of the State and maintained against foreign aggression by all its forces, have, by a cession which benefits both the public and still more themselves, acquired, so to speak, all that they gave up. This paradox may easily be explained by the distinction between the rights which the Sovereign and the proprietor have over the same estate, as we shall see later on.

It may also happen that men begin to unite one with another before they possess anything, and that, subsequently occupying a tract of country which is enough for all, they enjoy it in common, or share it out among themselves, either equally or according to a scale fixed by the Sovereign. However the acquisition be made, the right which each individual has to his own estate is always subordinate to the right which the community has over all: without this, there would be neither stability in the social tie, nor real force in the exercise of Sovereignty.

I shall end this chapter and this book by remarking on a fact on which the whole social system should rest: *i. e.* that, instead of destroying natural inequality, the fundamental compact substitutes, for such physical inequality as nature may have set up between men, an equality that is moral and legitimate, and that men, who may be unequal in strength or intelligence, become every one equal by convention and legal right.[1]

MAN AND GOVERNMENT

THOMAS HOBBES

Of the natural condition of mankind as concerning their felicity, and misery

Nature hath made men so equal, in the faculties of the body, and mind; as that though there be found one man sometimes manifestly stronger in body, or of quicker mind than another; yet when all is reckoned together, the difference between man, and man, is not so considerable, as that one man can thereupon claim to himself any benefit, to which another may not pretend, as well as he. For as to the strength of body, the weakest has strength enough to kill the strongest, either by secret machination, or by confederacy with others, that are in the same danger with himself.

And as to the faculties of the mind, setting aside the arts grounded upon words, and especially that skill of proceeding upon general, and infallible rules, called science; which very few have, and but in few things; as being not a native faculty, born with us; nor attained, as prudence, while we look after somewhat else, I find yet a greater equality amongst men, than that of strength. For prudence, is but experience; which equal time, equally bestows on all men, in those things they equally apply themselves unto. That which may perhaps make such equality incredible, is but a vain conceit of one's own wisdom, which almost all men think they have in a greater degree, than the vulgar; that is, than all men but themselves, and a few others, whom by fame, or for concurring with themselves, they approve. For such is the nature of men, that howsoever they may acknowledge many others to be more witty, or more eloquent, or more learned; yet they will hardly believe there be many so wise as themselves; for they see their own wit at hand, and other men's at a distance. But this proveth rather that men are in that point equal, than unequal. For there is not ordinarily a greater sign of the equal distribution of anything, than that every man is contented with his share.

From this equality of ability, ariseth equality of hope in the attaining of our ends. And therefore if any two men desire the same thing, which nevertheless they cannot both enjoy, they become enemies; and in the way to their end, which is principally their own conservation, and sometimes their delectation only, endeavour to destroy, or subdue one another. And from hence It comes to pass, that where an invader hath no more to fear, than another man's single power; if one plant, sow, build, or possess a convenient seat, others may probably be expected to come prepared with forces united, to dispossess, and deprive him, not only of the fruit of his labour, but also of his life, or liberty. And the invader again is in the like danger of another.

And from this diffidence of one another, there is no way for any man to secure himself, so reasonable, as anticipation; that is, by force, or wiles, to master the persons of all men he can, so long, till he see no other power great enough to endanger him: and this is no more than his own conservation requireth, and is generally allowed. Also because there be some, that taking pleasure in contemplating their own power in the acts of conquest, which they pursue farther than their security requires; if others, that otherwise would be glad to be at ease within modest bounds, should not by invasion increase their power, they would not be able, long time, by standing only on their defence, to subsist. And by consequence, such augmentation of dominion over men being necessary to a man's conservation, it ought to be allowed him.

Reprinted from Thomas Hobbes, *Leviathan*, 1839, Molesworth Edition, Chaps. 13, 14, 17.

Again, men have no pleasure, but on the contrary a great deal of grief, in keeping company, where there is no power able to over-awe them all. For every man looketh that his companion should value him, at the same rate he sets upon himself: and upon all signs of contempt, or undervaluing, naturally endeavours, as far as he dares, (which amongst them that have no common power to keep them in quiet, is far enough to make them destroy each other), to extort a greater value from his contemners, by damage; and from others, by the example.

So that in the nature of man, we find three principal causes of quarrel. First, competition; secondly, diffidence; thirdly, glory.

The first, maketh men invade for gain; the second, for safety; and the third, for reputation. The first use violence, to make themselves masters of other men's persons, wives, children, and cattle; the second, to defend them; the third, for trifles, as a word, a smile, a different opinion, and any other sign of undervalue, either direct in their persons, or by reflection in their kindred, their friends, their nation, their profession, or their name.

Hereby it is manifest, that during the time men live without a common power to keep them all in awe, they are in that condition which is called war; and such a war, as is of every man, against every man. For WAR, consisteth not in battle only, or the act of fighting; but in a tract of time, wherein the will to contend by battle is sufficiently known: and therefore the notion of *time*, is to be considered in the nature of war; as it is in the nature of weather. For as the nature of foul weather, lieth not in a shower or two of rain; but in an inclination thereto of many days together: so the nature of war, consisteth not in actual fighting; but in the known disposition thereto, during all the time there is no assurance to the contrary. All other time is PEACE.

Whatsoever therefore is consequent to a time of war, where every man is enemy to every man; the same is consequent to the time, wherein men live without other security, than what their own strength, and their own invention shall furnish them withal. In such condition, there is no place for industry; because the fruit thereof is uncertain: and consequently no culture of the earth; no navigation, nor use of the commodities that may be imported by sea; no commodious building; no instruments of moving, and removing, such things as require much force; no knowledge of the face of the earth; no account of time; no arts; no letters; no society; and which is worst of all, continual fear, and danger of violent death; and the life of man, solitary, poor, nasty, brutish, and short.

It may seem strange to some man, that has not well weighed these things; that nature should thus dissociate, and render men apt to invade, and destroy one another; and he may therefore, not trusting to this inference, made from the passions, desire perhaps to have the same confirmed by experience. Let him therefore consider with himself, when taking a journey, he arms himself, and seeks to go well accompanied; when going to sleep, he locks his doors; when even in his house he locks his chests; and this when he knows there be laws, and public officers, armed, to revenge all injuries shall be done him; what opinion he has of his fellow-subjects, when he rides armed; of his fellow citizens, when he locks his doors; and of his children, and servants, when he locks his chests. Does he not there as much accuse mankind by his actions, as I do by my words? But neither of us accuse man's nature in it. The desires, and other passions of man, are in themselves no sin. No more are the actions, that proceed from those passions, till they know a law that forbids them: which till laws be made they cannot know: nor can any law be made, till they have agreed upon the person that shall make it.

It may peradventure be thought, there was never such a time, nor condition of war as this; and I believe it was never generally so, over all the world: but there are many places, where they live so now. For the savage people in many places of America, except the government of small families, the concord whereof dependeth on natural lust, have no government at all; and live at this day in that brutish manner, as I said before. Howsoever, it may be perceived what manner of life there would be, where there were no common power to fear, by the manner of life, which men that have formerly lived under a peaceful government use to degenerate into, in a civil war.

But though there had never been any time, wherein particular men were in a condition of war one against another; yet in all times, kings, and persons of sovereign authority, because of their independency, are in continual jealousies, and in the state and posture of gladiators; having their weapons pointing, and their eyes fixed on one another; that is, their forts, garrisons, and guns upon the frontiers of their kingdoms; and continual spies upon their neighbours; which is a posture of war. But because they uphold thereby, the industry of their subjects; there does not follow from it, that misery, which accompanies the liberty of particular men.

To this war of every man, against every man, this also is consequent; that nothing can be unjust. The notions of right and wrong justice and injustice have there no place. Where there is no common power, there is no law; where no law, no injustice. Force, and fraud, are in war the two cardinal virtues. Justice, and injustice are none of the faculties neither of the body, nor mind. If they were, they might be in a man that were alone in the world, as well as his senses, and passions. They are qualities, that relate to men in society, not in solitude. It is consequent also to the same condition, that there be no propriety, no dominion, no *mine* and *thine* distinct; but only that to be every man's, that he can get; and for so long, as he can keep it. And thus much for the ill condition, which man by mere nature is actually placed in; though with a possibility to come out of it, consisting partly in the passions, partly in his reason.

The passions that incline men to peace, are fear of death; desire of such things as are necessary to commodious living; and a hope by their industry to obtain them. And reason suggesteth convenient articles of peace, upon which men may be drawn to agreement. These articles, are they, which otherwise are called the Laws of Nature: whereof I shall speak more particularly, in the two following chapters.

Of the first and second natural laws, and of contracts

The right of nature, which writers commonly call *jus naturale,* is the liberty each man hath, to use his own power, as he will himself, for the preservation of his own nature; that is to say, of his own life; and consequently, of doing any thing, which in his own judgment, and reason, he shall conceive to be the aptest means thereunto.

By *liberty,* is understood, according to the proper signification of the word, the absence of external impediments: which impediments, may oft take away part of a man's power to do what he would; but cannot hinder him from using the power left him, according as his judgment, and reason shall dictate to him.

A *law of nature, lex naturalls,* is a precept or general rule, found out by reason, by which a man is forbidden to do that, which is destructive of his life, or taketh away the means of preserving the same; and to omit that, by which he thinketh it may be best preserved. For though they that speak of this subject, use to confound *jus,* and *lex, right* and *law:* yet they ought to be distinguished; because *right,* consisteth in liberty to do, or to forbare; whereas *law,* determineth, and bindeth to one of them: so that law, and right, differ as much, as obligation, and liberty; which in one and the same matter are inconsistent.

And because the condition of man, as hath been declared in the precedent chapter, is a condition of war of every one against every one: in which case every one is governed by his own reason; and there is nothing he can make use of, that may not be a help unto him, in preserving his life against his enemies; it followeth, that in such a condition, every man has a right to every thing; even to one another's body. And therefore, as long as this natural right of every man to every thing endureth, there can be no security to any man, how strong or wise soever he be, of living out the time, which nature ordinarily alloweth men to live, and consequently it is a precept, or general rule of reason, *that every man, ought to endeavour peace, as far as he has hope of obtaining it; and when he cannot obtain it, that he may seek, and use, all helps, and advantages of war.* The first branch of which rule, containeth the first, and fundamental law of nature; which is, *to seek peace, and follow it.* The second, the sum of the right of nature; which is, *by all means we can, to defend ourselves.*

From this fundamental law of nature, by which men are commanded to endeavour peace, is derived this second law; *that a man be willing, when others are so too, as far-forth, as for peace, and defence of himself he shall think it necessary, to lay down this right to all things; and be contented with so much liberty against other men, as he would allow other men against himself.* For as long as every man holdeth this right, of doing any thing he liketh; so long are all men in the condition of war. But if other men will not lay down their right, as well as he; then there is no reason for any one, to divest himself of his: for that were to expose himself to prey, which no man is bound to, rather than to dispose himself to peace. This is that law of the Gospel; *whatsoever you require that others should do to you, that do ye to them.* And that law of all men, *quod tibi fieri non vis, alterl ne feceris.*

To *lay down* a man's *right* to any thing, is to *divest* himself of the *liberty,* of hindering another of the benefit of his own right to the same. For he that renounceth, or passeth away his right, giveth not to any other man a right which he had not before; because there is nothing to which every man had not right by nature: but only standeth out of his way, that he may enjoy his own original right, without hindrance from him; not without hindrance from another. So that the effect which redoundeth to one man, by another man's defect of right, is but so much diminution of impediments to the use of his own right original.

Right is laid aside, either by simply renouncing it; or by transferring it to another. By *simply renouncing;* when he cares not to whom the benefit thereof redoundeth. By *transferring;* when he intendeth the benefit thereof to some certain person, or persons. And when a man hath in either manner abandoned, or granted away his right; then he is said to be *obliged,* or *bound,* not to hinder those, to whom such right is granted, or abandoned, from the benefit of it: and that he *ought,* and it is his *duty,* not to make void that voluntary act of his own: and that such hindrance is *injustice,* and *injury,* as being *sine jure;* the right being before renounced, or transferred. So that *injury,* or *injustice,* in the controversies of the world, is somewhat like to that, which in the disputations of scholars is called *absurdity.* For as it is there called an absurdity, to contradict what one maintained in the beginning: so in the world, it is called injustice, and injury, voluntarily to undo that, which from the beginning he had voluntarily done. The way by which a man either simply renounceth, or transferreth his right, is a declaration, or signification, by some voluntary and sufficient sign, or signs, that he doth so renounce, or transfer; or hath so renounced, or transferred the same, to him that accepteth it. And these signs are either words only, or actions only; or, as it happeneth most often, both words, and actions. And the same are the *bonds,* by which men are bound, and obliged: bonds, that have their strength, not from their own nature, for nothing is more easily broken than a man's word, but from fear of some evil consequence upon that rupture.

Whensoever a man transferreth his right, or renounceth it; It is either in consideration of some right reciprocally transferred to himself; or for some other good he hopeth for thereby. For it is a voluntary act: and of the voluntary acts of every man, the object is some *good to himself.* And therefore there be some rights, which no man can be understood by any words, or other signs, to have abandoned, or transferred. As first a man cannot lay down the right of resisting them, that assault him by force, to take away his life; because he cannot be understood to aim thereby, at any good to himself. The same may be said of wounds, and chains, and imprisonment; both because there is no benefit consequent to such patience; as there is to the patience of suffering another to be wounded, or imprisoned: as also because a man cannot tell, when he seeth men proceed against him by violence, whether they intend his death or not. And lastly the motive, and end for which this renouncing, and transferring of right is introduced, is nothing else but the security of a man's person, in his life, and in the means of so preserving life, as not to be weary of it. And therefore if a man by words, or other signs, seem to despoil himself of the end, for which those signs were intended; he is not to be understood as if he meant it, or that it was his will; but that he was Ignorant of how such words and actions were to be interpreted.

The mutual transferring of right, is that which men call *contract.*

And though this may seem too subtle a deduction of the laws of nature, to be taken notice of by all men; whereof the most part are too busy in getting food, and the rest too negligent to understand; yet to leave all men inexcusable, they have been contracted into one easy sum, intelligible even to the meanest capacity; and that is, *Do not that to another, which thou wouldest not have done to thyself;* which sheweth him, that he has no more to do in learning the laws of nature, but, when weighing the actions of other men with his own, they seem too heavy, to put them into the other part of the balance, and his own into their place, that his own passions, and self-love, may add nothing to the weight; and then there is none of these laws of nature that will not appear unto him very reasonable.

The laws of nature oblige *in foro interno;* that is to say, they bind to a desire they should take place: but *in foro externo;* that is, to the putting them in act, not always. For he that should be modest, and tractable, and perform all he promises, in such time, and place, where no man else should do so, should but make himself a prey to others, and procure his own certain ruin, contrary to the ground of all laws of nature, which tend to nature's preservation. And again, he that having sufficient security, that others shall observe the same laws towards him, observes them not himself, seeketh not peace but war; and consequently the destruction of his nature by violence.

And whatsoever laws bind *in foro interno,* may be broken, not only by a fact contrary to the law, but also by a fact according to it, in case a man think it contrary. For though his action in this case, be according to the law; yet his purpose was against the law; which, where the obligation is *in foro interno,* is a breach.

The laws of nature are immutable and eternal; for injustice, ingratitude, arrogance, pride, iniquity, acception of persons, and the rest, can never be made lawful. For it can never be that war shall preserve life, and peace destroy it.

The same laws, because they oblige only to a desire, and endeavour, I mean an unfeigned and constant endeavour, are easy to be observed. For in that they require nothing but endeavour, he that endeavoureth their performance, fulfilleth them; and he that fulfilleth the law, is just.

And the science of them, is the true and only moral philosophy. For moral philosophy is nothing else but the science of what is *good,* and *evil,* in the conversation, and society of mankind. *Good,* and *evil,* are names that signify our appetites, and aversions; which in different tempers, customs, and doctrines of men, are different and divers men, differ not only in their judgment, on the senses of what is pleasant, and unpleasant to the taste, smell, hearing, touch, and sight; but also of what is conformable, or disagreeable to reason, in the actions of common life. Nay, the same man, in divers times, differs from himself; and one time praiseth, that is, calleth good, what another time he dispraiseth, and calleth evil: from whence arise disputes, controversies, and at last war. And therefore so long as a man is in the condition of mere nature, which is a condition of war, as private appetite is the measure of good, and evil: and consequently all men agree on this, that peace is good, and therefore also the way, or means of peace, which, as I have shewed before, are *justice, gratitude, modesty, equity, mercy,* and the rest of the laws of nature, are good; that is to say; *moral virtues;* and their contrary *vices,* evil.

Of the causes, generation, and definition of a commonwealth

The final cause, end, or design of men, who naturally love liberty, and dominion over others, in the introduction of that restraint upon themselves, in which we see them live in commonwealths, is the foresight of their own preservation, and of a more contented life thereby; that is to say, of getting themselves out from that miserable condition of war, which is necessarily consequent to the natural passions of men, when there is no visible power to keep them in awe, and tie them by fear of punishment to the performance of their covenants, and observation of those laws of nature set down in the fourteenth and fifteenth chapters.

For the laws of nature, as *justice, equity, modesty, mercy,* and, in sum, *doing to others, as we would be done to,* of themselves, without the terror of some power, to cause them to be observed, are contrary to our natural passions, that carry us to partiality, pride, revenge, and the like. And covenants, without the swords, are but words, and of no strength to secure a man at all. Therefore notwithstanding the laws of nature, which every one hath then kept, when he has the will to keep them, when he can do it safely, if there be no power erected, or not great enough for our security; every man will, and may lawfully rely on his own strength and art, for caution against all other men. And in all places, where men have lived by small families, to rob and spoil one another, has been a trade, and so far from being reputed against the law of nature, that the greater spoils they gained, the greater was their honour; and men observed no other laws therein, but the laws of honour; that is, to abstain from cruelty, leaving to men their lives, and instruments of husbandry. And as small families did then; so now do cities and kingdoms which are but greater families, for their own security, enlarge their dominions, upon all pretences of danger, and fear of invasion, or assistance that may be given to invaders, and endeavour as much as they can, to subdue, or weaken their neighbours, by open force, and secret arts, for want of other caution, justly; and are remembered for it in after ages with honour.

Nor is it the joining together of a small number of men, that gives them this security; because in small numbers, small additions on the one side or the other, make the advantage of strength so great, as is sufficient to carry the victory; and therefore gives encouragement to an invasion. The multitude sufficient to confide in for our security, is not determined by any certain number, but by comparison with the enemy we fear; and is then sufficient, when the odds of the enemy is not of so visible and conspicuous moment, to determine the event of war, as to move him to attempt.

And be there never so great a multitude; yet if their actions be directed according to their particular judgments, and particular appetites, they can expect thereby no defence, nor protection, neither against a common enemy, nor against the injuries of one another. For being distracted in opinions concerning the best use and application of their strength, they do not help but hinder one another; and reduce their strength by mutual opposition to nothing: whereby they are easily, not only subdued by a very few that agree together; but also when there is no common enemy, they make war upon each other, for their particular interests. For if we could suppose a great multitude of men to consent in the observation of Justice, and other laws of nature, without a common power to keep them all in awe; we might as well suppose all mankind to do the same; and then there neither would be, nor need to be any civil government, or commonwealth at all; because there would be peace without subjection.

Nor is it enough for the security, which men desire should last all the time of their life, that they be governed, and directed by one judgment, for a limited time; as in one battle, or one war. For though they obtain a victory by their unanimous endeavour against a foreign enemy; yet afterwards when either they have no common enemy, or he that by one part is held for an enemy, is by another part held for a friend, they must needs by the difference of their interests dissolve, and fall again into a war amongst themselves.

It is true, that certain living creatures, as bees, and ants, live sociably one with another, which are therefore by Aristotle numbered amongst political creatures; and yet have no other direction, than their particular judgments and appetites; nor speech, whereby one of them can signify to another, what he thinks expedient for the common benefit; and therefore some man may perhaps desire to know, why mankind cannot do the same. To which I answer.

First, that men are continually in competition for honour and dignity, which these creatures are not; and consequently amongst men there ariseth on that ground, envy and hatred, and finally war; but amongst these not so.

Secondly, that amongst these creatures, the common good differeth not from the private; and being by nature inclined to their private, they procure thereby the common benefit. But man, whose joy consisteth in comparing himself with other men, can relish nothing but what is eminent.

Thirdly, that these creatures, having not, as man, the use of reason, do not see, nor think they see any fault, in the administration of their common business; whereas amongst men, there are very many, that think themselves wiser, and abler to govern the public, better than the rest; and these strive to reform and innovate, one this way, another that way; and thereby bring it into distraction and civil war.

Fourthly, that these creatures, though they have some use of voice, in making known to one another their desires, and other affections; yet they want that art of words, by which some men can represent to others, that which is good, in the likeness of evil; and evil, in the likeness of good; and augment, or diminish the apparent greatness of good and evil; discontenting men, and troubling their peace at their pleasure.

Fifthly, irrational creatures cannot distinguish between *injury,* and *damage;* and therefore as long as they be at ease, they are not offended with their fellows: whereas man is then most troublesome, when he is most at ease: for then it is that he loves to shew his wisdom, and control the actions of them that govern the commonwealth.

Lastly, the agreement of these creatures is natural; that of men, is by covenant only, which is artificial: and therefore it is no wonder if there be somewhat else required, besides covenant, to make their agreement constant and lasting; which is a common power, to keep them in awe, and to direct their actions to the common benefit.

The only way to erect such a common power, as may be able to defend them from the invasion of foreigners, and the injuries of one another, and thereby to secure them in such sort, as that by their own industry, and by the fruits of the earth, they may nourish themselves and live contentedly; is, to confer all their power and strength upon one man, or upon one assembly of men, that may reduce all their wills, by plurality of voices, unto one will: which is as much as to say, to appoint one man, or assembly of men, to bear their person; and every one to own, and acknowledge himself to be author of whatsoever he that so beareth their person, shall act, or cause to be acted, in those things which concern the common peace and safety; and therein to submit their wills, every one to his will, and their judgments, to his judgment. This is more than consent, or concord; it is a real unity of them all, in one and the same person, made by covenant of every man with every man, in such manner, as if every man should say to every man, *I authorize and give up my right of governing myself, to this man, or to this assembly of men, on this condition, that thou give up thy right to him, and authorize all his actions in like manner.* This done, the multitude so united in one person, is called a *commonwealth,* in Latin *civitas.* This is the generation of the great *leviathan,* or rather, to speak more reverently, of that *mortal god,* to which we owe under the *immortal God,* our peace and defence. For by this authority, given him by every particular man in the commonwealth, he hath the use of so much power and strength conferred on him, that by terror thereof, he is enabled to perform the wills of them all, to peace at home, and mutual aid against their enemies abroad. And in him consisteth the essence of the commonwealth; which, to define it, is *one person, of whose acts a great multitude, by mutual covenants one with another, have made themselves every one the author, to the end he may use the strength and means of them all, as he shall think expedient, for their peace and common defence.*

And he that carrieth this person, is called *sovereign,* and said to have *sovereign power*; and every one besides, his *subject.*

The attaining to this sovereign power, is by two ways. One, by natural force; as when a man maketh his children, to submit themselves, and their children to his government, as being able to destroy them if they refuse; or by war subdueth his enemies to his will, giving them their lives on that condition. The other, is when men agree amongst themselves, to submit to some man, or assembly of men, voluntarily, on confidence to be protected by him against all others. This latter, may be called a political commonwealth, or commonwealth by *institution;* and the former, a commonwealth by *acquisition.*

SUMMA THEOLOGICA

ST. THOMAS AQUINAS

Question 75

Of Man Who is Composed of a Spiritual and a Corporeal Substance: And in The First Place, Concerning What Belongs to the Essence of the Soul (In Seven Articles)

Having treated of the spiritual and of the corporeal creature, we now proceed to treat of man, who is composed of a spiritual and corporeal substance. We shall treat first of the nature of man, and secondly of his origin. Now the theologian considers the nature of man in relation to the soul; but not in relation to the body, except in so far as the body has relation to the soul. Hence the first object of our consideration will be the soul. And since Dionysius (Ang. Hier. xi) says that three things are to be found in spiritual substances—essence, power, and operation—we shall treat first of what belongs to the essence of the soul; secondly, of what belongs to its power; thirdly, of what belongs to its operation.

Concerning the first, two points have to be considered; the first is the nature of the soul considered in itself; the second is the union of the soul with the body. Under the first head there are seven points of inquiry.

1. Whether the soul is a body?
2. Whether the human soul is a subsistence?
3. Whether the souls of brute animals are subsistent?
4. Whether the soul is man, or is man composed of soul and body?
5. Whether the soul is composed of matter and form?
6. Whether the soul is incorruptible?
7. Whether the soul is of the same species as an angel?

First Article [I, Q. 75, Art. 1]

Whether the soul is a Body?

Objection 1: It would seem that the soul is a body. For the soul is the moving principle of the body. Nor does it move unless moved. First, because seemingly nothing can move unless it is itself moved, since nothing gives what it has not; for instance, what is not hot does not give heat. Secondly, because if there be anything that moves and is not moved, it must be the cause of eternal, unchanging movement, as we find proved Phys. viii, 6; and this does not appear to be the case in the movement of an animal, which is caused by the soul. Therefore the soul is a mover moved. But every mover moved is a body. Therefore the soul is a body.

Obj. 2: Further, all knowledge is caused by means of a likeness. But there can be no likeness of a body to an incorporeal thing. If, therefore, the soul were not a body, it could not have knowledge of corporeal things.

Obj. 3: Further, between the mover and the moved there must be contact. But contact is only between bodies. Since, therefore, the soul moves the body, it seems that the soul must be a body.

On the contrary, Augustine says (De Trin. vi, 6) that the soul "is simple in comparison with the body, inasmuch as it does not occupy space by its bulk."

I answer that, To seek the nature of the soul, we must premise that the soul is defined as the first principle of life of those things which live: for we call living things "animate," [*i.e. having a soul] and those things which have no life, "inanimate." Now life is shown principally by two actions, knowledge and movement. The philosophers of old, not being able to rise above their imagination, supposed that the principle of these actions was something corporeal: for they asserted that only bodies were real things; and that what is not corporeal is nothing: hence they maintained that the soul is something corporeal. This opinion can be proved to be false in many ways; but we shall make use of only one proof, based on universal and certain principles, which shows clearly that the soul is not a body.

It is manifest that not every principle of vital action is a soul, for then the eye would be a soul, as it is a principle of vision; and the same might be applied to the other instruments of the soul: but it is the first principle of life, which we call the soul. Now, though a body may be a principle of life, as the heart is a principle of life in an animal, yet nothing corporeal can be the first principle of life. For it is clear that to be a principle of life, or to be a living thing, does not belong to a body as such; since, if that were the case, every body would be a living thing, or a principle of life. Therefore a body is competent to be a living thing or even a principle of life, as "such" a body. Now that it is actually such a body, it owes to some principle which is called its act. Therefore the soul, which is the first principle of life, is not a body, but the act of a body; thus heat, which is the principle of calefaction, is not a body, but an act of a body.

Reply Obj. 1: As everything which is in motion must be moved by something else, a process which cannot be prolonged indefinitely, we must allow that not every mover is moved. For, since to be moved is to pass from potentiality to actuality, the mover gives what it has to the thing moved, inasmuch as it causes it to be in act. But, as is shown in Phys. viii, 6, there is a mover which is altogether immovable, and not moved either essentially, or accidentally; and such a mover can cause an invariable movement. There is, however, another kind of mover, which, though not moved essentially, is moved accidentally; and for this reason it does not cause an invariable movement; such a mover, is the soul. There is, again, another mover, which is moved essentially—namely, the body. And because the philosophers of old believed that nothing existed but bodies, they maintained that every mover is moved; and that the soul is moved directly, and is a body.

Reply Obj. 2: The likeness of a thing known is not of necessity actually in the nature of the knower; but given a thing which knows potentially, and afterwards knows actually, the likeness of the thing known must be in the nature of the knower, not actually, but only potentially; thus color is not actually in the pupil of the eye, but only potentially. Hence it is necessary, not that the likeness of corporeal things should be actually in the nature of the soul, but that there be a potentiality in the soul for such a likeness. But the ancient philosophers omitted to distinguish between actuality and potentiality; and so they held that the soul must be a body in order to have knowledge of a body; and that it must be composed of the principles of which all bodies are formed in order to know all bodies.

Reply Obj. 3: There are two kinds of contact; of "quantity," and of "power." By the former a body can be touched only by a body; by the latter a body can be touched by an incorporeal thing, which moves that body.

Second Article [I, Q. 75, Art. 2]

Whether the Human Soul is Something Subsistent?

Objection 1: It would seem that the human soul is not something subsistent. For that which subsists is said to be "this particular thing." Now "this particular thing" is said not of the soul, but of that which is composed of soul and body. Therefore the soul is not something subsistent.

Obj. 2: Further, everything subsistent operates. But the soul does not operate; for, as the Philosopher says (De Anima i, 4), "to say that the soul feels or understands is like saying that the soul weaves or builds." Therefore the soul is not subsistent.

Obj. 3: Further, if the soul were subsistent, it would have some operation apart from the body. But it has no operation apart from the body, not even that of understanding: for the act of understanding does not take place without a phantasm, which cannot exist apart from the body. Therefore the human soul is not something subsistent.

On the contrary, Augustine says (De Trin. x, 7): "Who understands that the nature of the soul is that of a substance and not that of a body, will see that those who maintain the corporeal nature of the soul, are led astray through associating with the soul those things without which they are unable to think of any nature—i.e. imaginary pictures of corporeal things." Therefore the nature of the human intellect is not only incorporeal, but it is also a substance, that is, something subsistent.

I answer that, It must necessarily be allowed that the principle of intellectual operation which we call the soul, is a principle both incorporeal and subsistent. For it is clear that by means of the intellect man can have knowledge of all corporeal things. Now whatever knows certain things cannot have any of them in its own nature; because that which is in it naturally would impede the knowledge of anything else. Thus we observe that a sick man's tongue being vitiated by a feverish and bitter humor, is insensible to anything sweet, and everything seems bitter to it. Therefore, if the intellectual principle contained the nature of a body it would be unable to know all bodies. Now every body has its own determinate nature. Therefore it is impossible for the intellectual principle to be a body. It is likewise impossible for it to understand by means of a bodily organ; since the determinate nature of that organ would impede knowledge of all bodies; as when a certain determinate color is not only in the pupil of the eye, but also in a glass vase, the liquid in the vase seems to be of that same color.

Therefore the intellectual principle which we call the mind or the intellect has an operation per se apart from the body. Now only that which subsists can have an operation per se. For nothing can operate but what is actual: for which reason we do not say that heat imparts heat, but that what is hot gives heat. We must conclude, therefore, that the human soul, which is called the intellect or the mind, is something incorporeal and subsistent.

Reply Obj. 1: "This particular thing" can be taken in two senses. Firstly, for anything subsistent; secondly, for that which subsists, and is complete in a specific nature. The former sense excludes the inherence of an accident or of a material form; the latter excludes also the imperfection of the part, so that a hand can be called "this particular thing" in the first sense, but not in the second. Therefore, as the human soul is a part of human nature, it can indeed be called "this particular thing," in the first sense, as being something subsistent; but not in the second, for in this sense, what is composed of body and soul is said to be "this particular thing."

Reply Obj. 2: Aristotle wrote those words as expressing not his own opinion, but the opinion of those who said that to understand is to be moved, as is clear from the context. Or we may reply that to operate per se belongs to what exists per se. But for a thing to exist per se, it suffices sometimes that it be not inherent, as an accident or a material form; even though it be part of something. Nevertheless, that is rightly said to subsist per se, which is neither inherent in the above sense, nor part of anything else. In this sense, the eye or the hand cannot be said to subsist per se; nor can it for that reason be said to operate per se. Hence the operation of the parts is through each part attributed to the whole. For we say that man sees with the eye, and feels with the hand, and not in the same sense as when we say that what is hot gives heat by its heat; for heat, strictly speaking, does not give heat. We may therefore say that the soul understands, as the eye sees; but it is more correct to say that man understands through the soul.

Reply Obj. 3: The body is necessary for the action of the intellect, not as its origin of action, but on the part of the object; for the phantasm is to the intellect what color is to the sight. Neither does such a dependence on the body prove the intellect to be non-subsistent; otherwise it would follow that an animal is non-subsistent, since it requires external objects of the senses in order to perform its act of perception.

Third Article [I, Q. 75, Art. 3]

Whether the Souls of Brute Animals are Subsistent?

Objection 1: It would seem that the souls of brute animals are subsistent. For man is of the same genus as other animals; and, as we have just shown (A. 2), the soul of man is subsistent. Therefore the souls of other animals are subsistent.

Obj. 2: Further, the relation of the sensitive faculty to sensible objects is like the relation of the intellectual faculty to intelligible objects. But the intellect, apart from the body, apprehends intelligible objects. Therefore the sensitive faculty, apart from the body, perceives sensible objects. Therefore, since the souls of brute animals are sensitive, it follows that they are subsistent; just as the human intellectual soul is subsistent.

Obj. 3: Further, the soul of brute animals moves the body. But the body is not a mover, but is moved. Therefore the soul of brute animals has an operation apart from the body.

On the contrary, Is what is written in the book De Eccl. Dogm. xvi, xvii: "Man alone we believe to have a subsistent soul: whereas the souls of animals are not subsistent."

I answer that, The ancient philosophers made no distinction between sense and intellect, and referred both to a corporeal principle, as has been said (A. 1). Plato, however, drew a distinction between intellect and sense; yet he referred both to an incorporeal principle, maintaining that sensing, just as understanding, belongs to the soul as such. From this it follows that even the souls of brute animals are subsistent. But Aristotle held that of the operations of the soul, understanding alone is performed without a corporeal organ. On the other hand, sensation and the consequent operations of the sensitive soul are evidently accompanied with change in the body; thus in the act of vision, the pupil of the eye is affected by a reflection of color: and so with the other senses. Hence it is clear that the sensitive soul has no per se operation of its own, and that every operation of the sensitive soul belongs to the composite. Wherefore we conclude that as the souls of brute animals have no per se operations they are not subsistent. For the operation of anything follows the mode of its being.

Reply Obj. 1: Although man is of the same genus as other animals, he is of a different species. Specific difference is derived from the difference of form; nor does every difference of form necessarily imply a diversity of genus.

Reply Obj. 2: The relation of the sensitive faculty to the sensible object is in one way the same as that of the intellectual faculty to the intelligible object, in so far as each is in potentiality to its object. But in another way their relations differ, inasmuch as the impression of the object on the sense is accompanied with change in the body; so that excessive strength of the sensible corrupts sense; a thing that never occurs in the case of the intellect. For an intellect that understands the highest of intelligible objects is more able afterwards to understand those that are lower. If, however, in the process of intellectual operation the body is weary, this result is accidental, inasmuch as the intellect requires the operation of the sensitive powers in the production of the phantasms.

Reply Obj. 3: Motive power is of two kinds. One, the appetitive power, commands motion. The operation of this power in the sensitive soul is not apart from the body; for anger, joy, and passions of a like nature are accompanied by a change in the body. The other motive power is that which executes motion in adapting the members for obeying the appetite; and the act of this power does not consist in moving, but in being moved. Whence it is clear that to move is not an act of the sensitive soul without the body.

Fourth Article [I, Q. 75, Art. 4]

Whether the Soul is Man?

Objection 1: It would seem that the soul is man. For it is written (2 Cor. 4:16): "Though our outward man is corrupted, yet the inward man is renewed day by day." But that which is within man is the soul. Therefore the soul is the inward man.

Obj. 2: Further, the human soul is a substance. But it is not a universal substance. Therefore it is a particular substance. Therefore it is a "hypostasis" or a person; and it can only be a human person. Therefore the soul is man; for a human person is a man.

On the contrary, Augustine (De Civ. Dei xix, 3) commends Varro as holding "that man is not a mere soul, nor a mere body; but both soul and body."

I answer that, The assertion "the soul is man," can be taken in two senses. First, that man is a soul; though this particular man, Socrates, for instance, is not a soul, but composed of soul and body. I say this, forasmuch as some held that the form alone belongs to the species; while matter is part of the individual, and not the species. This cannot be true; for to the nature of the species belongs what the definition signifies; and in natural things the definition does not signify the form only, but the form and the matter. Hence in natural things the matter is part of the species; not, indeed, signate matter, which is the principle of individuality; but the common matter. For as it belongs to the notion of this particular man to be composed of this soul, of this flesh, and of these bones; so it belongs to the notion of man to be composed of soul, flesh, and bones; for whatever belongs in common to the substance of all the individuals contained under a given species, must belong to the substance of the species.

It may also be understood in this sense, that this soul is this man; and this could be held if it were supposed that the operation of the sensitive soul were proper to it, apart from the body; because in that case all the operations which are attributed to man would belong to the soul only; and whatever performs the operations proper to a thing, is that thing; wherefore that which performs the operations of a man is man. But it has been shown above (A. 3) that sensation is not the operation of the soul only. Since, then, sensation is an operation of man, but not proper to him, it is clear that man is not a soul only, but something composed of soul and body. Plato, through supposing that sensation was proper to the soul, could maintain man to be a soul making use of the body.

Reply Obj. 1: According to the Philosopher (Ethic. ix, 8), a thing seems to be chiefly what is princip[al] in it; thus what the governor of a state does, the state is said to do. In this way sometimes what is princip[al] in man is said to be man; sometimes, indeed, the intellectual part which, in accordance with truth, is called the "inward" man; and sometimes the sensitive part with the body is called man in the opinion of those whose observation does not go beyond the senses. And this is called the "outward" man.

Reply Obj. 2: Not every particular substance is a hypostasis or a person, but that which has the complete nature of its species. Hence a hand, or a foot, is not called a hypostasis, or a person; nor, likewise, is the soul alone so called, since it is a part of the human species.

Fifth Article [I, Q. 75, Art. 5]

Whether the Soul is Composed of Matter and Form?

Objection 1: It would seem that the soul is composed of matter and form. For potentiality is opposed to actuality. Now, whatsoever things are in actuality participate of the First Act, which is God; by participation of Whom, all things are good, are beings, and are living things, as is clear from the teaching of Dionysius (Div. Nom. v). Therefore whatsoever things are in potentiality participate of the first potentiality.

But the first potentiality is primary matter. Therefore, since the human soul is, after a manner, in potentiality; which appears from the fact that sometimes a man is potentially understanding; it seems that the human soul must participate of primary matter, as part of itself.

Obj. 2: Further, wherever the properties of matter are found, there matter is. But the properties of matter are found in the soul—namely, to be a subject, and to be changed, for it is a subject to science, and virtue; and it changes from ignorance to knowledge and from vice to virtue. Therefore matter is in the soul.

Obj. 3: Further, things which have no matter, have no cause of their existence, as the Philosopher says Metaph. viii (Did. vii, 6). But the soul has a cause of its existence, since it is created by God. Therefore the soul has matter.

Obj. 4: Further, what has no matter, and is a form only, is a pure act, and is infinite. But this belongs to God alone. Therefore the soul has matter.

On the contrary, Augustine (Gen. ad lit. vii, 7, 8, 9) proves that the soul was made neither of corporeal matter, nor of spiritual matter.

I answer that, The soul has no matter. We may consider this question in two ways. First, from the notion of a soul in general; for it belongs to the notion of a soul to be the form of a body. Now, either it is a form by virtue of itself, in its entirety, or by virtue of some part of itself. If by virtue of itself in its entirety, then it is impossible that any part of it should be matter, if by matter we understand something purely potential: for a form, as such, is an act; and that which is purely potentiality cannot be part of an act, since potentiality is repugnant to actuality as being opposite thereto. If, however, it be a form by virtue of a part of itself, then we call that part the soul: and that matter, which it actualize first, we call the "primary animate."

Secondly, we may proceed from the specific notion of the human soul inasmuch as it is intellectual. For it is clear that whatever is received into something is received according to the condition of the recipient. Now a thing is known in as far as its form is in the knower. But the intellectual soul knows a thing in its nature absolutely: for instance, it knows a stone absolutely as a stone; and therefore the form of a stone absolutely, as to its proper formal idea, is in the intellectual soul. Therefore the intellectual soul itself is an absolute form, and not something composed of matter and form. For if the intellectual soul were composed of matter and form, the forms of things would be received into it as individuals, and so it would only know the individual: just as it happens with the sensitive powers which receive forms in a corporeal organ; since matter is the principle by which forms are individualized. It follows, therefore, that the intellectual soul, and every intellectual substance which has knowledge of forms absolutely, is exempt from composition of matter and form.

Reply Obj. 1: The First Act is the universal principle of all acts; because It is infinite, virtually "precontaining all things," as Dionysius says (Div. Nom. v). Wherefore things participate of It not as a part of themselves, but by diffusion of Its processions. Now as potentiality is receptive of act, it must be proportionate to act. But the acts received which proceed from the First Infinite Act, and are participations thereof, are diverse, so that there cannot be one potentiality which receives all acts, as there is one act, from which all participated acts are derived; for then the receptive potentiality would equal the active potentiality of the First Act. Now the receptive potentiality in the intellectual soul is other than the receptive potentiality of first matter, as appears from the diversity of the things received by each. For primary matter receives individual forms; whereas the intelligence receives absolute forms. Hence the existence of such a potentiality in the intellectual soul does not prove that the soul is composed of matter and form.

Reply Obj. 2: To be a subject and to be changed belong to matter by reason of its being in potentiality. As, therefore, the potentiality of the intelligence is one thing and the potentiality of primary matter another, so in each is there a different reason of subjection and change. For the intelligence is subject to knowledge, and is changed from ignorance to knowledge, by reason of its being in potentiality with regard to the intelligible species.

Reply Obj. 3: The form causes matter to be, and so does the agent; wherefore the agent causes matter to be, so far as it actualizes it by transmuting it to the act of a form. A subsistent form, however, does not owe its existence to some formal principle, nor has it a cause transmuting it from potentiality to act. So after the words quoted above, the Philosopher concludes, that in things composed of matter and form "there is no other cause but that which moves from potentiality to act; while whatsoever things have no matter are simply beings at once." [*The Leonine edition has, "simpliciter sunt quod vere entia aliquid." The Parma edition of St. Thomas's Commentary on Aristotle has, "statim per se unum quiddam est . . . et ens quiddam."]

Reply Obj. 4: Everything participated is compared to the participator as its act. But whatever created form be supposed to subsist "per se," must have existence by participation; for "even life," or anything of that sort, "is a participator of existence," as Dionysius says (Div. Nom. v). Now participated existence is limited by the capacity of the participator; so that God alone, who is His own existence, is pure act and infinite. But in intellectual substances there is composition of actuality and potentiality, not, indeed, of matter and form, but of form and participated existence. Wherefore some say that they are composed of that "whereby they are" and that "which they are"; for existence itself is that by which a thing is.

Sixth Article [I, Q. 75, Art. 6]

Whether the Human Soul is Incorruptible?

Objection 1: It would seem that the human soul is corruptible. For those things that have a like beginning and process seemingly have a like end. But the beginning, by generation, of men is like that of animals, for they are made from the earth. And the process of life is alike in both; because "all things breathe alike, and man hath nothing more than the beast," as it is written (Eccles. 3:19). Therefore, as the same text concludes, "the death of man and beast is one, and the condition of both is equal." But the souls of brute animals are corruptible. Therefore, also, the human soul is corruptible.

Obj. 2: Further, whatever is out of nothing can return to nothingness; because the end should correspond to the beginning. But as it is written (Wis. 2:2), "we are born of nothing"; which is true, not only of the body, but also of the soul. Therefore, as is concluded in the same passage, "After this we shall be as if we had not been," even as to our soul.

Obj. 3: Further, nothing is without its own proper operation. But the operation proper to the soul, which is to understand through a phantasm, cannot be without the body. For the soul understands nothing without a phantasm; and there is no phantasm without the body as the Philosopher says (De Anima i, 1). Therefore the soul cannot survive the dissolution of the body.

On the contrary, Dionysius says (Div. Nom. iv) that human souls owe to Divine goodness that they are "intellectual," and that they have "an incorruptible substantial life."

I answer that, We must assert that the intellectual principle which we call the human soul is incorruptible. For a thing may be corrupted in two ways—per se, and accidentally. Now it is impossible for any substance to be generated or corrupted accidentally, that is, by the generation or corruption of something else. For generation and corruption belong to a thing, just as existence belongs to it, which is acquired by generation and lost by corruption. Therefore, whatever has existence per se cannot be generated or corrupted except "per se"; while things which do not subsist, such as accidents and material forms, acquire existence or lose it through the generation or corruption of composite things. Now it was shown above (AA. 2, 3) that the souls of brutes are not self-subsistent, whereas the human soul is; so that the souls of brutes are corrupted, when their bodies are corrupted; while the human soul could not be corrupted unless it were corrupted per se. This, indeed, is impossible, not only as regards the human soul, but also as regards anything subsistent that is a form alone. For it is clear that what belongs to a thing by virtue of itself is inseparable from it; but existence belongs to a form, which is an act, by virtue of itself. Wherefore matter acquires actual existence as it acquires the form; while it is corrupted so far as the form is separated from it. But it is impossible for a form to be separated from itself; and therefore it is impossible for a subsistent form to cease to exist.

Granted even that the soul is composed of matter and form, as some pretend, we should nevertheless have to maintain that it is incorruptible. For corruption is found only where there is contrariety; since generation and corruption are from contraries and into contraries. Wherefore the heavenly bodies, since they have no matter subject to contrariety, are incorruptible. Now there can be no contrariety in the intellectual soul; for it receives according to the manner of its existence, and those things which it receives are without contrariety; for the notions even of contraries are not themselves contrary, since contraries belong to the same knowledge. Therefore it is impossible for the intellectual soul to be corruptible. Moreover we may take a sign of this from the fact that everything naturally aspires to existence after its own manner. Now, in things that have knowledge, desire ensues upon knowledge. The senses indeed do not know existence, except under the conditions of "here" and "now," whereas the intellect apprehends existence absolutely, and for all time; so that everything that has an intellect naturally desires always to exist. But a natural desire cannot be in vain. Therefore every intellectual substance is incorruptible.

Reply Obj. 1: Solomon reasons thus in the person of the foolish, as expressed in the words of wisdom 2. Therefore the saying that man and animals have a like beginning in generation is true of the body; for all animals alike are made of earth. But it is not true of the soul. For the souls of brutes are produced by some power of the body; whereas the human soul is produced by God. To signify this it is written as to other animals: "Let the earth bring forth the living soul" (Gen. 1:24): while of man it is written (Gen. 2:7) that "He breathed into his face the breath of life." And so in the last chapter of Ecclesiastes (12:7) it is concluded: "(Before) the dust return into its earth from whence it was; and the spirit return to God Who gave it." Again the process of life is alike as to the body, concerning which it is written (Eccles. 3:19): "All things breathe alike," and (Wis. 2:2), "The breath in our nostrils is smoke." But the process is not alike of the soul; for man is intelligent, whereas animals are not. Hence it is false to say: "Man has nothing more than beasts." Thus death comes to both alike as to the body, by not as to the soul.

Reply Obj. 2: As a thing can be created by reason, not of a passive potentiality, but only of the active potentiality of the Creator, Who can produce something out of nothing, so when we say that a thing can be reduced to nothing, we do not imply in the creature a potentiality to non-existence, but in the Creator the power of ceasing to sustain existence. But a thing is said to be corruptible because there is in it a potentiality to non-existence.

Reply Obj. 3: To understand through a phantasm is the proper operation of the soul by virtue of its union with the body. After separation from the body it will have another mode of understanding, similar to other substances separated from bodies, as will appear later on (Q. 89, A. 1).

Seventh Article [I, Q. 75, Art. 7]

Whether the Soul is of the Same Species As an Angel?

Objection 1: It would seem that the soul is of the same species as an angel. For each thing is ordained to its proper end by the nature of its species, whence is derived its inclination for that end. But the end of the soul is the same as that of an angel—namely, eternal happiness. Therefore they are of the same species.

Obj. 2: Further, the ultimate specific difference is the noblest, because it completes the nature of the species. But there is nothing nobler either in an angel or in the soul than their intellectual nature. Therefore the soul and the angel agree in the ultimate specific difference: therefore they belong to the same species.

Obj. 3: Further, it seems that the soul does not differ from an angel except in its union with the body. But as the body is outside the essence of the soul, it seems that it does not belong to its species. Therefore the soul and angel are of the same species.

On the contrary, Things which have different natural operations are of different species. But the natural operations of the soul and of an angel are different; since, as Dionysius says (Div. Nom. vii), "Angelic minds have simple and blessed intelligence, not gathering their knowledge of Divine things from visible things." Subsequently he says the contrary to this of the soul. Therefore the soul and an angel are not of the same species.

I answer that, Origen (Peri Archon iii, 5) held that human souls and angels are all of the same species; and this because he supposed that in these substances the difference of degree was accidental, as resulting from their free-will: as we have seen above (Q. 47, A. 2). But this cannot be; for in incorporeal substances there cannot be diversity of number without diversity of species and inequality of nature; because, as they are not composed of matter and form, but are subsistent forms, it is clear that there is necessarily among them a diversity of species. For a separate form cannot be understood otherwise than as one of a single species; thus, supposing a separate whiteness to exist, it could only be one; forasmuch as one whiteness does not differ from another except as in this or that subject. But diversity of species is always accompanied with a diversity of nature; thus in species of colors one is more perfect than another; and the same applies to other species, because differences which divide a genus are contrary to one another. Contraries, however, are compared to one another as the perfect to the imperfect, since the "principle of contrariety is habit, and privation thereof," as is written, Metaph. x (Did. ix, 4). The same would follow if the aforesaid substances were composed of matter and form. For if the matter of one be distinct from the matter of another, it follows that either the form is the principle of the distinction of matter--that is to say, that the matter is distinct on account of its relation to divers forms; and even then there would result a difference of species and inequality of nature: or else the matter is the principle of the distinction of forms. But one matter cannot be distinct from another, except by a distinction of quantity, which has no place in these incorporeal substances, such as an angel and the soul. So that it is not possible for the angel and the soul to be of the same species. How it is that there can be many souls of one species will be explained later (Q. 76, A. 2, ad 1).

Reply Obj. 1: This argument proceeds from the proximate and natural end. Eternal happiness is the ultimate and supernatural end.

Reply Obj. 2: The ultimate specific difference is the noblest because it is the most determinate, in the same way as actuality is nobler than potentiality. Thus, however, the intellectual faculty is not the noblest, because it is indeterminate and common to many degrees of intellectuality; as the sensible faculty is common to many degrees in the sensible nature. Hence, as all sensible things are not of one species, so neither are all intellectual things of one species.

Reply Obj. 3: The body is not of the essence of the soul; but the soul by the nature of its essence can be united to the body, so that, properly speaking, not the soul alone, but the "composite," is the species. And the very fact that the soul in a certain way requires the body for its operation, proves that the soul is endowed with a grade of intellectuality inferior to that of an angel, who is not united to a body.

Questions

1. What is the conflict over human nature? How does each side view human nature?

2. What is the relationship between a philosophy of human nature and a philosophy of God?

3. In what ways can liberty be perceived from the varying views of human nature?

4. Understanding the various perspectives of human nature, how do the writers maintain a connection between justice and human nature?

Suggested Media

Movies

Human Nature
Thank You for Smoking
The Human Experience
Magnolia
Atlas Shrugged
I Heart Huckabees
A Bug's Life
Avatar
Lord of the Flies
The Hunger Games
Groundhog Day
Waking Life

Television

Lost
Century of the Self

Blog

Darwin and Human Nature: the blog

Social Relations and Intersections

Complex personhood means that even those who haunt our dominant institutions and their systems of values are haunted too by things they sometimes have names for and sometimes do not. At the very least, complex personhood is about conferring the respect on others that comes from presuming that life and people's lives are simultaneously straightforward and full of enormously subtle meaning.

Gordon, A. 2008 p.5.

When seeking to understand justice, it is first important to begin from the simple premise, as Avery Gordon (2008) points out, that "life is complicated" (p.3). By beginning here, it is easier to understand that power, personhood, and social relations are complex, contested, and, often, fragile. By addressing social relations, we seek to put into focus the relationships between people and everyday life. This section is centered around the understanding that people are engaged in and shaped by multiple relationships, events, and influences and pays close attention to the meanings and interpretations that justice theorists have attached to people's diverse experiences in everyday life.

As was seen in the previous section, *human nature* is frequently constructed in binary terms—good vs. evil, right vs. wrong, selfish vs. self-interested—but, as theorists throughout the rest of this text will argue, human nature is far more complex and dynamic than any dichotomy. Not all of the authors in this text explicitly start at a discussion or deconstruction of human nature. Instead, many of the authors that you will read in the following sections start from varying perspectives such as power, relations, or institutions. Though their arguments may be interpreted as referencing human nature, many of these authors would claim that their analyses of justice do not necessarily lend themselves to any direct analysis of human nature. Therefore, we emphasize that human nature is complicated and discussions of human nature may be explicit and implicit and that human nature is one of many beginning points for deconstructing notions of justice and injustice.

The concept of 'the individual' can, by definition, exist only in relational terms. A person constructs a sense of identity in relation to family, peers and other people, cultural and community practices, gender, race and ethnicity, socio-economic class, social and political systems, sexuality, geographic location, and physical and mental abilities. By engaging with these constructs, the theorists in this section are able to appreciate connections between individuals and the social, political, and cultural structures that impact the daily experiences of people. This section foregrounds the lived experiences of people as a continual process and invites and encourages engagement with relevant topical issues such as relationships including the family, community, as well as the intersections between race, class, gender, and other converging identities. Meanings are informed by culture, community, peer groups, and families, among others, and the meaning of human action depends on lived experiences.

By exploring theoretical underpinnings of social relations in everyday life, it is our hope to better enhance understandings of people's personal lives; their workplace experiences; their engagement and sense of belonging with the community; and the way they make sense of and engage with intersecting oppressions. The authors in this section enhance our understanding of the social and cultural issues and local contexts that play a part in developing and sustaining a theoretical understanding of human nature and experiences in justice within everyday life.

Just as an individual person constructs a sense of identity in relation to multiple others, they also acquire multiple layered identities that are derived from social relations, historical contexts, and power structures. Moreover, identities are fluid and changing over time and across situations and audiences; they are never static. People occupy multiple identities, are part of multiple communities simultaneously, and navigate experiences of oppression and privilege through, and in relation to, these institutions and identities. By acknowledging that people have multiple identities, theorists of justice have been able to advocate for *laws* and ideas about *governance* and *economy* that address these converging identities. The concept of intersectionality is used to grasp the many identities people have and seeks to bring to light the multiple contesting frames and situations of people's everyday lives. The theorists in this section seek to deconstruct the ways in which people conduct themselves and carry out their mundane, ordinary, and important activities and relations in life.

Intersectionality and intersectional analysis were first coined by legal scholar Kimberlé Crenshaw in "Mapping the Margins: Intersectionality, Identity Politics, and Violence Against Women of Color" (1991), wherein she documented that within the eyes of the law, black women were doubly marginalized. When bringing a suit against General Motors (GM), black women claimed that they were discriminated against based on the fact that they were both black *and* women. They were not able to obtain front office administrative jobs because they were black and they were not able to obtain factory jobs because they were women. The court, on the other hand, in *Degraffenreid v. General Motors,* claimed that because there were women and black men working for GM, discrimination was not occurring. The Court saw discrimination as running parallel rather than as overlapping and therefore black women were not seen as a group and their multiple identities (being black and being women) were not considered under the law.

In addition to legal definitions, social movements have tended also to focus specifically on one identity—feminism on gender, antiracism on race, LGBT movements on sexual orientation—but frequently these movements, and the scholarly theorists that wrote about them, failed to comprehend the countless ways their constituents confront discrimination and oppression on multiple fronts and failed to acknowledge that disadvantage is based on the confluence of multiple dimensions of identities. For example, antiracism movements often did not address the sexism that women of color face and LGBT movements did not address the struggles of gay and lesbian people of color. Because theories of justice are particularly concerned with whether, how, and why persons are treated differently from others, it is crucial that we reflect on the overlapping, intersecting, dynamic, and converging identities of people. This means addressing issues such as gender, race, socioeconomic class, power, and sexual orientation.

The following readings embrace an intersectional analysis of social situations. Realizing that people have a multiplicity of identities (including race, gender, class, sexual orientation, ability, and citizenship, among others) that are created, sustained, changed, and influenced by social structures (including family, community, institutions, and media), the justice theorists in this section engage in an intersectional framework in their attempts to understand how intersecting identities influence relationships with the social world. As you will see in the rest of this reader, the social construction of reality and the intersections of social relations all contribute to the ways people understand governance, law, and economy. Only by beginning with a multifaceted understanding of the way people interact with the structural and institutional powers that surround them can we begin to grasp how people view justice in relation to these other aspects of society.

An interesting place to begin the discussion of social relations and intersections is Hegel's (1807) parable of the master and slave. Hegel presents the master and slave as a thought experiment of the two self-consciousnesses. In this thought experiment, the two self-conscious beings are in a battle for mutual recognition, which in turn, undermines the notion of autonomy and reflects an interaction between the self and the social. This further confirms the understanding that we cannot understand individuals as outside of everyday life and social relations. Therefore, both master and slave are interconnected where the master cannot be defined outside of the slave and the slave cannot be defined outside of the master. The two are in mutual interdependence and relation.

As Hegel claims, we are mutually dependent on others. This is seen clearly in one of the most prominent social institutions that influence our understandings of justice, the family. Beginning as early as Frederick Engel's (1884) "The Monogamous Family," the supremacy of the family as a socializing institution remains one of the most influential social relationships today. Previous scholars considered the family to be an exemplar of kindness and consideration for others, but rarely examined it. The family was frequently viewed as a reflection of man. Family life and practices, however, are often structured around notions of gender inequality, particularly in patriarchal societies where the mother/wife and children are constructed as subordinate and are valued less. Innate sex has been constructed as one of the clearest legitimizers of rights and restrictions.

The first selection in this section is by an early influential feminist theorist, John Stuart Mill entitled "On the Subjection of Women" where he claims that the principle which regulates social relations between men and women is the legal subordination of women through marriage. In her piece "Justice as Fairness: For Whom?" Susan Okin interrogates Rawls's *A Theory of Justice*, and, specifically the original position. She claims that Rawls neglects gender in his analysis and offers, instead, a feminist critique of Rawls' fundamental ideas. Rawls's original position is a thought experiment wherein the parties select principles about the structure of the society based on a "veil of ignorance" which conceals all knowledge on their individual characteristics and social position. Therefore, when making decisions about justice and distribution, those making the decisions would not know where they would fall in the social hierarchy. This, would then, ideally create a just environment because participants would select principles impartially. Okin, however, believes that though Rawls mentions the family, the "veil of ignorance" neglects gender and reinforces the public/private dichotomy of the family.

In addition to family, other social institutions and relations complicate and influence how we understand each other, particularly how we understand "difference." Race relations play a significant role when it comes to understanding social relations and intersections because they are one of the guiding forces in how we understand our place compared to others. Race continues to be one of the most influential social categories. In "The Changing Meaning of Race," Michael Omi provides an historical overview of the changing meaning of race and advocates that we think about race in terms of multiplicity, intersectionality, and hybridity. For Omi, though race is a social construction, racism is real and has very real consequences and he urges researchers and scholars to look at the processes of racialization and the "many ways racial meanings are constructed and imparted to social groups and processes." Omi interrogates debates around multiculturalism and whiteness and argues against "racial essentialism." He claims that unfortunately most social science research on race tends to neglect the intersecting and overlapping forms of stratification and difference.

Along with the family and other socially constructed institutions, media too, particularly in our current time, play an influential role in the way people understand themselves in relation to the social world. One of the most salient issues woven into discussions of justice and social relations is the conception of power. Power is one of the key principles that regulates and defines social relations and intersections. Power is embedded in social relations and is relative, rather than absolute, to a given situation, relationship, or interaction. Building on Antonio Gramsci's term "hegemony," Lull attempts to provide an understanding of hegemony as a powerful, albeit fragile, conceptual tool. Hegemony, as defined by Lull, is "the power or dominance that one social group holds over others." Family, peer and social groups, political and social institutions, and the mass media all play particularly important roles in the maintenance and development of hegemony as dominant ideologies are reproduced and reinforced within these basic social units. Hegemony is both the power and dominance one group holds over another and is a method for gaining and maintaining power. Hegemony implies willing and/or tacit consent and agreement by those in the subordinated role and is sustained by the major socializing institutions. Lull pays particular attention to the way media maintains hegemonic control. When analyzing and critiquing Justice, hegemony is one of the most important concepts to understand and provides a place to begin building a theory of justice.

As previously stated, everyday life, personhood, and social relations are complex. As such, Iris Marion Young brings to light the complexity of a new critical theory of justice. She envisions a new theory on justice as socially and historically contextualized. Young advocates for a politics that recognizes, rather than represses, difference; a politics that acknowledges and affirms group identity and difference. She utilizes Habermas' "ideal speech situation" and claims that this "represents the idea of justice as a structure of institutionalized relations that are free from domination." Young points out that a critical theory of justice "focuses on relations of interaction . . . focuses primarily on forms of social organization . . . and contains an a priori universal aspect without producing a conception of justice which claims transhistorical application." Therefore, the study of justice takes into account social, historical, and contextual matters and works to include and bring to light the complexities of everyday life.

Lastly, social relations and intersections can be seen both at the micro-level (communities, families, etc.) and at the macro-level (dealings nationally, internationally, and with the state). Social relations must also be understood as power relations. Historically, power relations have been contextualized within the framework of dominance and subordination. These relations are depicted in colonial relationships. In his selection, Aimé Césaire makes clear the need to further interrogate the colonizer/colonized relationships that continue to exist today. The process of colonization in any form creates relationships based on oppression rather than reciprocity, domination rather than consensus.

Similarly, Gyan Prakash argues for the importance of the field of Subaltern Studies because of its ability to plunge into the historiographical contest over the representation of culture and politics of the people. By providing an overview of the emergence and evolution of Subaltern Studies, Prakash illustrates the complexity of the colonized/colonizer relationship, the importance of understanding historiography, and provides an example of navigating what Audre Lorde (whom you will read in the *Governance* section) calls using the Master's tools to dismantle the Master's house. By understanding the position of the subaltern, those who are subordinated in terms of class, caste, gender, race, language and/or culture, we can further critique the dominant/dominated relationship.

As will become clear in the governance section that follows, the relationship between people and the state is often conflictual. The relations between colonizer and colonized is one of domination and submission which leads us to ask, what do we owe other persons in life?

References

Crenshaw, K. (1991). Mapping the Margins: Intersectionality, Identity Politics, and Violence Against Women of Color in *Stanford Law Review* 43:6. 1241–1299.

Engels, F. (1884/2004). *The Origins of the Family, Private Property and the State*. Australia: Resistance Books.

Gordon, A. (2008). *Ghostly Matters: Haunting and the Sociological Imagination*. Minneapolis: University of Minnesota Press.

Gramsci, A. (1971). *Selections from the Prison Notebooks*. Q. Hoare and G. Smith (eds). New York: International Publishers Co.

Hegel, G.W.F. (translation 1977). *The Phenomenology of Spirit*. A.V. Miller (translator). Oxford: Oxford University Press.

THE SUBJECTION OF WOMEN

JOHN STUART MILL

The object of this essay is to explain as clearly as I am able, the grounds of an opinion which I have held from the very earliest period when I had formed any opinions at all on social or political matters, and which, instead of being weakened or modified, has been constantly growing stronger by the progress of reflection and the experience of life: That the principle which regulates the existing social relations between the two sexes—the legal subordination of one sex to the other—is wrong in itself, and now one of the chief hindrances to human improvements; and that it ought to be replaced by a principle of perfect equality, admitting no power or privilege on the one side, nor disability on the other.

The very words necessary to express the task I have undertaken, show how arduous it is. But it would be a mistake to suppose that the difficulty of the case must lie in the insufficiency or obscurity of the grounds of reason on which my conviction rests. The difficulty is that which exists in all cases in which there is a mass of feeling to be contended against. So long as an opinion is strongly rooted in the feelings, it gains rather than loses in stability by having a preponderating weight of argument against it. For if it were accepted as a result of argument, the refutation of the argument might shake the solidity of the conviction; but when it rests solely on feeling, the worse it fares in argumentative contest, the more persuaded its adherents are that their feeling must have some deeper grounds, which the arguments do not reach; and while the feeling remains, it is always throwing up fresh intrenchments of argument to repair any breach made in the old. And there are so many causes tending to make the feelings connected with this subject the most intense and most deeply rooted of all those which gather round and protect old institutions and customs, that we need not wonder to find them as yet less undermined and loosened than any of the rest by the progress of the great modern spiritual and social transition; nor suppose that the barbarisms to which men cling longest must be less barbarisms than those which they earlier shake off. . . .

In the first place, the opinion in favour of the present system, which entirely subordinates the weaker sex to the stronger, rests upon theory only; for there never has been trial made of any other; so that experience, in the sense in which it is vulgarly opposed to theory, cannot be pretended to have pronounced any verdict. And in the second place, the adoption of this system of inequality never was the result of deliberation, or forethought, or any social ideas, or any notion whatever of what conduced to the benefit of humanity or the good order of society. It arose simply from the fact that from the very earliest twilight of human society, every woman (owing to the value attached to her by men, combined with her inferiority in muscular strength) was found in a state of bondage to some man. Laws and systems of polity always begin by recognising the relations they find already existing between individuals. They convert what was a mere physical fact into a legal right, give it the sanction of society, and principally aim at the substitution of public and organized means of asserting and protecting these rights, instead of the irregular and lawless conflict of physical strength. Those who had already been compelled to obedience became in this manner legally bound to it. Slavery, from being a mere affair of force between the master and the slave, became regularized and a matter of compact among the masters, who, binding themselves to one another for common protection, guaranteed by their collective strength the private possessions of each, including his slaves. In early times, the great majority of the male sex were slaves, as well as the

From The Subjection of Women, *Chap. 1. First published in 1869.*

whole of the female. And many ages elapsed, some of them ages of high cultivation, before any thinker was bold enough to question the rightfulness and absolute social necessity, either of the one slavery or of the other . . . .

If people are mostly so little aware how completely, during the greater part of the duration of our species, the law of force was the avowed rule of general conduct—any other being only a special and exceptional consequence of peculiar ties—and from how very recent a date it is that the affairs of society in general have been even pretended to be regulated according to any moral law, as little do people remember or consider how institutions and customs, which never had any ground but the law of force, last on into ages and states of general opinion which never would have permitted their first establishment. Less than forty years ago, Englishmen might still by law hold human beings in bondage as saleable property; within the present century they might kidnap them and carry them off, and work them literally to death. This absolutely extreme case of the law of force, condemned by those who can tolerate almost every other from of arbitrary power, and which, of all others, presents features the most revolting to the feelings of all who look at it from an impartial position, was the law of civilized and Christian England within the memory of persons now living: and in one half of Anglo-Saxon America three or four years ago, not only did slavery exist, but the slave trade, and the breeding of slaves expressly for it, was a general practice between slave states. Yet not only was there a greater strength of sentiment against it, but, in England at least a less amount either of feeling or of interest in favour of it, than of any other of the customary abuses of force: for its motive was the love of gain, unmixed and undisguised; and those who profited by it were a very small numerical fraction of the country, while the natural feeling of all who were not personally interested in it, was unmitigated abhorrence. So extreme an instance makes it almost superfluous to refer to any other; but consider the long duration of absolute monarchy. In England at present it is the almost universal conviction that military despotism is a case of the law of force, having no other origin or justification. Yet in all the great nations of Europe except England it either still exists, or has only just ceased to exist, and has even now a strong party favourable to it in all ranks of the people, especially among persons of station and consequence. Such is the power of an established system, even when far from universal, when not only in almost every period of history there have been great and well-known examples of the contrary system, but these have almost invariably been afforded by the most illustrious and most prosperous communities. In this case, too, the possessor of the undue power, the person directly interested in it, is only one person, while those who are subject to it and suffer from it are literally all the rest. The yoke is naturally and necessarily humiliating to all persons, except the one who is on the throne, together with, at most, the one who expects to succeed to it. How different are these cases from that of the power of men over women! I am not now prejudging the question of its justifiableness. I am showing how vastly more permanent it could not but be, even if not justifiable, than these other dominations which have nevertheless lasted down to our own time. Whatever gratification of pride there is in the possession of power, and whatever personal interest in its exercise, is in this case not confined to a limited class, but common to the whole male sex. Instead of being, to most of its supporters, a thing desirable chiefly in the abstract, or, like the political ends usually contended for by factions, of little private importance to any but the leaders, it comes home to the person and hearth of every male head of a family, and of every one who looks forward to being so. The clodhopper exercises, or is to exercise, his share of the power equally with the highest nobleman. And the case is that in which the desire of power is the strongest: for every one who desires power, desires it most over those who are nearest to him with whom his life is passed, with whom he has most concerns in common, and in whom any independence of his authority is oftenest likely to interfere with his individual preferences. If, in the other cases specified, power manifestly grounded only on force, and having so much less to support them, are so slowly and with so much difficulty got rid of, much more must it be so with this, even if it rests on no better foundation than those. We must consider, too, that the possessors of the power have facilities in this case, greater than in any other, to prevent any uprising against it. Every one of the subjects lives under the very eye, and almost, it may be said, in the hands, of some of the masters—in closer intimacy with him than with any of her fellow-subjects—with no means of combining against him, no power of even locally overmastering him, and, on the other hand, with the strongest motives for seeking his favour and avoiding to give him offence. In struggles for political emancipation, everybody knows how often its champions are bought off by bribes, or daunted by terrors. In the case of women, each individual of the subject-class is in a chronic state of bribery and intimidation combined. In setting up the standard of resistance, a large number of the leaders, and still more of the followers, must make an almost complete sacrifice of the pleasures or the alleviations of their own individual lot. If ever any system of privilege and enforced subjection had its yoke tightly riveted on the necks of those who are kept down by it, this has. . . .

All causes, social and natural, combine to make it unlikely that women should be collectively rebellious to the power of men. They are so far in a position different from all other subject classes, that their masters require something more from them than actual service. Men do not want solely the obedience of women, they want their sentiments. All men, except the most brutish, desire to have in the woman most nearly connected with them, not a forced slave but a willing one, not a slave merely, but a favourite. They have therefore put everything in practice to enslave their minds. The masters of all other slaves rely, for maintaining obedience, on fear; either fear of themselves, or religious fears. The masters of women wanted more than simple obedience, and they turned the whole force of education to effect their purpose. All women are bought up from the very earliest years in the belief that their ideal of character is the very opposite to that of men; not self-will, and government by self-control, but submission, and yielding to the control of others. All the moralities tell them that it is the duty of women, and all the current sentimentalities that it is their nature, to live for others; to make complete abnegation of themselves, and to have no life but in their affections. And by their affections are meant the only ones they are allowed to have—those to the men with whom they are connected, or to the children who constitute an additional and indefeasible tie between them and a man. When we put together three things—first, the natural attraction between opposite sexes; secondly, the wife's entire dependence on the husband, every privilege or pleasure she has being either his gift, or depending entirely on his will; and lastly, that the principal object of human pursuit, consideration, and all objects of social ambition, can in general be sought or obtained by her only through him, it would be a miracle if the object of being attractive to men had not become the polar star of feminine education and formation of character. And, this great means of influence over the minds of women having been acquired, an instinct of selfishness made men avail themselves of it to the utmost as a means of holding women in subjection, by representing to them meekness, submissiveness, and resignation of all individual will into the hands of a man, as an essential part of sexual attractiveness. Can it be doubted that any other yokes which mankind have succeeded in breaking, would have subsisted till now if the same means had existed, and had been as sedulously used, to bow down their minds to it? If it had been made the object of the life of every young plebeian to find personal favour in the eyes of some patrician, of every young serf with some seigneur; if domestication with him, and a share of his personal affections, had been held out as the prize which they all should look out for, the most gifted and aspiring being able to reckon on the most desirable prizes; and if, when this prize had been obtained, they had been shut out by a wall of brass from all interests not centering in him, all feelings and desires but those which he shared or inculcated; would not serfs and seigneurs, plebeians and patricians, have been as broadly distinguished at this day as men and women are? and would not all but a thinker here and there, have believed the distinction to be a fundamental and unalterable fact in human nature?

The preceding considerations are amply sufficient to show that custom, however universal it may be, affords in this case no presumption, and ought not to create any prejudice, in favour of the arrangements which place women in social and political subjection to men. But I may go farther, and maintain that the course of history, and the tendencies of progressive human society, afford not only no presumption in favour of this system of inequality of rights, but a strong one against it; and that, so far as the whole course of human improvement up to this time, the whole stream of modern tendencies, warrants any inference on the subject, it is, that this relic of the past is discordant with the future, and must necessarily disappear.

For, what is the peculiar character of the modern world—the difference which chiefly distinguishes modern institutions, modern social ideas, modern life itself, from those of times long past? It is, that human beings are no longer born to their place in life, and chained down by an inexorable bond to the place they are born to, but are free to employ their faculties, and such favourable chances as offer, to achieve the lot which may appear to them most desirable. Human society of old was constituted on a very different principle. All were born to a fixed social position, were mostly kept in it by law, or interdicted from any means by which they could emerge from it. As some men are born white and others black, so some were born slaves and others freemen and citizens; some were born patricians, others plebeians; some were born feudal nobles, others commoners and *roturiers*. A slave or serf could never make himself free, nor, except by the will of his master, become so. In most European countries it was not till towards the close of the middle ages, and as a consequence of the growth of regal power, that commoners could be ennobled. Even among nobles, the eldest son was born the exclusive heir to the paternal possessions, and a long time elapsed before it was fully established that the father could disinherit him. Among the industrious classes, only those who were born members of a guild, or were admitted into it by its members, could lawfully practise their calling within its local limits; and nobody could practise any calling deemed important, in any but the legal manner—by processes authoritatively prescribed. Manufacturers have stood in the pilory for presuming to carry on their business by new and improved methods. In modern Europe, and most in those parts of it which have participated most largely in all other modern improvements, diametrically opposite doctrines now prevail. Law and government do not undertake to prescribe by whom any social or industrial operation shall or shall not be conducted, or what modes of conducting them shall be lawful. These things are left to the unfettered choice of individuals. Even the laws which required that workmen should serve an apprenticeship, have in this country been repealed: there being ample assurance that in all cases in which an apprenticeship is necessary, its necessity will suffice to enforce it. The old theory was, that the least possible should be left to the choice of the individual agent; that all he had to do should, as far as practicable, be laid down for him by superior wisdom. Left to himself he was sure to go wrong. The modern conviction, the fruit of a thousand years of experience is, that things in which the individual is the person directly interested, never go right but as they are left to his own discretion; and that any regulation of them by authority, except to protect the rights of others, is sure to be mischievous. This conclusion, slowly arrived at, and not adopted until almost every possible application of the contrary theory had been made with disastrous result, now (in the industrial department) prevails universally in the most advanced countries, almost universally in all that have pretensions to any sort of advancement. It is not that all processes are supposed to be equally good, or all persons to be equally qualified for everything; but that freedom of individual choice is now known to be the only thing which procures the adoption of the best processes, and throws each operation into the hands of those who are best qualified for it. Nobody thinks it necessary to make a law that only a strong-armed man shall be a blacksmith. Freedom and competition suffice to make blacksmiths strong-armed men, because the weak-armed can earn more by engaging in occupations for which they are more fit. In consonance with this doctrine, it is felt to be an overstepping of the proper bounds of authority to fit beforehand, on some general presumption, that certain persons are not fit to do certain things. It is now thoroughly known and admitted that if some such presumptions exist, no such presumption is infallible. Even if it be well grounded in a majority of cases, which it is very likely not to be, there will be a minority of exceptional cases in which it does not hold; and in those it is both an injustice to the individuals, and a detriment to society, to place barriers in the way of their using their faculties for their own benefit and for that of others. In the cases, on the other hand, in which the unfitness is real, the ordinary motives of human conduct will on the whole suffice to prevent the incompetent person from making, or from persisting in, the attempt.

If this general principle of social and economical science is not true; if individuals, with such help as they can derive from the opinion of those who know them, are not better judges than the law and the government, of their own capacities and vocation; the world cannot too soon abandon this principle, and return to the old system of regulations and disabilities. But if the principle is true, we ought to act as if we believed it, and not to ordain that to be born a girl instead of a boy, and more than to be born black instead of white, or a commoner instead of a nobleman, shall decide the person's position through all life—shall interdict people from all the more elevated social positions, and from all, except a few, respectable occupations. Even were we to admit the utmost that is ever pretended as to the superior fitness of men for all the functions now reserved to them, the same argument applies which forbids a legal qualification for members of Parliament. If only once in a dozen years the conditions of eligibility exclude a fit person, there is a real loss, while the exclusion of thousands of unfit persons is no gain; for if the constitution of the electoral body disposes them to choose unfit persons, there are always plenty of such persons to choose from. In all things of any difficulty and importance, those who can do them well are fewer than the need, even with the most unrestricted latitude of choice; and any limitation of the field of selection deprives society of some chances of being served by the competent, without ever saving it from the incompetent.

At present, in the more improved countries, the disabilities of women are the only case, save one, in which laws and institutions take persons at their birth, and ordain that they shall never in all their lives be allowed to compete for certain things. . . .

The social subordination of women thus stands out an isolated fact in modern social institutions; a solitary breach of what has become their fundamental law; a single relic of an old world of thought and practice exploded in everything else, but retained in the one thing of most universal interest. . . .

The least that can be demanded is, that the question should not be considered as prejudged by existing fact and existing opinion, but open to discussion on its merits, as a question of justice and expediency; the decision on this, as on any of the other social arrangements of mankind, depending on what an enlightened estimate of tendencies and consequences may show to be most advantageous to humanity in general, without distinction of sex. And the discussion must be a real discussion descending to foundations, and not resting satisfied with vague and general assertions. It will not do, for instance, to assert in general terms, that the experience of mankind has pronounced in favour of the existing system. Experience cannot possibly have decided between two courses, so long as there has only been experience of one. If it be said that the doctrine of the equality of the sexes rests only on theory, it must be remembered that the contrary doctrine also has only theory to rest upon. All that is proved in its favour by direct experience, is that mankind have been able to exist under it, and to attain the degree of improvement and prosperity which we now see; but whether that prosperity has been attained sooner, or is now greater, than it would have been under the other system, experience does not say. On the other hand, experience does say, that every step in improvement has been so invariably accompanied by a step made in raising the social position of women, that historians and philosophers have been led to adopt their elevation or debasement as on the whole the surest test and most correct measure of the civilization of a people or an age. Through all the progressive period of human history, the condition of women has been approaching nearer to equality with men. This does not of itself prove that the assimilation must go on to complete equality; but it assuredly affords some presumption that such is the case.

Neither does it avail anything to say that the *nature* of the two sexes adapts them to their present functions and position, and renders these appropriate to them. Standing on the ground of common sense and the constitutions of the human mind, I deny that any one knows, or can know, the nature of the two sexes, as long as they have only been seen in their present relation to one another. If men had ever been found in society without women, or women without men, or if there had been a society of men and women in which the women were not under the control of the men, something might have been positively known about the mental and moral differences which may be inherent in the nature of each. What is now called the nature of women is an eminently artificial thing—the result of forced repression in some directions, unnatural stimulation in others. It may be asserted without scruple, that no other class of dependents have had their character so entirely distorted from its natural proportions by their relation with their masters; for, if conquered and slave races have been, in some respects, more forcibly repressed, whatever in them has not been crushed down by an iron heel has generally been let alone, and if left with any liberty of development, it has developed itself according to its own laws; but in the case of women, a hot-house and stove cultivation has always been carried on of some of the capabilities of their nature, for the benefit and pleasure of their masters. . . .

Hence, in regard to that most difficult question, what are the natural differences between the two sexes—a subject on which it is impossible in the present state of society to obtain complete and correct knowledge—while almost everybody dogmatizes upon it, almost all neglect and make light of the only means by which any partial insight can be obtained into it. This is, an analytic study of the most important department of psychology, the laws of the influence of circumstances on character. For, however great and apparently ineradicable the moral and intellectual differences between men and women might be, the evidence of their being natural differences could only be negative. Those only could be inferred to be natural which could not possibly be artificial—the residuum, after deducting every characteristic of either sex which can admit of being explained from education or external circumstances. The profoundest knowledge of the laws of the formation of character is indispensable to entitle any one to affirm even that there is any difference, much more what the difference is, between the two sexes considered as moral and rational beings; and since no one, as yet, has the knowledge, (for there is hardly any subject which, in proportion to its importance, has been so little studied), no one is thus far entitled to any positive opinion on the subject. Conjectures are all that can at present be made; conjectures more or less probable, according as more or less authorized by such knowledge as we yet have of the laws of psychology, as applied to the formation of character.

Even the preliminary knowledge, what the differences between the sexes now are, apart from all questions as to how they are made what they are, is still in the crudest and most incomplete state. . . .

One thing we may be certain of—that what is contrary to women's nature to do, they never will be made to do by simply giving their nature free play. The anxiety of mankind to interfere in behalf of nature, for fear lest nature should not succeed in effecting its purpose, is an altogether necessary solicitude. What women by nature cannot do, it is quite superfluous to forbid them from doing. What they can do, but not so well as the men who are their competitors, competition suffices to exclude them from, since nobody asks for protective duties and bounties in favour of women; it is only asked that the present bounties and protective duties in favour of men should be recalled. If women have a greater natural inclination for some things than for others, there is no need of laws or social inculcation to make the majority of them do the former in preference to the latter. Whatever women's services are most wanted for, the free play of competition will hold out the strongest inducements to them to undertake. And, as the words imply, they are most wanted for the things for which they are most fit; by the apportionment of which to them, the collective faculties of the two sexes can be applied on the whole with greatest sum of valuable result.

The general opinion of men is supposed to be, that the natural vocation of a woman is that of a wife and mother. I say, is supposed to be, because, judging from acts—from the whole of the present constitution of society—one might infer that their opinion was the direct contrary. They might be supposed to think that the alleged natural vocation of women was of all things the most repugnant to their nature; insomuch that if they are free to do anything else—if any other means of living, or occupation of their time and faculties, is open, which has any chance of appearing desirable to them—there will not be enough of them who will be willing to accept the condition said to be natural to them. If this is the real opinion of men in general, it would be well that it should be spoken out. I should like to hear somebody openly enunciating the doctrine (it is already implied in much that is written on the subject)—"It is necessary to society that women should marry and produce children. They will not do so unless they are compelled. Therefore it is necessary to compel them." The merits of the case would then be clearly defined. It would be exactly that of the slaveholders of South Carolina and Louisiana. "It is necessary that cotton and sugar should be grown. White men cannot produce them. Negroes will not, for any wages which we choose to give. *Ergo* they must be compelled." An illustration still closer to the point is that of impressment. Sailors must absolutely be had to defend the country. It often happens that they will not voluntarily enlist. Therefore there must be the power of forcing them. How often has this logic been used! and, but for one flaw in it, without doubt it would have been successful up to this day. But it is open to the retort—First pay the sailors the honest value of their labour. When you have made it as well worth their while to serve you, as to work for other employers, you will have no more difficulty than others have in obtaining their services. To this there is no logical answer except "I will not": and as people are now not only ashamed, but are not desirous, to rob the labourer of his hire, impressment is no longer advocated. Those who attempt to force women into marriage by closing all other doors against them, lay themselves open to a similar retort. If they mean what they say, their opinion must evidently be, that men do not render the married condition so desirable to women, as to induce them to accept it for its own recommendations. It is not a sign of one's thinking the boon one offers very attractive, when one allows only Hobson's choice, "that or none." And here, I believe, is the clue to the feelings of those men, who have a real antipathy to the equal freedom of women. I believe they are afraid, not lest women should be unwilling to marry, for I do not think that any one in reality has that apprehension; but lest they should insist that marriage should be on equal conditions; lest all women of spirit and capacity should prefer doing almost anything else, not in their own eyes degrading, rather than marry, when marrying is giving themselves a master, and a master too of all their earthly possessions. And truly, if this consequence were necessarily incident to marriage, I think that the apprehension would be very well founded. I agree in thinking it probable that few women, capable of anything else, would, unless under an irresistible *entrainement*, rendering them for the time insensible to anything but itself, choose such a lot, when any other means were open to them of filling a conventionally honourable place in life: and if men are determined that the law of marriage shall be a law of despotism, they are quite right, in point of mere policy, in leaving to women only Hobson's choice. But, in that case, all that has been done in the modern world to relax the chain on the minds of women, has been a mistake. They never should have been allowed to receive a literary education. Women who read, much more women who write, are, in the existing constitution of things, a contradiction and a disturbing element: and it was wrong to bring women up with any acquirements but those of an odalisque, or of a domestic servant.

"JUSTICE AS FAIRNESS FOR WHOM?"

SUSAN MOLLER OKIN

There is strikingly little indication, throughout most of *A Theory of Justice*, that the modern liberal society to which the principles of justice are to be applied is deeply and pervasively gender-structured. Thus an ambiguity runs throughout the work, which is continually noticeable to anyone reading it from a feminist perspective. On the one hand, as I shall argue, a consistent and wholehearted application of Rawls's liberal principles of justice can lead us to challenge fundamentally the gender system of our society. On the other hand, in his own account of his theory, this challenge is barely hinted at, much less developed. After critiquing Rawls's theory for its neglect of gender, I shall ask two related questions: What effects does a feminist reading of Rawls have on some of his fundamental ideas (particularly those most attacked by critics); and what undeveloped potential does the theory have for feminist critique, and in particular for our attempts to answer the question, Can justice co-exist with gender?

Central to Rawls's theory of justice is a construct, or heuristic device, that is both his most important single contribution to moral and political theory and the focus of most of the controversy his theory still attracts, nearly twenty years after its publication. Rawls argues that the principles of justice that should regulate the basic institutions of society are those that would be arrived at by persons reasoning in what is termed "the original position." His specifications for the original position are that "the parties" who deliberate there are rational and mutually disinterested, and that while no limits are placed on the general information available to them, a "veil of ignorance" conceals from them all knowledge of their individual characteristics and their social position. Though the theory is presented as a contract theory, it is so only in an odd and metaphoric sense, since "no one knows his situation in society nor his natural assets, and therefore no one is in a position to tailor principles to his advantage." Thus they have "no basis for bargaining in the usual sense." This is how, Rawls explains, "the arbitrariness of the world . . . [is] corrected for," in order that the principles arrived at will be fair. Indeed, since no one knows who he is, all think identically and the standpoint of any one party represents that of all. Thus the principles of justice are arrived at unanimously. Later in this chapter, I shall address some of the criticisms that have been made of Rawls's original position and of the nature of those who deliberate there. I shall show that his theory can be read in a way that either obviates these objections or answers them satisfactorily. But first, let us see how the theory treats women, gender, and the family.

Justice for All?

Rawls, like almost all political theorists until very recently, employs in *A Theory of Justice* supposedly generic male terms of reference. *Men, mankind, he,* and *his* are interspersed with gender-neutral terms of reference such as *individual* and *moral person.* Examples of intergenerational concern are worded in terms of "fathers" and "sons," and the difference principle is said to correspond to "the principle of fraternity." This linguistic usage would perhaps be less significant if it were not for the fact that Rawls self-consciously subscribes to a long tradition of moral and political philosophy that has used in its arguments either such "generic" male terms or more inclusive terms of reference ("human beings," "persons," "all rational beings as such"), only to exclude women from the scope of its conclusions. Kant is a clear example. But when Rawls refers to the generality and universality of Kant's ethics, and when he compares the principles chosen in his own original position to those regulative of Kant's kingdom of ends, "acting from [which] expresses our nature as free and equal rational persons," he does not mention the fact that women were not included among those persons to whom Kant meant his moral theory to apply. Again, in a brief discussion of Freud's account of moral development, Rawls presents Freud's theory of the formation of the male superego in largely gender-neutral terms, without mentioning the fact that Freud considered women's moral development to be sadly deficient, on account of their incomplete resolution of the Oedipus complex. Thus there is a blindness to the sexism of the tradition in which Rawls is a participant, which tends to render his terms of reference more ambiguous than they might otherwise be. A feminist reader finds it difficult not to keep asking, Does this theory of justice apply to women?

This question is not answered in the important passages listing the characteristics that persons in the original position are not to know about themselves, in order to formulate impartial principles of justice. In a subsequent article, Rawls has made it clear that sex is one of those morally irrelevant contingencies that are hidden by the veil of ignorance. But throughout *A Theory of Justice*, while the list of things unknown by a person in the original position includes "his place in society, his class position or social status, . . . his fortune in the distribution of natural assets and abilities, his intelligence and strength, and the like, . . . his conception of the good, the particulars of his rational plan of life, even the special features of his psychology," "his" sex is not mentioned. Since the parties also "know the general facts about human society," presumably including the fact that it is gender-structured both by custom and still in some respects by law, one might think that whether or not they knew their sex might matter enough to be mentioned. Perhaps Rawls meant to cover it by his phrase "and the like," but it is also possible that he did not consider it significant.

The ambiguity is exacerbated by the statement that those free and equal moral persons in the original position who formulate the principles of justice are to be thought of not as "single individuals" but as "heads of families" or "representatives of families." Rawls says that it is not necessary to think of the parties as heads of families, but that he will generally do so. The reason he does this, he explains, is to ensure that each person in the original position cares about the well-being of some persons in the next generation. These "ties of sentiment" between generations, which Rawls regards as important for the establishment of intergenerational justice—his just savings principle—, would otherwise constitute a problem because of the general assumption that the parties in the original position are mutually disinterested. In spite of the ties of sentiment *within* families, then, "as representatives of families their interests are opposed as the circumstances of justice imply."

The head of a family need not necessarily, of course, be a man. Certainly in the United States, at least, there has been a striking growth in the proportion of female-headed households during the last several decades. But the very fact that, in common usage, the term "female-headed household" is used *only* in reference to households without resident adult males implies the assumption that any present male takes precedence over a female as the household or family head. Rawls does nothing to contest this impression when he says of those in the original position that "imagining themselves to be fathers, say, they are to ascertain how much they should set aside for their sons by noting what they would believe themselves entitled to claim of their fathers. He makes the "heads of families" assumption only in order to address the problem of justice between generations, and presumably does not intend it to be a sexist assumption. Nevertheless, he is thereby effectively trapped into the public/domestic diohotomy and, with it, the conventional mode of thinking that life within the family and relations between the sexes are not properly regarded as part of the subject matter of a theory of social justice.

Let me here point out that Rawls, for good reason, states at the outset of his theory that the family is part of the subject matter of a theory of social justice. "For us" he says, "the primary subject of justice is the basic structure of society, or more exactly, the way in which the major social institutions distribute fundamental rights and duties and determine the division of advantages from social cooperation." The political constitution and the principal economic and social arrangements are basic because "taken together as one scheme, [they] define men's rights and duties and influence their life prospects, what they can expect to be and how well they can hope to do. The basic structure is the primary subject of justice *because its effects are so profound and present from the start*" (emphasis added). Rawls specifies "the monogamous family" as an example of such major social institutions, together with the political constitution, the legal protection of essential freedoms, competitive markets, and private property. Although this initial inclusion of the family as a basic social institution to which the principles of justice should apply is surprising in the light of the history of liberal thought, with its dichotomy between domestic and public spheres, it is necessary, given Rawls's stated criteria for inclusion in the basic structure. It would scarcely be possible to deny that different family structures, and different distributions of rights and duties within families, affect men's "life prospects, what they can expect to be and how well they can hope to do," and even more difficult to deny their effects on the life prospects of women. There is no doubt, then, that in Rawls's initial definition of the sphere of social justice, the family is included and the public/domestic dichotomy momentarily cast in doubt. However, the family is to a large extent ignored, though assumed, in the rest of the theory. . . .

Rawls's Theory of Justice as a Tool for Feminist Criticism

The significance of Rawls's central, brilliant idea, the original position, is that it forces one to question and consider traditions, customs, and institutions from all points of view, and ensures that the principles of justice will be acceptable to everyone, regardless of what position "he" ends up in. The critical force of the original position becomes evident when one considers that some of the most creative critiques of Rawls's theory have resulted from more radical or broad interpretations of the original position than his own. The theory, in principle, avoids both the problem of domination that is inherent in theories of justice based on traditions or shared understandings and the partiality of libertarian theory to those who are talented or fortunate. For feminist readers, however, the problem of the theory as stated by Rawls himself is encapsulated in that ambiguous "he." As I have shown, while Rawls briefly rules out formal, legal discrimination on the grounds of sex (as on other grounds that he regards as "morally irrelevant"), he fails entirely to address the justice of the gender system, which, with its roots in the sex roles of the family and its branches extending into virtually every corner of our lives, is one of the fundamental structures of our society. If, however, we read Rawls in such a way as to take seriously both the notion that those behind the veil of ignorance do not know what sex they are and the requirement that the family and the gender system, as basic social institutions, are to be subject to scrutiny, constructive feminist criticism of these contemporary institutions follows. So, also, do hidden difficulties for the application of a Rawlsian theory of justice in a gendered society.

I shall explain each of these points in turn. But first, both the critical perspective and the incipient problems of a feminist reading of Rawls can perhaps be illuminated by a description of a cartoon I saw a few years ago. Three elderly, robed male justices are depicted, looking down with astonishment at their very pregnant bellies. One says to the others, without further elaboration: "Perhaps we'd better reconsider that decision." This illustration graphically demonstrates the importance, in thinking about justice, of a concept like Rawls's original position, which makes us adopt the positions of others—especially positions that we ourselves could never be in. It also suggests that those thinking in such a way might well conclude that more than formal legal equality of the sexes is required if justice is to be done. As we have seen in recent years, it is quite possible to enact and uphold "gender-neutral" laws concerning pregnancy, abortion, childbirth leave, and so on, that in effect discriminate against women. The United States Supreme Court decided in 1976, for example, that "an exclusion of pregnancy from a disability-benefits plan providing general coverage is not a gender-based discrimination at all." One of the virtues of the cartoon is its suggestion that one's thinking on such matters is likely to be affected by the knowledge that one might become "a pregnant person." The illustration also points out the limits of what is possible, in terms of thinking ourselves into the original position, as long as we live in a gender-structured society. While the elderly male justices can, in a sense, imagine themselves as pregnant, what is a much more difficult question is whether, in order to construct principles of justice, they can imagine themselves as women. This raises the question of whether, in fact, sex is a morally irrelevant and contingent characteristic in a society structured by gender.

Let us first assume that sex is contingent in this way, though I shall later question this assumption. Let us suppose that it is possible, as Rawls clearly considers it to be, to hypothesize the moral thinking of representative human beings, as ignorant of their sex as of all the other things hidden by the veil of ignorance. It seems clear that, while Rawls does not do this, we must consistently take the relevant positions of both sexes into account in formulating and applying principles of justice. In particular, those in the original position must take special account of the perspective of women, since their knowledge of "the general facts about human society" must include the knowledge that women have been and continue to be the less advantaged sex in a great number of respects. In considering the basic institutions of society, they are more likely to pay special attention to the family than virtually to ignore it. Not only is it potentially the first school of social justice, but its customary unequal assignment of responsibilities and privileges to the two sexes and its socialization of children into sex roles make it, in its current form, an institution of crucial importance for the perpetuation of sex inequality.

In innumerable ways, the principles of justice that Rawls arrives at are inconsistent with a gender-structured society and with traditional family roles. The critical impact of a feminist application of Rawls's theory comes chiefly from his second principle, which requires that inequalities be both "to the greatest benefit of the least advantaged" and "attached to offices and positions open to all." This means that if any roles or positions analogous to our current sex roles—including those of husband and wife, mother and father—were to survive the demands of the first requirement, the second requirement would prohibit any linkage between these roles and sex. Gender, with its ascriptive designation of positions and expectations of behavior in accordance with the inborn characteristic of sex, could no longer form a legitimate part of the social structure, whether inside or outside the family. . . .

There is, then, implicit in Rawls's theory of justice a potential critique of gender-structured social institutions, which can be developed by taking seriously the fact that those formulating the principles of justice do not know their sex. At the beginning of my brief account of this feminist critique, however, I made an assumption that I said would later be questioned—that a person's sex is, as Rawls at times indicates, a contingent and morally irrelevant characteristic, such that human beings really can hypothesize ignorance of this fact about them. First, I shall explain why, unless this assumption is a reasonable one, there are likely to be further feminist ramifications for a Rawlsian theory of justice, in addition to those I have just sketched out. I shall then argue that the assumption is very probably not plausible in any society that is structured along the lines of gender. I reach the conclusions not only that our current gender structure is incompatible with the attainment of social justice, but also that the disappearance of gender is a prerequisite for the *complete* development of a nonsexist, fully human theory of justice.

Although Rawls is clearly aware of the effects on individuals of their different places in the social system, he regards it as possible to hypothesize free and rational moral persons in the original position who, temporarily freed from the contingencies of actual characteristics and social circumstances, will adopt the viewpoint of the "representative" human being. He is under no illusions about the difficulty of this task: it requires a "great shift in perspective" from the way we think about fairness in everyday life. But with the help of the veil of ignorance, he believes that we can "take up a point of view that everyone can adopt on an equal footing," so that "we share a common standpoint along with others and do not make our judgments from a personal slant." The result of this rational impartiality or objectivity, Rawls argues, is that, all being convinced by the same arguments, agreement about the basic principles of justice will be unanimous. He does not mean that those in the original position will agree about all moral or social issues—"ethical differences are bound to remain"— but that complete agreement will be reached on all basic principles, or "essential understandings." A critical assumption of this argument for unanimity, however, is that all the parties have similar motivations and psychologies (for example, he assumes mutually disinterested rationality and an absence of envy) and have experienced similar patterns of moral development, and are thus presumed capable of a sense of justice. Rawls regards these assumptions as the kind of "weak stipulations" on which a general theory can safely be founded.

The coherence of Rawls's hypothetical original position, with its unanimity of representative human beings, however, is placed in doubt if the kinds of human beings we actually become in society differ not only in respect to interests, superficial opinions, prejudices, and points of view that we can discard for the purpose of formulating principles of justice, but also in their basic psychologies, conceptions of the self in relation to others, and experiences of moral development. A number of feminist theorists have argued in recent years that, in a gender-structured society, the different life experiences of females and males from the start in fact affect their respective psychologies, modes of thinking, and patterns of moral development in significant ways. Special attention has been paid to the effects on the psychological and moral development of both sexes of the fact, fundamental to our gendered society, that children of both sexes are reared primarily by women. It has been argued that the experience of individuation—of separating oneself from the nurturer with whom one is originally psychologically fused—is a very different experience for girls than for boys, leaving the members of each sex with a different perception of themselves and of their relations with others. . . . In addition, it has been argued that the experience of *being* primary nurturers (and of growing up with this expectation) also affects the psychological and moral perspective of women, as does the experience of growing up in a society in which members of one's sex are in many ways subordinate to the other sex. Feminist theorists have scrutinized and analyzed the different experiences we encounter as we develop, from our actual lived lives to our absorption of their ideological underpinnings, and have filled out in valuable ways Simone de Beauvoir's claim that "one is not born, but rather becomes, a woman."

What seems already to be indicated by these studies, despite their incompleteness so far, is that *in a gender-structured society* there is such a thing as the distinct standpoint of women, and that this standpoint cannot be adequately taken into account by male philosophers doing the theoretical equivalent of the elderly male justices depicted in the cartoon. The formative influence of female parenting on small children, especially, seems to suggest that sex difference is even more likely to affect one's thinking about justice in a gendered society than, for example, racial difference in a society in which race has social significance, or class difference in a class society. The notion of the standpoint of women, while not without its own problems, suggests that a fully human moral or political theory can be developed only with the full participation of both sexes. At the very least, this will require that women take their place with men in the dialogue in approximately equal numbers and in positions of comparable influence. In a society structured along the lines of gender, this cannot happen.

In itself moreover, it is insufficient for the development of a fully human theory of justice. For if principles of justice are to be adopted unanimously by representative human beings ignorant of their particular characteristics and positions in society, they must be persons whose psychological and moral development is in all essentials identical. This means that the social factors influencing the differences presently found between the sexes—from female parenting to all the manifestations of female subordination and dependence—would have to be replaced by genderless institutions and customs. Only children who are equally mothered and fathered can develop fully the psychological and moral capacities that currently seem to be unevenly distributed between the sexes. Only when men participate equally in what have been principally women's realms of meeting the daily material and psychological needs of those close to them, and when women participate equally in what have been principally men's realms of larger scale production, government, and intellectual and artistic life, will members of both sexes be able to develop a more complete *human* personality than has hitherto been possible. Whereas Rawls and most other philosophers have assumed that human psychology, rationality, moral development, and other capacities are completely represented by the males of the species, this assumption itself has now been exposed as part of the male-dominated ideology of our gendered society.

What effect might consideration of the standpoint of women in gendered society have on Rawls's theory of justice? It would place in doubt some assumptions and conclusions, while reinforcing others. For example, the discussion of rational plans of life and primary goods might be focused more on relationships and less exclusively on the complex activities that he values most highly, if it were to take account of, rather than to take for granted, the traditionally more female contributions to human life. Rawls says that self-respect or self-esteem is "perhaps the most important primary good," and that "the parties in the original position would wish to avoid at almost any cost the social conditions that undermine [it]." Good early physical and especially psychological nurturance in a favorable setting is essential for a child to develop self-respect or self-esteem. Yet there is no discussion of this in Rawls's consideration of the primary goods. Since the basis of self-respect is formed in very early childhood, just family structures and practices in which it is fostered and in which parenting itself is esteemed, and high-quality, subsidized child care facilities to supplement them, would surely be fundamental requirements of a just society. On the other hand, as I indicated earlier, those aspects of Rawls's theory, such as the difference principle, that require a considerable capacity to identify with others, can be strengthened by reference to conceptions of relations between self and others that seem in gendered society to be more predominantly female, but that would in a gender-free society be more or less evenly shared by members of both sexes.

The arguments of this chapter have led to mixed conclusions about the potential usefulness of Rawls's theory of justice from a feminist viewpoint, and about its adaptability to a genderless society. Rawls himself neglects gender and, despite his initial statement about the place of the family in the basic structure, does not consider whether or in what form the family is a just institution. It seems significant, too, that whereas at the beginning of *A Theory of Justice* he explicitly distinguishes the institutions of the basic structure (*including* the family) from other "private associations" and "various informal conventions and customs of everyday life," [in his most recent work] he distinctly reinforces the impression that the family belongs with those "private" and therefore nonpolitical associations, for which he suggests the principles of justice are less appropriate or relevant. He does this, moreover, despite the fact that his own theory of moral development rests centrally on the early experience of persons within a family environment that is both loving and just. Thus the theory as it stands contains an internal paradox. Because of his assumptions about gender, he has not applied the principles of justice to the realm of human nurturance, a realm that is essential to the achievement and the maintenance of justice.

On the other hand, I have argued that the feminist *potential* of Rawls's method of thinking and his conclusions is considerable. The original position, with the veil of ignorance hiding from its participants their sex as well as their other particular characteristics, talents, circumstances, and aims, is a powerful concept for challenging the gender structure. Once we dispense with the traditional liberal assumptions about public versus domestic, political versus nonpolitical spheres of life, we can use Rawls's theory as a tool with which to think about how to achieve justice between the sexes both within the family and in society at large.

THE CHANGING MEANING OF RACE

MICHAEL A. OMI

The 1997 President's Initiative on Race elicited numerous comments regarding its intent and focus. One such comment was made by Jefferson Fish, a psychologist at St. John's University in New York, who said: "This dialogue on race is driving me up the wall. Nobody is asking the question, 'What is race?' It is a biologically meaningless category" (quoted in Petit, 1998: A1).

Biologists, geneticists, and physical anthropologists, among others, long ago reached a common understanding that race is not a "scientific" concept rooted in discernible biological differences. Nevertheless, race is commonly and popularly defined in terms of biological traits—phenotypic differences in skin color, hair texture, and other physical attributes, often perceived as surface manifestations of deeper, underlying differences in intelligence, temperament, physical prowess; and sexuality. Thus, although race may have no biological meaning, as used in reference to human differences, it has an extremely important and highly contested *social* one.

Clearly, there is an enormous gap between the scientific rejection of race as a concept, and the popular acceptance of it as an important organizing principle of individual identity and collective consciousness. But merely asserting that race is socially constructed does not get a how specific racial concepts come into existence, what the fundamental determinants of racialization are, and how race articulates with other major axes of stratification and "difference," such as gender and class. Each of these topics would require an extensive treatise on possible variables shaping our collective notions of race. The following discussion is much more modest.

I attempt to survey ways of thinking about, bringing into context, and interrogating the changing meaning of race in the United States. My intent is to raise a series of points to be used as frames of reference, to facilitate and deepen the conversation about race.

My general point is that the meaning of race in the United States has been and probably always will be fluid and subject to multiple determinations. Race cannot be seen simply as an objective fact, nor treated as an independent variable. Attempting to do so only serves, ultimately, to emphasize the importance of critically examining how specific concepts of race are conceived of and deployed in areas such as social-science research, public-policy initiatives, cultural representations, and political discourse. Real issues and debates about race—from the Federal Standards for Racial and Ethnic Classification to studies of economic inequality—need to be approached from a perspective that makes the concept of race problematic.

A second point is the importance of discerning the relationship between race and racism, and being attentive to transformations in the nature of "racialized power." The distribution of power—and its expression in structures, ideologies, and practices at various institutional and individual levels—is significantly racialized in our society. Shifts in what "race" means are indicative of reconfigurations in the nature of "racialized power" and emphasize the need to interrogate specific concepts of racism.

Global And National Racial Change

The present historical moment is unique, with respect to racial meanings. Since the end of World War II, there has been an epochal shift in the global racial order that had persisted for centuries (Winant and Seidman, 1998). The horrors of fascism and a wave of anticolonialism facilitated a rupture with biologic and eugenic concepts of race, and challenged the ideology(ies) of White supremacy on a number of important fronts. Scholarly projects in genetics, cultural anthropology, and history, among others, were fundamentally rethought, and antiracist initiatives became a crucial part of democratic political projects throughout the world.

In the United States, the Civil Rights Movement was instrumental in challenging and subsequently dismantling patterns of Jim Crow[1] segregation in the South. The strategic push of the Movement in its initial phase was toward racial integration in various institutional arenas—e.g., schools, public transportation, and public accommodations—and the extension of legal equality for all regardless of "color." This took place in a national context of economic growth and the expansion of the role and scope of the federal government.

Times have changed and ironies abound. Domestic economic restructuring and the transnational flow of capital and labor have created a new economic context for situating race and racism. The federal government's ability to expand social programs, redistribute resources, and ensure social justice has been dramatically curtailed by fiscal constraints and the rejection of liberal social reforms of the 1960s. Demographically, the nation is becoming less White and the dominant Black-White paradigm of race relations is challenged by the dramatic growth and increasing visibility of Hispanics and Asians.

All these changes have had a tremendous impact on racial identity, consciousness, and politics. Racial discourse is now littered with confused and contradictory meanings. The notion of "color-blindness" is now more likely to be advanced by political groups seeking to dismantle policies, such as affirmative action, initially designed to mitigate racial inequality. Calls to get "beyond race" are popularly expressed, and any hint of race consciousness is viewed as racism.

In this transformed political landscape, traditional civil rights organizations have experienced a crisis of mission, political values, and strategic orientation. Integrationist versus "separate-but-equal" remedies for persistent racial disparities have been revisited in a new light. More often the calls are for "self-help" and for private support to tackle problems of crime, unemployment, and drug abuse. The civil rights establishment confronts a puzzling dilemma—formal, legal equality has been significantly achieved, but substantive racial inequality in employment, housing, and health care remains, and in many cases, has deepened.

All this provides an historical context in which to situate evolving racial meanings. Over the past 50 years, changes in the meaning of race have been shaped by, and in turn have shaped, broader global/epochal shifts in racial formation. The massive influx of new immigrant groups has destabilized specific concepts of race, led to a proliferation of identity positions, and challenged prevailing modes of political and cultural organization.

Demographic Change And Racial Transformation

In a discussion of Asian American cultural production and political formation, Lowe (1996) uses the concepts of *heterogeneity, hybridity,* and *multiplicity* to disrupt popular notions of a singular, unified Asian American subject. Refashioning these concepts, I use them to assess the changes in, and issues relevant to, racial meaning created by demographic shifts.

---

[1] The original "Jim Crow" was a character in a nineteenth-century act, a stereotype of a Black man. As encoded in laws discrimination the phrase refers to both legally enforced and traditionally sanctioned limitations of Blacks rights, primarily in the U.S. South.

Heterogeneity

Lowe defines heterogeneity as "the existence of differences and differential relationships within a bounded category" (1996:67). Over the past several decades, there has been increasing diversity among so-called racial groups. Our collective understanding of who Blacks, Hispanics, and Asians are has undergone a fundamental revision as new groups entered the country. The liberalization of immigration laws beginning in 1965, political instability in various areas of the world, and labor migration set in motion by global economic restructuring all contributed to an influx of new groups—Laotians, Guatemalans, Haitians, and Sudanese, among others.

In the United States, many of these immigrants encounter an interesting dilemma. Although they may stress their national origins and ethnic identities, they are continually racialized as part of a broader group. Many first-generation Black immigrants from, for example, Jamaica, Ethiopia, or Trinidad, distance themselves from, subscribe to negative stereotypes of, and believe that, as ethnic immigrants, they are accorded a higher status than, Black Americans (Kasinitz, 1992). Children of Black immigrants, who lack their parents' distinctive accents, have more choice in assuming different identities (Waters, 1994). Some try to defy racial classification as "Black Americans" by strategically asserting their ethnic identity in specific encounters with Whites. Others simply see themselves as "Americans."

Panethnic organization and identity constitute one distinct political/cultural response to increasing heterogeneity. Lopez and Espiritu define panethnicity as "the development of bridging organizations and solidarities among subgroups of ethnic collectivities that are often seen as homogeneous by outsiders" (1990:198); such a development, they claim, is a crucial feature of ethnic change, "supplanting both assimilation and ethnic particularism as the direction of change for racial/ethnic minorities" (1990:198).

Omi and Winant (1996) describe the rise of panethnicity as a response to racialization, driven by a dynamic relationship between the group being racialized and the state. Elites representing panethnic groups find it advantageous to make political demands backed by the numbers and resources panethnic formations can mobilize. The state, in turn, can more easily manage claims by recognizing and responding to large blocs, as opposed to dealing with specific claims from a plethora of ethnically defined interest groups. Different dynamics of inclusion and exclusion are continually expressed. Conflicts often occur over the precise definition and boundaries of various racially defined groups and their adequate representation in census counts, reapportionment debates, and minority set-aside programs. The increasing heterogeneity of racial categories raises several questions for research to answer.

Hybridity

Crouch, in his essay "Race Is Over" (1996), speculates that in the future, race will cease to be the basis of identity and "special-interest power" because of the growth in mixed-race people. It has been a long-standing liberal dream, most recently expressed by Warren Beatty in the film *Bulworth*, that increased "race mixing" would solve our racial problems. Multiraciality disrupts our fixed notions about race and opens up new possibilities with respect to dialogue and engagement across the color line. It does not, however, mean that "race is over."

Although the number of people of "mixed-racial descent" is unclear, and contingent on self-definition, the 1990 census counted two million children (under the age of 18) whose parents were of different races (Marriott, 1996). The demographic growth and increased visibility of "mixed-race" or "multiracial" individuals has resulted in a growing literature on multiracial identity and its meaning for a racially stratified society (Root, 1992; Zack, 1994).

In response to these demographic changes, there was a concerted effort from school boards and organizations such as Project RACE (Reclassify All Children Equally) to add a "multiracial" category to the 2000 Census form (Mathews, 1996). This was opposed by many civil rights organizations (e.g., Urban

League, National Council of La Raza) who feared a reduction in their numbers and worried that such a multiracial category would spur debates regarding the "protected status" of groups and individuals. According to various estimates, 75 to 90 percent of those who now check the "Black" box could check a multiracial one (Wright, 1994). In pretests by the Census Bureau in 1996, however, only 1 percent of the sample claimed to be multiracial (U.S. Bureau of the Census, 1996).

In October 1997, the Office of Management and Budget (OMB) decided to allow Americans the option of multiple checkoffs on the census with respect to the newly modified racial and ethnic classifications (Holmes, 1997). Initial debate centered on how to count people who assigned themselves to more than one racial/ethnic category. At issue is not only census enumeration, but also its impact on federal policies relevant to voting rights and civil rights.

It remains to be seen how many people will actually identify themselves as members of more than one race. Much depends on the prevailing consciousness of multiracial identity, the visibility of multiracial people, and representational practices. As Reynolds Farley notes, "At the time of the 2000 census, if we have another Tiger Woods . . . those figures could up to 5 percent—who knows?" (quoted in Holmes, 1997:A19).

The debate over a multiracial category reveals an intriguing aspect about our conceptualizations of race. The terms "mixed race" or "multiracial" in themselves imply the existence of "pure" and discrete races. By drawing attention to the socially constructed nature of "race," and the meanings attached to it, multiraciality reveals the inherent fluidity and slipperiness of our concepts of race. Restructuring concepts of race has a number of political implications. House Speaker Newt Gingrich (1997), for example, used the issue of multiraciality to illustrate the indeterminacy of racial categories and to vigorously advocate for their abolition in government data collection, much as advocates of color-blindness do.

In her definition of hybridity, Lowe refers to the formation of material culture and practices "produced by the histories of uneven and unsynthetic power relations" (Lowe, 1996:67). Indeed, the question of power cannot be elided in the discussion of multiraciality because power is deeply implicated in racial trends and in construction of racial meanings. The rigidity of the "one-drop rule,"[2] long-standing fears of racial "pollution," and the persistence (until the *Loving*, decision in 1967) of antimiscegenation laws demonstrate the ways in which the color line has been policed in the United States. This legacy to affect trends in interracial marriage. Lind (1998) suggests that both multiculturalists and nativists have misread trends, and that a new dichotomy between Black and non-Blacks is emerging. In the 21st century, he envisions "a White-Asian-Hispanic melting-pot majority—a hard-to-differentiate group of beige Americans—offset by a minority consisting of Blacks who have been left out of the melting pot once again" (p.39). Such a dire racial landscape raises a number of troubling political questions regarding group interests, the distribution of resources, and the organization of power.

Simultaneously, racial hybridity reveals the fundamental instability of all racial categories, helps us discern particular dimensions of racialized power, and raises a host of political issues.

The repeal of antimiscegenation laws, the marked lessening of social distance between racial groups, and interracial marriage among specific groups have contributed to the growth and increased visibility of a multiracial population. Studies thus far have focused on "cultural conflict" and psychological issues of individual adjustment. We need to assess more deeply how multiraciality affects the logic and organization of data on racial classification, and the political and policy issues that emanate from this.

---

[2] A person was legally Negrold, regardless of actual physical appearance, if there were any proof of African ancestry—i.e., one drop of African blood.

Multiplicity

It is, by now, obvious that the racial composition of the nation has been radically changing. In seven years, Hispanics will surpass Blacks as the largest "minority group" in the United States (Holmes, 1998). Trends in particular states and regions are even more dramatic. In 1970, Whites constituted 77 percent of the San Francisco Bay Area's population. Hispanics and Asians constituted 11 and 4 percent, respectively, of the population (McLeod, 1998). In 1997, Whites constituted 54 percent, and Hispanics and Asians each comprised nearly 20 percent of the population.

At the first Advisory Board meeting of the President's Initiative on Race (July 14, 1997), a brief debate ensued among the panelists. Linda Chavez-Thompson argued that the "American dilemma" had become a proliferation of racial and ethnic dilemmas. Angela Oh argued that the national conversation needed to move beyond discussions of racism as solely directed at Blacks. Advisory Board chairman John Hope Franklin, by contrast, affirmed the historical importance of Black-White relations and stressed the need to focus on unfinished business. Although the Board members subsequently downplayed their differences, their distinct perspectives continued to provoke debate within academic, policy, and community activist settings regarding the Black-White race paradigm.

How we think about, engage, and politically mobilize around racial issues have been fundamentally shaped by a prevailing "Black-White" paradigm of race relations. Historical accounts of other people of color in the United States are cast in the shadows of the Black-White encounter. Contemporary conflicts between a number of different racial/ethnic groups are understood in relationship to Black-White conflict, and the media uses the bipolar model as a master frame to present such conflicts.

Such biracial theorizing misses the complex nature of race relations in post-Civil Rights Movement America. Complex patterns of conflict and accommodation have developed among multiple racial/ethnic groups. In many major U.S. cities, Whites have fled to suburbia, leaving the inner city to the turf battles among different racial minorities for housing, public services, and economic development.

The dominant mode of biracial theorizing ignores the fact that a range of specific conditions and trends—such as labor-market stratification and residential segregation—cannot be adequately studied by narrowly assessing the relative situations of Whites and Blacks. Working within a "two-nations" framework of Black and White, Hacker (1992) needs to consider Asians in higher education at some length in order to address the issue of race-based affirmative action.

In suggesting that we get beyond the Black-White paradigm, I'm conscious of the consequences of such a move. On the one hand, I do not mean to displace or decenter the Black experience, which continues to define the fundamental contours of race and racism in our society. On the other hand, I do want to suggest that the prevailing Black-White model tends to marginalize, if not ignore, the experiences, needs, and political claims of other racialized groups. The challenge is to frame an appropriate language and analysis to help us understand the shifting dynamic of race that all groups are implicated in.

We would profit from more historical and contemporary studies that look at the patterns of interaction between, and among, a multiplicity of groups. Almaguer (1994), in his study of race in nineteenth-century California, breaks from the dominant mode of biracial theorizing to illustrate how American Indians, Mexicans, Chinese, and Japanese were racialized and positioned in relation to one another by the dominant Anglo elite. Horton (1995) takes a look at distinct sites of political and cultural engagement between different groups in Monterey Park, California—a city where Asians constitute the majority population. Such studies emphasize how different groups shape the conditions of each other's existence.

Research needs to consider how specific social policies (e.g., affirmative action, community economic development proposals) have different consequences for different groups. The meaning and impact of immigration reforms for Hispanics for example, may be quite distinct from its meaning and impact for Asians. In line with an eye toward heterogeneity, different ethnic groups (e.g., Cubans and Salvadorans) within a single racial category (Hispanic) may be differentially affected by particular policy initiatives and reforms. All this is important because politics, policies, and practices framed in dichotomous Black-White terms miss the ways in which specific initiatives structure the possibilities for conflict or accommodation among different racial minority groups.

The multiplicity of groups has transformed the nation's political and cultural terrain, and provoked a contentious debate regarding multiculturalism. New demographic realities have also provided a distinctive context in which to examine the changing dynamics of White racial identity. Both the debate over multiculturalism and the increasing salience of White racial identity are tied to changes in the meaning of race as a result of challenges to the logic and organization of White supremacy.

Multiculturalism And Whiteness

Controversies over the multiculturalism have been bitter and divisive. Proponents claim that a multicultural curriculum, for example, can facilitate an appreciation for diversity, increase tolerance, and improve relations between and among racial and ethnic groups. Opponents claim that multiculturalists devalue or relativize core national values and beliefs, shamelessly promote "identity politics," and unwittingly increase racial tensions.

One of problems of the multicultural debate is the conflation of "race" and "culture." I take seriously Hollinger's (1995) claim that we have reified what he calls the American "ethno-racial pentagon." Blacks, Hispanics, American Indians/Alaska Natives, Asians/Pacific Islanders, and Whites are now seen as the five basic demographic blocs we as the subjects of multiculturalism. The problem is that these groups do not represent distinct and mutually exclusive "cultures." American multiculturalism, Hollinger claims, has accomplished, in short order, a task that centuries of British imperial power could not complete: the making of the Irish as indistinguishable from English. Such a perspective argues for the need to rethink what we mean by the terms "race" and "culture," and to critically interrogate the manner in which we articulate the connection between the two in research and policy studies.

Another issue is how forms of multiculturalist discourse the organization and distribution of power. Multiculturalism is often posed as the celebration of "differences" and unique forms of material culture expressed, for example, in music, food, dance, and holidays. Such an approach tends to level the important differences and contradictions within and among racial and ethnic groups. Different groups possess different forms of power—the power to control resources, the power to push a political agenda, and the power to culturally represent themselves and other groups. In a recent study of perceived group competition in Los Angeles, Bobo and Hutchings (1996) found, among other things, that Whites felt least threatened by Blacks and most threatened by Asians, while Asians felt a greater threat from Blacks than Hispanics. Such distinct perceptions of "group position" are related to, and implicated in, the organization of power.

Some scholars and activists have defined racism as "prejudice plus power." Using this formula, they argue that people of color can't be racist because they don't have power. But things aren't that simple. In the post-Civil Rights era, some racial minority groups have carved out a degree of power in select urban areas—particularly with respect to administering social services and distributing economic resources. This has led, in cities like Oakland and Miami, to conflicts between Blacks and Hispanics over educational programs, minority business opportunities, and political power. We need to acknowledge and examine the historical and contemporary differences in power that different groups possess.

Dramatic challenges to ideologies and structures of White supremacy in the past 50 years, have caused some Whites to perceive a loss of power and influence. In 25 years, non-Hispanic Whites will constitute a minority in four states, including two of the most populous ones, and in 50 years, they will make up barely half of the U.S. population (Booth, 1998:A18). Whiteness has lost its transparency and self-evident meaning in a period of demographic transformation and racial reforms. White racial identity has recently been the subject of interrogation by scholars (Roediger, 1991; Lott, 1995; Ignatiev, 1995), who have explored how the social category of "White" has evolved and been implicated with racism and the labor movement. Contemporary works look at how White racial identities are constructed, negotiated, and transformed in institutional and everyday life (Hill, 1997).

Research on White Americans suggests that they do not experience their ethnicity as a definitive aspect of their social identity (Alba, 1990; Waters 1990). Rather, they perceive it dimly and irregularly, picking and choosing among its varied strands that allow them to exercise an "ethnic option" (Waters, 1990). Waters found that ethnicity was flexible, symbolic, and voluntary for her White respondents in ways that it was not for non-Whites.

The loose affiliation with specific European ethnicities does not necessarily suggest the demise of any coherent group consciousness and identity. In the "twilight of ethnicity," White racial identity may increase in salience. Indeed, in an increasingly diverse workplace and society. Whites experience a profound racialization.

The racialization process for Whites is evident on many college/university campuses as White students encounter a heightened awareness of race, which calls their own identity into question. Focus group interviews with White students at the University of California, Berkeley, reveals many of the themes and dilemmas of White identity in the current period: the "absence" of a clear culture and identity, the perceived "disadvantages" of being White with respect to the distribution of resources, and the stigma of being perceived as the "oppressors of the nation" (Institute for the Study of Social Change, 1991:37). Such comments underscore the new problematic meanings attached to "White," and debates about the meanings will continue, and perhaps deepen, in the years to come, fueled by such social issues as affirmative action, English-only initiatives, and immigration policies.

Racial meanings are profoundly influenced by state definitions and discursive practices. They are also shaped by interaction with prevailing forms of gender and class formation. An examination of both these topics reveals the fundamental instability of racial categories, their historically contingent character, and the ways they articulate with other axes of stratification and "difference." Extending this understanding, it is crucial to relate racial categories and meanings to concepts of racism. The idea of "race" and its persistence as a social category is only given meaning in a social order structured by forms of inequality—economic, political, and cultural—that are organized, to a significant degree, along racial lines.

Intersectionality

In a critique of racial essentialism, Hall (1996:444) states that "the central issues of race always appear historically in articulation; in a formation, with other categories and divisions and are constantly crossed and recrossed by categories of class, of gender and ethnicity." Although this may seem obvious, most social-science research tends to neglect an examination of the connections between distinct, yet overlapping, forms of stratification and "difference." The result is a compartmentalization of inquiry and analysis. Higginbotham (1993:14) notes that; "Race *only* comes up when we talk about African Americans and other people of color, gender *only* comes up when we talk about women, and class *only* comes up when we talk about the poor and working class."

Analyses that do grapple with more than one variable frequently reveal a crisis of imagination. Much of the race-class debate, for example, inspired by the work of Wilson (1978), suffers from the imposition of rigid categories and analyses that degenerate into dogmatic assertions of the primacy of one category over the other. In fairness, more recent work has examined the interactive effects of race and class on residential segregation (Massey and Denton, 1993) and inequalities in wealth accumulation (Oliver and Shapiro, 1995). Still, most work treats race and class as discrete and analytically distinct categories.

A new direction is reflected in scholarship that emphasizes the "intersectionality" of race, gender, and class (Collins, 1990). Such work does not simply employ an additive model of examining inequalities (e.g., assessing the relative and combined effects of race and gender "penalties" in wage differentials), but examines how different categories are constituted, transformed, and given meaning in dynamic engagement with each other. Glenn's (1992, 1999) work on the history of domestic and service work, for example, reveals how race is gendered and gender is raced. Frankenberg (1993) explores the ways in which White women experience, reproduce, and/or challenge the prevailing racial order. In so doing, she reveals how the very notion of racial privilege is experienced and articulated differently by women and men.

In institutional and everyday life, any clear demarcation of specific forms of "difference" is constantly being disrupted. This suggests the importance of understanding how changes in racial meaning are affected by transformations in gender and class relations. New research promises a break with the conception of race, class, and gender as relatively static categories, and emphasizes an approach that looks at the multiple and mutually determining ways that they shape each other. Such a framework of analysis is, however, still tentative, incomplete, and in need of further elaboration and refinement.

Race And Racism

Blauner (1994) notes that in classroom discussions of racism, White and Black students tend to talk past one another. Whites tend to locate racism in color consciousness and find its absence in color-blindness. In so doing, they see the affirmation of difference and racial identity among racially defined minority students as racist. Black students, by contrast, see racism as a system of power, and correspondingly argue that they cannot be racist because they lack power. Blauner concludes that there are two "languages" of race, one in which members of racial minorities, especially Blacks, see the centrality of race in history and everyday experience, and another in which Whites see race as a peripheral, nonessential reality.

Such discussions remind us of the crucial importance of discerning and articulating the connections between the changing meaning of race and concepts of racism. Increasingly, some scholars argue that the term "racism" has suffered from conceptual inflation, and been subject to so many different meanings as to render the concept useless. (Miles, 1989). Recently, John Bunzel, a former member of the U.S. Commission on Civil Rights and current senior research fellow at Stanford's Hoover Institution, argued that the President's Advisory Board on Race should call for a halt to the use of the term "racism" because it breeds "bitterness and polarization, not a spirit of pragmatic reasonableness in confronting our difficult problems" (Bunzel, 1998:D-7).

In academic and policy circles, the question of what racism is continues to haunt discussions. Prior to World War II, the term "racism" was not commonly used in public discourse or in the social-science literature. The term was originally used to characterize the ideology of White supremacy that was buttressed by biologically based theories of superiority/inferiority. In the 1950s and 1960s, the emphasis shifted to notions of individual expressions of prejudice and discrimination. The rise of the Black power movement in the 1960s and 1970s fostered a redefinition of racism that focused on its institutional nature. Current work in cultural studies looks at the often implicit and unconscious structures of racial privilege and racial representation in daily life and popular culture.

All this suggests that more precise terms are needed to examine racial consciousness, institutional bias, inequality, patterns of segregation, and the distribution of power. Racism is expressed differently at different levels and sites of social activity, and we need to be attentive to its shifting meaning in different contexts. As Goldberg (1990:xiii) states, "the presumption of a single monolithic racism is being displaced by a mapping of the multifarious historical formulations of *racisms*."

Looking Back, Thinking Ahead

Old theories, of course, are often revisited and remodeled. Traditional theories of assimilation, for example, have been substantially revised. No longer is assimilation posed and envisioned as a zero-sum game; the more "assimilated" one is, does mean that one is less "ethnic." Assimilation is also no longer read as "Anglo conformity"; there is no clearly discernible social and cultural "core" that immigrant groups gravitate toward. Forms of what Portes and Zhou (1993) label "segmented assimilation" are occurring, and they involve complex patterns of accommodation and conflict between increasingly diverse racial and ethnic groups.

That said, it is important to critically examine racial trends and their interpretation through a conceptual framework such as assimilation. What is missing is sufficient attentiveness to the processes of *racialization*—the ways racial meanings are constructed and imparted to social groups and processes. From an assimilationist vantage point, one could examine the intermarriage patterns among Asians to support the idea of their incorporation into the White mainstream. Indeed some social scientists (Hacker, 1992) believe that increasing Asian-White marriage rates, along with positive trends in income, education, and residential patterns, suggest that Asian Americans are becoming "White" as the very category of "Whiteness" is being expanded.

Such a conclusion draws on a troublesome aspect of the traditional assimilationist paradigm, namely, its lack of attention to differences in group *power*. Interracial marriage has been seen as a crucial subprocess of assimilation (Gordon, 1964). Increasing rates of marriage between minority and majority groups were read as an important indicator of narrowing of social distance, a reduction in group prejudice and discrimination, and the lessening of strict group boundaries. But increasing intermarriage could also illustrate inequalities in racial power and the complex articulation of race, gender, and sexuality (Shinagawa and Pang, 1996). Asian women, for example, are construed as desirable spouses/partners drawing on specific racial and gender representations (Marchetti, 1993). These ideas and images circulate in a variety of settings—in popular films, pornography, and "mail-order bride" services. Given the pervasiveness of these representations, can increased rates of intermarriage between Asian women and White men simply be read as an indicator of assimilation? I think not.

What it does suggest is the need to look at the cultural representations and discursive practices that shape racial meanings. This has crucial implications for the examination and interpretation of racial trends. By looking at levels of educational attainment, residential patterns, median family incomes; and poverty rates, Asians, as one group, do not appear to be structurally disadvantaged by race. But there lurks beneath these glowing social indicators a repertoire of ideologies and practices that can be evoked in particular moments to render Asians foreign, subversive, and suspect. The Asian campaign finance controversy (Wang, 1998; Nakanishi, 1998) and the recent Chinese spy scandal provide illustrations of this. Popular interpretations of these events have had a chilling effect on both Asian American political participation and employment in scientific research settings.

The point of all this is to underscore the necessity of an interdisciplinary, multidimensional approach to the study of race and its changing meaning. Social scientists often treat the category of race in an unproblematic fashion. Seeing it as an independent variable, correlations are established between a host of other variables, and trends are discerned with respect to life chances. But we need to problematize race in our work; to look more closely and critically at the connections between structures and discursive practices—linking, for example, labor-market stratification with cultural representations. In focusing on such dynamic relationships, we can more fully appreciate how racial meanings change, and what those changes mean to our collective identity as a people.

HEGEMONY

JAMES LULL

Hegemony is the power or dominance that one social group holds over others. This can refer to the "asymmetrical interdependence" of political-economic-cultural relations between and among nation-states (Straubhaar, 1991) or differences between and among social classes within a nation. Hegemony is "dominance and subordination in the field of relations structured by power" (Hall, 1985). But hegemony is more than social power itself; it is a method for gaining and maintaining power.

Classical Marxist theory, of course, stresses economic position as the strongest predictor of social differences. Today, more than a century after Karl Marx and Friedrich Engels wrote their treatises about capitalist exploitation of the working class, economic disparities still underlie and help reproduce social inequalities in industrialized societies. In that important, basic sense, Marxism and Marxist critical theory, which have been so badly maligned in the rhetoric surrounding the recent political transformation of communist nations, remain fundamentally on target. Technological developments in the twentieth century, however, have made the manner of social domination much more complex than before. Social class differences in today's world are not determined solely or directly by economic factors. Ideological influence is crucial now in the exercise of social power.

The Italian intellectual Antonio Gramsci—to whom the term hegemony is attributed—broadened materialist Marxist theory into the realm of ideology. Persecuted by his country's then fascist government (and writing from prison), Gramsci emphasized society's "super structure," its ideology producing institutions, in struggles over meaning and power (1971, 1973, 1978; see also Boggs, 1976; Sassoon, 1980; and Simon, 1982). A shift in critical theory thus was made away from a preoccupation with capitalist society's "base" (its economic foundation) and towards its dominant dispensaries of ideas. Attention was given to the structuring of authority and dependence in symbolic environments that correspond to, but are not the same as, economically determined class-based structures and processes of industrial production. Such a theoretical turn seems a natural and necessary development in an era when communications technology is such a pervasive and potent ideological medium. According to Gramsci's theory of ideological hegemony, mass media are tools that ruling elites use to "perpetuate their power, wealth, and status [by popularizing] their own philosophy, culture and morality" (Boggs, 1976: 39). The mass media uniquely "introduce elements into individual consciousness that would not otherwise appear there, but will not be rejected by consciousness because they are so commonly shared in the cultural community" (Nordenstreng, 1977: 276). Owners and managers of media industries can produce and reproduce the content, inflections, and tones of ideas favorable to them far more easily than other social groups because they manage key socializing institutions, thereby guaranteeing that their points of view are constantly and attractively cast into the public arena.

Mass-mediated ideologies are corroborated and strengthened by an interlocking system of efficacious information-distributing agencies and taken-for-granted social practices that permeate every aspect social and cultural reality. Messages supportive of the status quo emanating from schools, businesses, political organizations, trade unions, religious groups, the military, and the mass media all dovetail together ideologically. This inter-articulating, mutually reinforcing process of ideological influence is the essence of hegemony. Society's most entrenched and powerful institutions—which all depend in one way or another on the same sources for economic support—fundamentally agree with each other ideologically.

Hegemony is not a *direct* stimulation of thought or action, but, according to Stuart Hall, is a "framing [of] all competing definitions of reality within [the dominant class's] range, bringing all alternatives within their horizons of thought. [The dominant class] sets the limits—mental and structural—within which subordinate classes 'live' and make sense of their subordination in such a way as to sustain the dominance of those ruling over them" (1977: 333). British social theorist Philip Elliott suggested similarly that the most potent effect of mass media is how they subtly influence their audiences to perceive social roles and routine personal activities. The controlling economic forces in society use the mass media to provide a "rhetoric [through] which these [concepts] are labeled, evaluated, and explained" (1974: 262). Television commercials, for example, encourage audiences to think of themselves as "markets rather than as a public, as consumers rather than citizens" (Gitlin, 1979: 255).

But hegemony does not mature strictly from ideological articulation. Dominant ideological streams must be subsequently reproduced in the activities of our most basic social units—families, workplace networks, and friendship groups in the many sites and undertakings of everyday life. Gramsci's theory of hegemony, therefore, connects ideological representation to culture. Hegemony requires that ideological assertions become self-evident cultural assumptions. Its effectiveness depends on subordinated peoples accepting the dominant ideology as "normal reality or common sense . . . in active forms of experience and consciousness" (Williams, 1976: 145). Because information and entertainment technology is so thoroughly integrated into the everyday realities of modern societies, mass media's social influence is not always recognized, discussed, or criticized, particularly in societies where the overall standard of living is relatively high. Hegemony, therefore, can easily go undetected (Bausinger, 1984).

Hegemony implies a willing agreement by people to be governed by principles, rules, and laws they believe operate in their best interests, even though in actual practice they may not. Social consent can be a more effective means of control than coercion or force. Again, Raymond Williams: "The idea of hegemony, in its wide sense, is . . . especially important in societies [where] electoral politics and public opinion are significant factors, and in which social practice is seen to depend on consent to certain dominant ideas which in fact express the needs of a dominant class" (1976: 145). Thus, in the words of Colombian communication theorist Jesús Martín-Barbero, "one class exercises hegemony to the extent that the dominating class has interests which the subaltern classes recognize as being in some degree their interests too" (1993: 74).

Relationships between and among the major information-diffusing, socializing agencies of a society and the interacting, cumulative, socially accepted ideological orientations they create and sustain is the essence of hegemony. The American television industry, for instance, connects with other large industries, especially advertising companies but also national and multinational corporations that produce, distribute, and market a wide range of commodities. So, for example, commercial TV networks no longer buy original children's television shows. Network executives only want new program ideas associated with successful retail products already marketed to children. By late 1990 more than 20 toy-based TV shows appeared on American commercial TV weekly. Television also has the ability to absorb other major social institutions—organized religion, for instance—and turn them into popular culture. The TV industry also connects with government institutions, including especially the federal agencies that are supposed to regulate telecommunications. The development of American commercial broadcasting is a vivid example of how capitalist economic forces assert their power. Evacuation of the legislatively mandated public service ideal could only have taken place because the Federal Communications Commission stepped aside while commercial interests amassed power and expanded their influence. Symptomatic of the problem is the fact that government regulators typically are recruited from, and return to, the very industries they are supposed to monitor.

Transmedia and transgenre integrations with mutually reinforcing ideological consequences are also commonplace. Popular radio and video songs, for example, can also be commercials. . . . Commercial logos become products themselves and are reproduced on tee-shirts, posters, beach towels, and other informal media. The rhetoric of TV commercials and programs is recycled in the lyrics of rap music and in the routines of stand-up comedians performing live and on television. . . . There are films made for television, magazines published about television, and television news magazines. The most well-known national newspaper in the United States, *USA Today*, is sold nationwide in vending boxes that resemble TV sets. Television commercial appear on Channel One, an educational news channel shown to students in American elementary school classrooms. Logos that advertise only national gasoline, food, and motel chains appear on government highway signs, advising travelers of their availability at upcoming freeway exits. Expensive public relations campaigns of major corporations distribute "informational" supplementary textbooks to elementary and secondary school systems. Major business organizations send digests of their annual reports and other promotional materials to college instructors, hoping this biased information will be incorporated into teaching and research. Similar materials are sent to political and religious leaders so they will pass the information along to their constituencies and congregations.

In the United States, advocacy of alternative political ideologies, parties, and candidates, or suggestions of viable consumer alternatives to the commercial frenzy stimulated and reinforced by advertising and other marketing techniques, are rarely seen on the popular media. Radical ideas typically appear only on underfinanced, non-commercial radio and TV stations and in low-budget print media. These media have tiny public followings compared to commercial television and video outlets, metropolitan daily newspapers, and national magazines. When genuinely divergent views appear on mainstream media, the information is frequently shown in an unfavorable light or is modified and co-opted to surrender to the embrace of mainstream thought. . . . The mass media help create an impression that even society's roughest edges ultimately must conform to the conventional contours of dominant ideologies.

Hegemony has been central to the management of ideology in communist nations too, though it develops differently. Central ideological planning and the creation of propaganda to advise "the people" represent the same intention—to protect the interests of ruling elites. . . .

The collapse of political authority in Eastern and Central Europe and the former Soviet Union was a breakdown in communist ideological hegemony. Conflict between culture producers and young audiences in East Germany and Hungary is typical of what happened in the Soviet bloc (Wicke, 1992; Szemere, 1985). Young rock musicians and their enthusiastic audiences led a cultural and political struggle against the repressive institutions and the ideology behind them. Trying to contain and control rebellious youth, the former communist governments attempted in sinister ways to defuse the politically charged musical and cultural activity of youth by incorporating and sponsoring them. Young people and other dissenters saw through the strategy, however, challenged the hegemony, and stimulated policy changes that later contributed to the dramatic downfall of the European communist governments. In China, the extraordinary student and worker uprising in 1989 is but the most visible sign of wide-spread resistance among that country's disaffected urban population.[1] Recent popular revolutions in communist countries developed from widespread discontent with an interacting spectrum of economic, political, and cultural conditions. Ironically, the workers' uprising that Marx and Engels theorized would take place in repressive, class-based capitalist economies developed instead in communist nations which had proven in many respects to be even more repressive.

Hegemony as an Incomplete Process

Two of our leading critical theorists, Raymond Williams and Stuart Hall, remind us that hegemony in any political context is indeed fragile. It requires renewal and modification through the assertion and reassertion of power. Hall suggests that "it is crucial to the concept that hegemony is not a 'given' and permanent state of affairs, but it has to be actively won and secured; it can also be lost" (1977: 333). Ideological work is the winning and securing of hegemony over time. . . . Ideology is composed of "texts that are not closed" according to Hall, who also notes that ideological "counter-tendencies" regularly appear in the seams and cracks of dominant forms (Hall, 1985). Mediated communications ranging from popular television shows to rap and rock music, even graffiti scrawled over surfaces of public spaces, all inscribe messages that challenge central political positions and cultural assumptions.

Counter-hegemonic tendencies do not inhere solely in texts. They are formulated in processes of communication—in the interpretations, social circulation, and uses of media content. As with the American soldiers' use of military gas masks as inhaling devices to heighten the effect of marijuana smoke, or the homeless's transformation of supermarket shopping carts into personal storage vehicles, ideological resistance and appropriation frequently involve reinventing institutional messages for purposes that differ greatly from their creators' intentions. Expressions of the dominant ideology are sometimes reformulated to assert alternative, often completely resistant or contradictory messages. . . .

Furthermore, resistance to hegemony is not initiated solely by media consumers. Texts themselves are implicated. Ideology can never be stated purely and simply. Ways of thinking are always reflexive and embedded in a complex, sometimes contradictory, ideological regress. . . .

Audience interpretations and uses of media imagery also eat away at hegemony. Hegemony fails when dominant ideology is weaker than social resistance. Gay subcultures, feminist organizations, environmental groups, radical political parties, music-based formations such as punks, B-boys, Rastafarians, and metal heads all use media and their social networks to endorse counter-hegemonic values and lifestyles. Indeed, we have only just begun to examine the complex relationship between ideological representation and social action.

Note

1. It's important to realize that the military suppression of the student-worker uprising in Beijing in 1989 did not stop the Chinese revolutionary movement. It made possible the dramatic and far-reaching (if less visually spectacular) economic and cultural changes that characterize the People's Republic today.

TOWARD A CRITICAL THEORY OF JUSTICE

IRIS M. YOUNG

Contemporary radical criticisms of the liberal paradigm of justice carry less weight than they might because they fail to offer a positive alternative framework for reasoning about justice. Some authors do indeed offer principles of justice or images of the just society which they claim will help justify a political practice aiming to alter fundamentally the basic institutions, especially the economic institutions, of our society.[1] Such efforts, however, lack grounding in a critically oriented framework of reasoning about justice. Lacking such grounding, proposals for radical egalitarian or socialist conceptions of justice constitute little more in the way of an alternative positive theory of justice than do mere criticisms of the dominant framework.

I argue that formulation of questions of justice exclusively in distributive terms tends toward conceptual confusion and fails to be basic enough. I also argue that the sort of criticism of traditional theories of justice that Fisk outlines leaves us with the apparently impossible task of developing a theory which can make universalistic claims without abandoning or disguising the historical embeddedness of its origins and application.

To solve both these problems with traditional theories of justice, I offer some suggestions for an alternative framework for theorizing about justice. To outline a theory of justice, I develop certain elements of the communicative ethics which Habermas has proposed. In particular, I take up his unelaborated suggestion that the ideal speech situation, which he argues any act of speaking presup poses, expresses the ideal of justice. I argue that the ideal speech situation offers the potential foundation for a framework of theorizing about justice which focuses not primarily on distribution, but on more fundamental questions of institutional relations and domination. I argue, further, that the application of the ideal speech situation to particular social configurations constitutes a means for solving the problem of how to construct an objective and critical conception of justice which does not merely reflect actual social circumstances at the same time that it remains historically specific.

1

Since Adam Smith, almost every theory of social justice has focused primarily on questions of how social benefits should be allocated among members of the society. Insofar as it entails a theory of justice, utilitarianism is a paradigm of this distributive focus. Utilitarian methodology calls for treating all values as greater or lesser "bundles" of goods and comparing alternative distributions of bundles.

Contemporary criticisms of classical utilitarian theory as ignoring the most important questions of justice—merit, desert, rights, and so forth—may be apt. Most contemporary critics of utilitarianism, however, continue to formulate the question of justice primarily as a question of distribution.

The distributive paradigm of questioning about justice so dominates philosophical thinking that even critics of the traditional liberal framework continue to formulate the focus of justice in exclusively distributive terms.

A distributive focus on theorizing about justice is so much a part of our moral conceptualization that it does not appear possible to have any other. To find such another focus we must look back to the ancient conception of justice, in particular that enunciated in the Platonic dialogues. For the ancients, justice refers to the whole of virtue insofar as it concerns relations with others.[12] For Plato the question of justice does not concern primarily the proper distribution of social benefits and burdens. Rather, justice concerns first the organization of the community as a whole. We develop a conception of justice by constructing a vision of the organization of social positions and relations which will produce a harmonious and cooperative whole.[13]

I do not wish to adopt the Platonic conception of justice, for there is much in it that is inappropriate for us, or indeed positively pernicious. I will argue, however, that a theory of justice which takes as its primary question the structural and institutional relations of the society in its totality is better than one which focuses exclusively or primarily on questions of distribution. There are, in particular, two objections to the distributive orientation. First, formulation of many apt questions of justice in distributive terms tends to render them conceptually confused. Second, a distributive orientation tends to focus on the evaluation of the effects of given institutional forms and relations, instead of evaluating the institutional structures themselves.

Questions about the principles and procedures according to which a society ought to distribute the material benefits of social production obviously constitute crucial questions of social justice. By no means all questions most theorists would admit as questions of justice fall into that class, however. They also ask questions about the rights and liberties a society ought to protect for its members, the structure of power and decision-making, and so on. Here are some examples of such questions of justice that are not distributive in any immediate sense: Is a division between mental and manual labor just? Is it just to raise taxes without the mandate of a popular referendum? Is marriage just?

True to the utilitarian tradition, most modern theories of justice answer questions like these in terms of the relative quantity of benefits that accrue to persons. They conceptualize questions of rights, liberties, the justice of institutionalized positions, decision-making procedures, relations of authority, and so on, as questions of the proper distribution of bundles of non-material goods. Such distributively oriented treatment of questions of rights, liberties, power, and so on, however, tends to obscure the meaning of those concepts. I shall concentrate on the examples of rights and power.

Talk of distribution of power within society is perhaps the most common way political theories wrongly construe questions of social justice in distributive terms. Democratic arrangements are frequently held to entail an equal distribution of power, while more hierarchical arrangements are defined by an unequal distribution of power. The conceptual confusion here may ultimately lie in an equivocation on the term "equality." Equality in the distribution of goods refers to sameness of quantity or value, whereas equality in relations of power and powerlessness means something like "peership."[15]

Discussion of power as some kind of "stock" which can be distributed obscures the fact that power, unlike wealth, for example, does not exist except through social relations. Having social power means standing in relation with others such that one can control their actions or the conditions of their actions. One can have a plot of land without being related to anyone else, but having the power to levy rent on it essentially entails specific relation to others and a whole supporting set of institutions. It is thus misleading to conceptualize relations of power on analogy with the distribution of an amount of goods. If the social relations of power change in such a way that a person or group gains autonomy, this does not mean that some quantity of power has been redistributed. It means, rather, that a relation of power has been eliminated.[16]

This criticism that a distributively oriented theory of justice distorts the meaning of important social and political concepts, however, does not reach to the core of the problem with distributively oriented theories. The main criticism of a distributively oriented theory of justice is that it tends to focus on patterns of distribution without even bringing into direct theoretical focus the structure of the institutional relations and the movement of social processes which bring this pattern of distribution about.

Like nearly all other modern theories of justice, then, Rawls's approach avoids asking about the justice of specific institutional structures themselves, along with the relations of power, exploitation and dependency they can produce. Several writers have argued, for example, that Rawls fails to focus on the institutional relations which underlie economic classes, and fails to justify his assumption that class inequality is inevitable.[22] In his theory Rawls implicitly assumes many institutions as given, moreover, such as competitive markets, political bureaucracies, and monogamous heterosexual families, without ever raising questions about whether the positions and relations these institutions entail are just.

In sum, distributively oriented theories conceptualize questions of justice, whether of particular actions or practices, or of the pattern of rights and inequalities of a whole society, primarily as questions concerning the fair allocation of social goods, including non-material goods, among individuals. The approach advocated here, on the other hand, focuses on the structures of social organization that allow some individuals to have power over others, on the structure of decision making within and among institutions, and on the definition of social positions themselves. I am not arguing, of course, that questions of distribution are not important to a theory of justice, only that these questions of institutional structure should be considered first.

In section 2, I interpret Habermas's notion of the ideal speech situation as embodying a conception of justice which focuses evaluation primarily on this level of social structure and institutional relations. Section 3 shows among other things that a major reason that many theories of justice tend to ignore questions about basic forms of social organization is that they lack the historically specific focus that can bring such forms into view. I will argue in section 4 that a particular application of the ideal speech situation in a theory of justice yields such specificity.

2

One of Habermas's most central concerns has been to lay the philosophical foundation for an expanded conception of rationality that applies to normative claims as well as facts. The positivist spirit appropriately spurned traditional efforts to ground normative reason in a theological or metaphysical basis. In so doing, however, the positivist spirit we inherit abandoned entirely the project of providing the rational ground to normative discourse. Thus since norms have been judged to lack an objective basis comparable to that given to scientific reason, moral and political discourse has been reduced either to technical reason or the expressions of preference. In several works Habermas discusses the implications this dominance of technical reason over political life has for the continuance of contemporary forms of domination. He suggests that emancipatory interests can be expressed only if appeals to normative ideals regain a place in public discourse.[24] Thus the concern to give a rational foundation to normative discourse is not merely theoretical, but practical as well.

Habermas claims we can find the foundations of all rationality, both normative and non-normative, in the conditions of the possibility of communication which underlie and are presupposed by any speech act. He provides a theory of what he calls "universal pragmatics" to elaborate these conditions. I shall not summarize that theory here, but only touch enough of its outlines to indicate the place of the ideal speech situation in it.[25]

Any act of speaking which aims to be understood, according to Habermas, implicitly involves four validity claims. The speaker makes a claim to (1) comprehensibility, that the speech itself makes sense in terms of the grammar and syntax of the speakers; (2) truth, that the asserted relation to the world made by the speech is true; (3) truthfulness, that the speaker himself or herself speaks sincerely and does not deceive or hide his or her motives, feeling, interests, and so forth; (4) rightness, that in speaking the speaker acts in accordance with intersubjectively recognized norms that apply in this situation.[26]

In situations of ongoing interaction when persons understand each other and act on projects together in harmony, these four validity claims remain entirely implicit. Any one of them is, however, open to challenge, at which point they become explicit. A challenge obliges the speaker to make good on the claims. One can make good on claims to comprehensibility and truthfulness by appropriate actions. One makes good on claims to truth and rightness, on the other hand, only by entering another level of discourse which calls the claims explicitly into question and in which reasoned justification must be offered for them. The possibility of entering such argumentative discourse, Habermas claims, lies behind any act of speaking insofar as it aims to be understood. It is a condition for the possibility of such speaking.

Discourse takes place within the normative context Habermas describes as the ideal speech situation. This describes the formal conditions of a community of speakers engaged in discourse in which they have removed themselves from the immediacy of action in order to test a claim. The ideal speech situation expresses those conditions of interaction necessary for participants in such a discussion to reach a rationally motivated consensus. In a rationally motivated consensus the participants assent to a conclusion solely on the grounds that it is most reasonable.

Habermas states three conditions which must be met in the ideal speech situation:[27] (1) All those standing in the speaking situation have the same opportunity to speak and to criticize the speeches of others, and there are no limits on the content of speeches; (2) all participants must have the same opportunity to express their attitudes, feelings, intentions, interests and motives; all have the equal opportunity, that is, to require recognition of their individuality; (3) all the participants have the equal right to give commands to the others and to require others to justify themselves in terms of mutually recognized norms and rules of interaction.

Since the ideal speech situation abstracts from all contents of social interaction other than speech, and from all interests other than that of arriving at consensus in discussion, it is necessarily unrealizable.[28] As emptied of all material content and reference to material needs, it is a pure, formal ideal.

As such a formal ideal, however, it actually underlies communication as a universal condition. Insofar as any act of speaking aims at being understood and accepted, it anticipates the ideal speech situation as the condition for achieving understanding and acceptance. We would never try to achieve understanding unless we implicitly grasped the conditions required for achieving it. Thus even though the ideal speech situation is unrealizable, it has a real influence on interaction, as the motive of our attempts to achieve understanding.[29]

In this way Habermas intends to ground normative reason in the conditions of actual speaking life. Communication itself depends on the implicit understanding of a situation of interaction guided by norms that participants in discourse appeal to and abide by in order to guarantee the objectivity and freedom of their consensus.[30] These norms that define the ideal speech situation, according to Habermas, embody the universal ideals of truth, freedom and justice.

The ideal speech situation represents the idea of justice as a structure of institutionalized relations that are free from domination. The attainment of a rationally motivated consensus requires that the organization of interaction contains relations of equality, mutual recognition of the individuality of each, and reciprocity. Structures of domination create conflicts of interest that prevent commitment to consensus. These structures also prevent individuals from knowing their real interests, or expressing them even if they know them.[31] To the degree that such structural asymmetries exist, an interaction situation declines from the ideal of justice.

I have suggested, then, that the ideal speech situation can direct a theory of justice to focus its questioning on forms of social organization and relations of domination. It is important to note, however, that the ideal speech situation does not itself constitute a standard or set of principles by which actual social arrangements ought to be evaluated. The ideal speech situation expresses the ideal of justice in a purely formal way that abstracts from all particular social and historical content. As I will argue in the next section, it is not possible to have a substantive conception of justice which lacks historical specificity. Thus, as the final section will show, the ideal speech situation must be applied within concretely specified circumstances before it yields a substantive set of evaluative principles of justice.

3

Philosophers generally stipulate that a conception of justice should be held independently of particular social or historical circumstances, or practices, as a necessary condition for objectivity. In the effort to achieve this universality and objectivity, most modern philosophical accounts seek correct normative principles of social life by adopting a strategy of deriving such principles from a hypothetical starting point. Whether called the state of nature, the original position, the moral point of view, the ideal observer, and so on, this hypothetical starting point purportedly escapes the specificity of actual historical circumstances. The starting point aims to remove all natural and social contingency from human life, leaving only its formal and universal elements. Then political theorists can claim to derive the correct conception of the just social order from this universal and formal starting point.

As we have seen, however, each account smuggles into the starting point substantive premises derived more or less directly from the theorist's social circumstances. The theory of the just social order which emerges, then, merely reflects in idealized and systematized form the actual structure of the society in which the theorist dwells.

Thus many writers argue that classical liberalism makes substantive assumptions about human nature (for example, that human beings are essentially acquisitive) which reflect the particular needs of an emergent bourgeois and capitalist social order.[36]

This presents us with a dilemma. If one cannot derive a substantive conception of justice from a formal starting point alone, then it appears inevitable that substantive theories must have substantive premises derived from particular social circumstances. Theories do not err in introducing substantive premises into the starting point, since this is logically necessary if they are to arrive at substantive conclusions. Rather, the error lies in presenting these substantive premises as ahistorical and thus claiming that the substantive conception applies across different social and historical circumstances.

Most contemporary social theorists conclude from this that the philosophical ideal of a rationally grounded conception of justice independent of particular social circumstances is a pipe dream, and a dangerous one at that. Many Marxists, for example, argue that the search for correct, rationally grounded, universal principles of justice is illusory. Each social formation has its own normative principles which arise from and serve to reproduce the particular social relations of that society. Juridical forms, and the principles of justice that govern them, are specific to modes of production. There is, moreover, no transhistorical conception of justice by which these social practices can be judged unjust. There can be no "justice in itself" independent of the particular economic forms and social relations which engender and embody particular conceptions and principles of justice. It follows that any claim to have a universal and objective theory of justice is necessarily ideological; it masks as disinterested truth what really expresses the interests and values of the dominant class.[39]

Similarly, many contemporary non-Marxist social scientists regard with scepticism the possibility of arriving at a normative conception of justice that is not a mere reflection of norms actually operative in a society. For much contemporary social science norms exist only as facts: One can give an account of the norms people actually adhere to and follow in a society. One can show their social origins and give a functional account of how they contribute to the maintenance of social integration. No basis exists, however, for saying that some norms are right while others are not.

Given the logical problem outlined above, the traditional philosophical search for a rationally grounded theory of justice appears to be illusory. Yet this conclusion leads to undesirable consequences. The thesis of the impossibility of a rationally grounded conception of justice that is more than a mere reflection of actual social circumstances implies the impossibility of rational social criticism. To criticize a set of social circumstances, and to judge them unjust, one should be able to take a sufficient distance from them that they no longer appear normal or inevitable. This seems to imply that one needs some means of transhistorical evaluation.

Marcuse has argued that the traditional appeal to normative universals like truth, beauty, freedom and justice serves just this critical function. The projection of universalistic ideas of what ought to be opens up possibilities for thinking, which otherwise would be conditioned by what actually exists. The absence of such philosophical ideals creates the one-dimensional thinking characteristic of contemporary culture.[40]

Yet the appeal to universals is necessarily abstract. In the classical philosophical tradition while the motive for the development of an ideal conception of justice may have been critical, the outcome more often than not has been ineffectual. Reflection on the philosophic ideal of the just society has most often served as a means of turning one's back on the real social circumstances and retreating into rarified contemplation.[41]

A theory of justice is thus presented with a dilemma. It must provide a means of distancing social criticism from the concrete social conditions under evaluation. The tradition of philosophical criticism has found such a means of distancing only in an a priori formal ideal. For a conception of justice to have any substance, however, it must be anchored in the particular social circumstances in which it exists and which it purports to evaluate, and hence be limited in application only to them. So the project of a properly critical theory of justice appears to be contradictory. It must develop a conception of justice independent of particular social circumstances, and yet at the same time derive from particular circumstances and be applicable only to them. I suggest that utilization of the ideal speech situation in what Habermas calls the "model of the suppression of generalizable interests" does just this.

4

In its crucial features the ideal speech situation is strictly formal. To arrive at it we abstract from all social circumstances and institutions, as well as particular technical economic, political and cultural circumstances. The ideal speech situation abstracts out any interests speakers might have other than an interest in discursive consensus, and assumes for the speakers that all their experience and feeling is communicable. It also abstracts from the speaking situation those real material factors that require us to cut discussions short (such as having to eat, sleep, and so forth) and to acquire the means for doing so.

Only this complete formality of the ideal speech situation permits it to have a universal character. Given the correctness of the theory of communication in which it is embedded, the ideal speech situation implicitly underlies any act of speaking which aims at understanding, as a quasi-transcendental condition for that speaking. This universality provides a theory of justice with a grounding that makes it less arbitrary than some other starting points. It also can provide a critical theory of justice with its needed capacity to distance itself from any and all actual social circumstances.

There is a price for this universalizing distance, however. Because the ideal speech situation is formal and abstract, it cannot itself serve as a standard or goal of justice. The ideal speech situation offers the vision of social relations free from domination, the ideal of pure democracy and social reciprocity. It offers this as a mere vision, however; it is no more than an unreal projection that interests thought. It is too abstract to serve as a means of evaluating particular social circumstances. Nor can principles of the evaluation of a society be derived from the ideal speech situation directly. As we have already seen, it is illegitimate to derive substantive normative principles from a purely formal beginning.

To use the ideal speech situation for developing a conception of justice applicable to the evaluation of actual societies, we must introduce material premises derived from actual social circumstances. Habermas suggests a method for the introduction of such material content into the ideal speech situation.

In this model we are asked to reason hypothetically about how the members of society would choose the organization of their institutions if they stood in the relations that define the ideal speech situation.

Utilization of the ideal speech situation, on the other hand, entails incorporating specific knowledge of the particular society one seeks to evaluate. The participants in the discussion know at least the following things about their society: They know the basic natural constraints of their location, such as climate, topography, the character and general amount of land and material resources to which they have access, and so on. They have basic demographic knowledge such as how much relative space they have and how much food can be produced relative to the given and projected population. They know the sort of problems their technology can solve and the general level of productive capacity they have at their disposal. All the above says in concrete terms that the persons here know approximately at what point their society lies on a scale between social scarcity and social abundance. As I interpret this model, moreover, the members of the discussion also know much about the culture and traditions of their particular society. They have a notion of the tastes of their artistic and decorative tradition and a set of shared symbols and stories. They know their language, the games they play, their educational practices, and so on.

In principle, in this model of reasoning about justice, the only things abstracted from real society are those conditions of domination which prevent people in real society from pressing interests that all would agree to as legitimate if they were in a situation of equality and reciprocity. This model of reasoning must be purely hypothetical, of course, since in reality material conditions and relations of domination are inextricably linked. Imagining persons with these material constraints as standing in the ideal speech situation—even though no such persons could exist—provides a means of locating the sources of domination.

Given discussion unconstrained by domination, the model has individuals choose first the principles of social organization that best serve what they judge as their collective needs and legitimate individual interests, given the material constraints under which they operate. They choose, that is, the basic rules of interaction, authority relations, and forms of decision making within and among institutions. Among the principles and rules chosen, of course, are those relating to the distribution of the benefits of social cooperation. Such principles of distribution, however, would be dependent on prior determination of institutional forms, conditions and relations of production and authority relations, as well as on the level of material abundance of which the society is capable. For without the prior knowledge of the forms of social organization, we do not know what sorts of social benefits are to be distributed, nor what sorts of social positions and interest groups there are to decide among in distributing.

The conception and principles of justice which emerge in this way from the application of the formal conditions of the ideal speech situation to the material situation of a particular society are thus quite particular. Unlike most theories of justice, this model of reasoning about justice does not call for constructing an idea of *the* just society in general. Rather, the model allows for, even requires, a multitude of conceptions of justice, each derived from the particular conditions of the society and applicable only to them.

The model thus satisfies the condition developed in the previous section, that a theory of justice recognize the historical specificity of conceptions of justice. It grants that it is not in fact possible to articulate a substantive conception of justice that applies to the evaluation of all or many societies.

This form of reasoning about justice in effect measures a society against itself rather than measuring the society directly against an ahistorical set of principles. The conception of justice resulting from application of the ideal speech situation to particular social conditions, expresses the interests of all insofar as they are compatible. It thus shows the latent possibilities of the society given its historical and material conditions with the systemic sources of its conflicts of interest removed.

This process of reasoning about justice serves two purposes. Its main function is to identify sources of domination in the social arrangements of a particular society. The thought experiment discovers relations of domination in the process of setting up its starting point of reasoning. For every social relation whose justice one wishes to examine one asks whether there are aspects of it that tend to create asymmetries in the situation of discussion. The hypothetical model abstracts from them, but not from the material conditions and constraints. The second function served by the model is to project a vision of an alternative organization of that society which is free from domination.

To summarize, utilization of the ideal speech situation in a model of reasoning about justice that applies it to the particular material and cultural situation of a given society satisfies both the requirements for a theory of justice which have been raised in this essay. First, since the ideal speech situation focuses on relations of interaction and its application reveals the sources of domination, a theory of justice that uses it focuses primarily on forms of social organization. Secondly, the method of applying the ideal speech situation to particular material and cultural conditions points to a theory of justice that contains an a priori universal aspect without producing a conception of justice which claims transhistorical application.[44]

DISCOURSE ON COLONIALISM

AIMÉ CÉSAIRE

Translated by Joan Pinkham. This version published by Monthly Review Press: New York and London, 1972. Originally published as *Discours sur le colonialisme* by Editions Presence Africaine, 1955.

Discourse on Colonialism

A civilization that proves incapable of solving the problems it creates is a decadent civilization.

A civilization that chooses to close its eyes to its most crucial problems is a stricken civilization.

A civilization that uses its principles for trickery and deceit is a dying civilization.

The fact is that the so-called European civilization—"Western" civilization—as it has been shaped by two centuries of bourgeois rule, is incapable of solving the two major problems to which its existence has given rise: the problem of the proletariat and the colonial problem; that Europe is unable to justify itself either before the bar of "reason" or before the bar of "conscience"; and that, increasingly, it takes refuge in a hypocrisy which is all the more odious because it is less and less likely to deceive.

Europe is indefensible.

Apparently that is what the American strategists are whispering to each other.

That in itself is not serious.

What is serious is that "Europe" is morally, spiritually indefensible.

And today the indictment is brought against it not by the European masses alone, but on a world scale, by tens and tens of millions of men who, from the depths of slavery, set themselves up as judges.

The colonialists may kill in Indochina, torture in Madagascar, imprison in Black Africa, crackdown in the West Indies. Henceforth, the colonized know that they have an advantage over them. They know that their temporary, "masters" are lying.

Therefore, that their masters are weak.

And since I have been asked to speak about colonization and civilization, let us go straight to the principal lie which is the source of all the others.

Colonization and civilization?

In dealing with this subject, the commonest curse is to be the dupe in good faith of a collective hypocrisy that cleverly misrepresents problems, the better to legitimize the hateful solutions provided for them.

In other words, the essential thing here is to see clearly, to think clearly—that is, dangerously—and to answer clearly the innocent first question: what, fundamentally, is colonization? To agree on what it is not: neither evangelization, nor a philanthropic enterprise, nor a desire to push back the frontiers of ignorance, disease, and tyranny, nor a project undertaken for the greater glory of God, nor an attempt to extend the rule of law. To admit once for all, without flinching at the consequences, that the decisive actors here are the adventurer and the pirate, the wholesale grocer and the ship owner, the gold digger and the merchant, appetite and force, and behind them, the baleful projected shadow of a form of civilization which, at a certain point in its history, finds itself obliged, for internal reasons, to extend to a world scale the competition of its antagonistic economies.

Pursuing my analysis, I find that hypocrisy is of recent date; that neither Cortez discovering Mexico from the top of the great teocalli, nor Pizzaro before Cuzco (much less Marco Polo before Cambaluc), claims that he is the harbinger of a superior order; that they kill; that they plunder; that they have helmets, lances, cupidities; that the slavering apologists came later; that the chief culprit in this domain is Christian pedantry, which laid down the dishonest equations *Christianity=civilization, paganism=savagery*, from which there could not but ensue abominable colonialist and racist consequences, whose victims were to be the Indians, the yellow peoples, and the Negroes.

That being settled, I admit that it is a good thing to place different civilizations in contact with each other that it is an excellent thing to blend different worlds; that whatever its own particular genius may be, a civilization that withdraws into itself atrophies; that for civilizations, exchange is oxygen; that the great good fortune of Europe is to have been a crossroads, and that because it was the locus of all ideas, the receptacle of all philosophies, the meeting place of all sentiments, it was the best center for the redistribution of energy.

But then I ask the following question: has colonization really *placed civilizations in contact?* Or, if you prefer, of all the ways of *establishing contact*, was it the best?

I answer no.

And I say that between *colonization* and *civilization* there is an infinite distance; that out of all the colonial expeditions that have been undertaken, out of all the colonial statutes that have been drawn up, out of all the memoranda that have been dispatched by all the ministries, there could not come a single human value.

First we must study how colonization works to *decivilize* the colonizer, to *brutalize* him in the true sense of the word, to degrade him, to awaken him to buried instincts, to covetousness, violence, race hatred, and moral relativism; and we must show that each time a head is cut off or an eye put out in Vietnam and in France they accept the fact, each time a little girl is raped and in France they accept the fact, each time a Madagascan is tortured and in France they accept the fact, civilization acquires another dead weight, a universal regression takes place, a gangrene sets in, a center of infection begins to spread; and that at the end of all these treaties that have been violated, all these lies that have been propagated, all these punitive expeditions that have been tolerated, all these prisoners who have been tied up and "interrogated, all these patriots who have been tortured, at the end of all the racial pride that has been encouraged, all the boastfulness that has been displayed, a poison has been instilled into the veins of Europe and, slowly but surely, the continent proceeds toward *savagery*.

And then one fine day the bourgeoisie is awakened by a terrific reverse shock: the gestapos are busy, the prisons fill up, the torturers around the racks invent, refine, discuss.

People are surprised, they become indignant. They say: "How strange! But never mind-it's Nazism, it will. pass!" And they wait, and they hope; and they hide the truth from themselves, that it is barbarism, but the supreme barbarism, the crowning barbarism that sums up all the daily barbarisms; that it is Nazism, yes, but that before they were its victims, they were its accomplices; that they tolerated that Nazism before it was inflicted on them, that they absolved it, shut their eyes to it, legitimized it, because, until then, it had been applied only to non-European peoples; that they have cultivated that Nazism, that they are responsible for it, and that before engulfing the whole of Western, Christian civilization in its reddened waters, it oozes, seeps, and trickles from every crack.

Yes, it would be worthwhile to study clinically, in detail, the steps taken by Hitler and Hitlerism and to reveal to the very distinguished, very humanistic, very Christian bourgeois of the twentieth century that without his being aware of it, he has a Hitler inside him, that Hitler *inhabits* him, that Hitler is his *demon*, that if he rails against him, he is being inconsistent and that, at bottom, what he cannot forgive Hitler for is not *crime* in itself, *the crime against man*, it is not *the humiliation of man as such*, it is the crime against the white man, the humiliation of the white man, and the fact that he applied to Europe colonialist procedures which until then had been reserved exclusively for the Arabs of Algeria, the coolies of India, and the blacks of Africa.

And that is the great thing I hold against pseudo-humanism: that for too long it has diminished the rights of man, that its concept of those rights has been—and still is—narrow and fragmentary, incomplete and biased and, all things considered, sordidly racist.

I have talked a good deal about Hitler. Because he deserves it: he makes it possible to see things on a large scale and to grasp the fact that capitalist society, at its present stage, is incapable of establishing a concept of the rights of all men, just as it has proved incapable of establishing a system of individual ethics. Whether one likes it or not, at the end of the blind alley that is Europe, I mean the Europe of Adenauer, Schuman, Bidault, and a few others, there is Hitler. At the end of capitalism, which is eager to outlive its day, there is Hitler. At the end of formal humanism and philosophic renunciation, there is Hitler.

What am I driving at? At this idea: that no one colonizes innocently, that no one colonizes with impunity either; that a nation which colonizes, that a civilization which justifies colonization—and therefore force—is already a sick civilization, a civilization that is morally diseased, that irresistibly, progressing from one consequence to another, one repudiation to another, calls for its Hitler, I mean its punishment.

Colonization: bridgehead in a campaign to civilize barbarism, from which there may emerge at any moment the negation of civilization, pure and simple.

But let us speak about the colonized.

I see clearly what colonization has destroyed: the wonderful Indian civilizations—and neither Deterding nor Royal Dutch nor Standard Oil will ever console me for the Aztecs and the Incas.

I see clearly the civilizations; condemned to perish at a future date, into which it has introduced a principle of ruin: the South Sea islands, Nigeria, Nyasaland. I see less clearly the contributions it has made.

Security? Culture? The rule of law? In the meantime, I look around and wherever there are colonizers and colonized face to face, I see force, brutality, cruelty, sadism, conflict, and, in a parody of education, the hasty manufacture of a few thousand subordinate functionaries, "boys," artisans, office clerks, and interpreters necessary for the smooth operation of business.

I spoke of contact.

Between colonizer and colonized there is room only for forced labor, intimidation, pressure, the police, taxation, theft, rape, compulsory crops, contempt, mistrust, arrogance, self-complacency, swinishness, brainless elites, degraded masses.

No human contact, but relations of domination and submission which turn the colonizing man into a class-room monitor, an army sergeant, a prison guard, a slave driver, and the indigenous man into an instrument of production.

My turn to state an equation: colonization = "thing-ification."

I hear the storm. They talk to me about progress, about "achievements," diseases cured, improved standards of living.

I am talking about societies drained of their essence, cultures trampled underfoot, institutions undermined, lands confiscated, religions smashed, magnificent artistic creations destroyed, extraordinary *possibilities* wiped out.

They throw facts at my head, statistics, mileages of roads, canals, and railroad tracks.

I am talking about thousands of men sacrificed to the Congo-Ocean. I am talking about those who, as I write this, are digging the harbor of Abidjan by hand. I am talking about millions of men torn from their gods, their land, their habits, their life-from life, from the dance, from wisdom.

I am talking about millions of men in whom fear has been cunningly instilled, who have been taught to have an inferiority complex, to tremble, kneel, despair, and behave like flunkeys.

They dazzle me with the tonnage of cotton or cocoa that has been exported, the acreage that has been planted with olive trees or grapevines.

I am talking about natural *economies* that have been disrupted—harmonious and viable economies adapted to the indigenous population—about food crops destroyed, malnutrition permanently introduced, agricultural development oriented solely toward the benefit of the metropolitan countries, about the looting of products, the looting of raw materials.

They pride themselves on abuses eliminated.

I too talk about abuses, but what I say is that on the old ones—very real—they have superimposed others—very detestable. They talk to me about local tyrants brought to reason; but I note that in general the old tyrants get on very well with the new ones, and that there has been established between them, to the detriment of the people, a circuit of mutual services and complicity.

They talk to me about civilization. I talk about proletarianization and mystification.

For my part, I make a systematic defense of the non-European civilizations.

Every day that passes, every denial of justice, every beating by the police, every demand of the workers that is drowned in blood, every scandal that is hushed tip, every punitive expedition, every police van, every gendarme and every militiaman, brings home to us the value of our old societies.

They were communal societies, never societies of the many for the few.

They were societies that were not only ante-capitalist, as has been said, but also *anti-capitalist*.

They were democratic societies, always.

They were cooperative societies, fraternal societies.

I make a systematic defense of the societies destroyed by imperialism.

They were the fact, they did not pretend to be the idea; despite their faults, they were neither to be hated nor condemned. They were content to be. In them, neither the word *failure* nor the word *avatar* had any meaning. They kept hope intact.

Whereas those are the only words that can, in all honesty, be applied to the European enterprises outside Europe. My only consolation is that periods of colonization pass, that nations sleep only for a time, and that peoples remain.

This being said, it seems that in certain circles they pretend to have discovered in me an "enemy of Europe" and a prophet of the return to the ante-European past.

For my part, I search in vain for the place where I could have expressed such views; where I ever underestimated the importance of Europe in the history of human thought; where I ever preached a *return* of any kind; where I ever claimed that there could be a *return*.

The truth is that I have said something very different: to wit, that the great historical tragedy of Africa has beennot so much that it was too late in making contact with the rest of the world, as the manner in which that contact was brought about; that Europe began to "propagate" at a time when it had fallen into the hands of the most unscrupulous financiers and captains of industry; that it was our misfortune to encounter that particular Europe on our path, and that Europe is responsible before the human community for the highest heap of corpses in history.

In another connection, in judging colonization, I have added that Europe has gotten on very well indeed with all the local feudal lords who agreed to serve, woven a villainous complicity with them, rendered their tyranny more effective and more efficient, and that it has actually tended to prolong artificially the survival of local pasts in their most pernicious aspects.

I have said—and this is something very different—that colonialist Europe has grafted modern abuse onto ancient injustice, hateful racism onto old inequality.

That if I am attacked on the grounds of intent, I maintain that colonialist Europe is dishonest in trying to justify its colonizing activity a *posteriori* by the obvious material progress that has been achieved in certain fields under the colonial regime—since *sudden change* is always possible, in history as elsewhere; since no one knows at what stage of material development these same countries would have been if Europe had not intervened; since the technical outfitting of Africa and Asia, their administrative reorganization, in a word, their "Europeanization," was (as is proved by the example of Japan) in no way tied to the European *occupation*; since the Europeanization of the non-European continents could have been accomplished otherwise than under the heel of Europe; since this movement of Europeanization *was in progress*; since it was even slowed down; since in any case it was distorted by the European takeover.

The proof is that at present it is the indigenous peoples of Africa and Asia who are demanding schools, and colonialist Europe which refuses them; that it is the African who is asking for ports and roads, and colonialist Europe which is niggardly on this score; that it is the colonized man who wants to move forward, and the colonizer who holds things back.

And in this connection, I cite as examples (purposely taken from very different disciplines):

—From Gourou, his book *Les Pays tropicaux*, in which, amid certain correct observations, there is expressed the fundamental thesis, biased and unacceptable, that there has never been a great tropical civilization, that great civilizations have existed only in temperate climates, that in every tropical country the germ of civilization comes, and can only come, from some other place outside the tropics, and that if the tropical countries are not under the biological curse of the racists, there at least hangs over them, with the same consequences, a no less effective geographical curse.

—From the Rev. Tempels, missionary and Belgian, his "Bantu philosophy," as slimy and fetid as one could wish, but discovered very opportunely, as Hinduism was discovered by others, in order to counteract the "communistic materialism" which, it seems, threatens to turn the Negroes into "moral vagabonds."

—From the historians or novelists of civilization (it's the same thing)—not from this one or that one, but from all of them, or almost all-their false objectivity, their chauvinism, their sly racism, their depraved passion for refusing to acknowledge any merit in the nonwhite races, especially the black-skinned races, their obsession with monopolizing all glory for their own race.

—From the psychologists, sociologists *et al.*, their views on "primitivism," their rigged investigations, their self-serving generalizations, their tendentious speculations, their insistence on the marginal, "separate" character of the non-whites, and-although each of these gentlemen, in order to impugn on higher authority the weakness of primitive thought, claims that his own is based on the firmest rationalism-their barbaric repudiation, for the sake of the cause, of Descartes' statement, the charter of universalism, that "reason . . . is found whole and entire in each man," and that "where individuals of the same species are concerned, there may be degrees in respect of their accidental qualities, but not in respect of their forms, or natures."

One of the values invented by the bourgeoisie in former times and launched throughout the world was *man*—and we have seen what has become of that. The other was the *nation*.

It is a fact: the *nation* is a bourgeois phenomenon.

Exactly; but if I turn my attention from *man* to *nations*, I note that here too there is great danger; that colonial enterprise is to the modern world what Roman imperialism was to the ancient world: the prelude to Disaster and the forerunner of Catastrophe. Come, now! The Indians massacred, the Moslem world drained of itself, the Chinese world defiled and perverted for a good century; the Negro world disqualified; mighty voices stilled forever; homes scattered to the wind; all this wreckage, all this waste, humanity reduced to a monologue, and you think that all that does not have its price? The truth is that this policy *cannot but bring about the ruin of Europe itself*, and that Europe, if it is not careful, will perish from the void it has created around itself.

They thought they were only slaughtering Indians, or Hndus, or South Sea islanders, or Africans. They have in fact overthrown, one after another, the ramparts behind which European civilization could have developed freely.

I know how fallacious historical parallels are, particularly the one I am about to draw. Neverthe-less, permit me to quote a page from Edgar Quinet for the not inconsiderable element of truth which it contains and which is worth pondering.

Here it is:

> People ask why barbarism emerged all at once in ancient civilization. I believe I know the answer. It is surprising that so simple a cause is not obvious to everyone. The system of ancient civilization was composed of a certain number of nationalities, of coun-tries which, although they seemed to be enemies, or were even ignorant of each other, protected, supported, and guarded one another. When the expanding Roman Empire undertook to conquer and destroy these groups of nations, the dazzled sophists thought they saw at the end of this road humanity triumphant in Rome. They talked about the unity of the human spirit; it was only a dream. It happened that these nationalities were so many bulwarks protecting Rome itself . . . Thus when Rome, in its alleged triumphal march toward a single civilization, had destroyed, one after the other, Carthage, Egypt, Greece, Judea, Persia, Dacia, and Cisalpine and Transalpine Gaul, it came to pass that it had itself swallowed up the dikes that protected it against the human ocean under which it was to perish. The magnanimous Caesar, by crushing the two Gauls, only paved the way for the Teutons. So many societies, so many languages extinguished, so many cities, rights, homes annihilated, created a void around Rome, and in those places which were not invaded by the barbarians, barbarism was born spontaneously. The vanquished Gauls changed into Bagaudes. Thus the violent downfall, the progressive extirpation of individual cities, caused the crumbling of ancient civilization. That social edifice was supported by the various nationalities as by so many different columns of marble or porphyry. When, to the applause of the wise men of the time, each of these living columns had been demolished, the edifice came crashing down; and the wise men of our day are still trying to understand how such mighty ruins could have been made in a moment's time.

And now I ask: what else has bourgeois Europe done? It has undermined civilizations, destroyed countries, ruined nationalities, extirpated "the root of diversity." No more dikes, no more bulwarks. The hour of the barbarian is at hand. The modern barbarian. The American hour. Violence, excess, waste, mercantilism, bluff, gregariousness, stupidity, vulgarity, disorder.

In 1913, Ambassador Page wrote to Wilson:

"The future of the world belongs to us . . . Now what are we going to do with the leadership of the world presently when it clearly falls into our hands?"

And in 1914: "What are we going to do with this England and this Empire, presently, when eco-nomic forces unmistakably put the leadership of the race in our hands?"

This Empire . . . And the others . . .

And indeed, do you not see how ostentatiously these gentlemen have just unfurled the banner of anti-colonialism?

"Aid to the disinherited countries," says Truman. "The time of the old colonialism has passed." That's also Truman.

Which means that American high finance considers that the time has come to raid every colony in the world. So, dear friends, here you have to be careful!

I know that some of you, disgusted with Europe, with all that hideous mess which you did not wit-ness by choice, are turning—oh! in no great numbers—toward America and getting used to looking upon that country as a possible liberator.

"What a godsend" you think.

"The bulldozers! The massive investments of capital! The roads! The ports!"

"But American racism!"

"So what? European racism in the colonies has inured us to it!"

And there we are, ready to run the great Yankee risk.

So, once again, be careful!

American domination—the only domination from which one never recovers. I mean from which one never recovers unscarred.

And since you are talking about factories and industries, do you not see the tremendous factory hysterically spitting out its cinders in the heart of our forests or deep in the bush, the factory for the production of lackeys; do you not see the prodigious mechanization, the mechanization of man; the gigantic rape of everything intimate, undamaged, undefiled that, despoiled as we are, our human spirit has still managed to preserve; the machine, yes, have you never seen it, the machine for crushing, for grinding, for degrading peoples?

So that the danger is immense.

So that unless, in Africa, in the South Sea islands, in Madagascar (that is, at the gates of South Africa), in the West Indies (that is, at the gates of America), Western Europe undertakes on its own initiative a policy of *nationalities*, a new policy founded on respect for peoples and cultures—nay, more —unless Europe galvanizes the dying cultures or raises up new ones, unless it becomes the awakener of countries and civilizations (this being said without taking into account the admirable resistance of the colonial peoples primarily symbolized at present by Vietnam, but also by the Africa of the Rassemblement Democratique Africain), Europe will have deprived itself of its last chance and, with its own hands, drawn up over itself the pall of mortal darkness.

Which comes down to saying that the salvation of Europe is not a matter of a revolution in methods. It is a matter of the Revolution—the one which, until such time as there is a classless society, will substitute for the narrow tyranny of a dehumanized bourgeoisie the preponderance of the only class that still has a universal mission, because it suffers in its flesh from all the wrongs of history, from all the universal wrongs: the proletariat.

AHR FORUM
SUBALTERN STUDIES AS POSTCOLONIAL CRITICISM

GYAN PRAKASH

To note the ferment created by Subaltern Studies in disciplines as diverse as history, anthropology, and literature is to recognize the force of recent postcolonial criticism. This criticism has compelled a radical rethinking of knowledge and social identities authored and authorized by colonialism and Western domination. Of course, colonialism and its legacies have faced challenges before. One has only to think of nationalist rebellions against imperialist domination and Marxism's unrelenting critiques of capitalism and colonialism. But neither nationalism nor Marxism broke free from Eurocentric discourses. As nationalism reversed Orientalist thought, and attributed agency and history to the subjected nation, it staked a claim to the order of Reason and Progress instituted by colonialism. When Marxists turned the spotlight on colonial exploitation, their criticism was framed by a historicist scheme that universalized Europe's historical experience. The emergent postcolonial critique, by contrast, seeks to undo the Eurocentrism produced by the institution of the West's trajectory, its appropriation of the other as History. It does so, however, with the acute realization that its own critical apparatus does not enjoy a panoptic distance from colonial history but exists as an aftermath, as an after—after being worked over by colonialism. Criticism formed as an aftermath acknowledges that it inhabits the structures of Western domination that it seeks to undo. In this sense, postcolonial criticism is deliberately interdisciplinary, arising in the interstices of disciplines of power/knowledge that it critiques. This is what Homi Bhabha calls an in-between, hybrid position of practice and negotiation, or what Gayatri Chakravorty Spivak terms catachresis: "reversing, displacing, and seizing the apparatus of value-coding."

The dissemination of Subaltern Studies, beginning in 1982 as an intervention in South Asian historiography and developing into a vigorous postcolonial critique, must be placed in such a complex, catachrestic reworking of knowledge. The challenge it poses to the existing historical scholarship has been felt not only in South Asian studies but also in the historiography of other regions and in disciplines other than history. The term "subaltern" now appears with growing frequency in studies on Africa, Latin America, and Europe, and subalternist analysis has become a recognizable mode of critical scholarship in history, literature, and anthropology.

The formation of subaltern studies as an intervention in South Asian historiography occurred in the wake of the growing crisis of the Indian state in the 1970s. The dominance of the nation-state, cobbled together through compromises and coercion during the nationalist struggle against British rule, became precarious as its program of capitalist modernity sharpened social and political inequalities and conflicts. Faced with the outbreak of powerful movements of different ideological hues that challenged its claim to represent the people, the state resorted increasingly to repression to preserve its dominance. But repression was not the only means adopted. The state combined coercive measures with the powers of patronage and money, on the one hand, and the appeal of populist slogans and programs, on the other, to make a fresh bid for its legitimacy. These measures, pioneered by the Indira Gandhi government, secured the dominance of the state but corroded the authority of its institutions. The key components of the modern nation-state—political parties, the electoral process, parliamentary bodies, the bureaucracy, law, and the ideology of development—survived, but their claim to represent the culture and politics of the masses suffered crippling blows.

In the field of historical scholarship, the perilous position of the nation-state in the 1970s became evident in the increasingly embattled nationalist historiography. Attacked relentlessly by the "Cambridge School," which represented India's colonial history as nothing but a chronicle of competition among its elites, nationalism's fabric of legitimacy was torn apart. This school exposed the nationalist hagiography, but its elite-based analysis turned the common people into dupes of their superiors. Marxists contested both nationalist historiography and the "Cambridge School" interpretation, but their mode-of-production narratives merged imperceptibly with the nation-state's ideology of modernity and progress. This congruence meant that while championing the history of the oppressed classes and their emancipation through modern progress, the Marxists found it difficult to deal with the hold of "backward" ideologies of caste and religion. Unable to take into account the oppressed's "lived experience" of religion and social customs, Marxist accounts of peasant rebellions either overlooked the religious idiom of the rebels or viewed it as a mere form and a stage in the development of revolutionary consciousness. Thus, although Marxist historians produced impressive and pioneering studies, their claim to represent the history of the masses remained debatable.

Subaltern Studies plunged into this historiographical contest over the representation of the culture and politics of the people. Accusing colonialist, nationalist, and Marxist interpretations of robbing the common people of their agency, it announced a new approach to restore history to the subordinated. Started by an editorial collective consisting of six scholars of South Asia spread across Britain, India, and Australia, Subaltern Studies was inspired by Ranajit Guha. A distinguished historian whose most notable previous work was *A Rule of Property for Bengal* (1963), Guha edited the first six Subaltern Studies volumes. After he relinquished the editorship, Subaltern Studies was published by a rotating two-member editorial team drawn from the collective. Guha continues, however, to publish in Subaltern Studies, now under an expanded and reconstituted editorial collective.

The establishment of subaltern studies was aimed to promote, as the preface by Guha to the first volume declared, the study and discussion of subalternist themes in South Asian studies. The term "subaltern," drawn from Antonio Gramsci's writings, refers to subordination in terms of class, caste, gender, race, language, and culture and was used to signify the centrality of dominant/ dominated relationships in history. Guha suggested that while Subaltern Studies would not ignore the dominant, because the subalterns are always subject to their activity, its aim was to "rectify the elitist bias characteristic of much research and academic work" in South Asian studies. The act of rectification sprang from the conviction that the elites had exercised dominance, not hegemony, in Gramsci's sense, over the subalterns. A reflection of this belief was Guha's argument that the subalterns had acted in history "*on their own*, that is, *independently of the elite*"; their politics constituted "an autonomous domain, for it neither originated from elite politics nor did its existence depend on the latter."

While the focus on subordination has remained central to Subaltern Studies, the conception of subalternity has witnessed shifts and varied uses. Individual contributors to the volumes have also differed, not surprisingly, in their orientation. A shift in interests, focus, and theoretical grounds is also evident through the eight volumes of essays produced so far and several monographs by individual subalternists. Yet what has remained consistent is the effort to rethink history from the perspective of the subaltern.

How the adoption of the subaltern's perspective aimed to undo the "spurious primacy assigned to them [the elites]" was not entirely clear in the first volume. The essays, ranging from agrarian history to the analysis of the relationship between peasants and nationalists, represented excellent though not novel scholarship. Although all the contributions attempted to highlight the lives and the historical presence of subaltern classes, neither the thorough and insightful research in social and economic history nor the critique of the Indian nationalist appropriation of peasant movements was new; Marxist historians, in particular, had done both. It was with the second volume that the novelty and insurgency of Subaltern Studies became clear.

The second volume made forthright claims about the subaltern subject and set about demonstrating how the agency of the subaltern in history had been denied by elite perspectives anchored in colonialist, nationalist, and or Marxist narratives. Arguing that these narratives had sought to represent the subaltern's consciousness and activity according to schemes that encoded elite dominance, Guha asserted that historiography had dealt with "the peasant rebel merely as an empirical person or member of a class, but not as an entity whose will and reason constituted the praxis called rebellion." Historians were apt to depict peasant rebellions as spontaneous eruptions that "break out like thunder storms, heave like earthquakes, spread like wildfires"; alternatively, they attributed rebellions as a reflex action to economic and political oppression. "Either way insurgency is regarded as external to the peasant's consciousness and Cause is made to stand in as a phantom surrogate for Reason, the logic of consciousness."

How did historiography develop this blind spot? Guha asked. In answering this question, his "Prose of Counter-Insurgency" offers a methodological tour de force and a perceptive reading of the historical writings on peasant insurgency in colonial India. Describing these writings as counter-insurgent texts, Guha begins by distinguishing three types of discourses—primary, secondary, and tertiary. These differ from one another in terms of the order of their appearance in time and the degree of their acknowledged or unacknowledged identification with the official point of view. Analyzing each in turn, Guha shows the presence, transformation, and redistribution of a "counter-insurgent code." This code, present in the immediate accounts of insurgency produced by officials (primary discourse), is processed into another time and narrative by official reports and memoirs (secondary discourse) and is then incorporated and redistributed by historians who have no official affiliation and are farthest removed from the time of the event (tertiary discourse). The "code of pacification," written into the "raw" data of primary texts and the narratives of secondary discourses, survives, and it shapes the tertiary discourse of historians when they fail to read in it the presence of the excluded other, the insurgent. Consequently, while historians produce accounts that differ from secondary discourses, their tertiary discourse also ends up appropriating the insurgent. Consider, for example, the treatment of peasant rebellions. When colonial officials, using on-the-spot accounts containing "the code of pacification," blamed wicked landlords and wily moneylenders for the occurrence of these events, they used causality as a counter-insurgent instrument: to identify the cause of the revolt was a step in the direction of control over it and constituted a denial of the insurgent's agency. In nationalist historiography, this denial took a different form, as British rule, rather than local oppression, became the cause of revolts and turned peasant rebellions into nationalist struggles. Radical historians, too, ended up incorporating the counter-insurgent code of the secondary discourse as they explained peasant revolts in relation to a revolutionary continuum leading to socialism. Each tertiary account failed to step outside the counter-insurgent paradigm, Guha argues, by refusing to acknowledge the subjectivity and agency of the insurgent.

Clearly, the project to restore the insurgent's agency involved, as Rosalind O'Hanlon pointed out in a thoughtful review essay, the notion of the "recovery of the subject." Thus, while reading records against their grain, these scholars have sought to uncover the subaltern's myths, cults, ideologies, and revolts that colonial and nationalist elites sought to appropriate and that conventional historiography has laid waste by the deadly weapon of cause and effect. Ranajit Guha's *Elementary Aspects of Peasant Insurgency in Colonial India* (1983) is a powerful example of scholarship that seeks to recover the peasant from elite projects and positivist historiography. In this wide-ranging study full of brilliant insights and methodological innovation, Guha returns to nineteenth-century peasant insurrections in colonial India. Reading colonial records and historiographical representations with an uncanny eye, he offers a fascinating account of the peasant's insurgent consciousness, rumors, mythic visions, religiosity, and bonds of community. From Guha's account, the subaltern emerges with forms of sociality and political community at odds with nation and class, defying the models of rationality and social action that conventional historiography uses. Guha argues persuasively that such models are elitist insofar as they deny the subaltern's autonomous consciousness and that they are drawn from colonial and liberal-nationalist projects of appropriating the subaltern.

It is true that the effort to retrieve the autonomy of the subaltern subject resembled the "history from below" approach developed by social history in the West. But the subalternist search for a humanist subject-agent frequently ended up with the discovery of the failure of subaltern agency: the moment of rebellion always contained within it the moment of failure. The desire to recover the subaltern's autonomy was repeatedly frustrated because subalternity, by definition, signified the impossibility of autonomy: subaltern rebellions only offered fleeting moments of defiance, "a night-time of love," not "a life-time of love." While these scholars failed to recognize fully that the subalterns' resistance did not simply oppose power but was also constituted by it, their own work showed this to be the case. Further complicating the urge to recover the subject was the fact that, unlike British and U.S. social history, Subaltern Studies drew on anti-humanist structuralist and poststructuralist writings. Ranajit Guha's deft readings of colonial records, in particular, drew explicitly from Ferdinand de Sassure, Claude Lévi-Strauss, Roman Jakobson, Roland Barthes, and Michel Foucault. Partly, the reliance on such theorists and the emphasis on "textual" readings arose from, as Dipesh Chakrabarty points out, the absence of workers' diaries and other such sources available to British historians. Indian peasants had left no sources, no documents from which their own "voice" could be retrieved. But the emphasis on "readings" of texts and the recourse to theorists such as Foucault, whose writings cast a shroud of doubt over the idea of the autonomous subject, contained an awareness that the colonial subaltern was not just a form of "general" subalternity. While the operation of power relations in colonial and metropolitan theaters had parallels, the conditions of subalternity were also irreducibly different. Subaltern Studies, therefore, could not just be the Indian version of the "history from below" approach; it had to conceive the subaltern differently and write different histories.

This difference has grown in subsequent Subaltern Studies volumes as the desire to recover the subaltern subject became increasingly entangled in the analysis of how subalternity was constituted by dominant discourses. Of course, the tension between the recovery of the subaltern as a subject outside the elite discourse and the analysis of subalternity as an effect of discursive systems was present from the very beginning. It also continues to characterize Subaltern Studies scholarship today, as Florencia Mallon notes in her essay in this issue of the *AHR*. Recent volumes, however, pay greater attention to developing the emergence of subalternity as a discursive effect without abandoning the notion of the subaltern as a subject and agent. This perspective, amplified since *Subaltern Studies III*, identifies subalternity as a position of critique, as a recalcitrant difference that arises not outside but inside elite discourses to exert pressure on forces and forms that subordinate it.

The attention paid to discourse in locating the process and effects of subordination can be seen in Partha Chatterjee's influential *Nationalist Thought and the Colonial World* (1986). A study of how Indian nationalism achieved dominance, this book traces critical shifts in nationalist thought, leading to a "passive revolution"—a concept that he draws from Gramsci to interpret the achievement of Indian independence in 1947 as a mass revolution that appropriated the agency of the common people. In interpreting the shifts in nationalist thought, Chatterjee stresses the pressure exerted on the dominant discourse by the problem of representing the masses. The nationalists dealt with this problem by marginalizing certain forms of mass action and expression that run counter to the modernity-driven goals that they derived from the colonial discourse. Such a strategy secures elite dominance but not hegemony over subaltern culture and politics. His recent *The Nation and Its Fragments* (1993) returns once again to this theme of appropriation of subalternity, sketching how the nation was first imagined in the cultural domain and then readied for political contest by an elite that "normalized" various subaltern aspirations for community and agency in the drive to create a modern nation-state.

Investigating the process of "normalization" means a complex and deep engagement with elite and canonical texts. This, of course, is not new to Subaltern Studies. Earlier essays, most notably Guha's "Prose of Counter-Insurgency," engaged and interrogated elite writings with enviable skill and imagination. But these analyses of elite texts sought to establish the presence of the subalterns as subjects of their own history. The engagement with elite themes and writings, by contrast, emphasizes the analysis of the operation of dominance as it confronted, constituted, and subordinated certain forms of culture and politics. This approach is visible in the treatment of the writings of authoritative political figures such as Mahatma Gandhi and Jawaharlal Nehru and in the analyses of the activities of the Indian National Congress—the dominant nationalist party. These strive to outline how elite nationalism rewrote history and how its rewriting was directed at both contesting colonial rule and protecting its flanks from the subalterns. Another theme explored with a similar aim is the intertwined functioning of colonialism, nationalism, and "communalism" in the partition of British India into India and Pakistan—a theme that has taken on added importance with the recent resurgence of Hindu supremacists and outbreaks of Hindu-Muslim riots.

The importance of such topics is self-evident, but the real significance of the shift to the analysis of discourses is the reformulation of the notion of the subaltern. It is tempting to characterize this shift as an abandonment of the search for subaltern groups in favor of the discovery of discourses and texts. But this would be inaccurate. Although some scholars have rejected the positivistic retrieval of the subalterns, the notion of the subalterns' radical heterogeneity with, though not autonomy from, the dominant remains crucial. It is true, however, that scholars locate this heterogeneity in discourses, woven into the fabric of dominant structures and manifesting itself in the very operation of power. In other words, subalterns and subalternity do not disappear into discourse but appear in its interstices, subordinated by structures over which they exert pressure. Thus Shahid Amin shows that Indian nationalists in 1921–1922, confronted with the millennial and deeply subversive language of peasant politics, were quick to claim peasant actions as their own and Gandhian. Unable to acknowledge the peasants' insurgent appropriation of Gandhi, Indian nationalists represented it in the stereotypical saint-devotee relationship. Amin develops this point further in his innovative monograph on the peasant violence in 1922 that resulted in the death of several policemen and led Gandhi to suspend the noncooperation campaign against British rule. Returning to this emotive date in Indian nationalist history, Amin shows that this violent event, "criminalized" in the colonial judicial discourse, was "nationalized" by the elite nationalists, first by an "obligatory amnesia" and then by selective remembrance and reappropriation. To take another example, Gyanendra Pandey suggests that the discourse of the Indian nation-state, which had to imagine India as a national community, could not recognize community (religious, cultural, social, and local) as a political form; thus it pitted nationalism (termed good because it "stood above" difference) against communalism (termed evil because it did not "rise above" difference).

Such reexaminations of South Asian history do not invoke "real" subalterns, prior to discourse, in framing their critique. Placing subalterns in the labyrinth of discourse, they cannot claim an unmediated access to their reality. The actual subalterns and subalternity emerge between the folds of the discourse, in its silences and blindness, and in its overdetermined pronouncements. Interpreting the 1922 peasant violence, Amin identifies the subaltern presence as an effect in the discourse. This effect manifests itself in a telling dilemma the nationalists faced. On the one hand, they could not endorse peasant violence as nationalist activity, but, on the other, they had to acknowledge the peasant "criminals" as part of the nation. They sought to resolve this dilemma by admitting the event in the narrative of the nation while denying it agency: the peasants were shown to act the way they did because they were provoked, or because they were insufficiently trained in the methods of nonviolence.

Subalternity thus emerges in the paradoxes of the functioning of power, in the functioning of the dominant discourse as it represents and domesticates peasant agency as a spontaneous and "pre-political" response to colonial violence. No longer does it appear outside the elite discourse as a separate domain, embodied in a figure endowed with a will that the dominant suppress and overpower but do not constitute. Instead, it refers to that impossible thought, figure, or action without which the dominant discourse cannot exist and which is acknowledged in its subterfuges and stereotypes.

This portrait of subalternity is certainly different from the image of the autonomous subject, and it has emerged in the confrontation with the systematic fragmentation of the record of subalternity. Such records register both the necessary failure of subalterns to come into their own and the pressure they exerted on discursive systems that, in turn, provoked their suppression and fragmentation. The representation of this discontinuous mode of subalternity demands a strategy that recognizes both the emergence and displacement of subaltern agency in dominant discourses. It is by adopting such a strategy that the Subaltern Studies scholars have redeployed and redefined the concept of the subaltern, enhancing, not diminishing, its recalcitrance.

The Subaltern Studies' relocation of subalternity in the operation of dominant discourses leads it necessarily to the critique of the modern West. For if the marginalization of "other" sources of knowledge and agency occurred in the functioning of colonialism and its derivative, nationalism, then the weapon of critique must turn against Europe and the modes of knowledge it instituted. It is in this context that there emerges a certain convergence between Subaltern Studies and postcolonial critiques originating in literary and cultural studies. To cite only one example, not only did Edward Said's *Orientalism* provide the grounds for Partha Chatterjee's critique of Indian nationalism, Said also wrote an appreciative foreword to a collection of Subaltern Studies essays. It is important to recognize that the critique of the West is not confined to the colonial record of exploitation and profiteering but extends to the disciplinary knowledge and procedures it authorized—above all, the discipline of history.

In a recent essay, Dipesh Chakrabarty offers a forceful critique of the academic discipline of history as a theoretical category laden with power. Finding premature the celebration of Subaltern Studies as a case of successful decolonization of knowledge, Chakrabarty writes that,

> insofar as the academic discourse of history—that is, "history" as a discourse produced at the institutional site of the university—is concerned, "Europe" remains the sovereign, theoretical subject of all histories, including the ones we call "Indian," "Chinese," "Kenyan," and so on. There is a peculiar way in which all these other histories tend to become variations on a master narrative that could be called "the history of Europe." In this sense, "Indian" history itself is in a position of subalternity; one can only articulate subaltern subject positions in the name of this history.

The place of Europe as a silent referent works in many ways. First, there is the matter of "asymmetric ignorance": non-Westerners must read "great" Western historians (E. P. Thompson or Emmanuel Le Roy Ladurie or Carlo Ginzburg) to produce the good histories, while the Western scholars are not expected to know non-Western works. Indeed, non-Western scholars are recognized for their innovation and imagination when they put into practice genres of inquiry developed for European history; a "total history" of China, the history of *mentalité* in Mexico, the making of the working class in India are likely to be applauded as fine studies.

Even more important, Chakrabarty suggests, is the installation of Europe as the theoretical subject of all histories. This universalization of Europe works through the representation of histories as History; even "Marx's methodological/epistemological statements have not always successfully resisted historicist readings." Chakrabarty's study of jute workers in Bengal runs up against precisely the same Eurocentrism that undergirds Marx's analysis of capital and class struggle. In his study, Chakrabarty finds that deeply hierarchical notions of caste and religion, drawn from India's traditions, animated working-class organization and politics in Bengal. This posed a problem for Marxist historiography. If India's traditions lacked the "Liberty Tree" that had nourished, according to E. P. Thompson, the consciousness of the English working class, were Indian workers condemned to "low classness"? The alternative was to envision that, sooner or later, the Indian working class would reach the desired state of emancipatory consciousness. This vision, of course, assumes the universality of such notions as the rights of "free-born Englishmen" and "equality before the law," and it posits that "workers all over the world, irrespective of their specific cultural pasts, experience 'capitalist production' in the same way." This possibility can only arise if it is assumed that there is a universal subject endowed with an emancipatory narrative. Such an assumption, Chakrabarty suggests, is present in Marx's analysis, which, while carefully contrasting the proletariat from the citizen, falls back nonetheless on Enlightenment notions of freedom and democracy to define the emancipatory narrative. As a result, the jute workers, who resisted the bourgeois ideals of equality before the law with their hierarchical vision of a pre-capitalist community, are condemned to "backwardness" in Marxist accounts. Furthermore, it allows the nation-state to step onto the stage as the instrument of liberal transformation of the hierarchy-ridden masses.

It is not surprising, therefore, that themes of historical transition occupy a prominent place in the writing of non-Western histories. Historians ask if these societies achieved a successful transition to development, modernization, and capitalism and frequently answer in the negative. A sense of failure overwhelms the representation of the history of these societies. So much so that even contestatory projects, including Subaltern Studies, Chakrabarty acknowledges, write of non-Western histories in terms of failed transitions. Such images of aborted transitions reinforce the subalternity of non-Western histories and the dominance of Europe as History.

The dominance of Europe as history not only subalternizes non-Western societies but also serves the aims of their nation-states. Indeed, Subaltern Studies developed its critique of history in the course of its examination of Indian nationalism and the nation-state. Guha's reconstruction of the language of peasant politics in his *Elementary Aspects of Peasant Insurgency in Colonial India* is premised on the argument that nationalist historiography engaged in a systematic appropriation of peasants in the service of elite nationalism. Chatterjee's work contains an extended analysis of Jawaharlal Nehru's *Discovery of India*, a foundational nationalist text, showing the use of History, Reason, and Progress in the normalization of peasant "irrationality." The inescapable conclusion from such analyses is that "history," authorized by European imperialism and the Indian nation-state, functions as a discipline, empowering certain forms of knowledge while disempowering others.

If history functions as a discipline that renders certain forms of thought and action "irrational" and subaltern, then should not the critique extend to the techniques and procedures it utilizes? Addressing this question, Chakrabarty turns to "one of the most elementary rules of evidence in academic history-writing: that your sources must be verifiable." Pointing out that this rule assumes the existence of a "public sphere," which public archives and history writing are expected to reproduce, he suggests that the canons of historical research cannot help but live a problematic life in societies such as India. The idea of "public life" and "free access to information" must contend with the fact that knowledge is privileged and "belongs and circulates in the numerous and particularistic networks of kinship, community, gendered spaces, [and] ageing structures." If this is the case, then, Chakrabarty asks, how can we assume the universality of the canons of history writings: "Whose universals are they?"

It is important to note that "Europe" or "the West" in Subaltern Studies refers to an imaginary though powerful entity created by a historical process that authorized it as the home of Reason, Progress, and Modernity. To undo the authority of such an entity, distributed and universalized by imperialism and nationalism, requires, in Chakrabarty's words, the "provincialization of Europe." But neither nativism nor cultural relativism animates this project of provincializing Europe; there are no calls for reversing the Europe/India hierarchy and no attempts to represent India through an "Indian," not Western, perspective. Instead, the recognition that the "third-world historian is condemned to knowing 'Europe' as the original home of the 'modern,' whereas the 'European' historian does not share a comparable predicament with regard to the pasts of the majority of humankind," serves as the condition for a deconstructive rethinking of history. Such a strategy seeks to find in the functioning of history as a discipline (in Foucault's sense) the source for another history.

This move is a familiar one for postcolonial criticism and should not be confused with approaches that insist simply on the social construction of knowledge and identities. It delves into the history of colonialism not only to document its record of domination but also to identify its failures, silences, and impasses; not only to chronicle the career of dominant discourses but to track those (subaltern) positions that could not be properly recognized and named, only "normalized." The aim of such a strategy is not to unmask dominant discourses but to explore their fault lines in order to provide different accounts, to describe histories revealed in the cracks of the colonial archaeology of knowledge.

This perspective draws on critiques of binary oppositions that, as Frederick Cooper notes in his essay in this *Forum*, historians of former empires look upon with suspicion. It is true, as Cooper points out, that binary oppositions conceal intertwined histories and engagements across dichotomies, but the critique must go further. Oppositions such as East/West and colonizer/colonized are suspect not only because these distort the history of engagements but also because they edit, suppress, and marginalize everything that upsets founding values. It is in this respect that Jacques Derrida's strategy to undo the implacable oppositions of Western dominance is of some relevance.

> Metaphysics—the white mythology which reassembles and reflects the culture of the West: the white man takes his own mythology, Indo-European mythology, his own *logos*, that is, the *mythos* of his idiom, for the universal form that he must still wish to call Reason . . . White mythology—metaphysics has erased within itself the fabulous scene that has produced it, the scene that nevertheless remains active and stirring, inscribed in white ink, an invisible design covered over in the palimpsest.

If the production of white mythology has nevertheless left "an invisible design covered over in the palimpsest," Derrida suggests that the structure of signification, of "différance," can be rearticulated differently than that which produced the West as Reason. Further, the source of the rearticulation of structures that produce foundational myths (History as the march of Man, of Reason, Progress) lies inside, not outside, their ambivalent functioning. From this point of view, critical work seeks its basis not without but within the fissures of dominant structures. Or, as Gayatri Chakravorty Spivak puts it, the deconstructive philosophical position (or postcolonial criticism) consists in saying an "impossible 'no' to a structure, which one critiques, yet inhabits intimately."

The potential of this deconstructive position has been explored effectively in the recent readings of the archival documents on the abolition of *sati*, the Hindu widow sacrifice in the early nineteenth century. The historian encounters these records, as I have suggested elsewhere, as evidence of the contests between the British "civilizing mission" and Hindu heathenism, between modernity and tradition, and as a story of the beginning of the emancipation of Hindu women and about the birth of modern India. This is so because, Lata Mani shows, the very existence of these documents has a history that entails the use of women as the site for both the colonial and the indigenous male elite's constructions of authoritative Hindu traditions. The questions asked of accumulated sources on *sati*—whether or not the burning of widows was sanctioned by Hindu codes, did women go willingly to the funeral pyre, on what grounds could the immolation of women be abolished—come to us marked by their early nineteenth-century history. The historian's confrontation today with sources on *sati*, therefore, cannot escape the echo of that previous rendezvous. In repeating that encounter, how does the historian today not replicate the early nineteenth-century staging of the issue as a contest between tradition and modernity, between the slavery of women and efforts toward their emancipation, between barbaric Hindu practices and the British "civilizing mission"? Mani tackles this dilemma by examining how such questions were asked and with what consequences. She shows that the opposing arguments assumed the authority of the law-giving scriptural tradition as the origin of Hindu customs: both those who supported and those who opposed *sati* sought the authority of textual origins for their beliefs. In other words, the nineteenth-century debate fabricated the authority of texts as Hinduism without acknowledging its work of authorization; indigenous patriarchy and colonial power colluded in constructing the origins for and against *sati* while concealing their collusion. Consequently, as Spivak states starkly, the debate left no room for the widow's enunciatory position. Caught in the contest over whether traditions did or did not sanction *sati* and over whether or not the widow self-immolated willingly, the colonized subaltern woman disappeared: she was literally extinguished for her dead husband in the indigenous patriarchal discourse, or offered the choice to speak in the voice of a sovereign individual authenticated by colonialism. The problem here is not one of sources (the absence of the woman's testimony) but of the staging of the debate: it left no position from which the widow could speak.

The silencing of subaltern women, Spivak argues, marks the limit of historical knowledge. It is impossible to retrieve the woman's voice when she was not given a subject-position from which to speak. This argument appears to run counter to the historiographical convention of retrieval to recover the histories of the traditionally ignored—women, workers, peasants, and minorities. Spivak's point, however, is not that such retrievals should not be undertaken but that the very project of recovery depends on the historical erasure of the subaltern "voice." The possibility of retrieval, therefore, is also a sign of its impossibility. Recognition of the aporetic condition of the subaltern's silence is necessary in order to subject the intervention of the historian-critic to persistent interrogation, to prevent the refraction of "what might have been the absolutely Other into a domesticated Other."

These directions of postcolonial criticism make it an ambivalent practice, perched between traditional historiography and its failures, within the folds of dominant discourses and seeking to rearticulate their pregnant silence—sketching "an invisible design covered over in the palimpsest." This should not be mistaken for the postmodern pastiche, although the present currency of concepts such as decentered subjects and parodic texts may provide a receptive and appropriative frame for postcolonial criticism. Postcolonial criticism seizes on discourse's silences and aporetic moments neither to celebrate the polyphony of native voices nor to privilege multiplicity. Rather, its point is that the *functioning* of colonial power was heterogeneous with its founding oppositions. The "native" was at once an other and entirely knowable; the Hindu widow was a silenced subaltern who was nonetheless sought as a sovereign subject asked to declare whether or not her immolation was voluntary. Clearly, colonial discourses operated as the structure of *writing*, with the structure of their enunciation remaining heterogeneous with the binary oppositions they instituted.

This perspective on history and the position within it that the postcolonial critic occupies keeps an eye on both the conditions of historical knowledge and the possibility of its reinscription. It is precisely this double vision that allows Shahid Amin to use the limits of historical knowledge for its reinscription. His monograph on the 1922 peasant violence in Chauri Chaura is at once scrupulously "local" and "general." It offers a "thick description" of a local event set on a larger stage by nationalism and historiographical practice. Amin seizes on this general (national) staging of the local not only to show that the Indian nation emerged in its narration but also to mark the tension between the two as the point at which the subaltern memory of 1922 can enter history. This memory, recalled for the author during his field work, is not invoked either to present a more "complete" account of the event or to recover the subaltern. In fact, treating gaps, contradictions, and ambivalences as constitutive, necessary components of the nationalist narrative, Amin inserts memory as a device that both dislocates and reinscribes the historical record. The result is not an archaeology of nationalism that yields lifeless layers of suppressed evidence and episodes. Instead, we get a stage on which several different but interrelated dramas are performed, jostling for attention and prominence; curtains are abruptly drawn on some, and often the voices of the peasant actors can only be heard in the din of the other, more powerful, voices.

To read Amin's work in this way shows, I hope, that his deconstructive strategy does not "flatten" the tension that has existed, as Florencia Mallon notes correctly, in this scholarship from the very beginning. To be sure, Amin's account is not animated by the urge to recover the subaltern as an autonomous subject. But he places his inquiry in the tension between nationalism's claim to know the peasant and its representation of the subalterns as the "criminals" of Chauri Chaura. The subaltern remains a recalcitrant presence in discourse, at once part of the nation and outside it. Amin trafficks between these two positions, demonstrating that subaltern insurgency left its mark, however disfigured, on the discourse— "an invisible design covered over in the palimpsest."

Neither Amin's retelling of the 1922 event nor Chakrabarty's project of "provincializing Europe" can be separated from postcolonial critiques of disciplines, including the discipline of history. Thus, even as Subaltern Studies has shifted from its original goal of recovering the subaltern autonomy, the subaltern has emerged as a position from which the discipline of history can be rethought. This rethinking does not entail the rejection of the discipline and its procedures of research. Far from it. As Chakrabarty writes, "it is not possible to simply walk out of the deep collusion between 'history' and the modernizing narrative(s)." Nor is it possible to abandon historical research so long as it is pursued as an academic discipline in universities and functions to universalize capitalism and the nation-state. There is no alternative but to inhabit the discipline, delve into archives, and push at the limits of historical knowledge to turn its contradictions, ambivalences, and gaps into grounds for its rewriting.

IF SUBALTERN STUDIES' POWERFUL INTERVENTION in South Asian historiography has turned into a sharp critique of the discipline of history, this is because South Asia is not an isolated arena but is woven into the web of historical discourse centered, as Chakrabarty argues, in the modern West. Through the long histories of colonialism and nationalism, the discourse of modernity, capitalism, and citizenship has acquired a strong though peculiar presence in the history of the region. The institutions of higher education in South Asia, relatively large and thriving, have functioned since the mid-nineteenth century in relation to the metropolitan academy, including centers for South Asian studies in the West. For all these reasons, India's historical scholarship has been uniquely placed to both experience and formulate searching critiques of metropolitan discourses even as its object remains the field of South Asia. To its credit, Subaltern Studies turned South Asia's entanglement with the modern West as the basis for rendering its intervention in South Asian history into a critique of discourses authorized by Western domination.

Subaltern Studies has arrived at its critique by engaging both Marxism and poststructuralism. But the nature of these engagements is complex. If the influence of Gramsci's Marxism is palpable in the concept of the subaltern and in treatments of such themes as hegemony and dominance, Marxism is also subjected to the poststructuralist critique of European humanism. It should be noted, however, as Spivak points out, that while "there is an affinity between the imperialist subject and the subject of humanism," the European critique of humanism does not provide the primary motive force for the Subaltern Studies project. Thus, even as this project utilizes Foucault's genealogical analysis to unravel the discourse of modernity, it relies on the subaltern as the vantage point of critique. The recalcitrant presence of the subaltern, marking the limits of the dominant discourse and the disciplines of representation, enables Subaltern Studies to identify the European provenance of Marx's account of capital, to disclose Enlightenment thought as the unthought of his analysis. It is outside Europe, in subaltern locations, that Marx's emancipatory narrative is disclosed as a telos deeply implicated in a discourse that was once part of colonialism and now serves to legitimate the nation-state. Such a critical and complex engagement with Marxism and poststructuralism, deriving its force from the concept of the subaltern, defines the Subaltern Studies project.

Clearly, Subaltern Studies obtains its force as postcolonial criticism from a catachrestic combination of Marxism, poststructuralism, Gramsci and Foucault, the modern West and India, archival research and textual criticism. As this project is translated into other regions and disciplines, the discrepant histories of colonialism, capitalism, and subalternity in different areas would have to be recognized. It is up to the scholars of these fields, including Europeanists, to determine how to use Subaltern Studies' insights on subalternity and its critique of the colonial genealogy of the discourse of modernity. But it is worth bearing in mind that Subaltern Studies itself is an act of translation. Representing a negotiation between South Asian historiography and the discipline of history centered in the West, its insights can be neither limited to South Asia nor globalized. Trafficking between the two, and originating as an ambivalent colonial aftermath, Subaltern Studies demands that its own translation also occur between the lines.

Questions

1. What is intersectionality? How can this concept be utilized to discuss social relations?

2. How do each of the authors in this section describe justice, or how do they envision a just world?

3. Take one of the authors from this section and put them in dialogue with Locke. What would they agree on? Where would their opinions diverge?

4. "The Changing Meaning of Race" was written more than ten years ago. Is Omi's account still accurate today? What is Whiteness and why is it an important concept?

5. These authors do not necessarily make the claim that they are addressing human nature as represented by the authors in the first section. In what ways can you see human nature in each of these pieces?

Suggested Media

Movies

The Human Experience
9500 Liberty
Crash
Avatar
The Social Network
Inception

Television

Race the Power of an Illusion (PBS)
Big Love (HBO)

Books and Articles

K. Crenshaw (1989) Mapping the Margins: Intersectionality, Identity Politics, and Violence Against Women of Color
A. Gordon (2008) *Ghostly Matters: Haunting and the Sociological Imagination*
G. Hegel (1977 translation) *The Phenomenology of Spirit*

Governance

Governance is more than just the structure and administration of a nation's government. It is the rules and rulers, the law, and the bureaucracy embedded in the system of that government, it is about the relationship between the state and the individual. In this section, the readings on governance will discuss various theories of justice that comment on the polity, law, structure, communication, and administration of governance. Most of the readings are western civilization-centered and regionally specific to the United States, although this section, as well as this text, will include readings outside of this tradition. These various theories of justice may have roots in the foundations of differing notions of human nature.

This section will highlight various systems of governance and the theories of justice that are rooted in each of them:

- Democracy is a governance system that emphasizes the "rule by the people" and citizenship, participation, and communication.
- A republic is a governance system in which the constitution is seen as an essential document organizing the collective will and rule of law.

- Governance systems of anarchy promote the idea that humankind should have the individual liberty to act in accordance to their own will and absent of constraint.
- Communism and theocracy are both governance ideas which emphasize a government that is "absolute" in rule and regulation in order to maintain a stronger communal liberty.

This section will also look at a critique on the Western notions of governance, and instead assert a de-colonial system of difference in governance dealing with race, gender, sexuality, class, and more.

Alexis de Tocqueville provides essential thoughts on democracy for the United States. His famous book *Democracy in America,* which originated as a research project, began by studying the American prison system in 1831. Tocqueville's illustration of a democratic government, in which the social conditions were fair and just, was what he saw when he traveled throughout the United States. His enthusiasm for the democracy he witnessed in the United States came at a time when nations around the world were ruled by the injustices of aristocracy. In his writings, he noted that equality in the United States was so great in both "fortune and intellect" that the strength of democracy will spread throughout the world. Though Tocqueville talked a lot about the democracy he experienced, in actuality the system he portrayed was that of a democratic republic. Within this democratic republic were core theories of justice, such as contractarianism and egalitarianism. This view holds that a social contract is assembled by the collective will of the people, along with guiding principles of equality and joint responsibility. Tocqueville's writings show how the integration of differing theories of justice intersect and work in agreement toward a stronger and fairer governance structure of a democratic republic, and how this self-governance is the goal of justice.

Frédéric Bastiat's essential writing, *The Law* (1850), was spurred by his family's business experience with governmental trade intervention and tariffs, which put their company out of business. It was because of this difficult experience that Bastiat began to evaluate the system of governance in France and critique it. Bastiat writes from a critical perspective about all and any intervention in the market by the government. He writes, "The law [is] guilty of that very iniquity which it was its mission to punish!" This critique led to the advocacy of a free-market and an anarchic governance system. This governance system is highlighted by a libertarian system of justice, one that maintains that all "men have a right of defending, even by force, his person, his liberty, and his property". A libertarian theory of justice, one that yields free-markets and an anarchist governance, will defend the core principles of justice as freedom from any constraints, ability to defend your own liberty, and the protection of your property and yourself.

Kai Nielson is a contemporary social and political philosopher who writes about utilitarian and egalitarian theories of justice. The specific reading, *Radical Egalitarianism,* in his 1985 book *Equality and Liberty*, paints a picture of a communistic system of governance. Nielson discusses how systems of justice within governance must reflect the goal of "equality of basic conditions for everyone". He constructs this governance by dealing with the problems of scarcity and surplus, entitlements, meritocracy, and talents. Using an egalitarian theory of justice, along with elements of utilitarianism, Nielson shows how a system of governance like communism is based on "absolute" controls and regulations within a society, and reflects the goal of shared responsibility and equal conditions for all within the community.

In Seyla Benhabib's 1994 essay, titled *Toward a Deliberative Model of Democratic Legitimacy*, she writes about a democratic governance system which is integrated with justice theories of egalitarianism and critical theory. Her addition to the discussion of the governance structure of democracy is that of its legitimacy. This standard of legitimacy is only obtained when the decisions that produce outcomes for the collective population are reached based on this ideal of deliberation. Furthermore, the process of deliberation must be inclusive of differences and maintain a discourse model that makes the implicit, explicit; the unstated, known. Within this framework of critical theory as the foundation to legitimate

Governance **113**

a democracy, there are also principles of egalitarianism as conditions for participation and input into the process and creating an equal opportunity to influence governance. Benhabib states that governance should be "conceived as an anonymous, plural, and multiple medium of communication and deliberation, the public sphere need not homogenize and repress difference". Benhabib deconstructs this idea of democracy, and reconstructs a more holistic system that is reflective of the difference that exists in the community.

Audre Lorde (1979) writes about de-colonization and alternate voices for justice in a short piece called *The Master's Tools Will Never Dismantle the Master's House*. Lorde begins her essay by describing the situation that occurred at an N.Y.U. conference, at which she was asked to speak about difference. Lorde continues to critique the situation because of the lack of alternative voices that were glaringly absent at this conference in which her role reflected the tokenism that the dominant culture uses to placate different groups. This section centers on not only the feminist critique, but a post-colonial perspective toward the paternalist, Eurocentric culture. Lorde's famous saying about not being able to dismantle the master's house with the master's tools is explained even more clearly. She states, "(the tools) may allow us temporarily to beat him at his own game, but they will never enable us to bring about genuine change". The feminist system of justice which Lorde uses calls into question the system of governance as a whole, along with how the system is defined and who does the defining.

This section discusses the concept of governance and its role as a structure in society. By examining various theories of justice (egalitarianism, utilitarianism, contractarianism, libertarianism, feminism, and critical theory), this section helps to shape how those theories construct and critique systems of governance (such as democratic republics, legitimate democracies, anarchies, communistic systems and post-colonialism).

DEMOCRACY IN AMERICA

ALEXIS DE TOCQUEVILLE

Chapter III

Social Condition Of The Anglo-Americans

A social condition is commonly the result of circumstances, sometimes of laws, oftener still of these two causes united; but wherever it exists, it may justly be considered as the source of almost all the laws, the usages, and the ideas, which regulate the conduct of nations: whatever it does not produce, it modifies.

It is, therefore, necessary, if we would become acquainted with the legislation and the manners of a nation, to begin by the study of its social condition.

The Striking Characteristic of The Social Condition of The Anglo-Americans is Its Essential Democracy

The first Emigrants of New England.—Their Equality.—Aristocratic Laws introduced in the South.—Period of the Revolution.—Change in the Law of Descent.—Effects produced by this Change.—Democracy carried to its utmost Limits in the new States of the West.—Equality of Education.

Many important observations suggest themselves upon the social condition of the Anglo-Americans; but there is one which takes precedence of all the rest. The social condition of the Americans is eminently democratic; this was its character at the foundation of the colonies, and is still more strongly marked at the present day.

I have stated in the preceding chapter that great equality existed among the emigrants who settled on the shores of New England The germe of aristocracy was never planted in that part of the Union. The only influence which obtained there was that of intellect; the people were used to reverence certain names as the emblems of knowledge and virtue. Some of their fellow-citizens acquired a power over the rest which might truly have been called aristocratic, if it had been capable of invariable transmission from father to son.

This was the state of things to the east of the Hudson : to the southwest of that river, and in the direction of the Floridas, the case was different. In most of the states situated to the southwest of the Hudson some great English proprietors had settled, who had imported with them aristocratic principles and the English law of descent. I have explained the reasons why it was impossible ever to establish a powerful aristocracy in America; these reasons existed with less force to the south west of the Hudson. In the south, one man, aided by slaves, could cultivate a great extent of country: it was therefore common to see rich landed proprietors. But their influence was not altogether aristocratic as that term is understood in Europe, since they possessed no privileges; and the cultivation of their estates being carried on by slaves, they had no tenants depending on them, and consequently no patronage. Still, the great proprietors south of the Hudson constituted a superior class, having ideas and tastes of its own, and forming the centre of political action. This kind of aristocracy sympathized with the body of the people, whose passions and interests it easily embraced; but it was too weak and too short-lived to excite either love or hatred for itself. This was the class which headed the insurrection in the south, and furnished the best leaders of the American revolution.

At the period of which we are now speaking, society was shaken to its centre: the people, in whose name the struggle had taken place, conceived the desire of exercising the authority which it had acquired;

its democratic tendencies were awakened; and having thrown off the yoke of the mother-country, it aspired to independence of every kind. The influence of individuals gradually ceased to be felt, and custom and law united together to produce the same result.

But the law of descent was the last step to equality. I am surprised that ancient and modern jurists have not attributed to this law a greater influence on human affairs.* It is true that these laws belong to civil affairs: but they ought nevertheless to be placed at the head of all political institutions; for, while political laws are only the symbol of a nation's condition, they exercise an incredible influence upon its social state. They have, moreover, a sure and uniform manner of operating upon society, affecting, as it were, generations yet unborn.

Through their means man acquires a kind of preternatural power over the future lot of his fellow-creatures. When the legislator has once regulated the law of inheritance, he may rest from his labour. The machine once put in motion will go on for ages, and advance, as if self-guided, toward a given point. When framed in a particular manner, this law unites, draws together, and vests property and power in a few hands: its tendency is clearly aristocratic. On opposite principles its action is still more rapid; it divides, distributes, and disperses both property and power. Alarmed by the rapidity of its progress, those who despair of arresting its motion endeavour to obstruct by difficulties and impediments; they vainly seek to counteract its effect by contrary efforts: but it gradually reduces or destroys every obstacle, until by its incessant activity the bulwarks of the influence of wealth are ground down to the fine and shifting sand which is the basis of democracy. When the law of inheritance permits, still more when it decrees, the equal division of a father's property among all his children, its effects are of two kinds: it is important to distinguish them from each other, although they tend to the same end.

In virtue of the law of partible inheritance, the death of every proprietor brings about a kind of revolution in property: not only do his possessions change hands, but their very nature is altered; since they are parcelled into shares, which become smaller and smaller at each division. This is the direct, and, as it were, the physical effect of the law. It follows, then, that in countries where equality of inheritance is established by law, property, and especially landed property, must have a tendency to perpetual diminution. The effects, however, of such legislation would only be perceptible after a lapse of time, if the law was abandoned to its own working; for supposing a family to consist of two children (and in a country peopled as France is, the average number is not above three), these children, sharing among them the fortune of both parents, would not be poorer than their father or mother.

But the law of equal division exercises its influence not merely upon the property itself, but it affects the minds of the heirs, and brings their passions into play. These indirect consequences tend powerfully to the destruction of large fortunes, and especially of large domains.

Among the nations whose law of descent is founded upon the right of primogeniture, landed estates often pass from generation to generation without undergoing division. The consequence of which is, that family feeling is to a certain degree incorporated with the estate. The family represents the estate, the estate the family; whose name, together with its origin, its glory, its power, and its virtues, is thus perpetuated in an imperishable memorial of the past, and a sure pledge of the future.

When the equal partition of property is established by law, the intimate connexion is destroyed between family feeling and the preservation of the paternal estate; the property ceases to represent the family; for, as it must inevitably be divided after one or two generations, it has evidently a constant tendency to diminish, and must in the end be completely dispersed. The sons of the great landed proprietor,

---

* I understand by the law of descent all those laws whose principal object it is to regulate the distribution of property after the death of its owner. The law of entail is of this number: it certainly prevents the owner from disposing of his possessions before his death; but this is solely with a view of preserving them entire for the heir. The principal object, therefore, of the law of entail is to regulate the descent of property after the death of its owner: its other provisions are merely means to this end.

if they are few in number, or if fortune befriend them, may indeed entertain the hope of being as wealthy as their father, but not that of possessing the same property as he did; their riches must necessarily be composed of elements different from his.

Now, from the moment when you divest the land-owner of that interest in the preservation of his estate which he derives from association, from tradition, and from family pride, you may be certain that sooner or later he will dispose of it; for there is a strong pecuniary interest in favour of selling, as floating capital produces higher interest than real property, and is more readily available to gratify the passions of the moment.

Great landed estates which have once been divided, never come together again; for the small proprietor draws from his land a better revenue in proportion, than the large owner does from his; and of course he sells it at a higher rate.* The calculations of gain, therefore, which decided the rich man to sell his domain, will still more powerfully influence him against buying small estates to unite them into a large one.

What is called family pride is often founded upon an illusion of self-love. A man wishes to perpetuate and immortalize himself, as it were, in his great-grandchildren. Where the *esprit de famille* ceases to act, individual selfishness comes into play. When the idea of family becomes vague, indeterminate, and uncertain, a man thinks of his present convenience; he provides for the establishment of the succeeding generation, and no more.

Either a man gives up the idea of perpetuating his family, or at any rate he seeks to accomplish it by other means than that of a landed estate.

Thus not only does the law of partible inheritance render it difficult for families to preserve their ancestral domains entire, but it deprives them of the inclination to attempt it, and compels them in some measure to co-operate with the law in their own extinction.

The law of equal distribution proceeds by two methods: by acting upon things, it acts upon persons; by influencing persons, it affects things. By these means the law succeeds in striking at the root of landed property, and dispersing rapidly both families and fortunes.†

Most certainly is it not for us, Frenchmen of the nineteenth century, who daily behold the political and social changes which the law of partition is bringing to pass, to question its influence. It is perpetually conspicuous in our country, overthrowing the walls of our dwellings and removing the landmarks of our fields. But although it has produced great effects in France, much still remains for it to do. Our recollections, opinions, and habits, present powerful obstacles to its progress.

In the United States it has nearly completed its work of destruction, and there we can best study its results. The English laws concerning the transmission of property were abolished in almost all the states at the time of the revolution. The law of entail was so modified as not to interrupt the free circulation of property.* The first having passed away, estates began to be parcelled out; and the change became more and more rapid with the progress of time. At this moment, after a lapse of little more than sixty

---

* I do not mean to say that the small proprietor cultivates his land better, but he cultivates it with more ardour and care; so that he makes up by his labour for his want of skill.

† Land being the most stable kind of property, we find, from time to time, rich individuals who are disposed to make great sacrifices in order to obtain it, and who willingly forfeit a considerable part of their income to make sure of the rest. But these are accidental cases. The preference for landed property is no longer found habitually in any class but among the poor. The small land-owner, who has less information, less imagination, and fewer passions, than the great one, is generally occupied with the desire of increasing his estate; and it often happens that by inheritance, by marriage, or by the chances of trade, he is gradually furnished with the means. Thus, to balance the tendency which leads men to divide their estates, there exists another, which incites them to add to them. This tendency, which is sufficient to prevent estates from being divided *ad infinitum*, is not strong enough to create great territo rial possessions, certainly not to keep them up in the same family.

years, the aspect of society is totally altered; the families of the great landed proprietors are almost all commingled with the general mass. In the state of New York, which formerly contained many of these, there are but two who still keep their heads above the stream; and they must shortly disappear. The sons of these opulent citizens have become merchants, lawyers, or physicians. Most of them have lapsed into obscurity. The last trace of hereditary ranks and distinctions is destroyed—the law of partition has reduced all to one level.

I do not mean that there is any deficiency of wealthy individuals in the United States; I know of no country, indeed, where the love of money has taken stronger hold on the affections of men, and where a profounder contempt is expressed for the theory of the permanent equality of property. But wealth circulates with inconceivable rapidity, and experience shows that it is rare to find two succeeding generations in the full enjoyment of it.

This picture, which may perhaps be thought overcharged, still gives a very imperfect idea of what is taking place in the new states of the west and southwest. At the end of the last century a few bold adventurers began to penetrate into the valleys of the Mississippi, and the mass of the population very soon began to move in that direction: communities unheard of till then were seen to emerge from their wilds: states, whose names were not in existence a few years before, claimed their place in the American Union; and in the western settlements we may behold democracy arrived at its utmost extreme. In these states, founded off hand, and as it were by chance, the inhabitants are but of yesterday. Scarcely known to one another, the nearest neighbours are ignorant of each other's history. In this part of the American continent, therefore, the population has not experienced the influence of great names and great wealth, nor even that of the natural aristocracy of knowledge and virtue. None are there to wield that respectable power which men willingly grant to the remembrance of a life spent in doing good before their eyes. The new states of the west are already inhabited; but society has no existence among them.

It is not only the fortunes of men which are equal in America; even their aquirements partake in some degree of the same uniformity. I do not believe there is a country in the world where, in proportion to the population, there are so few uninstructed, and at the same time so few learned individuals. Primary instruction is within the reach of everybody; superior instruction is scarcely to be obtained by any. This is not surprising; it is in fact the necessary consequence of what we have advanced above. Almost all the Americans are in easy circumstances, and can therefore obtain the first elements of human knowledge.

In America there are comparatively few who are rich enough to live without a profession. Every profession requires an apprenticeship, which limits the time of instruction to the early years of life. At fifteen they enter upon their calling, and thus their education ends at the age when ours begins. Whatever is done afterward, is with a view to some special and lucrative object; a science is taken up as a matter of business, and the only branch of it which is attended to is such as admits of an immediate practical application.

[This paragraph does not fairly render the meaning of the author. The original French is as follows:—

"En Amérique il y a peu de riches; presque tous les Américains ont done besoin d'exercer une profession. Or, toute profession exige un apprentissage. Les Américains ne peuvent done donner a la culture générale de l'intelligence que les premières années de la vie: à quinze ans, ils entrent dans une carrière: ainsi leur education finit le plus souvent à l'époque où la nótre commence."

What is meant by the remark, that "at fifteen they enter upon a career, and thus their education is very often finished at the epoch when ours commences," is not clearly perceived. Our professional men enter upon their course of preparation for their respective professions, wholly between eighteen and twenty-one years of age. Apprentices to trades are bound out, ordinarily, at fourteen, but what general education they receive is after that period. Previously, they have acquired the mere elements of reading, writing, and arithmetic. But it is supposed there is nothing peculiar to America, in the age at which apprenticeship commences. In England, they commence at the same age, and it is believed that the same thing occurs throughout Europe. It is feared that the author has not here expressed himself with his usual clearness and precision.—*American Editor.*]

In America most of the rich men were formerly poor: most of those who now enjoy leisure were absorbed in business during their youth; the consequence of which is, that when they might have had a taste for study they had no time for it, and when the time is at their disposal they have no longer the inclination.

There is no class, then, in America in which the taste for intellectual pleasures is transmitted with hereditary fortune and leisure, and by which the labours of the intellect are held in honour. Accordingly there is an equal want of the desire and the power of application to these objects.

A middling standard is fixed in America for human knowledge. All approach as near to it as they can; some as they rise, others as they descend. Of course, an immense multitude of persons are to be found who entertain the same number of ideas on religion, history, science, political economy, legislation, and government. The gifts of intellect proceed directly from God, and man cannot prevent their unequal distribution. But in consequence of the state of things which we have here represented, it happens, that although the capacities of men are widely different, as the Creator has doubtless intended they should be, they are submitted to the same method of treatment.

In America the aristocratic element has always been feeble from its birth; and if at the present day it is not actually destroyed, it is at any rate so completely disabled that we can scarcely assign to it any degree of influence in the course of affairs.

The democratic principle, on the contrary, has gained so much strength by time, by events, and by legislation, as to have become not only predominant but all-powerful. There is no family or corporate authority, and it is rare to find even the influence of individual character enjoy any durability.

America, then, exhibits in her social state a most extraordinary phenomenon. Men are there seen on a greater equality in point of fortune and intellect, or in other words, more equal in their strength, than in any other country of the world, or, in any age of which history has preserved the remembrance.

Political Consequences Of The Social Condition Of The Anglo-Americans.

The political consequences of such a social condition as this are easily deducible.

It is impossible to believe that equality will not eventually find its way into the political world as it does everywhere else. To conceive of men remaining for ever unequal upon one single point, yet equal on all others, is impossible; they must come in the end to be equal upon all.

Now I know of only two methods of establishing equality in the political world: every citizen must be put in possession of his rights, or rights must be granted to no one. For nations which have arrived at the same stage of social existence as the Anglo-Americans, it is therefore very difficult to discover a medium between the sovereignty of all and the absolute power of one man: and it would be vain to deny that the social condition which I have been describing is equally liable to each of these consequences.

There is, in fact, a manly and lawful passion for equality, which excites men to wish all to be powerful and honoured. This passion tends to elevate the humble to the rank of the great; but there exists also in the human heart a depraved taste for equality, which impels the weak to attempt to lower the powerful to their own level, and reduces men to prefer equality in slavery to inequality with freedom. Not that those nations whose social condition is democratic naturally despise liberty; on the contrary, they have an instinctive love of it. But liberty is not the chief and constant object of their desires; equality is their idol: they make rapid and sudden efforts to obtain liberty, and if they miss their aim, resign themselves to their disappointment; but nothing can satisfy them excent equality, and rather than lose it they resolve to perish.

On the other hand, in a state where the citizens are nearly on an equality, it becomes difficult for them to preserve their independence against the aggressions of power. No one among them being strong enough to engage singly in the struggle with advantage, nothing but a general combination can protect their liberty: and such a union is not always to be found.

From the same social position, then, nations may derive one or the other of two great political results; these results are extremely different from each other, but they may both proceed from the same cause.

The Anglo-Americans, are the first who, having been exposed to this formidable alternative, have been happy enough to escape the dominion of absolute power. They have been allowed by their circumstances, their origin, their intelligence, and especially by their moral feeling, to establish and maintain the sovereignty of the people.

Chapter XIV

What The Real Advantages Are Which American Society Derives From The Government of The Democracy

Before I enter upon the subject of the present chapter, I am induced to remind the reader of what I have more than once adverted to in the course of this book. The political institutions of the United States appear to me to be one of the forms of government which a democracy may adopt: but I do not regard the American constitution as the best, or as the only one which a democratic people may establish. In showing the advantages which the Americans derive from the government of democracy, I am therefore very far from meaning, or from believing, that similar advantages can be obtained only from the same laws.

General Tendency of The Laws Under The Rule of The American Democracy, And Habits of Those Who Apply Them

Defects of a democratic Government easy to be discovered.—Its Advantages only to be discerned by long Observation.—Democracy in America often inexpert, but the general Tendency of the Laws advantageous.—In the American Democracy public Officers have no permanent interests distinct from those of the Majority.—Result of this State of Things.

The defects and the weaknesses of a democratic government may very readily be discovered; they are demonstrated by the most flagrant instances, while its beneficial influence is less perceptibly exercised. A single glance suffices to detect its evil consequences, but its good qualities can only be discerned by long observation The laws of the American democracy are frequently defective or incomplete; they sometimes attack vested rights, or give a sanction to others which are dangerous to the community; but even if they were good, the frequent changes which they undergo would be an evil. How comes it, then, that the American republics prosper, and maintain their position?

In the consideration of laws, a distinction must be carefully observed between the end at which they aim, and the means by which they are directed to that end; between their absolute and their relative excellence. If it be the intention of the legislator to favour the interests of the minority at the expense of the majority, and if the measures he takes are so combined as to accomplish the object he has in view with the least possible expense of time and exertion, the law may be well drawn up, although its purpose be bad; and the more efficacious it is, the greater is the mischief which it causes.

Democratic laws generally tend to promote the welfare of the greatest possible number; for they emanate from a majority of the citizens, who are subject to error, but who cannot have an interest opposed to their own advantage. The laws of an aristocracy tend, on the contrary, to concentrate wealth and power in the hands of the minority, because an aristocracy, by its very nature, constitutes a minority. It may therefore be asserted, as a general proposition, that the purpose of a democracy, in the conduct of its legislation, is useful to a greater number of citizens than that of an aristocracy. This is, however, the sum total of its advantages.

Aristocracies are infinitely more expert in the science of legislation than democracies ever can be. They are possessed of a self-control which protects them from the errors of a temporary excitement; and they form lasting designs which they mature with the assistance of favourable opportunities. Aristocratic government proceeds with the dexterity of art; it understands how to make the collective force of all its laws converge at the same time to a given point. Such is not the case with democracies, whose laws are almost always ineffective or in inopportune. The means of democracy are therefore more imperfect than those of aristocracy, and the measures which it unwittingly adopts are frequently opposed to its own cause; but the object it has in view is more useful.

Let us now imagine a community so organized by nature, or by its constitution, that it can support the transitory action of bad laws, and that it can await, without destruction, the general tendency of the legislation: we shall then be able to conceive that a democratic government, notwithstanding its defects, will be most fitted to conduce to the prosperity of this community. This is precisely what has occurred in the United States; and I repeat, what I have before remarked, that the great advantage of the Americans consists in their being able to commit faults which they may afterward repair.

An analogous observation may be made respecting public officers. It is easy to perceive that the American democracy frequently errs in the choice of the individuals to whom it intrusts the power of the administration; but it is more difficult to say why the state prospers under their rule. In the first place it is to be remarked, that if in a democratic state the governors have less honesty and less capacity than elsewhere, the governed on the other hand are more enlightened and more attentive to their interests. As the people in democracies is more incessantly vigilant in its affairs, and more jealous of its rights, it prevents its representatives from abandoning that general line of conduct which its own interest prescribes. In the second place, it must be remembered that if the democratic magistrate is more apt to misuse his power, he possesses it for a shorter period of time. But there is yet another reason which is still more general and conclusive. It is no doubt of importance to the welfare of nations that they should be governed by men of talents and virtue; but it is perhaps still more important than the interests of those men should not differ from the interests of the community at large; for if such were the case, virtues of a high order might become useless, and talents might be turned to a bad account.

I say that it is important that the interests of the persons in authority should not conflict with or oppose the interests of the community at large; but I do not insist upon their having the same interests as the *whole* population, because I am not a ware that such a state of things ever existed in any country.

No political form has hitherto been discovered, which is equally favourable to the prosperity and the development of all the classes into which society is divided. These classes continue to form, as it were, a certain number of distinct nations in the same nation; and experience has shown that it is no less dangerous to place the fate of these classes exclusively in the hands of any one of them, than it is to make one people the arbiter of the destiny of another. When the rich alone govern, the interest of the poor is always endangered; and when the poor make the laws, that of the rich incurs very serious risks. The advantage of democracy does not consist, therefore, as has sometimes been asserted, in favouring the prosperity of all, but simply in contributing to the well-being of the greatest possible number.

The men who are intrusted with the direction of public affairs in the United States, are frequently inferior, both in point of capacity and of morality, to those whom aristocratic institutions would raise to power. But their interest is identified and confounded with that of the majority of their fellow-citizens. They may frequently be faithless, and frequently mistake; but they will never systematically adopt a line of conduct opposed to the will of the majority; and it is impossible that they should give a dangerous or an exclusive tendency to the government.

The mal-administration of a democratic magistrate is a mere isolated fact, which only occurs during the short period for which he is elected. Corruption and incapacity do not act as common interests, which may connect men permanently with one another. A corrupt or an incapable magistrate will not concert his measures with another magistrate, simply because that individual is as corrupt and as incapable as himself; and these two men will never unite their endeavors to promote the corruption and inaptitude of their remote posterity. The ambition and the manœuvres of the one will serve, on the contrary, to unmask the other. The vices of a magistrate, in democratic states, are usually peculiar to his own person.

But under aristocratic governments public men are swayed by the interest of their order, which, if it is sometimes confounded with the interests of the majority, is very frequently distinct from them. This interest is the common and lasting bond which unites them together; it induces them to coalesce, and to combine their efforts in order to attain an end which does not always ensure the greatest happiness of the greatest number; and it serves not only to connect the persons in authority, but to unite them to a considerable portion of the community, since a numerous body of citizens belongs to the aristocracy, without being invested with official functions. The aristocratic magistrate is therefore constantly supported by a portion of the community, as well as by the government of which he is a member.

The common purpose which connects the interest of the magistrates in aristocracies, with that of a portion of their contemporaries, identifies it with that of future generations; their influence belongs to the future as much as to the present. The aristocratic magistrate is urged at the same time toward the same point, by the passions of the community, by his own, and I may almost add, by those of his posterity. Is it, then, wonderful that he does not resist such repeated impulses? And, indeed, aristocracies are often carried away by the spirit of their order without being corrupted by it; and they unconsciously fashion society to their own ends, and prepare it for their own descendants.

The English aristocracy is perhaps the most liberal which ever existed, and no body of men has ever, uninterruptedly, furnished so many honorable and enlightened individuals to the government of a country. It cannot, however, escape observation, that in the legislation of England the good of the poor has been sacrificed to the advantage of the rich, and the rights of the majority to the privileges of the few. The consequence is, that England, at the present day, combines the extremes of fortune in the bosom of her society; and her perils and calamities are almost equal to her power and her renown.

In the United States, where the public officers have no interests to promote connected with their caste, the general and constant influence of the government is beneficial, although the individuals who conduct it are frequently unskilful and sometimes contemptible. There is, indeed, a secret tendency in democratic institutions to render the exertions of the citizens subservient to the prosperity of the community, notwithstanding their private vices and mistakes; while in aristocratic institutions there is a secret propensity, which, not withstanding the talents and the virtue of those who conduct the government, leads them to contribute to the evils which oppress their fellow-creatures. In aristocratic governments public men may frequently do injuries which they do not intend; and in democratic states they produce advantages which they never thought of.

Chapter II

That The Notions Of Democratic Nations On Government Are Naturally Favourable To The Concentration Of Power.

The notion of secondary powers, placed between the sovereign and his subjects, occurred naturally to the imagination of aristocratic nations, because those communities contained individuals or families raised above the common level, and apparently destined to command by their birth, their education, and their wealth. This same notion is naturally wanting in the minds of men in democratic ages, for converse reasons; it can only be introduced artificially, it can only be kept there with difficulty; whereas they conceive, as it were, without thinking upon the subject, the notion of a sole and central power which governs the whole community by its direct influence. Moreover in politics, as well as in philosophy and in religion, the intellect of democratic nations is peculiarly open to simple and general notions. Complicated systems are repugnant to it, and its favourite conception is that of a great nation composed of citizens all resembling the same pattern, and all governed by a single power.

The very next notion to that of a sole and central power, which presents itself to the minds of men in the ages of equality, is the notion of uniformity of legislation. As every man sees that he differs but little from those about him, he cannot understand why a rule which is applicable to one man should not be equally applicable to all others. Hence the slightest privileges are repugnant to his reason; the faintest dissimilarities in the political institutions of the same people offend him, and uniformity of legislation appears to him to be the first condition of good government.

I find, on the contrary, that this same notion of a uniform rule, equally binding on all the members of the community, was almost unknown to the human mind in aristocratic ages; it was either never entertained, or it was rejected.

These contrary tendencies of opinion ultimately turn on either side to such blind instincts and such ungovernable habits, that they still direct the actions of men, in spite of particular exceptions. Notwithstanding the immense variety of conditions in the middle ages, a certain number of persons existed at that period in precisely similar circumstances; but this did not prevent the laws then in force from assigning to each of them distinct duties and different rights. On the contrary, at the present time all the powers of government are exerted to impose the same customs and the same laws on populations which have as yet but few points of resemblance.

As the conditions of men become equal among a people, individuals seem of less importance, and society of greater dimensions; or rather, every citizen, being assimilated to all the rest, is lost in the crowd, and nothing stands conspicuous but the great and imposing image of the people at large. This naturally gives the men of democratic periods a lofty opinion of the privileges of society, and a very humble notion of the rights of individuals; they are ready to admit that the interests of the former are everything, and those of the latter nothing. They are willing to acknowledge that the power which represents the community has far more information and wisdom than any of the members of that community; and that it is the duty, as well as the right, of that power to guide as well as govern each private citizen.

If we closely scrutinize our contemporaries, and penetrate to the root of their political opinions, we shall detect some of the notions which I have just pointed out, and we shall perhaps be surprised to find so much accordance between men who are so often at variance.

The Americans hold, that in every state the supreme power ought to emanate from the people; but when once that power is constituted, they can conceive, as it were, no limits to it, and they are ready to admit that it has the right to do whatever it pleases. They have not the slightest notion of peculiar privileges granted to cities, families, or persons; their minds appear never to have foreseen that it might be possible not to apply with strict uniformity the same laws to every part, and to all the inhabitants.

These same opinions are more and more diffused in Europe; they even insinuate themselves among those nations which most vehemently reject the principle of the sovereignty of the people. Such nations assign a different origin to the supreme power, but they ascribe to that power the same characteristics. Among them all, the idea of intermediate powers is weakened and obliterated: the idea of rights inherent in certain individuals is rapidly disappearing from the minds of men; the idea of the omnipotence and sole authority of society at large rises to fill its place. These ideas take root and spread in proportion as social conditions become more equal, and men more alike; they are engendered by equality, and in turn they hasten the progress of equality.

In France, where the revolution of which I am speaking has gone further than in any other European country, these opinions have got complete hold of the public mind. If we listen attentively to the language of the various parties in France, we shall find that there is not one which has not adopted them. Most of these parties censure the conduct of the government, but they all hold that the government ought perpetually to act and interfere in everything that is done. Even those which are most at variance are nevertheless agreed upon this head. The unity, the ubiquity, the omnipotence of the supreme power, and the uniformity of its rules, constitute the principal characteristics of all the political systems which have been put forward in our age. They recur even in the wildest visions of political regeneration: the human mind pursues them in its dreams.

If these notions spontaneously arise in the minds of private individuals, they suggest themselves still more forcibly to the minds of princes. While the ancient fabric of European society is altered and dissolved, sovereigns acquire new conceptions of their opportunities and their duties; they learn for the first time that the central power which they represent may and ought to administer by its own agency, and on a uniform plan, all the concerns of the whole community. This opinion, which, I will venture to say, was never conceived before our time by the monarchs of Europe, now sinks deeply into the minds of kings, and abides there amid all the agitation of more unsettled thoughts.

Our contemporaries are therefore much less divided than is commonly supposed; they are constantly disputing as to the hands in which supremacy is to be vested, but they readily agree upon the duties and the rights of that supremacy. The notion they all form of government is that of a sole, simple, providential and creative power.

All secondary opinions in politics are unsettled; this one remains fixed, invariable, and consistent. It is adopted by statesmen and political philosophers; it is eagerly laid hold of by the multitude; those who govern and those who are governed agree to pursue it with equal ardour; it is the foremost notion of their minds, it seems conatural with their feelings. It originates therefore in no caprice of the human intellect, but it is a necessary condition of the present state of mankind.

Chapter III.

That The Sentiments Of Democratic Nations Accord With Then Opinions In Leading Them To Concentrate Political Power.

If it be true that, in ages of equality, men readily adopt the notion of a great central power, it cannot be doubted on the other hand that their habits and sentiments predispose them to recognise such a power and to give it their support.* This may be demonstrated in a few words, as the greater part of the reasons, to which the fact may be attributed, have been previously stated.

As the men who inhabit democratic countries have no superiors, no inferiors, and no habitual or necessary partners in their undertakings, they readily fall back upon themselves and consider themselves as beings apart. I had occasion to point this out at considerable length in treating of individualism.

---

* Men connect the greatness of their idea of unity with means, God with ends; hence this idea of greatness, as men conceive it, leads us into infinite littlenesses. To compel all men to follow the same course toward the same object is a human notion;—to introduce infinite variety of action, but so combined that all these acts lead by a multitude of different courses to the accomplishment of one great design, is a conception of the Deity.

The human idea of unity is almost always barren; the divine idea pregnant with abundant results. Men think they manifest their greatness by simplifying the means they use; but it is the purpose of God which is simple—his means are infinitely varied.

Hence such men can never, without an effort, tear themselves from their private affairs to engage in public business; their natural bias leads them to abandon the latter to the sole visible and permanent representative of the interests of the community, that is to say, to the State. Not only are they naturally wanting in a taste for public business, but they have frequently no time to attend to it. Private life is so busy in democratic periods, so excited, so full of wishes and of work, that hardly any energy or leisure remains to each individual for public life. I am the last man to contend that these propensities are unconquerable, since my chief object in writing this book has been to combat them. I only maintain that at the present day a secret power is fostering them in the human heart, and that if they are not checked they will wholly overgrow it.

I have also had occasion to show how the increasing love of well-being, and the fluctuating character of property, cause democratic nations to dread all violent disturbance. The love of public tranquillity is frequently the only passion which these nations retain, and it becomes more active and powerful among them in proportion as all other passions droop and die. This naturally disposes the members of the community constantly to give or to surrender additional rights to the central power, which alone seems to be interested in defending them by the same means that it uses to defend itself.

As in ages of equality no man is compelled to lend his assistance to his fellow-men, and none has any right to expect much support from them, every one is at once independent and powerless. These two conditions, which must never be either separately considered or confounded together, inspire the citizen of a democratic country with very contrary propensities. His independence fills him with self-reliance and pride among his equals; his debility makes him feel from time to time the want of some outward assistance, which he cannot expect from any of them, because they are all impotent and unsympathizing. In this predicament he naturally turns his eyes to that imposing power which alone rises above the level of universal depression. Of that power his wants and especially his desires continually remind him, until he ultimately views it as the sole and necessary support of his own weakness.*

This may more completely explain what frequently takes place in democratic countries, where the very men who are so impatient of superiors patiently submit to a master, exhibiting at once their pride and their servility.

The hatred which men bear to privilege increases in proportion as privileges become more scarce and less considerable, so that democratic passions would seem to burn most fiercely at the very time

---

* In democratic communities nothing but the central power has any stability in its position or any permanence in its undertakings. All the members of society are in ceaseless stir and transformation. Now it is in the nature of all governments to seek constantly to enlarge their sphere of action: hence it is almost impossible that such a government should not ultimately succeed, because it acts with a fixed principle and a constant will, upon men, whose position, whose notions, and whose desires are in continual vacillation.

It frequently happens that the members of the community promote the influence of the central power without intending it. Democratic age are periods of experiment, innovation, and adventure. At such times there are always a multitude of men engaged in difficult or novel undertakings, which they follow alone, without caring for their fellow-men. Such persons may be ready to admit, as a general principle, that the public authority ought not to interfere in private concerns; but, by an exception to that rule, each of them craves for its assistance in the particular concern on which he is engaged, and seeks to draw upon the influence of the government for his own benefit, though he would restrict it on all other occasions. If a large number of men apply this particular exception to a great variety of different purposes, the sphere of the central power extends insensibly in all directions, although each of them wishes it to be circumscribed.

Thus a democratic government increases its power simply by the fact of its permanence. Time is on its side; every incident befriends it; the passions of individuals unconsciously promote it; and it may be asserted, that the older a democratic community is, the more centralized will its government become.

when they have least fuel. I have already given the reason of this phenomenon. When all conditions are unequal, no inequality is so great as to offend the eye; whereas the slightest dissimilarity is odious in the midst of general uniformity: the more complete is this uniformity, the more insupportable does the sight of such a difference become. Hence it is natural that the love of equality should constantly increase together with equality itself, and that it should grow by what it feeds upon.

This never-dying, ever-kindling hatred, which sets a democratic people against the smallest privileges, is peculiarly favourable to the gradual concentration of all political rights in the hands of the representative of the state alone. The sovereign, being necessarily and incontestably above all the citizens, excites not their envy, and each of them thinks that he strips his equals of the prerogative which he concedes to the crown.

The man of a democratic age is extremely reluctant to obey his neighbour who is his equal; he refuses to acknowledge in such a person ability superior to his own; he mistrusts his justice, and is jealous of his power; he fears and he contemns him; and he loves continually to remind him of the common dependance in which both of them stand to the same master.

Every central power which follows its natural tendencies courts and encourages the principle of equality; for equality singularly facilitates, extends, and secures the influence of a central power.

In like manner it may be said that every central government worships uniformity: uniformity relieves it from inquiry into an infinite number of small details which must be attended to if rules were to be adapted to men, instead of indiscriminately subjecting men to rules: thus the government likes what the citizens like, and naturally hates what they hate. These common sentiments, which, in democratic nations, constantly unite the sovereign and every member of the community in one and the same conviction, establish a secret and lasting sympathy between them. The faults of the government are pardoned for the sake of its tastes; public confidence is only reluctantly withdrawn in the midst even of its excesses and its errors, and it is restored at the first call. Democratic nations often hate those in whose hands the central power is vested; but they always love that power itself.

Thus, by two separate paths, I have reached the same conclusion. I have shown that the principle of equality suggests to men the notion of a sole, uniform, and strong government: I have now shown that the principle of equality imparts to them a taste for it. To governments of this kind the nations of our age are therefore tending. They are drawn thither by the natural inclination of mind and heart; and in order to reach that result, it is enough that they do not check themselves in their course.

I am of opinion, that, in the democratic ages which are opening upon us, individual independence and local liberties will ever be the produce of artificial contrivance; that centralization will be the natural form of government.*

---

* A democratic people is not only led by its own tastes to centralize its government, but the passions of all the men by whom it is governed constantly urge it in the same direction. It may easily be foreseen that almost all the able and ambitious members of a democratic community will labour without ceasing to extend the powers of government, because they all hope at some time or other to wield those powers. It is a waste of time to attempt to prove to them that extreme centralization may be injurious to the State, since they are centralizing for their own benefit. Among the public men of democracies there are hardly any but men of great disinterestedness or extreme mediocrity who seek to oppose the centralization of government: the former are scarce, the latter powerless.

THE LAW[1]

FRÉDÉRIC BASTIAT

The law perverted! The law—and, in its wake, all the collective forces of the nation—the law, I say, not only diverted from its proper direction, but made to pursue one entirely contrary! The law become the tool of every kind of avarice, instead of being its check! The law guilty of that very iniquity which it was its mission to punish! Truly, this is a serious fact, if it exists, and one to which I feel bound to call the attention of my fellow citizens.

We hold from God the gift that, as far as we are concerned, contains all others, Life—physical, intellectual, and moral life.

But life cannot support itself. He who has bestowed it, has entrusted us with the care of supporting it, of developing it, and of perfecting it. To that end, He has provided us with a collection of wonderful faculties; He has plunged us into the midst of a variety of elements. It is by the application of our faculties to these elements that the phenomena of assimilation and of appropriation, by which life pursues the circle that has been assigned to it are realized.

Existence, faculties, assimilation—in other words, personality, liberty, property—this is man.

It is of these three things that it may be said, apart from all demagogic subtlety, that they are anterior and superior to all human legislation.

It is not because men have made laws, that personality, liberty, and property exist. On the contrary, it is because personality, liberty, and property exist beforehand, that men make laws. What, then, is law? As I have said elsewhere, it is the collective organization of the individual right to lawful defense.

Nature, or rather God, has bestowed upon every one of us the right to defend his person, his liberty, and his property, since these are the three constituent or preserving elements of life; elements, each of which is rendered complete by the others, and that cannot be understood without them. For what are our faculties, but the extension of our personality? and what is property, but an extension of our faculties?

If every man has the right of defending, even by force, his person, his liberty, and his property, a number of men have the right to combine together to extend, to organize a common force to provide regularly for this defense.

Collective right, then, has its principle, its reason for existing, its lawfulness, in individual right; and the common force cannot rationally have any other end, or any other mission, than that of the isolated forces for which it is substituted. Thus, as the force of an individual cannot lawfully touch the person, the liberty, or the property of another individual—for the same reason, the common force cannot lawfully be used to destroy the person, the liberty, or the property of individuals or of classes.

For this perversion of force would be, in one case as in the other, in contradiction to our premises. For who will dare to say that force has been given to us, not to defend our rights, but to annihilate the equal rights of our brethren? And if this be not true of every individual force, acting independently, how can it be true of the collective force, which is only the organized union of isolated forces?

Nothing, therefore, can be more evident than this: The law is the organization of the natural right of lawful defense; it is the substitution of collective for individual forces, for the purpose of acting in the sphere in which they have a right to act, of doing what they have a right to do, to secure persons, liberties, and properties, and to maintain each in its right, so as to cause justice to reign over all.

---

[1] First published in 1850.

And if a people established upon this basis were to exist, it seems to me that order would prevail among them in their acts as well as in their ideas. It seems to me that such a people would have the most simple, the most economical, the least oppressive, the least to be felt, the most restrained, the most just, and, consequently, the most stable Government that could be imagined, whatever its political form might be.

For under such an administration, everyone would feel that he possessed all the fullness, as well as all the responsibility of his existence. So long as personal safety was ensured, so long as labor was free, and the fruits of labor secured against all unjust attacks, no one would have any difficulties to contend with in the State. When prosperous, we should not, it is true, have to thank the State for our success; but when unfortunate, we should no more think of taxing it with our disasters than our peasants think of attributing to it the arrival of hail or of frost. We should know it only by the inestimable blessing of Safety.

It may further be affirmed, that, thanks to the non-intervention of the State in private affairs, our wants and their satisfactions would develop themselves in their natural order. We should not see poor families seeking for literary instruction before they were supplied with bread. We should not see towns peopled at the expense of rural districts, nor rural districts at the expense of towns. We should not see those great displacements of capital, of labor, and of population, that legislative measures occasion; displacements that render so uncertain and precarious the very sources of existence, and thus enlarge to such an extent the responsibility of Governments.

Unhappily, law is by no means confined to its own sphere. Nor is it merely in some ambiguous and debatable views that it has left its proper sphere. It has done more than this. It has acted in direct opposition to its proper end; it has destroyed its own object; it has been employed in annihilating that justice which it ought to have established, in effacing amongst Rights, that limit which it was its true mission to respect; it has placed the collective force in the service of those who wish to traffic, without risk and without scruple, in the persons, the liberty, and the property of others; it has converted plunder into a right, that it may protect it, and lawful defense into a crime, that it may punish it.

How has this perversion of law been accomplished? And what has resulted from it?

The law has been perverted through the influence of two very different causes—naked greed and misconceived philanthropy.

Let us speak of the former. Self-preservation and development is the common aspiration of all men, in such a way that if every one enjoyed the free exercise of his faculties and the free disposition of their fruits, social progress would be incessant, uninterrupted, inevitable.

But there is also another disposition which is common to them. This is to live and to develop, when they can, at the expense of one another. This is no rash imputation, emanating from a gloomy, uncharitable spirit. History bears witness to the truth of it, by the incessant wars, the migrations of races, sectarian oppressions, the universality of slavery, the frauds in trade, and the monopolies with which its annals abound. This fatal disposition has its origin in the very constitution of man—in that primitive, and universal, and invincible sentiment that urges it towards its well-being, and makes it seek to escape pain.

Man can only derive life and enjoyment from a perpetual search and appropriation; that is, from a perpetual application of his faculties to objects, or from labor. This is the origin of property.

But also he may live and enjoy, by seizing and appropriating the productions of the faculties of his fellow men. This is the origin of plunder.

Now, labor being in itself a pain, and man being naturally inclined to avoid pain, it follows, and history proves it, that wherever plunder is less burdensome than labor, it prevails; and neither religion nor morality can, in this case, prevent it from prevailing.

When does plunder cease, then? When it becomes more burdensome and more dangerous than labor. It is very evident that the proper aim of law is to oppose the fatal tendency to plunder with the powerful obstacle of collective force; that all its measures should be in favor of property, and against plunder.

But the law is made, generally, by one man, or by one class of men. And as law cannot exist without the sanction and the support of a preponderant force, it must finally place this force in the hands of those who legislate.

This inevitable phenomenon, combined with the fatal tendency that, we have said, exists in the heart of man, explains the almost universal perversion of law. It is easy to conceive that, instead of being a check upon injustice, it becomes its most invincible instrument.

It is easy to conceive that, according to the power of the legislator, it destroys for its own profit, and in different degrees amongst the rest of the community, personal independence by slavery, liberty by oppression, and property by plunder.

It is in the nature of men to rise against the injustice of which they are the victims. When, therefore, plunder is organized by law, for the profit of those who perpetrate it, all the plundered classes tend, either by peaceful or revolutionary means, to enter in some way into the manufacturing of laws. These classes, according to the degree of enlightenment at which they have arrived, may propose to themselves two very different ends, when they thus attempt the attainment of their political rights; either they may wish to put an end to lawful plunder, or they may desire to take part in it.

Woe to the nation where this latter thought prevails amongst the masses, at the moment when they, in their turn, seize upon the legislative power!

Up to that time, lawful plunder has been exercised by the few upon the many, as is the case in countries where the right of legislating is confined to a few hands. But now it has become universal, and the equilibrium is sought in universal plunder. The injustice that society contains, instead of being rooted out of it, is generalized. As soon as the injured classes have recovered their political rights, their first thought is not to abolish plunder (this would suppose them to possess enlightenment, which they cannot have), but to organize against the other classes, and to their own detriment, a system of reprisals—as if it was necessary, before the reign of justice arrives, that all should undergo a cruel retribution—some for their iniquity and some for their ignorance.

It would be impossible, therefore, to introduce into society a greater change and a greater evil than this—the conversion of the law into an instrument of plunder.

What would be the consequences of such a perversion? It would require volumes to describe them all. We must content ourselves with pointing out the most striking.

In the first place, it would efface from everybody's conscience the distinction between justice and injustice. No society can exist unless the laws are respected to a certain degree, but the safest way to make them respected is to make them respectable. When law and morality are in contradiction to each other, the citizen finds himself in the cruel alternative of either losing his moral sense, or of losing his respect for the law—two evils of equal magnitude, between which it would be difficult to choose.

It is so much in the nature of law to support justice that in the minds of the masses they are one and the same. There is in all of us a strong disposition to regard what is lawful as legitimate, so much so that many falsely derive all justice from law. It is sufficient, then, for the law to order and sanction plunder, that it may appear to many consciences just and sacred. Slavery, protection, and monopoly find defenders, not only in those who profit by them, but in those who suffer by them. If you suggest a doubt as to the morality of these institutions, it is said directly—"You are a dangerous experimenter, a utopian, a theorist, a despiser of the laws; you would shake the basis upon which society rests."

If you lecture upon morality, or political economy, official bodies will be found to make this request to the Government:

> That henceforth science be taught not only with sole reference to free exchange (to liberty, property, and justice), as has been the case up to the present time, but also, and

especially, with reference to the facts and legislation (contrary to liberty, property, and justice) that regulate French industry.

That, in public lecterns salaried by the treasury, the professor abstain rigorously from endangering in the slightest degree the respect due to the laws now in force.[2]

So that if a law exists that sanctions slavery or monopoly, oppression or plunder, in any form whatever, it must not even be mentioned—for how can it be mentioned without damaging the respect that it inspires? Still further, morality and political economy must be taught in connection with this law—that is, under the supposition that it must be just, only because it is law.

Another effect of this deplorable perversion of the law is that it gives to human passions and to political struggles, and, in general, to politics, properly so called, an exaggerated importance.

I could prove this assertion in a thousand ways. But I shall confine myself, by way of an illustration, to bringing it to bear upon a subject which has of late occupied everybody's mind: universal suffrage.

Whatever may be thought of it by the adepts of the school of Rousseau, which professes to be very far advanced, but which I consider 20 centuries behind, universal suffrage (taking the word in its strictest sense) is not one of those sacred dogmas with respect to which examination and doubt are crimes.

Serious objections may be made to it.

In the first place, the word universal conceals a gross sophism. There are, in France, 36,000,000 inhabitants. To make the right of suffrage universal, 36,000,000 electors should be reckoned. The most extended system reckons only 9,000,000. Three persons out of four, then, are excluded; and more than this, they are excluded by the fourth. Upon what principle is this exclusion founded? Upon the principle of incapacity. Universal suffrage, then, means: universal suffrage of those who are capable. In point of fact, who are the capable? Are age, sex, and judicial condemnations the only conditions to which incapacity is to be attached?

On taking a nearer view of the subject, we may soon perceive the reason why the right of suffrage depends upon the presumption of incapacity; the most extended system differing from the most restricted in the conditions on which this incapacity depends, and which constitutes not a difference in principle, but in degree.

This motive is, that the elector does not stipulate for himself, but for everybody.

If, as the republicans of the Greek and Roman tone pretend, the right of suffrage had fallen to the lot of every one at his birth, it would be an injustice to adults to prevent women and children from voting. Why are they prevented? Because they are presumed to be incapable. And why is incapacity a reason for exclusion? Because the elector does not reap alone the responsibility of his vote; because every vote engages and affects the community at large; because the community has a right to demand some assurances, as regards the acts upon which its well-being and its existence depend.

I know what might be said in answer to this. I know what might be objected. But this is not the place to settle a controversy of this kind. What I wish to observe is this, that this same controversy (in common with the greater part of political questions) that agitates, excites, and unsettles the nations, would lose almost all its importance if the law had always been what it ought to be.

In fact, if law were confined to causing all persons, all liberties, and all properties to be respected—if it were merely the organization of individual right and individual defense—if it were the obstacle, the check, the chastisement opposed to all oppression, to all plunder—is it likely that we should dispute much, as citizens, on the subject of the greater or lesser universality of suffrage? Is it likely that it would compromise that greatest of advantages, the public peace? Is it likely that the excluded classes would

[2] General Council of Manufactures, Agriculture, and Commerce, 6th of May, 1850.

not quietly wait for their turn? Is it likely that the enfranchised classes would be very jealous of their privilege? And is it not clear, that the interest of all being one and the same, some would act without much inconvenience to the others?

But if the fatal principle should come to be introduced, that, under pretense of organization, regulation, protection, or encouragement, the law may take from one party in order to give to another, help itself to the wealth acquired by all the classes that it may increase that of one class, whether that of the agriculturists, the manufacturers, the ship owners, or artists and comedians; then certainly, in this case, there is no class which may not try, and with reason, to place its hand upon the law, that would not demand with fury its right of election and eligibility, and that would overturn society rather than not obtain it. Even beggars and vagabonds will prove to you that they have an incontestable title to it. They will say:

> We never buy wine, tobacco, or salt, without paying the tax, and a part of this tax is given by law in perquisites and gratuities to men who are richer than we are. Others make use of the law to create an artificial rise in the price of bread, meat, iron, or cloth.
>
> Since everybody traffics in law for his own profit, we should like to do the same. We should like to make it produce the right to assistance, which is the poor man's plunder. To effect this, we ought to be electors and legislators, that we may organize, on a large scale, alms for our own class, as you have organized, on a large scale, protection for yours. Don't tell us that you will take our cause upon yourselves, and throw to us 600,000 francs to keep us quiet, like giving us a bone to pick. We have other claims, and, at any rate, we wish to stipulate for ourselves, as other classes have stipulated for themselves!

How is this argument to be answered? Yes, as long as it is admitted that the law may be diverted from its true mission, that it may violate property instead of securing it, everybody will be wanting to manufacture law, either to defend himself against plunder, or to organize it for his own profit. The political question will always be prejudicial, predominant, and absorbing; in a word, there will be fighting around the door of the Legislative Palace. The struggle will be no less furious within it. To be convinced of this, it is hardly necessary to look at what passes in the Chambers in France and in England; it is enough to know how the question stands.

With this understanding, let us examine the value, the origin, and the tendency of this popular aspiration, which pretends to realize the general good by general plunder.

The Socialists say, since the law organizes justice, why should it not organize labor, instruction, and religion?

Why? Because it could not organize labor, instruction, and religion, without disorganizing justice.

For remember, that law is force, and that consequently the domain of the law cannot properly extend beyond the domain of force.

When law and force keep a man within the bounds of justice, they impose nothing upon him but a mere negation. They only oblige him to abstain from doing harm. They violate neither his personality, his liberty, nor his property. They only guard the personality, the liberty, the property of others. They hold themselves on the defensive; they defend the equal right of all. They fulfill a mission whose harmlessness is evident, whose utility is palpable, and whose legitimacy is not to be disputed. This is so true that, as a friend of mine once remarked to me, to say that the aim of the law is to cause justice to reign, is to use an expression that is not rigorously exact. It ought to be said, the aim of the law is to prevent injustice from reigning. In fact, it is not justice that has an existence of its own, it is injustice. The one results from the absence of the other.

But when the law, through the medium of its necessary agent—force—imposes a form of labor, a method or a subject of instruction, a creed, or a worship, it is no longer negative; it acts positively upon men. It substitutes the will of the legislator for their own will, the initiative of the legislator for their own initiative. They have no need to consult, to compare, or to foresee; the law does all that for them. The intellect is for them a useless encumbrance; they cease to be men; they lose their personality, their liberty, their property.

Try to imagine a form of labor imposed by force, that is not a violation of liberty; a transmission of wealth imposed by force, that is not a violation of property. If you cannot succeed in reconciling this, you are bound to conclude that the law cannot organize labor and industry without organizing injustice.

When, from the seclusion of his office, a politician takes a view of society, he is struck with the spectacle of inequality that presents itself. He mourns over the sufferings that are the lot of so many of our brethren, sufferings whose aspect is rendered yet more sorrowful by the contrast of luxury and wealth.

He ought, perhaps, to ask himself whether such a social state has not been caused by the plunder of ancient times, exercised in the way of conquests; and by plunder of more recent times, effected through the medium of the laws? He ought to ask himself whether, granting the aspiration of all men to well-being and improvement, the reign of justice would not suffice to realize the greatest activity of progress, and the greatest amount of equality compatible with that individual responsibility that God has awarded as a just retribution of virtue and vice?

He never gives this a thought. His mind turns towards combinations, arrangements, legal or factitious organizations. He seeks the remedy in perpetuating and exaggerating what has produced the evil.

For, justice apart, which we have seen is only a negation, is there any one of these legal arrangements that does not contain the principle of plunder?

You say, "There are men who have no money," and you apply to the law. But the law is not a self-supplied fountain, whence every stream may obtain supplies independently of society. Nothing can enter the public treasury, in favor of one citizen or one class, but what other citizens and other classes have been forced to send to it. If everyone draws from it only the equivalent of what he has contributed to it, your law, it is true, is no plunderer, but it does nothing for men who want money—it does not promote equality. It can only be an instrument of equalization as far as it takes from one party to give to another, and then it is an instrument of plunder. Examine, in this light, the protection of tariffs, subsidies, right to profit, right to labor, right to assistance, free public education, progressive taxation, gratuitousness of credit, social workshops, and you will always find at the bottom legal plunder, organized injustice.

You say, "There are men who want knowledge," and you apply to the law. But the law is not a torch that sheds light that originates within itself. It extends over a society where there are men who have knowledge, and others who have not; citizens who want to learn, and others who are disposed to teach. It can only do one of two things: either allow a free operation to this kind of transaction, i.e., let this kind of want satisfy itself freely; or else preempt the will of the people in the matter, and take from some of them sufficient to pay professors commissioned to instruct others for free. But, in this second case there cannot fail to be a violation of liberty and property—legal plunder.

You say, "Here are men who are wanting in morality or religion," and you apply to the law; but law is force, and need I say how far it is a violent and absurd enterprise to introduce force in these matters?

As the result of its systems and of its efforts, it would seem that socialism, notwithstanding all its self-complacency, can scarcely help perceiving the monster of legal plunder. But what does it do? It disguises it cleverly from others, and even from itself, under the seductive names of fraternity, solidarity, organization, association. And because we do not ask so much at the hands of the law, because we only ask it for justice, it alleges that we reject fraternity, solidarity, organization, and association; and they brand us with the name of individualists.

We can assure them that what we repudiate is not natural organization, but forced organization.

It is not free association, but the forms of association that they would impose upon us.

It is not spontaneous fraternity, but legal fraternity.

It is not providential solidarity, but artificial solidarity, which is only an unjust displacement of responsibility.

Socialism, like the old policy from which it emanates, confounds Government and society. And so, every time we object to a thing being done by Government, it concludes that we object to its being done at all. We disapprove of education by the State—then we are against education altogether. We object to a State religion—then we would have no religion at all. We object to an equality which is brought about by the State then we are against equality, etc., etc. They might as well accuse us of wishing men not to eat, because we object to the cultivation of corn by the State.

How is it that the strange idea of making the law produce what it does not contain—prosperity, in a positive sense, wealth, science, religion—should ever have gained ground in the political world? The modern politicians, particularly those of the Socialist school, found their different theories upon one common hypothesis; and surely a more strange, a more presumptuous notion, could never have entered a human brain.

They divide mankind into two parts. Men in general, except one, form the first; the politician himself forms the second, which is by far the most important.

In fact, they begin by supposing that men are devoid of any principle of action, and of any means of discernment in themselves; that they have no initiative; that they are inert matter, passive particles, atoms without impulse; at best a vegetation indifferent to its own mode of existence, susceptible of assuming, from an exterior will and hand an infinite number of forms, more or less symmetrical, artistic, and perfected.

Moreover, every one of these politicians does not hesitate to assume that he himself is, under the names of organizer, discoverer, legislator, institutor or founder, this will and hand, this universal initiative, this creative power, whose sublime mission it is to gather together these scattered materials, that is, men, into society.

Starting from these data, as a gardener according to his caprice shapes his trees into pyramids, parasols, cubes, cones, vases, espaliers, distaffs, or fans; so the Socialist, following his chimera, shapes poor humanity into groups, series, circles, subcircles, honeycombs, or social workshops, with all kinds of variations. And as the gardener, to bring his trees into shape, needs hatchets, pruning hooks, saws, and shears, so the politician, to bring society into shape, needs the forces which he can only find in the laws; the law of tariffs, the law of taxation, the law of assistance, and the law of education.

It is so true, that the Socialists look upon mankind as a subject for social experiments, that if, by chance, they are not quite certain of the success of these experiments, they will request a portion of mankind, as a subject to experiment upon. It is well known how popular the idea of trying all systems is, and one of their chiefs has been known seriously to demand of the Constituent Assembly a parish, with all its inhabitants, upon which to make his experiments.

It is thus that an inventor will make a small machine before he makes one of the regular size. Thus the chemist sacrifices some substances, the agriculturist some seed and a corner of his field, to make trial of an idea.

But think of the difference between the gardener and his trees, between the inventor and his machine, between the chemist and his substances, between the agriculturist and his seed! The Socialist thinks, in all sincerity, that there is the same difference between himself and mankind.

No wonder the politicians of the nineteenth century look upon society as an artificial production of the legislator's genius. This idea, the result of a classical education, has taken possession of all the thinkers and great writers of our country.

To all these persons, the relations between mankind and the legislator appear to be the same as those that exist between the clay and the potter.

Moreover, if they have consented to recognize in the heart of man a capability of action, and in his intellect a faculty of discernment, they have looked upon this gift of God as a fatal one, and thought that mankind, under these two impulses, tended fatally towards ruin. They have taken it for granted that if abandoned to their own inclinations, men would only occupy themselves with religion to arrive at atheism, with instruction to come to ignorance, and with labor and exchange to be extinguished in misery.

I shall now resume the subject by remarking, that immediately after the economical part[4] of the question, and before the political part, a leading question presents itself. It is the following:

What is law? What ought it to be? What is its domain? What are its limits? Where, in fact, does the prerogative of the legislator stop?

I have no hesitation in answering, Law is common force organized to prevent injustice;—in short, Law is Justice.

It is not true that the legislator has absolute power over our persons and property, since they pre-exist, and his work is only to secure them from injury.

It is not true that the mission of the law is to regulate our consciences, our ideas, our will, our education, our sentiments, our works, our exchanges, our gifts, our enjoyments. Its mission is to prevent the rights of one from interfering with those of another, in any one of these things.

Law, because it has force for its necessary sanction, can only have the domain of force, which is justice.

I cannot avoid coming to this conclusion—that there are too many great men in the world; there are too many legislators, organizers, institutors of society, conductors of the people, fathers of nations, etc., etc. Too many persons place themselves above mankind, to rule and patronize it; too many persons make a trade of looking after it. It will be answered—"You yourself are occupied upon it all this time." Very true. But it must be admitted that it is in another sense entirely that I am speaking; and if I join the reformers it is solely for the purpose of inducing them to relax their hold.

I am not doing as Vaucauson did with his automaton, but as a physiologist does with the human frame; I would study and admire it.

I am acting with regard to it in the spirit that animated a celebrated traveler. He found himself in the midst of a savage tribe. A child had just been born, and a crowd of soothsayers, magicians, and quacks were around it, armed with rings, hooks, and bandages. One said—"This child will never smell the perfume of a calumet, unless I stretch his nostrils." Another said—"He will be without the sense of hearing, unless I draw his ears down to his shoulders." A third said—"He will never see the light of the sun, unless I give his eyes an oblique direction." A fourth said—"He will never be upright, unless I bend his legs." A fifth said—"He will not be able to think, unless I press his brain." "Stop!" said the traveler. "Whatever God does, is well done; do not pretend to know more than He; and as He has given organs to this frail creature, allow those organs to develop themselves, to strengthen themselves by exercise, use, experience, and liberty."

God has implanted in mankind also all that is necessary to enable it to accomplish its destinies. There is a providential social physiology, as well as a providential human physiology. The social organs are constituted so as to enable them to develop harmoniously in the grand air of liberty. Away, then, with quacks and organizers! Away with their rings, and their chains, and their hooks, and their pincers! Away with their artificial methods! Away with their social laboratories, their governmental whims, their centralization, their tariffs, their universities, their State religions, their inflationary or monopolizing banks, their limitations, their restrictions, their moralizations, and their equalization by taxation! And now, after having vainly inflicted upon the social body so many systems, let them end where they ought to have begun—reject all systems, and try liberty—liberty, which is an act of faith in God and in His work.

RADICAL EGALITARIANISM

KAI NIELSON

I

I have talked of equality as a right and of equality as a goal. And I have taken, as the principal thing, to be able to state what goal we are seeking when we say equality is a goal. When we are in a position actually to achieve that goal, then that same equality becomes a right. The goal we are seeking is an equality of basic condition for everyone. Let me say a bit what this is: everyone, as far as possible, should have equal life prospects, short of genetic engineering and the like and the rooting out of any form of the family and the undermining of our basic freedoms. There should, where this is possible, be an equality of access to equal resources over each person's life as a whole, though this should be qualified by people's varying needs. Where psychiatrists are in short supply only people who are in need of psychiatric help should have equal access to such help. This equal access to resources should be such that it stands as a barrier to there being the sort of differences between people that allow some to be in a position to control and to exploit others; such equal access to resources should also stand as a barrier to one person having power over other adult persons that does not rest on the revokable consent on the part of the persons over whom he comes to have power. Where, because of some remaining scarcity in a society of considerable productive abundance, we cannot reasonably distribute resources equally, we should first, where considerations of desert are not at issue, distribute according to stringency of need, second according to the strength of unmanipulated preferences and third, and finally, by lottery. We should, in trying to attain equality of condition, aim at a condition of autonomy (the fuller and the more rational the better) for everyone and at a condition where everyone alike, to the fullest extent possible, has his or her needs and wants satisfied. The limitations on the satisfaction of people's wants should be only where the satisfaction is incompatible with everyone getting the same treatment. Where we have conflicting wants, such as where two persons want to marry the same person, the fair thing to do will vary with the circumstances. In the marriage case, freedom of choice is obviously the fair thing. But generally, what should be aimed at is having everyone have their wants satisfied as far as possible. To achieve equality of condition would be, as well, to achieve a condition where the necessary burdens of the society are equally shared, where to do so is reasonable, and where each person has an equal voice in deciding what these burdens shall be. Moreover, everyone, as much as possible, should be in a position—and should be equally in that position—to control his own life. The goals of egalitarianism are to achieve such equalities.

Minimally, classlessness is something we should all aim at if we are egalitarians. It is necessary for the stable achievement of equalities of the type discussed in the previous paragraph. Beyond that, we should also aim at a statusless society, though not at an undifferentiated society or a society which does not recognize merit... It is only in such a classless, statusless society that the ideals of equality (the conception of equality as a very general goal to be achieved) can be realized. In aiming for a statusless society, we are aiming for a society which, while remaining a society of material abundance, is a society in which there are to be no extensive difference in life prospects between people because some have far greater income, power, authority or prestige than others. This is the *via negativa* of the egalitarian way.

The *via positiva* is to produce social conditions, where there is generally material abundance, where well-being and satisfaction are not only maximized (the utilitarian thing) but, as well, a society where this condition, as far as it is achievable, is sought equally for all (the egalitarian thing). This is the underlying conception of the egalitarian commitment to equality of condition.

II

Robert Nozick asks, "How do we decide how much equality is enough?"[1] In the preceding section we gestured in the direction of an answer. I should now like to be somewhat more explicit. Too much equality, as we have been at pains to point out, would be to treat everyone identically, completely ignoring their differing needs. Various forms of "barracks equality" approximating that would also be too much. Too little equality would be to limit equality of condition, as did the old egalitarianism, to achieving equal legal and political rights, equal civil liberties, to equality of opportunity and to a redistribution of gross disparities in wealth sufficient to keep social peace, the rationale for the latter being that such gross inequalities if allowed to stand would threaten social stability. This Hobbesist stance indicates that the old egalitarianism proceeds in a very pragmatic manner. Against the old egalitarianism I would argue that we must at least aim at an equality of whole life prospects, where that is not ready simply as the right to compete for scarce positions of advantage, but where there is to be brought into being the kind of equality of condition that would provide everyone equally, as far as possible, with the resources and the social conditions to satisfy their needs as fully as possible compatible with everyone else doing likewise. (Note that between people these needs will be partly the same but will still often be importantly different as well.) Ideally, as a kind of ideal limit for a society of wondrous abundance, a radical egalitarianism would go beyond that to a similar thing for wants. We should, that is, provide all people equally, as far as possible, with the resources and social conditions to satisfy their wants, as fully as possible compatible with everyone else doing likewise. (I recognize that there is a slide between wants and needs. As the wealth of a society increases and its structure changes, things that started out as wants tend to become needs, e.g. someone in the Falkland Islands might merely reasonably want an auto while someone in Los Angeles might not only want it but need it as well. But this does not collapse the distinction between wants and needs. There are things in any society people need, if they are to survive at all in anything like a commodious condition, whether they want them or not, e.g., they need food, shelter, security, companionship and the like. An egalitarian starts with basic needs, or at least with what are taken in the cultural environment in which a given person lives to be basic needs, and moves out to other needs and finally to wants as the productive power of the society increases.)

I qualified my above formulations with "as far as possible" and with "as fully as possible compatible with everyone else doing likewise." These are essential qualifications. Where, as in societies that we know, there are scarcities, even rather minimal scarcities, not everyone can have the resources or at least all the resources necessary to have their needs satisfied. Here we must first ensure that, again as far as possible, their basic needs are all satisfied and then we move on to other needs and finally to wants. But sometimes, to understate it, even in very affluent societies, everyone's needs cannot be met, or at least they cannot be equally met. In such circumstances we have to make some hard choices. I am thinking of a situation where there are not enough dialysis machines to go around so that everyone who needs one can have one. What then should we do? The thing to aim at, to try as far as possible to approximate, if only as a heuristic ideal, is the full and equal meeting of needs and wants of everyone. It is when we have that much equality that we have enough equality. But, of course, "ought implies can," and where we can't achieve it we can't achieve it. But where we reasonably can, we ought to do it. It is something that fairness requires.

The "reasonably can" is also an essential modification: we need situations of sufficient abundance so that we do not, in going for such an equality of condition, simply spread the misery around or spread very Spartan conditions around. Before we can rightly aim for the equality of condition I mentioned, we must first have the productive capacity and resource conditions to support the institutional means that would make possible the equal satisfaction of basic needs and the equal satisfaction of other needs and wants as well.

Such achievements will often not be possible; perhaps they will never be fully possible, for, no doubt, the physically handicapped will always be with us. Consider, for example, situations where our scarcities are such that we cannot, without causing considerable misery, create the institutions and mechanisms that would work to satisfy all needs, even all basic needs. Suppose we have the technology in place to develop all sorts of complicated life-sustaining machines all of which would predictably provide people with a quality of life that they, viewing the matter clearly, would rationally choose if they were simply choosing for themselves. But suppose, if we put such technologies in place, we will then not have the wherewithal to provide basic health care in outlying regions in the country or adequate educational services in such places. We should not, under those circumstances, put those technologies in place. But we should also recognize that where it becomes possible to put these technologies in place without sacrificing other more pressing needs, we should do so. The underlying egalitarian rationale is evident enough: produce the conditions for the most extensive satisfaction of needs for everyone. Where A's need and B's need are equally important (equally stringent) but cannot both be satisfied, satisfy A's need rather than B's if the satisfaction of A's need would be more fecund for the satisfaction of the needs of others than B's, or less undermining of the satisfaction of the needs of others than B's. (I do not mean to say that this is our only criterion of choice but it is the criterion most relevant for us here.) We should seek the satisfaction of the greatest compossible set of needs where the conditions for compossibility are (a) that everyone's needs be considered, (b) that everyone's needs be *equally* considered and where two sets of needs cannot both be satisfied, the more stringent set of needs shall first be satisfied. (Do not say we have no working criteria for what they are. If you need food to keep you from starvation or debilitating malnutrition and I need a vacation to relax after a spate of hard work, your need is plainly more stringent than mine. There would, of course, be all sorts of disputable cases, but there are also a host of perfectly determinate cases indicating that we have working criteria.) The underlying rationale is to seek compossible sets of needs so that we approach as far as possible as great a satisfaction of needs as possible for everyone.

This might, it could be said, produce a situation in which very few people got those things that they needed the most, or at least wanted the most. Remember Nozick with his need for the resources of Widener Library in an annex to his house. People, some might argue, with expensive tastes and extravagant needs, say a need for really good wine, would never, with a stress on such compossibilia, get things they are really keen about.[2] Is that the kind of world we would reflectively want? Well, *if* their not getting them is the price we have to pay for everyone having their basic needs met, then it is a price we ought to pay. I am very fond of very good wines as well as fresh ripe mangoes, but if the price of my having them is that people starve or suffer malnutrition in the Sahel, or indeed anywhere else, then plainly fairness, if not just plain human decency, requires that I forgo them.

In talking about how much equality is enough, I have so far talked of the benefits that equality is meant to provide. But egalitarians also speak of an equal sharing of the necessary burdens of the society as well. Fairness requires a sharing of the burdens and for a radical egalitarian this comes to an equal sharing of the burdens where people are equally capable of sharing them. Translated into the concrete this does *not* mean that a child or an old man or a pregnant woman are to be required to work in the mines or that they be required to collect garbage, but it would involve something like requiring every able bodied person, say from nineteen to twenty, to take his or her turn at a fair portion of the necessary unpleasant jobs in the world. In that way all, where we are able to do it, would share equally in these burdens—in doing the things that none of us want to do but that we, if we are at all reasonable, recognize the necessity of having done. (There are all kinds of variations and complications concerning this—what do we do with the youthful wonder at the violin? But, that notwithstanding, the general idea is clear enough.) And, where we think this is reasonably feasible, it squares with our considered judgments about fairness.

I have given you, in effect appealing to my considered judgments but considered judgments I do not think are at all eccentric, a picture of what I would take to be enough equality, too little equality and not enough equality. But how can we know that my proportions are right? I do not think we can avoid or should indeed try to avoid an appeal to considered judgments here. But working with them there are some arguments we can appeal to get them in wide reflective equilibrium. Suppose we go back to the formal principle of justice, namely that we must treat like cases alike. Because it does not tell us *what* are like cases, we cannot derive substantive criteria from it. But it may, indirectly, be of some help here. We all, if we are not utterly zany, want a life in which our needs are satisfied and in which we can live as we wish and do what we want to do. Though we differ in many ways, in our abilities, capacities for pleasure, determination to keep on with a job, we do not differ about wanting our needs satisfied or being able to live as we wish. Thus, *ceterus paribus*, where questions of desert, entitlement and the like do not enter, it is only fair that all of us should have our needs equally considered and that we should, again *ceterus paribus*, all be able to do as we wish in a way that is compatible with others doing likewise. From the formal principle of justice and a few key facts about us, we can get to the claim that *ceterus paribus* we should go for this much equality. But this is the core content of a radical egalitarianism.

However, how do we know that *ceterus* is *paribus* here? What about our entitlements and deserts? Suppose I have built my house with my own hands, from materials I have purchased and on land that I have purchased and that I have lived in it for years and have carefully cared for it. The house is mine and I am entitled to keep it even if by dividing the house into two apartments greater and more equal satisfaction of need would obtain for everyone. Justice requires that such an entitlement be respected here. (Again, there is an implicit *ceterus paribus* clause. In extreme situations, say after a war with housing in extremely short supply, that entitlement could be rightly overridden.)

There is a response on the egalitarian's part similar to a response utilitarianism made to criticisms of a similar logical type made of utilitarians by pluralistic deontologists. One of the things that people in fact need, or at least reflectively firmly want, is to have such entitlements respected. Where they are routinely overridden to satisfy other needs or wants, we would *not* in fact have a society in which the needs of everyone are being maximally met. To the reply, but what if more needs for everyone were met by ignoring or overriding such entitlements, the radical egalitarian should respond that that is, given the way we are, a thoroughly hypothetical situation and that theories of morality cannot be expected to give guidance for all logically possible worlds but only for worlds which are reasonably like what our actual world is or plausibly could come to be. Setting this argument aside for the moment, even if it did turn out that the need satisfaction linked with having other things—things that involved the overriding of those entitlements—was sufficient to make it the case that more need satisfaction all around for *everyone* would be achieved by overriding those entitlements, then, for reasonable people who clearly saw that, these entitlements would not have the weight presently given to them. They either would not have the importance presently attached to them or the need for the additional living space would be so great that their being overridden would seem, everything considered, the lesser of two evils (as in the example of the postwar housing situation).

There are without doubt genuine entitlements and a theory of justice must take them seriously, but they are not absolute. If the need is great enough we can see the merit in overriding them, just as in law as well as morality the right of eminent domain is recognized. Finally, while I have talked of entitlements here, parallel arguments will go through for desert.

III

I want now to relate this articulation of what equality comes to to my radically egalitarian principles of justice. My articulation of justice is a certain spelling out of the slogan proclaimed by Marx "From each according to his ability, to each according to his needs." The egalitarian conception of society argues for the desirability of bringing into existence a world, once the springs of social wealth flow freely, in which everyone's needs are as fully satisfied as possible and in which everyone gives according to his ability. Which means, among other things, that everyone, according to his ability, shares the burdens of society. There is an equal giving and equal responsibility here according to ability. It is here, with respect to giving according to ability and with respect to receiving according to need, that a complex equality of result, i.e., equality of condition, is being advocated by the radical egalitarian. What it comes to is this: each of us, where each is to count for one and none to count for more than one, is to give according to ability and receive according to need.

My radical egalitarian principles of justice read as follows:

1. Each person is to have an equal right to the most extensive total system of equal basic liberties and opportunities (including equal opportunities for meaningful work, for self-determination and political and economic participation) compatible with a similar treatment of all. (This principle gives expression to a commitment to attain and/or sustain equal moral autonomy and equal self-respect.)
2. After provisions are made for common social (community) values, for capital overhead to preserve the society's productive capacity, allowances made for differing unmanipulated needs and preferences, and due weight is given to the just entitlements of individuals, the income and wealth (the common stock of means) is to be so divided that each person will have a right to an equal share. The necessary burdens requisite to enhance human well-being are also to be equally shared, subject, of course, to limitations by differing abilities and differing situations. (Here I refer to different natural environments and the like and not to class position and the like.)

Here we are talking about equality as a right rather than about equality as a goal as has previously been the subject matter of equality in this chapter. These principles of egalitarianism spell out rights people have and duties they have under *conditions of very considerable productive abundance*. We have a right to certain basic liberties and opportunities and we have, subject to certain limitations spelled out in the second principle, a right to an equal share of the income and wealth in the world. We also have a duty, again subject to the qualifications mentioned in the principle, to do our equal share in shouldering the burdens necessary to protect us from ills and to enhance our well-being.

What is the relation between these rights and the ideal of equality of condition discussed earlier? That is a goal for which we can struggle now to bring about conditions which will some day make its achievement possible, while these rights only become rights when the goal is actually achievable. We have no such rights in slave, feudal or capitalist societies or such duties in those societies. In that important way they are not natural rights for they depend on certain social conditions and certain social structures (socialist ones) to be realizable. What we can say is that it is always desirable that socio-economic conditions come into being which would make it possible to achieve the goal of equality of condition so that these rights and duties I speak of could obtain. But that is a far cry from saying we have such rights and duties now.

It is a corollary of this, if these radical egalitarian principles of justice are correct, that capitalist societies (even capitalist welfare state societies such as Sweden) and statist societies such as the Soviet Union or the People's Republic of China cannot be just societies or at least they must be societies, structured as they are, which are defective in justice. (This is not to say that some of these societies are not juster than others. Sweden is juster than South Africa, Canada than the United States and Cuba and Nicaragua than Honduras and Guatemala.) But none of these statist or capitalist societies can satisfy these radical egalitarian principles of justice, for equal liberty, equal opportunity, equal wealth or equal sharing of burdens are not at all possible in societies having their social structure. So we do not have such rights now but we can take it as a goal that we bring such a society into being with a commitment to an equality of condition in which we would have these rights and duties. Here we require first the massive development of productive power.

The connection between equality as a goal and equality as a right spelled out in these principles of justice is this. This equality of condition appealed to in equality as a goal would, if it were actually to obtain, have to contain the rights and duties enunciated in those principles. There could be no equal life prospects between all people or anything approximating an equal satisfaction of needs if there were not in place something like the system of equal basic liberties referred to in the first principle. Furthermore, without the rough equality of wealth referred to in the second principle, there would be disparities in power and self-direction in society which would render impossible an equality of life prospects or the social conditions required for an equal satisfaction of needs. And plainly, without a roughly equal sharing of burdens, there cannot be a situation where everyone has equal life prospects or has the chance equally to satisfy his needs. The principles of radical egalitarian justice are implicated in its conception of an ideally adequate equality of condition.

IV

The principles of radical egalitarian justice I have articulated are meant to apply globally and not just to particular societies. But it is certainly fair to say that not a few would worry that such principles of radical egalitarian justice, if applied globally, would force the people in wealthier sections of the world to a kind of financial hari-kari. There are millions of desperately impoverished people. Indeed millions are starving or malnourished and things are not getting any better. People in the affluent societies cannot but worry about whether they face a bottomless pit. Many believe that meeting, even in the most minimal way, the needs of the impoverished is going to put an incredible burden on people—people of all classes—in the affluent societies. Indeed it will, if acted on non-evasively, bring about their impoverishment, and this is just too much to ask. Radical egalitarianism is forgetting Rawls' admonitions about "the strains of commitment"—the recognition that in any rational account of what is required of us, we must at least give a minimal healthy self-interest its due. We must construct our moral philosophy for human beings and not for saints. Human nature is less fixed than conservatives are wont to assume, but it is not so elastic that we can reasonably expect people to impoverish themselves to make the massive transfers between North and South—the industrialized world and the Third World— required to begin to approach a situation where even Rawls' principles would be in place on a global level, to say nothing of my radical egalitarian principles of justice.[3]

The first thing to say in response to this is that my radical egalitarian principles are meant actually to guide practice, to directly determine what we are to do, only in a world of extensive abundance where, as Marx put it, the springs of social wealth flow freely. If such a world cannot be attained with the underminings of capitalism and the full putting into place, stabilizing, and developing of socialist relations of production, then such radical egalitarian principles can only remain as heuristic ideals against which to measure the distance of our travel in the direction of what would be a perfectly just society.

Aside from a small capitalist class, along with those elites most directly and profitably beholden to it (together a group constituting not more than 5 percent of the world's population), there would, in taking my radical egalitarian principles as heuristic guides, be no impoverishment of people in the affluent societies, if we moved in a radically more egalitarian way to start to achieve a global fairness.

There would be massive transfers of wealth between North and South, but this could be done in stages so that, for the people in the affluent societies (capitalist elites apart), there need be no undermining of the quality of their lives. Even what were once capitalist elites would not be impoverished or reduced to some kind of bleak life though they would, the incidental Spartan types aside, find their life styles altered. But their health and general well being, including their opportunities to do significant and innovative work, would, if anything, be enhanced. And while some of the sources of their enjoyment would be a thing of the past, there would still be a considerable range of enjoyments available to them sufficient to afford anyone a rich life that could be lived with verve and zest.

A fraction of what the United States spends on defense spending would take care of immediate problems of starvation and malnutrition for most of the world. For longer range problems such as bringing conditions of life in the Third World more in line with conditions of life in Sweden and Switzerland, what is necessary is the dismantling of the capitalist system and the creation of a socio-economic system with an underlying rationale directing it toward producing for needs—everyone's needs. With this altered productive mode, the irrationalities and waste of capitalist production would be cut. There would be no more built-in obsolescence, no more merely cosmetic changes in consumer durables, no more fashion roulette, no more useless products and the like. Moreover, the enormous expenditures that go into the war industry would be a thing of the past. There would be great transfers from North to South, but it would be from the North's capitalist fat and not from things people in the North really need. (There would, in other words, be no self-pauperization of people in the capitalist world.)...

V

It has been repeatedly argued that equality undermines liberty. Some would say that a society in which principles like my radical egalitarian principles were adopted, or even the liberal egalitarian principles of Rawls or Dworkin were adopted, would not be a free society. My arguments have been just the reverse. I have argued that it is only in an egalitarian society that full and extensive liberty is possible.

Perhaps the egalitarian and the anti-egalitarian are arguing at cross purposes? What we need to recognize, it has been argued, is that we have two kinds of rights both of which are important to freedom but to rather different freedoms and which are freedoms which not infrequently conflict.[4] We have rights to *fair terms of cooperation* but we also have rights to non-interference. If a right of either kind is overridden our freedom is diminished. The reason why it might be thought that the egalitarian and the anti-egalitarian may be arguing at cross purposes is that the egalitarian is pointing to the fact that rights to fair terms of cooperation and their associated liberties require equality while the anti-egalitarian is pointing to the fact that rights to noninterference and their associated liberties conflict with equality. They focus on different liberties.

What I have said above may not be crystal clear, so let me explain. People have a right to fair terms of cooperation. In political terms this comes to the equal right of all to effective participation in government and, in more broadly social terms, and for a society of economic wealth, it means people having a right to a roughly equal distribution of the benefits and burdens of the basic social arrangements that affect their lives and for them to stand in such relations to each other such that no one has the power to dominate the life of another. By contrast, rights to non-interference come to the equal right of all to be left alone by the government and more broadly to live in a society in which people have a right peacefully to pursue their interests without interference.

The conflict between equality and liberty comes down to, very essentially, the conflicts we get in modern societies between rights to fair terms of cooperation and rights to noninterference. As Joseph Schumpeter saw and J. S. Mill before him, one could have a thoroughly democratic society (at least in conventional terms) in which rights to noninterference might still be extensively violated. A central anti-egalitarian claim is that we cannot have an egalitarian society in which the very precious liberties that go with the rights to non-interference would not be violated.

Socialism and egalitarianism plainly protect rights to fair terms of cooperation. Without the social (collective) ownership and control of the means of production, involving with this, in the initial stages of socialism at least, a workers' state, economic power will be concentrated in the hands of a few who will in turn, as a result, dominate effective participation in government. Some right-wing libertarians blind themselves to that reality, but it is about as evident as can be. Only an utter turning away from the facts of social life could lead to any doubts about this at all. But then this means that in a workers' state, if some people have capitalistic impulses, that they would have their rights peacefully to pursue their own interests interfered with. They might wish to invest, retain and bequeath in economic domains. In a workers' state these capitalist acts in many circumstances would have to be forbidden, but that would be a violation of an individual's right to non-interference and the fact, if it was a fact, that we by democratic vote, even with vast majorities, had made such capitalist acts illegal would still not make any difference because individuals' rights to noninterference would still be violated.

We are indeed driven, by egalitarian impulses, of a perfectly understandable sort, to accept interference with laissez-faire capitalism to protect non-subordination and non-domination of people by protecting the egalitarian right to fair terms of cooperation and the enhanced liberty that that brings. Still, as things stand, this leads inevitably to violations of the right to non-interference and this brings with it a diminution of liberty. There will be people with capitalist impulses and they will be interfered with. It is no good denying, it will be said, that egalitarianism and particularly socialism will not lead to interference with very precious individual liberties, namely with our right peacefully to pursue our interests without interference.[5]

The proper response to this, as should be apparent from what I have argued throughout, is that to live in any society at all, capitalist, socialist or whatever, is to live in a world in which there will be some restriction or other on our rights peacefully to pursue our interests without interference. I can't lecture in Albanian or even in French in a standard philosophy class at the University of Calgary, I can't jog naked on most beaches, borrow a book from your library without your permission, fish in your trout pond without your permission, take your dog for a walk without your say so and the like. At least some of these things have been thought to be things which I might peacefully pursue in my own interests. Stopping me from doing them is plainly interfering with my peaceful pursuit of my own interests. And indeed it is an infringement on liberty, an interference with my doing what I may want to do.

However, for at least many of these activities, and particularly the ones having to do with property, even right-wing libertarians think that such interference is perfectly justified. But, justified or not, they still plainly constitute a restriction on our individual freedom. However, what we must also recognize is that there will always be some such restrictions on freedom in any society whatsoever, just in virtue of the fact that a normless society, without the restrictions that having norms implies, is a contradiction in terms.[6] Many restrictions are hardly felt as restrictions, as in the attitudes of many people toward seat-belt legislation, but they are, all the same, plainly restriction on our liberty. It is just that they are thought to be unproblematically justified.

To the question would a socialism with a radical egalitarianism restrict some liberties, including some liberties rooted in rights to noninterference, the answer is that it indeed would; but so would laissez-faire capitalism, aristocratic conceptions of justice, liberal conceptions or any social formations at all, with their associated conceptions of justice. The relevant question is which of these restrictions are justified.

The restrictions on liberty preferred by radical egalitarianism and socialism, I have argued, are justified for they, of the various alternatives, give us both the most extensive and the most abundant system of liberty possible in modern conditions with their thorough protection of the right to fair terms of cooperation. Radical egalitarianism will also, and this is central for us, protect our civil liberties and these liberties are, of course, our most basic liberties. These are the liberties which are the most vital for us to protect. What it will not do is to protect our unrestricted liberties to invest, retain and bequeath in the economic realm and it will not protect our unrestricted freedom to buy and sell. There is, however, no good reason to think that these restrictions are restrictions of anything like a basic liberty. Moreover, we are justified in restricting our freedom to buy and sell if such restrictions strengthen, rather than weaken, our total system of liberty. This is in this way justified, for only by such market restrictions can the rights of the vast majority of people to effective participation in government and an equal role in the control of their social lives be protected. I say this because if we let the market run free in this way, power will pass into the hands of a few who will control the lives of the many and determine the fundamental design of the society. The actual liberties that are curtailed in a radically egalitarian social order are inessential liberties whose restriction in contemporary circumstances enhances human well-being and indeed makes for a firmer entrenchment of basic liberties and for their greater extension globally. That is to say, we here restrict some liberty in order to attain more liberty and a more equally distributed pattern of liberty. More people will be able to do what they want and have a greater control over their own lives than in a capitalist world order with its at least implicit inegalitarian commitments.

However, some might say I still have not faced the most central objection to radical egalitarianism, namely its statism. (I would prefer to say its putative statism.) The picture is this. The egalitarian state must be in the redistribution business. It has to make, or make sure there is made, an equal relative contribution to the welfare of every citizen. But this in effect means that the socialist state or, for that matter, the welfare state, will be deeply interventionist in our personal lives. It will be in the business, as one right-winger emotively put it, of cutting one person down to size in order to bring about that person's equality with another person who was in a previously disadvantageous position.[7] That is said to be morally objectionable and it would indeed be deeply morally objectionable in many circumstances. But it isn't in the circumstances in which the radical egalitarian presses for redistribution. (I am not speaking of what might be mere equalizing upwards.) The circumstances are these: Capitalist A gets his productive property confiscated so that he could no longer dominate and control the lives of proletarians C, D, E, F, and G. But what is wrong with it where this "cutting down to size"—in reality the confiscation of productive property or the taxation of the capitalist—involves no violation of A's civil liberties or the harming of his actual well-being (health, ability to work, to cultivate the arts, to have fruitful personal relation, to live in comfort and the like) and where B, C, D, E, F, and G will have their freedom and their well-being thoroughly enhanced if such confiscation or taxation occurs? Far from being morally objectionable, it is precisely the sort of state of affairs that people ought to favor. It certainly protects more liberties and more significant liberties that it undermines.

There is another familiar anti-egalitarian argument designed to establish the liberty-undermining qualities of egalitarianism. It is an argument we have touched upon in discussing meritocracy. It turns on the fact that in any society there will be both talents and handicaps. Where they exist, what do we want to do about maintaining equal distribution? Egalitarians, radical or otherwise, certainly do not want to penalize people for talent. That being so, then surely people should be allowed to retain the benefits of superior talent. But this in some circumstances will lead to significant inequalities in resources and in the meeting of needs. To sustain equality there will have to be an ongoing redistribution in the direction of the less talented and less fortunate. But this redistribution from the more to the less talented does plainly penalize the talented for their talent. That, it will be said, is something which is both unfair and an undermining of liberty.

The following, it has been argued, makes the above evident enough.[8] If people have talents they will tend to want to use them. And if they use them they are very likely to come out ahead. Must not egalitarians say they ought not to be able to come out ahead no matter how well they use their talents and no matter how considerable these talents are? But that is intolerably restrictive and unfair.

The answer to the above anti-egalitarian argument is implicit in a number of things I have already said. But here let me confront this familiar argument directly. Part of the answer comes out in probing some of the ambiguities of "coming out ahead." Note, incidentally, that (1) not all reflective, morally sensitive people will be so concerned with that, and (2) that being very concerned with that is a mentality that capitalism inculcates. Be that as it may, to turn to the ambiguities, note that some take "coming out ahead" principally to mean "being paid well for the use of those talents" where "being paid well" is being paid sufficiently well so that it creates inequalities sufficient to disturb the preferred egalitarian patterns. (Without that, being paid well would give one no relative advantage.) But, as we have seen, "coming out ahead" need not take that form at all. Talents can be recognized and acknowledged in many ways. First, in just the respect and admiration of a fine employment of talents that would naturally come from people seeing them so displayed where these people were not twisted by envy; second, by having, because of these talents, interesting and secure work that their talents fit them for and they merit in virtue of those talents. Moreover, having more money is not going to matter much—for familiar marginal utility reasons—where what in capitalist societies would be called the welfare floors are already very high, this being made feasible by the great productive wealth of the society. Recall that in such a society of abundance everyone will be well off and secure. In such a society people are not going to be very concerned about being a little better off than someone else. The talented are in no way, in such a situation, robbed to help the untalented and handicapped or penalized for their talents. They are only prevented from amassing wealth (most particularly productive wealth), which would enable them to dominate the untalented and the handicapped and to control the social life of the world of which they are both a part. . . .

I think that the moral authority for abstract egalitarianism, for the belief that the interests of everyone matter and matter equally, comes from its being the case that it is *required by the moral point of view*.[9] What I am predicting is that a person who has a good understanding of what morality is, has a good knowledge of the facts, is not ideologically mystified, takes an impartial point of view, and has an attitude of impartial caring, would, if not conceptually confused, come to accept the abstract egalitarian thesis. I see no way of arguing someone into such an egalitarianism who does not in this general way have a love of humankind.[10] A hard-hearted Hobbesist is not reachable here. But given that a person has that love of humankind—that impartial and impersonal caring—together with the other qualities mentioned above, then, I predict, that that person would be an egalitarian at least to the extent of accepting the abstract egalitarian thesis. What I am claiming is that if these conditions were to obtain (if they ceased to be just counterfactuals), then there would be a consensus among moral agents about accepting the abstract egalitarian thesis. . . .

TOWARD A DELIBERATIVE MODEL OF DEMOCRATIC LEGITIMACY

SEYLA BENHABIB

Democratic Legitimacy and Public Goods

Complex modern democratic societies since the Second World War face the task of securing three public goods. These are legitimacy, economic welfare, and a viable sense of collective identity. These are "goods" in the sense that their attainment is considered worthy and desirable by most members of such societies; furthermore, not attaining one or a combination thereof would cause problems in the functioning of these societies such as to throw them into crises.

These goods stand in a complex relation to one another: excessive realization of one such good may be in conflict with and may jeopardize the realization of others. For example, economic welfare may be attained at the cost of sacrificing legitimacy by curtailing union rights, by limiting a more rigorous examination of business accounting practices, or by encouraging the unfair use of protectionist state measures. Too great an emphasis on collective identity may come at the cost of minorities and dissidents whose civil and political rights may be impinged upon by a revival of a sense of collective identity. Thus legitimacy claims and collective identity demands, particularly if they take a nationalist tone, may come into conflict. There can also be conflicts between the claims of economic welfare and the demands of collective identity, as when excessive forms of protectionism and nationalism isolate countries in the world economic context, possibly leading to declining standards of living. Conversely, too great an emphasis on economic welfare may undermine a sense of collective identity by increasing competition among social groups and by weakening the claims of political sovereignty vis-à-vis other states. In a well-functioning democratic society the demands of legitimacy, economic welfare, and collective identity ideally exist in some form of equilibrium.

The present essay is concerned with one good among others which democratic societies must attain: the good of legitimacy. I am concerned to examine the philosophical foundations of democratic legitimacy. I will argue that legitimacy in complex democratic societies must be thought to result from the free and unconstrained public deliberation of all about matters of common concern. Thus a public sphere of deliberation about matters of mutual concern is essential to the legitimacy of democratic institutions.

Democracy, in my view, is best understood as a model for organizing the collective and public exercise of power in the major institutions of a society on the basis of the principle that decisions affecting the well being of a collectivity can be viewed as the outcome of a procedure of free and reasoned deliberation among individuals considered as moral and political equals. Certainly any definition of essentially contested concepts like democracy, freedom, and justice is never a mere definition; the definition itself already articulates the normative theory that justifies the term. Such is the case with the preceding definition. My understanding of democracy privileges a deliberative model over other kinds of normative considerations. This is not to imply that economic welfare, institutional efficiency, and cultural stability would not be relevant in judging the adequacy of a normative definition of democracy. Economic welfare claims and collective identity needs must also be satisfied for democracies to function over time. However, the normative basis of democracy as a form of organizing our collective life is neither the fulfillment of economic welfare nor the realization of a stable sense of collective identity. For just as the attainment of certain levels of economic welfare may be compatible with authoritarian political rule, so too antidemocratic regimes may be more successful in assuring a sense of collective identity than democratic ones.

My goal in the first half of this article will be to examine the relationship between the normative presuppositions of democratic deliberation and the idealized content of practical rationality. The approach I follow is consonant with what John Rawls has called "Kantian constructivism," and what Jürgen Habermas refers to as "reconstruction."[1] In this context, the differences in their methodologies are less significant than their shared assumption that the institutions of liberal democracies embody the idealized content of a form of practical reason. This idealized content can be elucidated and philosophically articulated; in fact, the task of a philosophical theory of democracy would consist in the clarification and articulation of the form of practical rationality represented by democratic rule.[2]

The methodology of "philosophical reconstruction" differs from "ethnocentric liberalism" (Richard Rorty) as well as from more a prioristic forms of Kantianism.[3] As distinguished from certain kinds of Kantianism, I would like to acknowledge the historical and sociological specificity of the project of democracy while, against ethnocentric liberalism, I would like to insist that the practical rationality embodied in democratic institutions has a culture-transcending validity claim. This form of practical reason has become the collective and anonymous property of cultures, institutions, and traditions as a result of the experiments and experiences, both ancient and modern, with democratic rule over the course of human history.[4] The insights and perhaps illusions resulting from these experiments and experiences are sedimented in diverse constitutions, institutional arrangements, and procedural specifics. When one thinks through the form of practical rationality at the core of democratic rule, Hegel's concept of "objective Spirit" (*objektiver Geist*) appears to me particularly appropriate.[5] To make this concept useful today we have to think of it without recourse to the metaphorical presence of a super-subject; we have to desubstantialize the model of a thinking and acting supersubject that still governs Hegelian philosophy. Without this metaphor of the subject implicitly governing it, the term "objective spirit" would refer to those *anonymous yet intelligible* collective rules, procedures, and practices that form a way of life. It is the rationality intrinsic to these anonymous yet intelligible rules, procedures and practices that any attempt aiming at the reconstruction of the logic of democracies must focus upon.

A Deliberative Model of Democracy

According to the deliberative model of democracy, it is a necessary condition for attaining legitimacy and rationality with regard to collective decision-making processes in a polity, that the institutions of this polity are so arranged that what is considered in the common interest of all results from processes of collective deliberation conducted rationally and fairly among free and equal individuals.[6] The more collective decision making processes approximate this model the more increases the presumption of their legitimacy and rationality. Why?

The basis of legitimacy in democratic institutions is to be traced back to the presumption that the instances which claim obligatory power for themselves do so because their decisions represent an impartial standpoint said to be equally in the interests of all. This presumption can be fulfilled only if such decisions are in principle open to appropriate public processes of deliberation by free and equal citizens.

The discourse model of ethics formulates the most *general principles* and *moral intuitions* behind the validity claims of a deliberative model of democracy.[7] The basic idea behind this model is that only those norms (i.e., general rules of action and institutional arrangements) can be said to be valid (i.e., morally binding), which would be agreed to by all those affected by their consequences, if such agreement were reached as a consequences, of a process of deliberation that had the following features: 1) participation in such deliberation is governed by the norms of equality and symmetry; all have the same chances to initiate speech acts, to question, to interrogate, and to open debate; 2) all have the right to question the assigned topics of conversation; and 3) all have the right to initiate reflexive arguments about the very rules of the discourse procedure and the way in which they are applied or carried out. There are no prima facie rules limiting the agenda of the conversation, or the identity of the participants, as long as each excluded person or group can justifiably show that they are relevantly affected by the proposed norm under question. In certain circumstances this would mean that citizens of a democratic community would have to enter into a practical discourse with noncitizens who may be residing in their countries, at their borders, or in neighboring communities if there are matters that affect them all. Ecology and environmental issues in general are a perfect example of such instances when the boundaries of discourses keep expanding because the consequences of our actions expand and affect increasingly more people.

The procedural specifics of those special argumentation situations called "practical discourses" are not automatically transferable to a macro-institutional level, nor is it necessary that they should be so transferable. A theory of democracy, as opposed to a general moral theory, would have to be concerned with the question of institutional specifications and practical feasibility. Nonetheless, the procedural constraints of the discourse model can act as test cases for critically evaluating the criteria of membership and the rules for agenda setting, and for the structuring of public discussions within and among institutions. . . .

According to the deliberative model, procedures of deliberation generate legitimacy as well as assure some degree of practical rationality.[8] But what are the claims to practical rationality of such deliberative democratic processes? Deliberative processes are essential to the rationality of collective decision-making processes for three reasons. First, as Bernard Manin has observed in an excellent article "On Legitimacy and Deliberation," deliberative processes are also processes that impart information.[9] New information is imparted because 1) no single individual can anticipate and foresee all the variety of perspectives through which matters of ethics and politics would be perceived by different individuals; and 2) no single individual can possess all the information deemed relevant to a certain decision affecting all.[10] Deliberation is a procedure for being informed.

Furthermore, much political theory under the influence of economic models of reasoning in particular proceeds from a methodological fiction: this is the methodological fiction of an individual with an ordered set of coherent preferences. This fiction does not have much relevance in the political world. On complex social and political issues, more often than not, individuals may have views and wishes but no ordered set of preferences, since the latter would imply that they would be enlightened not only about the preferences but about the consequences and relative merits of each of their preferred choices in advance. It is actually the deliberative process itself that is likely to produce such an outcome by leading the individual to further critical reflection on his already held views and opinions; it is incoherent to assume that individuals can start a process of public deliberation with a level of conceptual clarity about their choices and preferences that can actually result only from a successful process of deliberation. Likewise, the formation of coherent preferences cannot precede deliberation; it can only succeed it. Very often individuals' wishes as well as views and opinions conflict with one another. In the course of deliberation and the exchange of views with others, individuals become more aware of such conflicts and feel compelled to undertake a coherent ordering.

More significantly, the very procedure of articulating a view in public imposes a certain reflexivity on individual preferences and opinions. When presenting their point of view and position to others, individuals must support them by articulating good reasons in a public context to their codeliberators. This process of *articulating good reasons in public* forces the individual to think of what would count as a good reason for all others involved. One is thus forced to think from the standpoint of all involved for whose agreement one is "wooing." Nobody can convince others in public of her point of view without being able to state why what appears good, plausible, just, and expedient to her can also be considered so from the standpoint of all involved. Reasoning from the standpoint of all involved not only forces a certain coherence upon one's own views but also forces one to adopt a standpoint that Hannah Arendt, following Kant, had called the "enlarged mentality."[11]

A deliberative model of democracy suggests a necessary but not sufficient condition of practical rationality, because, as with any procedure, it can be misinterpreted, misapplied, and abused. Procedures can neither dictate outcomes nor define the quality of the reasons advanced in argumentation nor control the quality of the reasoning and rules of logic and inference used by participants. Procedural models of rationality are underdetermined. Nonetheless, the discourse model makes some provisions against its own misuses and abuses in that the reflexivity condition built into the model allows abuses and misapplications at the first level to be challenged at a second, metalevel of discourse. Likewise, the equal chance of all affected to initiate such discourse of deliberation suggests that no outcome is prima facie fixed but can be revised and subjected to reexamination. Such would be the normative justification of majority rule as a decision procedure following from this model: in many instances the majority rule is a fair and rational decision procedure, not because legitimacy resides in numbers but because if a majority of people are convinced at one point on the basis of reasons formulated as closely as possible as a result of a process of discursive deliberation that conclusion A is the right thing to do, then this conclusion can remain valid until challenged by good reasons by some other group. It is not the sheer numbers that support the rationality of the conclusion, but the presumption that if a large number of people see certain matters a certain way as a result of following certain kinds of rational procedures of deliberation and decision-making, then such a conclusion has a presumptive claim to being rational until shown to be otherwise. The simple practice of having a ruling and an opposition party in democracies in fact incorporates this principle: we accept the will of the majority at the end of an electoral process that has been fairly and correctly carried out, but even when we accept the legitimacy of the process we may have grave doubts about the rationality of the outcome. The practice of there being parliamentary opposition says that the grounds on which the majority party claims to govern can be examined, challenged, tested, criticized, and rearticulated. Parliamentary procedures of opposition, debate, questioning, and even impeachment proceedings, and investigatory commissions incorporate this rule of deliberative rationality that majoritarian decisions are temporarily agreed-upon conclusions, the claim to rationality and validity of which can be publicly reexamined.

This deliberative model of democracy is proceduranst in that it emphasizes first and foremost certain institutional procedures and practices for attaining decisions on matters that would be binding on all. Three additional points are worthy of note with respect to such a conception of democracy: first, I proceed from the assumption of value pluralism. Disagreement about the highest goods of human existence and the proper conduct of a morally righteous life are a fundamental feature of our modern value-universe since the end of natural law cosmologies in the sixteenth and seventeenth centuries, and the eventual separation of church and state.[12] The challenge to democratic rationality is to arrive at acceptable formulations of the common good despite this inevitable value-pluralism. We cannot resolve conflicts among value systems and visions of the good by reestablishing a strong unified moral and religious code without forsaking fundamental liberties. Agreements in societies living with value pluralism are to be sought for not at the level of substantive beliefs but at that of procedures, processes, and practices for attaining and revising beliefs. Proceduralism is a rational answer to persisting value conflicts at the substantive level.[13]

Second, the deliberative model of democracy proceeds not only from a conflict of values but also from a conflict of interests in social life. Social life necessitates both conflict of interests and cooperation. Democratic procedures have to convince, even under conditions when one's interests as an individual or as a group are negatively affected, that the conditions of mutual cooperation are still legitimate. Procedures can be regarded as methods for articulating, sifting through, and weighing conflicting interests. The more conflicts of interests there are the more it is important to have procedural solutions of conflict adjudication through which parties whose interests are negatively affected can find recourse to other methods of the articulation and representation of their grievances. Proceduralist models of democracy allow the articulation of conflicts of interests under conditions of social cooperation mutually acceptable to all.[14]

Finally, any proceduralist and deliberative model of democracy is prima facie open to the argument, that no modern society can organize its affairs along the fiction of a mass assembly carrying out its deliberations in public and collectively. Here more than an issue of size is at stake. The argument that there may be an invisible limit to the size of a deliberative body that, when crossed, affects the nature of the reasoning process is undoubtedly true. Nonetheless the reason why a deliberative and proceduralist model of democracy does not need to operate with the fiction of a general deliberative assembly is that the procedural specifications of this model privilege a *plurality of modes of association* in which all affected can have the right to articulate their point of view. These can range from political parties, to citizens' initiatives, to social movements, to voluntary associations, to consciousness-raising groups, and the like. *It is through the interlocking net of these multiple forms of associations, networks, and organizations that an anonymous "public conversation" results. It is central to the model of deliberative democracy that it privileges such a public sphere of mutually interlocking and overlapping networks and associations of deliberation, contestation, and argumentation.* The fiction of a general deliberative assembly in which the united people expressed their will belongs to the early history of democratic theory; today our guiding model has to be that of a medium of loosely associated, multiple foci of opinion formation and dissemination which affect one another in free and spontaneous processes of communication.[15]

Such a strong model of deliberative democracy is subject to three different kinds of criticism; first, liberal theorists will express concern that such a strong model would lead to the corrosion of individual liberties and may in fact destabilize the rule of law. In his earlier work, Bruce Ackerman had formulated a theory of "conversational neutrality" to voice some of these concerns.[16] Stephen Holmes has defended the plausibility of certain "gag rules" on public conversation.[17] Second, feminist theorists are skeptical about this model, because they see it as privileging a certain mode of discourse at the cost of silencing other: this is the rationalist, male, univocal, hegemonic discourse of a transparent polity that disregards the emotions, polyvocity, multiplicity, and differences in the articulation of the voice of the public. . . .

Basic Rights and Deliberative Democracy

Deliberative democracy models often seem subject to the argument that they do not protect individuals' basic rights and liberties sufficiently.[18] This objection is rooted in two assumptions: first, insofar as deliberative models appear to make a high degree of consensus or unanimity of public issues a value, it is fair to suspect that such unanimity could only be attained at the cost of silencing dissent and curtailing minority viewpoints. Second, what protection does a deliberative model allow against the tyranny of democratic majorities from imposing its choices and norms upon the minority?

I believe that these objections are fair when raised against most versions of radical participatory democratic theories that also prioritize political deliberation. I think it is fair to ask whether the radical democratic theories of Hannah Arendt, Benjamin Barber, or Mouffe and Laclau allow for a coherent theory of rights such as would protect both basic rights and liberties for all, and defend minority rights against the tyranny of the majority. But such objections are not applicable to the model of deliberative democracy developed here.

Precisely because I share with the Kantian liberal tradition the assumption that moral respect for the autonomous personality is a fundamental norm of morality and democracy, the deliberative model of democracy presupposes a discourse theory of ethics to supply it with the most general moral principles upon which rights claims would be based.[19] Insofar as a discourse theory of ethics considers participants to be equal and free beings, equally entitled to take part in those discourses which determine the norms that are to affect their lives, it proceeds from a view of persons as beings entitled to certain "moral rights." I have named this moral right the entitlement to *universal moral respect*, and have attempted in *Situating the Self* to give a nonfoundationalist but principled justification for the recognition of this norm.[20] I further maintain that within a discourse theory each individual has the same symmetrical rights to various speech acts, to initiate new topics, to ask for reflection about the presuppositions of the conversations, and so on. I call this the principle of *egalitarian reciprocity*. In my view the norms of universal moral respect and egalitarian reciprocity are moral rights in that they are entitlements that accrue to individuals insofar as we view them as moral persons.

The step that would lead from a recognition of these two moral rights to the formulation of a principle of basic rights and liberties is certainly not very wide.[21] Basically it would involve a hypothetical answer to the question, If it is plausible for individuals to view one another as beings entitled to universal moral respect and egalitarian reciprocity, which most general principles of basic rights and liberties would such individuals also be likely to accept as determining the conditions of their collective existence?[22]

Although the discourse theory shares this kind of hypothetical and counter-factual moral reasoning procedure with Kant and Rawls, it would be different from a Kantian deduction of the concept of right and from a Rawlsian construction of the "original position," in that it would privilege a discourse model of practical debate as being the appropriate forum for determining rights claims. But are we not thereby landing in a vicious circle, that is, discourses, even to get started, presuppose the recognition of one another's moral rights among discourse participants; on the other hand, such rights are said to be specified as a result of the discursive situation.

I have indicated elsewhere that this is not a vicious circle but rather the hermeneutic circle that characterizes all reasoning about morals and politics.[23] We never begin our deliberations concerning these matters at a "moral ground zero." Rather, in moral theory as in everyday morality, in political theory as in everyday political discourse, we are always situated within a horizon of presuppositions, assumptions, and power relations, the totality of which can never become wholly transparent to us. This much we must have learned from all the criticisms of rationalism in the last three centuries. Discourse ethics in this sense presupposes the reciprocal moral recognition of one another's claims to be participants in the moral political dialogue. I am still enough of a Hegelian to maintain, however, that such reciprocal recognition of one another's rights to moral personality is a result of a world-historical process that involves struggle, battle and resistance, as well as defeat, carried out by social classes, genders, groups, and nations.

What is distinctive about the discourse model is that although it presupposes that participants must recognize one another's entitlement to moral respect and reciprocity in some sense, the determination of the precise content and extent of these principles would be a consequence of discourses themselves.[24] Insofar as the precise meaning and entailment of the norms of universal moral respect and egalitarian reciprocity would be subject to discursive validation, we can speak here of a procedure of "recursive validation."[25] The methodological procedure of recursive validation rules out the two consequences most feared by liberals vis-à-vis the model of deliberative democracy—namely, too strong a formulation of the conditions of consent, and the tyranny of the majority. The norms of universal moral respect and egalitarian reciprocity allow minorities and dissenters both the right to withhold their assent and the right to challenge the rules as well as the agenda of public debate. For what distinguishes discourses from compromises and other agreements reached under conditions of coercion is that only the *freely given assent of all concerned* can count as a condition of having reached agreement in the discourse situation.[26]

Deliberative Democracy and Constitutionalism

Upon reflection, we can see that institutionally as well, complex constitutional democracies, and particularly those in which a *public sphere* of opinion formation and deliberation has been developed, engage in such recursive validation continually. Basic human civil and political rights, as guaranteed by the Bill of Rights to the U.S. Constitution and as embodied in the constitution of most democratic governments, are never really "off the agenda" of public discussion and debate. They are simply constitutive and regulative institutional norms of debate in democratic societies that cannot be transformed and abrogated by simple majority decisions. The language of keeping these rights off the agenda mischaracterizes the nature of democratic debate in our kinds of societies: although we cannot change these rights without extremely elaborate political and juridical procedures, we are always disputing their meaning, their extent, and their jurisdiction. Democratic debate is like a ball game where there is no umpire to interpret the rules of the game and their application definitively. Rather, in the game of democracy the rules of the game no less than their interpretation and even the position of the umpire are essentially contestable. Contestation means neither the complete abrogation of these rules nor silence about them. When basic rights and liberties are violated the game of democracy is suspended and becomes either martial rule, civil war, or dictatorship; when democratic politics is in full session, the debate about the meaning of these rights, what they do or do not entitle us to, their scope and enforcement, is what politics is all about. One cannot challenge the specific interpretation of basic rights and liberties in a democracy without taking these absolutely seriously.

The deliberative theory of democracy transcends the traditional opposition of majoritarian politics vs. liberal guarantees of basic rights and liberties to the extent that the normative conditions of discourses, like basic rights and liberties, are to be viewed as rules of the game that can be contested within the game but only insofar as one first accepts to abide by them and play the game at all. This formulation seems to me to correspond to the reality of democratic debate and public speech in real democracies much more accurately than the liberal model of deliberation upon constitutional essentials or the reasoning of the Supreme Court. Crucial to the deliberative model of democracy is the idea of a "public sphere" of opinion-formation, debate, deliberation, and contestation among citizens, groups, movements, and organizations in a polity. When this concept of a public sphere is introduced as the concrete embodiment of discursive democracy in practice, it also becomes possible to think of the issue of conversational constraints in a more nuanced way. While the deliberative model of democracy shares with liberalism a concern for the protection of the rights to autonomy of equal citizens, the conceptual method of discursive validation and the institutional reality of a differentiated public sphere of deliberation and contestation provide plausible beginning points for a mediation of the stark opposition between liberalism and deliberative democracy.

Bruce Ackerman's conception of dualist democracy is based upon a similar strategy of overcoming the opposition between the standpoint of foundationalist rights-liberals on the one hand and monist majoritarian democrats on the other: "The basic mediating device is the dualist's two-track system of democratic lawmaking. It allows an important place for the foundationalist's view of 'rights as trumps' without violating the monist's deeper commitment to the primacy of democracy."[27] In a constitutional democracy the question as to which aspects of the higher law are entrenched against revision by the people as opposed to which aspects may be repealed is itself always open and contestable. Conceptually as well as sociologically, models of deliberative and dualistic democracy focus on this process of "recursive" and "hermeneutic" interdependence between constitution-making and democratic politics.[28]

Feminist Suspicions toward Deliberative Democracy

While liberals criticize the model of deliberative democracy for possibly overextending itself and corroding the sphere of individual privacy, feminist theorists criticize this model for not extending itself broadly enough to be truly inclusive. In an illuminating article entitled "Impartiality and the Civic Public," Iris Young, for example, has argued:

The distinction between public and private as it appears in modern political theory expresses a will for homogeneity that necessitates the exclusion of many persons and groups, particularly women and radicalized groups culturally identified with the body, wildness and rationality. In conformity with the modern idea of normative reason, the idea of the public in modern political theory and practice designates a sphere of human existence in which citizens express their rationality and universality, abstracted from their particular situations and need, and opposed to feeling. . . . Examination of the exclusionary and homogeneous ideal in modern political theory, however, shows that we cannot envision such renewal of public life as a recovery of Enlightenment ideals. Instead, we need to transform the distinction between public and private that does not correlate with an opposition between reason and affectively and desire, or universal and particular.[29]

Iris Young's cogent and penetrating feminist critique of the ideal of the impartial public applies to the model of deliberative democracy suggested in the preceding only in certain respects. Certainly, the model of a general deliberative assembly that governed our conceptions of the public sphere well into the twentieth century was historically, socially, and culturally a space for male bodies. I mean this not only in the sense that only men were active citizens entitled to hold office and appear in public, but also in the sense that the institutional iconography of early democratic theory privileged the male mode of self-representation.[30]

Yet here we must distinguish between the *institutional* and the *conceptual* critiques. There is a certain ambivalence in the feminist critique of such models of the public sphere and deliberative democracy. On the one hand, the critique appears to take democratic institutions at their principled best and to criticize their biased and restrictive implementations in practice; on the other hand, the feminist critique appears to aim at a rejection of the ideals of free public reason and impartiality altogether. As Joan Landes puts it, the democratic public sphere appears to be essentially and not just accidentally "masculinist."[31] A normative theory of deliberative democracy requires a strong concept of the public sphere as its institutional correlate. The public sphere replaces the model of the general deliberative assembly found in early democratic theory. In this context, it is important for feminist theorists to specify the level of their conceptual objection, and to differentiate among institutional and normative presuppositions.[32]

Iris Young does not reject the ideal of a public sphere, only its Enlightenment variety. She proposes to replace the ideal of the "civil public" with that of a heterogeneous public. In her recent work she has advocated a number of institutional measures that would guarantee and solidify group representation in such a public sphere.[33] Yet wanting to retain the public sphere and according it a place in democratic theory is not compatible with the more radical critique of the ideal of impartial reason that Young also develops in some of her essays.

In her essay "Communication and the Other: Beyond Deliberative Democracy" Iris Young distinguishes between "deliberative" and "communicative" democracy on the grounds that most theories of deliberative democracy offer too narrow a conception of the democratic process because they continue to privilege an ideal of "a common good in which [the discussion participants] are all supposed to leave behind their particular experience and interests"(126).

By contrast, Young advocates a theory of communicative democracy according to which individuals would attend to one another's differences in class, gender, race, religion, and so on. Each social position has a partial perspective on the public that it does not abandon; but through the communicative process participants transcend and transform their initial situated knowledges (127). Instead of critical argumentation, such processes of communicative confrontation privilege modalities of communication like "greeting, rhetoric, and storytelling"(120).

I think this distinction between deliberative and communicative democracy is more apparent than real. To sustain her critique of the ideals of impartiality and objectivity, which she associates with the deliberative model, Young must be able to distinguish the kind of *transformation* and *transcendence* of partial perspectives that occurs in communicative democracy from the *mutual agreement* to be reached in processes of deliberative democracy. Yet how can we distinguish between the emergence of common opinion among members of one group, if we do not apply to such processes of communication or deliberation some standards of fairness and impartiality in order to judge the manner in which opinions were allowed to be brought forth, groups were given chances to express their points of view, and the like? The model of communicative democracy, far from dispensing with the need for standards of impartiality and fairness, requires them to make sense of its own formulations. Without some such standards, Young could not differentiate the genuine transformation of partial and situated perspectives from mere agreements of convenience or apparent unanimity reached under conditions of duress.

With respect to modes of communication like "greeting, rhetoric, and storytelling," I would say that each of these modes may have their place within the *informally structured process of everyday communication among individuals who share a cultural and historical life world*. However, it is neither necessary for the democratic theorist to try to formalize and institutionalize these aspects of communicative everyday competence, nor is it plausible—and this is the more important objection—to build an opposition between them and critical argumentation. Greeting, storytelling, and rhetoric, although they may be aspects of informal communication in our everyday life, cannot become the public language of institutions and legislatures in a democracy for the following reason: to attain legitimacy, democratic institutions require the articulation of the bases of their actions and policies in discursive language that appeals to commonly shared and accepted public reasons. In constitutional democracies such public reasons take the form of general statements consonant with the rule of law. The rule of law has a certain rhetorical structure of its own: it is general, applies to all members of a specified reference group on the basis of legitimate reasons. Young's attempt to transform the language of the rule of law into a more partial, affective, and situated mode of communication would have the consequence of inducing arbitrariness, for who can tell how far the power of a greeting can reach? It would further create capriciousness—what about those who simply cannot understand my story? It would limit rather than enhance social justice because rhetoric moves people and achieves results without having to render an account of the bases upon which it induces people to engage in certain courses of action rather than others. In short, some moral ideal of impartiality is a regulative principle that should govern not only our *deliberations* in public but also the *articulation* of reasons by public institutions. What is considered impartial has to be "in the best interests of all equally." Without such a normative principle, neither the ideal of the rule of law can be sustained nor deliberative reasoning toward a common good occur. Some Enlightenment ideals are part of any conception of democratic legitimacy and the public sphere. The point therefore is not a rejection of the Enlightenment in toto but a critical renegotiation of its legacy.

Expanding on the model of a heterogeneous, dispersed network of many publics, Nancy Fraser has suggested how, in fact, once the unitary model of the public sphere is abandoned, women's concerns, as well as those of other excluded groups, can be accommodated. Such a nonunitary and dispersed network of publics can accommodate women's desires for their own spaces, in their own terms. In such "subaltern counterpublics," to use Fraser's term,[34] the lines between the public and the private, for example, can be renegotiated, rethought, challenged, and reformulated. It is nonetheless a long step from the cultural and social rethinking and reformulation of such distinctions as between the public and the private to their implementation in legislation and governmental regulation. While sharing the concern of liberal theorists that the precipitous reformulation of such a divide may corrode individual liberties, Fraser rightly points out that there is a distinction between "opinion-making" and "policy-making" public bodies, and that the same kinds of constraints may not apply to each alike.[35] Opinion-making publics, as found in social movements, for example, can lead us to reconsider and rethink very controversial issues about privacy, sexuality, and intimacy; but this does not imply that the only or even most desirable consequence of such processes of public deliberation should be general legislation. Thus when conceived as an anonymous, plural, and multiple medium of communication and deliberation, the public sphere need not homogenize and repress difference. Heterogeneity, otherness, and difference can find expression in the multiple associations, networks, and citizens' forums, all of which constitute public life under late capitalism.[36]

Institutionalist Distrust of Deliberative Democracy

. . . My goal in this essay has been to outline a deliberative model of democracy that incorporates features of practical rationality. Central to practical rationality is the possibility of free public deliberation about matters of mutual concern to all. The discourse model of ethics and politics suggests a procedure for such free public deliberation among all concerned. Such processes of public deliberation have a claim to rationality because they increase and make available necessary information, because they allow the expression of arguments in the light of which opinions and beliefs need to be revised, and because they lead to the formation of conclusions that can be challenged publicly for good reasons. Furthermore, such procedures allow self-referential critique of their own uses and abuses. The chief institutional correlate of such a model of deliberative democracy is a multiple, anonymous, heterogeneous network of many publics and public conversations. In other domains of social life as well, the model of deliberative democracy based on the centrality of public deliberation can inspire the proliferation of many institutional designs.

THE MASTER'S TOOLS WILL NEVER DISMANTLE THE MASTER'S HOUSE

AUDRE LORDE

I agreed to take part in a New York University Institute for the Humanities conference a year ago, with the understanding that I would be commenting upon papers dealing with the role of difference within the lives of American women: difference of race, sexuality, class, and age. The absence of these considerations weakens any feminist discussion of the personal and the political.

It is a particular academic arrogance to assume any discussion of feminist theory without examining our many differences, and without a significant input from poor women, Black and Third World women, and lesbians. And yet, I stand here as a Black lesbian feminist, having been invited to comment within the only panel at this conference where the input of Black feminists and lesbians is represented. What this says about the vision of this conference is sad, in a country where racism, sexism, and homophobia are inseparable. To read this program is to assume that lesbian and Black women have nothing to say about existentialism, the erotic, women's culture and silence, developing feminist theory, or heterosexuality and power. And what does it mean in personal and political terms when even the two Black women who did present here were literally found at the last hour? What does it mean when the tools of a racist patriarchy are used to examine the fruits of that same patriarchy? It means that only the most narrow perimeters of change are possible and allowable.

The absence of any consideration of lesbian consciousness or the consciousness of Third World women leaves a serious gap within this conference and within the papers presented here. For example, in a paper on material relationships between women, I was conscious of an either/or model of nurturing which totally dismissed my knowledge as a Black lesbian. In this paper there was no examination of mutuality between women, no systems of shared support, no interdependence as exists between lesbians and women-identified women. Yet it is only in the patriarchal model of nurturance that women "who attempt to emancipate themselves pay perhaps too high a price for the results," as this paper states.

For women, the need and desire to nurture each other is not pathological but redemptive, and it is within that knowledge that our real power is rediscovered. It is this real connection which is so feared by a patriarchal world. Only within a patriarchal structure is maternity the only social power open to women.

Interdependency between women is the way to a freedom which allows the *I* to *be*, not in order to be used, but in order to be creative. This is a difference between the passive *be* and the active *being*.

Advocating the mere tolerance of difference between women is the grossest reformism. It is a total denial of the creative function of difference in our lives. Difference must be not merely tolerated, but seen as a fund of necessary polarities between which our creativity can spark like a dialectic. Only then does the necessity for interdependency become unthreatening. Only within that interdependency of different strengths, acknowledged and equal, can the power to seek new ways of being in the world generate, as well as the courage and sustenance to act where there are no charters.

Within the interdependence of mutual (nondominant) differences lies that security which enables us to descend into the chaos of knowledge and return with true visions of our future, along with the concomitant power to effect those changes which can bring that future into being. Difference is that raw and powerful connection from which our personal power is forged.

As women, we have been taught either to ignore our differences, or to view them as causes for separation and suspicion rather than as forces for change. Without community there is no liberation, only the most vulnerable and temporary armistice between an individual and her oppression. But community must not mean a shedding of our differences, nor the pathetic pretense that these differences do not exist.

Those of us who stand outside the circle of this society's definition of acceptable women; those of us who have been forged in the crucibles of difference—those of us who are poor, who are lesbians, who are Black, who are older—know that *survival is not an academic skill.* It is learning how to stand alone, unpopular and sometimes reviled, and how to make common cause with those others identified as outside the structures in order to define and seek a world in which we can all flourish. It is learning how to take our differences and make them strengths. *For the master's tools will never dismantle the master's house.* They may allow us temporarily to beat him at his own game, but they will never enable us to bring about genuine change. And this fact is only threatening to those women who still define the master's house as their only source of support.

Poor women and women of Color know there is a difference between the daily manifestations of marital slavery and prostitution because it is our daughters who line 42nd Street. If white American feminist theory need not deal with the differences between us, and the resulting difference in our oppressions, then how do you deal with the fact that the women who clean your houses and tend your children while you attend conferences on feminist theory are, for the most part, poor women and women of Color? What is the theory behind racist feminism?

In a world of possibility for us all, our personal visions help lay the groundwork for political action. The failure of academic feminists to recognize difference as a crucial strength is a failure to reach beyond the first patriarchal lesson. In our world, divide and conquer must become define and empower.

Why weren't other women of Color found to participate in this conference? Why were two phone calls to me considered a consultation? Am I the only possible source of names of Black feminists? And although the Black panelist's paper ends on an important and powerful connection of love between women, what about interracial cooperation between feminists who don't love each other?

In academic feminist circles, the answer to these questions is often, "We did not know who to ask." But that is the same evasion of responsibility, the same cop-out, that keeps Black women's art out of women's exhibitions, Black women's work out of most feminist publications except for the occasional "Special Third World Women's Issue," and Black women's texts off your reading lists. But as Adrienne Rich pointed out in a recent talk, white feminists have educated themselves about such an enormous amount over the past ten years, how come you haven't also educated yourselves about Black women and the differences between us—white and Black—when it is key to our survival as a movement?

Women of today are still being called upon to stretch across the gap of male ignorance and to educate men as to our existence and our needs. This is an old and primary tool of all oppressors to keep the oppressed occupied with the master's concerns. Now we hear that it is the task of women of Color to educate white women—in the face of tremendous resistance—as to our existence, our differences, our relative roles in our joint survival. This is a diversion of energies and a tragic repetition of racist patriarchal thought.

Simone de Beauvoir once said: "It is in the knowledge of the genuine conditions of our lives that we must draw our strength to live and our reasons for acting."

Racism and homophobia are real conditions of all our lives in this place and time. *I urge each one of us here to reach down into that deep place of knowledge inside herself and touch that terror and loathing of any difference that lives there. See whose face it wears.* Then the personal as the political can begin to illuminate all our choices.

Questions

1. In what ways can we critique contemporary American democracy compared to de Tocqueville's ideal of democracy?

2. What would a contemporary government look like according to Bastiat?

3. How is liberty differentiated between libertarianism and egalitarianism?

4. What is the goal of justice according to egalitarian principles?

5. How can justice be obtained using communicative rationality?

Suggested Media

Movies

Mr. Smith Goes to Washington
Citizen Kane
Brazil
In the Name of the Father
Fight Club
V for Vendetta
Reds
The Burning Season
Manufacturing Consent

Television

The West Wing

Books

1984
Animal Farm

Blogs

Ron Paul Blog
Dailykos

Law

Lawrence Friedman (2002), a professor at Stanford, has an interesting way to begin his first lecture for his course on American law: he waves around a newspaper. No matter what day or year, he has always been successful at demonstrating that a discussion of law is present on the front-cover of a national newspaper (Friedman, 2002). This is because law permeates American society. Further, many justice theories discussed within this text have originated from discussions regarding law; consequently, additional explanation and discussion will be provided within this section introduction.

Laws have been defined as a system of rules. Another way to think about this is to think in terms of Law and laws. While laws (little "l") are the specific rules that we have to restrict, regulate, and/or promote behavior, Law (big "L") is a larger concept: an ideal that is based in the values, structure, process, procedures, and purpose of a legal system. For example, the Civil Rights Act of 1964 was put on the books as a "law" that outlawed forms of discrimination, while the *value* of equality is promoted in the United States' "Law." There are different notions of Law. For some, such as human rights advocates, the purpose of Law is to promote and uplift human personality, while for others, such as libertarians, its purpose is to protect individual property rights (see Donnelly, 2003; King, Jr. 1963; Nozick, 1974). In evaluating the little "l" (law) in relation to justice, we ultimately are discussing the big "L"

(Law). One can evaluate their agreement with a particular law based upon the larger perspective of Law they uphold.

In the United States, Law is frequently associated with the norm "equal justice under law," which emphasizes the value of equality in the legal process, procedures, and structure. Some theorists argue that this value is not being achieved in the current United States' legal structure (see Rhode, 2004). Others critique what they see are the current norms and values promoted by the structures of the United States' legal system. Catherine MacKinnon (1983/1991) notes that the equality norm can be viewed and implemented in different ways. For example, you can treat likes alike, and unlikes unlike, or you can endorse equality of status in which unlikes are valued equally. Favoring the latter, MacKinnon argues that the current United States' legal system promotes the former, an understanding of equality that does not adequately address gender inequality.

Law, as a concept, can also be understood by juxtaposing it with the other subject material in this text. In relation to *economy*, some argue that the economy should not be regulated, while others favor laws and institutions regulating the economy and issues such as workers' rights and workplace discrimination. Additionally, although laws can attempt to regulate *social relations*, they have frequently failed to do so justly. As previously highlighted in section three of this text, Crenshaw (1989) discusses the need to recognize intersectionality in order to identify workplace discrimination against African American women. Crenshaw explains how legal procedures to identify discrimination did not allow the legal recognition of these women's experiences because of their particular experience as both African Americans *and* women. This work brings to light how legal structures and processes in the courtroom impact particular groups of people who need the aid of courts.

How can law be made more responsive to the actual conditions in which oppressed groups find themselves? It might be useful in this connection to consider the work of feminist legal scholars. Building on the work of Catherine MacKinnon, for example, Angela Harris argues for a feminist approach that challenges the privileged unitary voice of the legal system and the failure of laws to recognize real differences. But Harris wants to avoid gender essentialism, which she defines as a unitary approach toward women. Gender essentialism tends to equate the challenges that white, privileged women face as those of all women. Harris, like Crenshaw, wants legal theory to hear and respond to the voices of African American women. More broadly, the concern is how the legal system sees and addresses the intersecting identities of everyone.

The feminist critique is a reminder that laws are an institutional response to certain human behaviors that can be destructive. Some would argue that laws are a reaction to *human nature*, and that the legal system and its laws must be consistent with the morality of human nature in order to be considered legal. Additionally, laws are used in the *governance* of many societies and human behaviors. This brings us to the issue of politics. Politics is the process through which societies create laws. But in the application of law, politics is supposed to be absent. This is why lady justice has a blindfold—she cannot see the disputant and therefore cannot show favoritism. These issues are central in a series of debates between Lon Fuller, John Austin, and H.L.A. Hart. Colleagues at Harvard, Fuller and Austin had different perspectives. Fuller argued that the legal system requires a connection with morality in order for it to be considered truly legal (Murphy & Coleman, 1990, p.19). Austin disagreed. He (1832/2001) argued, famously, that laws are "commands, backed by threat of sanctions, from a sovereign, to whom people have a habit of obedience." Austin proposed that laws are not necessarily based in morality, and he defined them as an expression of the sovereign will, backed by sanctions. H.L.A. Hart was critical of Austin's argument, saying that Austin's position made the legal system look like nothing more than a "gunman writ large" (as cited in Murphy & Coleman, 1990, p.27). Instead, he argued, that the legal system should be viewed as a facilitator, a problem solver (Murphy & Coleman, 1990, pp.27–28). Hart saw the legal system as one of rules that imposed obligations. Some obligations are direct injunctions and requirements (primary rules): drive on the right-hand side of the road; no smoking in classrooms; income taxes due on April 15. Other rules, secondary rules, are about the creation and application of these primary rules: the Treasury Department will collect taxes; the Board of Regents has jurisdiction over classroom safety and health. These rules determine who has the power to make (primary) rules.

Jurisprudence

Jurisprudence is the theory behind law, the philosophy of law. Scholars discuss what law is in analytic jurisprudence, and what it ought to be in normative jurisprudence (Murphy & Coleman, 1990, pp.1 & 19). There are different schools of thought on jurisprudence, such as natural law, legal positivism, legal realism, and critical legal studies:

- Natural law theories connect morality and law. Natural law, in this school of thought, is different than "man-made law." Existing outside any state structure or society, natural law is seen as natural to human beings and thus consistent with human nature. Any law that is not consistent with human nature is not a true law; as St. Augustine famously said "an unjust law is no law at all" (as cited in Murphy & Coleman, 1990, p.11). This position should remind you of Lon Fuller's argument about the morality of law and of claims that human nature can be a test of a valid law. (Murphy & Coleman, 1990)
- Largely reacting to natural law theories, legal positivists believe that there is not necessarily a connection between morality and law. Law is a practical endeavor that varies over time and space. Legal positivists believe that law is a human construct. Both John Austin and H.L.A. Hart were legal positivists. (Murphy & Coleman, 1990)
- Legal realists include Justice Oliver Wendall Holmes, who said "Law is a prediction of what the courts will decide" (as cited in Murphy & Coleman, 1990, p.34). Holmes critiqued legal positivism, arguing that law is not a system of rules that the judge mechanically applies; he instead claimed that judges make law. The "rules" allow free play and, consequently, other factors (such as class, temperament, etc.) help determine judicial decisions. Legal realists believe that it is the real world practice of law that determines what law is. (Murphy & Coleman, 1990)
- Critical legal studies, the newest of these schools, began to develop in the 1970s (Fitzpatrick & Hunt, 1987). An early formative statement adopted by the Critical Legal Conference states: "The central focus of the critical legal approach is to explore the manner in which legal doctrine and legal education and the practices of legal institutions work to buttress and support a pervasive system of oppressive, inegalitarian relations" (as cited in Fitzpatrick & Hunt, 1987, pp.1–2). The statement continues: "Critical theory works to develop radical alternatives, and to explore and debate the role of law in the creation of social, economic and political relations that will advance human emancipation" (p.2). This multifaceted field is critical of traditional understandings of law. Scholars in this field argue that legal doctrines are hegemonic. They propose that legal doctrines reflect the ideas of the dominant, most powerful social groups, and so they rationalize and support existing inequality. (Murphy & Coleman, 1990)

There are many other ideas about law but the preceding four paradigms are major contributions on which others have built.

Case Study: (Un)just Laws

Let's apply the typology of jurisprudence that we developed above with Plato's "Crito," Martin Luther King, Jr.'s "Letter from a Birmingham Jail," and the work of John Rawls, a theorist whose work you will read in the economy section of this text.

A reading within this section, Plato's "Crito" (360 BCE) is a dialogue between Socrates and Socrates' friend Crito. Socrates awaits his execution after his trial and conviction for impiety and corrupting the youth. Crito has come to Socrates having prepared to smuggle him out of prison and into exile. Although both agree that the trial and decree of execution were unjust, the two men enter into a dialogue about whether or not Socrates should escape and, therefore, disobey Athenian law. Ultimately, Socrates decides not to attempt escape because of his commitment to Athenian laws, rooted ultimately in his belief that all laws must be obeyed because to do otherwise risks chaos and unhappiness. Socrates believes that human nature, as unwieldy as it is, needs to be controlled by laws, and thus he supports, and therefore must abide by, the laws in place, whether or not it currently results in just outcomes. Of all the pieces you will read, this argument exemplifies the tradition of legal positivism.

Martin Luther King, Jr. (1963), on the other hand, argues that sometimes a just person must openly disobey an unjust law. He believes in higher law principles that guarantee, among other things, equality for all mankind in law. For King, an unjust law is one that conflicts with God's laws; it degrades human personality. A just law can be recognized by its tendency to uplift humans, treating them with respect. King supports civil disobedience to resist unjust laws, but this requires a willingness to accept suffering. King's position typifies the natural-law approach.

Rawls (1971) does not accept King's natural-law criterion for the adequacy of law. Instead, he proposes that we test justice in law via a thought experiment. This thought experiment begins with the "original position," a room in which individuals enter and communicate. These individuals are cloaked in a "veil of ignorance," which does not allow them to see their own personal characteristics (such as their race, gender, class, nationality, age, or other distinctions). They are aware, however, of the societal conditions outside the room (such as the existence of poverty and its deleterious impact). Rawls suggests that their ignorance about where they fit in the scheme of things will enable them to come up with just and fair principles about how to treat one another outside this room. Each individual must be aware that, when they leave the room, they may discover that they are in the worst position in society. This will encourage them to agree on a reasonable social safety net that improves the position of the people worst-off in society. In the end, Rawls argues, these individuals will decide upon the following principles: (1) everyone should have equal opportunities and (2) there can be inequality but only when it benefits all individuals. Laws, if consistent with these principles, would be considered just. For Rawls, a legal positivist, the only thing one can say about human nature is that it is rational and self-interested.

Case Study: Punishment

If someone breaks a law and harms someone else, what should happen? Your perspective on humans, jurisprudence, and law will help determine your response. In a reading within this section, Jeremy Bentham offers a utilitarian perspective. Bentham (1823/1907) argues that justice is promoted by pursuing "utility." Utility is measured by examining the potential "happiness" (+) and unhappiness (i.e., "mischief") (–) created by an act. According to this theory, good laws should increase the total happiness of the community and exclude what subtracts from it. Punishments are mischief; thus, punishment should only occur if it promises to exclude a greater evil. It is interesting to contrast Bentham's 'greatest good for the greatest number' approach with that of Immanuel Kant (1797/2000). Kant argues for retribution where a wrong occurs. Against utilitarianism, and for a priori principles and not a set of feelings, Kant argues for the principle of equality between the crime and the penalty (like for like, murder for murder). In fact, he argues the famous premise that, even if a society is dissolving, it should still kill the last murderer because, if it did not, the bloodguiltiness would remain with the people.

Punishment is more than an abstraction. It occurs every day in the United States, where it is a highly institutionalized, bureaucratic process. We can consider the reality of punishment as it is practiced in the contemporary United States, asking under what conditions (if any) it can be considered just or unjust. A helpful guide in this process is Michel Foucault; a selection of his work is included within this section.

In *Discipline and Punish*, Foucault (1975) describes the development of the prison in Western society. He discusses that acts were once considered punishable when committed against the sovereign (such as a king). Punishment occurred to the body and was a public spectacle (such as hangings, quarterings, and beheadings). Enlightenment thinkers critiqued these methods of punishment and argued for reform. Society changed, as did punishment. Although not promoted by reformers, imprisonment became the preferred method of punishment. The development of prisons occurred alongside other social developments designed to condition individuals to societal norms. Punishable acts became considered as those committed against the public/community and punishment would occur largely behind closed doors, in prisons that focused on correcting the individual and their soul. As opposed to grotesque scenes in public, punishment now functions to condition people to societal norms, not only within the prison, but also within a society. According to Foucault, by promoting societal norms amongst each other, we bring the punitive procedure to the entire society. Those not adhering to societal norms become delinquents. Consequently, a central theme in Foucault's work is the issue of power. To be able to define the good and the bad is power. Therefore, as punishment occurs to condition individuals to societal norms, punishment is connected with power and prisons are mechanisms of power.

While Foucault critically traces the development of prisons and the relationship with power, the work of Angela Davis and Jeffrey Reimen further this discussion to present day. Davis describes a "prison industrial complex" that supports an ever-expanding prison system. The prison industrial complex recognizes the societal, economic, and political conditions that exist and support the use of prisons as punishment. Davis calls for a re-imagining of our system of punishment that does not rely as much as we do on prisons today. Reiman (1998) examines the criminal justice system as a whole. He shows how individuals belonging to a lower economic class or racial minority are hindered in the criminal justice system: for example, they do not have the resources that other groups have to afford private legal defense and the acts they are more likely to be charged with (as compared to other acts such as white collar crime) are punished more harshly.

Foucault, Davis, and Reiman are all critical of the current criminal justice system and punishments. Other critics have suggested alternatives to our system of punishment. If not prisons, then what? If not our current system, then what? These can be very difficult questions to ask ourselves. They require imagining new ways that we may not be familiar with, struggle with, and feel uncomfortable with. They require us to question ourselves, our culture, and our assumptions. Some, like Reimen, offer us positions favoring re-evaluating particular laws, such as drug laws. Perhaps changing our definitions of "crime" will impact the legal process, prisons/jails, and justice. What about punishment? Some, like Angela Davis, suggest that we could reduce our reliance on prisons if we focused more on education. In the last article for this section, Lois Presser (2007) discusses her struggle in thinking of new ways towards justice, new ways to deal with crime. In the end, she favors redefining how we see success in dealing with crime. She argues for restorative justice: a form of justice that emphasizes having a just, humane legal process and focuses on communication and attempts to restore those impacted by criminal activity: victims, perpetrators, and the community. Foucault allows us to see how various historical circumstances and discourse came together to allow punishment to go from quartering and prison, to see jail-time as favorable to quartering. Could we move away from primarily responding to crime with prisons and other techniques of our current criminal system to engaging in new practices to deal with crime? Presser would like us to. The question left to a justice studies student inspired by Foucault's type of theoretical analysis: what circumstances and discourse today may support and/or hinder such a move towards the system favored by Presser?

References

Austin, J. (2001). *The Providence of Jurisprudence Determined.* W.E. Rumble (Ed.). Cambridge: Cambridge University Press. (Originally published 1832).

Crenshaw, K. (1989). Demarginalizing the Intersection of Race and Sex: A Black Feminist Critique of Antidiscrimination Doctrine, Feminist Theory and Antiracist Politics. *Legal Forum*, pp.139–168.

Davis, A. (2003). *Are prisons obsolete?* New York: Seven Stories Press.

Donnelly, J. (2003). *Universal human rights in theory and practice* (2nd ed.). Ithaca: Cornell University Press.

Fitzpatrick, P. & Hunt, A. (1987). Critical legal studies: introduction. In Fitzpatrick, P. & Hunt, A., (Eds.), *Critical legal studies* (pp.1–3). Oxford: Basil Blackwell.

Friedman, L. M. (2002). *Law in America: a short history.* New York: Modern Library.

Kant, I. (2000). "A retributivist theory of punishment," from *The Philosophy of Law* (1797). In Solomon & Murphy (Eds.), *What is justice?: classical and contemporary readings* (pp.221–224). New York: Oxford University Press. (Originally published 1797).

King Jr., M. L. (1963). Letter from a Birmingham Jail. *The Martin Luther King, Jr. Research and Education Institute.* Retrieved from http:mlk-kpp01.standford.edu/index.php/resources/article/annotated_letter_from_birmingham/

MacKinnon, C. A. (1991). Feminism, Marxism, method, and the state: toward feminists jurisprudence. In K. Bartlett & R. Kennedy (Eds.), *Feminist legal theory: readings in law and gender.* Boulder, CO: Westview Press. (Originally published 1983).

Murphy, J. G. & Coleman, J. L. (1990). *Philosophy of law: an introduction to jurisprudence.* Boulder, CO: Westview Press.

Nozick, R. (1974). *Anarchy, state, and utopia.* Malden: Basic Books, Inc.

Rawls, J. (1971). *A theory of justice.* Cambridge, MA: Harvard University Press.

Reimen, J. (1998). *The rich get richer and the poor get prison: ideology, class, and criminal justice.* Boston, MA: Allyn and Bacon.

Rhode, D. (2004). *Access to justice.* Oxford: Oxford University Press.

RACE AND ESSENTIALISM IN FEMINIST LEGAL THEORY

ANGELA P. HARRIS

Bein alive & bein a woman & bein colored is a metaphysical dilemma[1]

—ntozake shange

In an essay, Cynthia Ozick describes a comment she once overheard at a party: "For me, the Holocaust and a corncob are the same."[9] Ozick understands this comment to mean that for a writer, all experience is equal. Literature has no moral content, for it exists purely in the domain of the imagination, a place where only aesthetics matter. Thus, a poet may freely replace the Holocaust with a corncob. Poetic language is only a game of words; the poet need not and in fact should not worry about social responsibility. Literary language is purely self-referential.

Law, however, has not been much tempted by the sound of the first voice. Lawyers are all too aware that legal language is not a purely self-referential game, for "legal interpretive acts signal and occasion the imposition of violence upon others."[10] In their concern to avoid the social and moral irresponsibility of the first voice, legal thinkers have veered in the opposite direction, toward the safety of the second voice, which speaks from the position of "objectivity" rather than "subjectivity," "neutrality" rather than "bias." This voice, like the voice of "We the People," is ultimately authoritarian and coercive in its attempt to speak for everyone.[11]

In both law and literature there are theorists who struggle against their discipline's grain. Literary theorists such as Henry Louis Gates, Jr., Gayatri Spivak, and Abdul JanMohamed are attempting to "read specific verbal and visual texts against complex cultural codes of power, assertion, and domination which these texts both reflect and, indeed, reinforce."[12] Legal theorists such as Mari Matsuda, Pat Williams, and Derrick Bell juxtapose the voice that "allows theorists to discuss liberty, property, and rights in the aspirational mode of liberalism with no connection to what those concepts mean in real people's lives"[13] with the voices of people whose voices are rarely heard in law. In neither law nor literature, however, is the goal merely to replace one voice with its opposite. Rather, the aim is to understand both legal and literary discourse as the complex struggle and unending dialogue between these voices.

The metaphor of "voice" implies a speaker. I want to suggest, however, that both the voices I have described come from the same source, a source I term "multiple consciousness." It is a premise of this article that we are not born with a "self," but rather are composed of a welter of partial, sometimes contradictory, or even antithetical "selves." A unified identity, if such can ever exist, is a product of will, not a common destiny or natural birthright. Thus, consciousness is "never fixed, never attained once and for all";[14] it is not a final outcome or a biological given, but a process, a constant contradictory state of becoming, in which both social institutions and individual wills are deeply implicated. A multiple consciousness is home both to the first and second voices, and all the voices in between.

As I use the phrase, "multiple consciousness" as reflected in legal or literary discourse is not a golden mean or static equilibrium between two extremes, but rather a process in which propositions are constantly put forth, challenged, and subverted. Cynthia Ozick argues that "a redemptive literature, a literature that interprets and decodes the world, beaten out for the sake of humanity, must wrestle with its own body, with its own flesh and blood, with its own life."[15] Similarly, Mari Matsuda, while arguing that in the legal realm "[h]olding on to a multiple consciousness will allow us to operate both within the abstractions of standard jurisprudential discourse, *and* within the details of our own special knowledge,"[16] acknowledges that "this constant shifting of consciousness produces sometimes madness, sometimes genius, sometimes both."[17]

B. Race and Essentialism in Feminist Legal Theory

1. Methodology

In this article, I discuss some of the writings of feminist legal theorist Catharine MacKinnon. I argue that her work, though powerful and brilliant in many ways, relies on what I call gender essentialism—the notion that a unitary, "essential" women's experience can be isolated and described independently of race, class, sexual orientation, and other realities of experience. The result of this tendency toward gender essentialism, I argue, is not only that some voices are silenced in order to privilege others (for this is an inevitable result of categorization, which is necessary both for human communication and political movement), but that the voices that are silenced turn out to be the same voices silenced by the mainstream legal voice of "We the People"—among them, the voices of black women.

This result troubles me for two reasons. First, the obvious one: As a black woman, in my opinion the experience of black women is too often ignored both in feminist theory and in legal theory, and gender essentialism in feminist legal theory does nothing to address this problem. A second and less obvious reason for my criticism of gender essentialism is that, in my view, contemporary legal theory needs less abstraction and not simply a different sort of abstraction. To be fully subversive, the methodology of feminist legal theory should challenge not only law's content but its tendency to privilege the abstract and unitary voice, and this gender essentialism also fails to do.

In accordance with my belief that legal theory, including feminist legal theory, is in need of less abstraction, in this article I destabilize and subvert the unity of MacKinnon's "woman" by introducing the voices of black women, especially as represented in literature. Before I begin, however, I want to make three cautionary points to the reader. First, my argument should not be read to accuse MacKinnon of "racism" in the sense of personal antipathy to black people. MacKinnon is steadfastly anti-racist, which in a sense is my point. Just as law itself, in trying to speak for all persons, ends up silencing those without power, feminist legal theory is in danger of silencing those who have traditionally been kept from speaking, or who have been ignored when they spoke, including black women. The first step toward avoiding this danger is to give up the dream of gender essentialism.

Second, in using a racial critique to attack gender essentialism in feminist legal theory, my aim is not to establish a new essentialism in its place based on the essential experience of black women. Nor should my focus on black women be taken to mean that other women are not silenced either by the mainstream culture or by feminist legal theory. Accordingly, I invite the critique and subversion of my own generalizations.

Third and finally, I do not mean in this article to suggest that either feminism or legal theory should adopt the voice of Funes the Memorious, for whom every experience is unique and no categories or generalizations exist at all. Even a jurisprudence based on multiple consciousness must categorize; without categorization each individual is as isolated as Funes, and there can be no moral responsibility or social change. My suggestion is only that we make our categories explicitly tentative, relational, and unstable, and that to do so is all the more important in a discipline like law, where abstraction and "frozen" categories are the norm. Avoiding gender essentialism need not mean that the Holocaust and a corncob are the same.

2. Feminist Legal Theory

> As a Black lesbian feminist comfortable with the many different ingredients of my identity, and a woman committed to racial and sexual freedom from oppression. I find I am constantly being encouraged to pluck out some one aspect of myself and present this as the meaningful whole, eclipsing or denying the other parts of self.[18]
>
> —Audre Lorde

The need for multiple consciousness in feminist movement—a social movement encompassing law, literature, and everything in between—has long been apparent. Since the beginning of the feminist movement in the United States, black women have been arguing that their experience calls into question the notion of a unitary "women's experience."[19] In the first wave of the feminist movement, black women's[20] realization that the white leaders of the suffrage movement intended to take neither issues of racial oppression nor black women themselves seriously was instrumental in destroying or preventing political alliances between black and white women within the movement.[21] In the second wave, black women are again speaking loudly and persistently,[22] and at many levels our voices have begun to be heard. Feminists have adopted the notion of multiple consciousness as appropriate to describe a world in which people are not oppressed only or primarily on the basis of gender, but on the bases of race, class, sexual orientation, and other categories in inextricable webs.[23] Moreover, multiple consciousness is implicit in the precepts of feminism itself. In Christine Littleton's words, "[f]eminist method starts with the very radical act of taking women seriously, believing that what we say about ourselves and our experience is important and valid, even when (or perhaps especially when) it has little or no relationship to what has been or is being said *about* us."[24] If a unitary "women's experience" or "feminism" must be distilled, feminists must ignore many women's voices.[25]

In feminist legal theory, however, the move away from univocal toward multivocal theories of women's experience and feminism has been slower than in other areas. In feminist legal theory, the pull of the second voice, the voice of abstract categorization, is still powerfully strong: "We the People" seems in danger of being replaced by "We the Women." And in feminist legal theory, as in the dominant culture, it is mostly white, straight, and socioeconomically privileged people who claim to speak for all of us. Not surprisingly, the story they tell about "women," despite its claim to universality, seems to black women to be peculiar to women who are white, straight, and socioeconomically privileged—a phenomenon Adrienne Rich terms "white solipsism."[27]

Elizabeth Spelman Notes:

> [T]he real problem has been how feminist theory has confused the condition of one group of women with the condition of all.
>
> . . . A measure of the depth of white middle-class privilege is that the apparently straightforward and logical points and axioms at the heart of much of feminist theory guarantee the direction of its attention to the concerns of white middle-class women.[28]

The notion that there is a monolithic "women's experience" that can be described independent of other facets of experience like race, class, and sexual orientation is one I refer to in this essay as "gender essentialism."[29] The source of gender and racial essentialism (and all other essentialisms, for the list of categories could be infinitely multiplied) is the second voice, the voice that claims to speak for all. The result of essentialism is to reduce the lives of people who experience multiple forms of oppression to addition problems: "racism + sexism = straight black women's experience," or "racism + sexism + homophobia = black lesbian experience."[30] Thus, in an essentialist world, black women's experience will always be forcibly fragmented before being subjected to analysis, as those who are "only interested in race" and those who are "only interested in gender" take their separate slices of our lives.

Moreover, feminist essentialism paves the way for unconscious racism. Spelman puts it this way:

> [T]hose who produce the "story of woman" want to make sure they appear in it. The best way to ensure that is to be the storyteller and hence to be in a position to decide which of all the many facts about women's lives ought to go into the story, which ought to be left out. Essentialism works well in behalf of these aims, aims that subvert the very process by which women might come to see where and how they wish to make common cause. For essentialism invites me to take what I understand to be true of me "as a woman" for some golden nugget of womanness all women have as women; and it makes the participation of other women inessential to the production of the story. How lovely: the many turn out to be one, and the one that they are is me.[31]

In a racist society like this one, the storytellers are usually white, and so "woman" turns out to be "white woman."

Why, in the face of challenges from "different" women and from feminist method itself, is feminist essentialism so persistent and pervasive? I think the reasons are several. Essentialism is intellectually convenient, and to a certain extent cognitively ingrained. Essentialism also carries with it important emotional and political payoffs. Finally, essentialism often appears (especially to white women) as the only alternative to chaos, mindless pluralism (the Funes trap), and the end of the feminist movement. In my view, however, as long as feminists, like theorists in the dominant culture, continue to search for gender and racial essences, black women will never be anything more than a crossroads between two kinds of domination, or at the bottom of a hierarchy of oppressions; we will always be required to choose pieces of ourselves to present as wholeness. . . .

Modified Women and Unmodified Feminism: Black Women in Dominance Theory

Catharine MacKinnon describes her "dominance theory," like the Marxism with which she likes to compare it, as "total": "[T]hey are both theories of the totality, of the whole thing, theories of a fundamental and critical under-pinning of the whole they envision."[35] Both her dominance theory (which she identifies as simply "feminism") and Marxism "focus on that which is most one's own, that which most makes one the being the theory addresses, as that which is most taken away by what the theory criticizes. In each theory you are made who you are by that which is taken away from you by the social relations the theory criticizes."[36] In Marxism, the "that" is work; in feminism, it is sexuality.

MacKinnon defines sexuality as "that social process which creates, organizes, expresses, and directs desire, creating the social beings we know as women and men, as their relations create society."[37] Moreover, "the organized expropriation of the sexuality of some for the use of others defines the sex, woman. Heterosexuality is its structure, gender and family its congealed forms, sex roles its qualities generalized to social persona, reproduction a consequence, and control its issue."[38] Dominance theory, the analysis of this organized expropriation, is a theory of power and its unequal distribution.

In MacKinnon's view, "[t]he idea of gender difference helps keep the reality of male dominance in place."[39] That is, the concept of gender difference is an ideology which masks the fact that genders are socially constructed, not natural, and coercively enforced, not freely consented-to. Moreover, "the social relation between the sexes is organized so that men may dominate and women must submit and this relation is sexual—in fact, is sex."[40]

For MacKinnon, male dominance is not only "perhaps the most pervasive and tenacious system of power in history, but . . . it is metaphysically nearly perfect."[41] The masculine point of view is point-of-viewlessness; the force of male dominance "is exercised as consent, its authority as participation, its supremacy as the paradigm of order, its control as the definition of legitimacy."[42] In such a world, the very existence of feminism is something of a paradox. "Feminism claims the voice of women's silence, the sexuality of our eroticized desexualization, the fullness of 'lack,' the centrality of our marginality and exclusion, the public nature of privacy, the presence of our absence."[41] The wonder is how feminism can exist in the face of its theoretical impossibility.

In MacKinnon's view, men have their foot on women's necks,[44] regardless of race or class, or of mode of production: "Feminists do not argue that it means the same to women to be on the bottom in a feudal regime, a capitalist regime, and a socialist regime; the commonality argued is that, despite real changes, bottom is bottom."[45] As a political matter, moreover, MacKinnon is quick to insist that there is only one "true," "unmodified" feminism: that which analyzes women *as women*, not as subsets of some other group and not as gender-neutral beings.[46]

Despite its power, MacKinnon's dominance theory is flawed by its essentialism. MacKinnon assumes, as does the dominant culture, that there is an essential "woman" beneath the realities of differences between women[47]—that in describing the experiences of "women" issues of race, class, and sexual orientation can therefore be safely ignored, or relegated to footnotes.[48] In her search for what is essential womanhood, however, MacKinnon rediscovers white womanhood and introduces it as universal truth. In dominance theory, black women are white women, only more so.

Essentialism in feminist theory has two characteristics that ensure that black women's voices will be ignored. First, in the pursuit of the essential feminine, Woman leached of all color and irrelevant social circumstance, issues of race are bracketed as belonging to a separate and distinct discourse—a process which leaves black women's selves fragmented beyond recognition. Second, feminist essentialists find that in removing issues of "race" they have actually only managed to remove black women—meaning that white women now stand as the epitome of Woman. Both processes can be seen at work in dominance theory.

A. Dominance Theory and the Bracketing of Race

MacKinnon repeatedly seems to recognize the inadequacy of theories that deal with gender while ignoring race, but having recognized the problem, she repeatedly shies away from its implications. Thus, she at times justifies her essentialism by pointing to the essentialism of the dominant discourse: "My suggestion is that what we have in common is not that our conditions have no particularity in ways that matter. But we are all measured by a male standard for women, a standard that is not ours."[50] At other times she deals with the challenge of black women by placing it in footnotes.

Finally, MacKinnon postpones the demand of black women until the arrival of a "general theory of social inequality";[53] recognizing that "gender in this country appears partly to comprise the meaning of, as well as bisect, race and class, even as race and class specificities make up, as well as cross-cut, gender,"[54] she nevertheless is prepared to maintain her "colorblind" approach to women's experience until that general theory arrives (presumably that is someone else's work).

B. Dominance Theory and White Women as All Women

The second consequence of feminist essentialism is that the racism that was acknowledged only in brackets quietly emerges in the feminist theory itself—both a cause and an effect of creating "Woman" from white woman. In MacKinnon's work, the result is that black women become white women only more so.

In a passage in *Signs I,* MacKinnon borrows a quote from Toni Cade Bambara describing a black woman with too many children and no means with which to care for them as "grown ugly and dangerous from being nobody for so long," and then explains:

> By using her phrase in altered context, I do not want to distort her meaning but to extend it. Throughout this essay, I have tried to see if women's condition is shared, even when contexts or magnitudes differ. (Thus, it is very different to be "nobody" as a Black woman than as a white lady, but neither is "somebody" by male standards.) This is the approach to race and ethnicity attempted throughout. I aspire to include all women in the term "women" in some way, without violating the particularity of any woman's experience. Whenever this fails, the statement is simply wrong and will have to be qualified or the aspiration (or the theory) abandoned.[66]

I call this the "nuance theory" approach to the problem of essentialism[67]: by being sensitive to the notion that different women have different experiences, generalizations can be offered about "all women" while qualifying statements, often in footnotes, supplement the general account with the subtle nuances of experience that "different" women add to the mix. Nuance theory thus assumes the commonality of all women—differences are a matter of "context" or "magnitude"; that is, nuance.

The problem with nuance theory is that by defining black women as "different," white women quietly become the norm, or pure, essential woman.[68] Just as MacKinnon would argue that being female is more than a "context" or a "magnitude" of human experience,[69] being black is more than a context or magnitude of all (white) women's experience. But not in dominance theory.

MacKinnon's essentialist, "color-blind" approach also distorts the analysis of rape that constitutes the heart of *Signs II.* By ignoring the voices of black female theoreticians of rape, she produces an ahistorical account that fails to capture the experience of black women.

MacKinnon sees sexuality as "a social sphere of male power of which forced sex is paradigmatic."[78] As with beauty standards, black women are victimized by rape just like white women, only more so: "Racism in the United States, by singling out Black men for allegations of rape of white women, has helped obscure the fact that it is men who rape women, disproportionately women of color."[79] In this peculiar fashion MacKinnon simultaneously recognizes and shelves racism, finally reaffirming that the divide between men and women is more fundamental and that women of color are simply "women plus." MacKinnon goes on to develop a powerful analysis of rape as the subordination of women to men, with only one more mention of color: "[R]ape comes to mean a strange (read Black) man knowing a woman does not want sex and going ahead anyway."[80]

This analysis, though rhetorically powerful, is an analysis of what rape means to white women masquerading as a general account; it has nothing to do with the experience of black women.[81] For black women, rape is a far more complex experience, and an experience as deeply rooted in color as in gender.

For example, the paradigm experience of rape for black women has historically involved the white employer in the kitchen or bedroom as much as the strange black man in the bushes. During slavery, the sexual abuse of black women by white men was commonplace.[82] Even after emancipation, the majority of working black women were domestic servants for white families, a job which made them uniquely vulnerable to sexual harassment and rape.[83]

Moreover, as a legal matter, the experience of rape did not even exist for black women. During slavery, the rape of a black woman by any man, white or black, was simply not a crime.[84] Even after the Civil War, rape laws were seldom used to protect black women against either white or black men, since black women were considered promiscuous by nature.[85] In contrast to the partial or at least formal protection white women had against sexual brutalization, black women frequently had no legal protection whatsoever. "Rape," in this sense, was something that only happened to white women; what happened to black women was simply life.

Finally, for black people, male and female, "rape" signified the terrorism of black men by white men, aided and abetted, passively (by silence) or actively (by "crying rape"), by white women. Black women have recognized this aspect of rape since the nineteenth century. For example, social activist Ida B. Wells analyzed rape as an example of the inseparability of race and gender oppression in *Southern Horrors: Lynch Law in All Its Phases,* published in 1892. Wells saw that both the law of rape and Southern miscegenation laws were part of a patriarchal system through which white men maintained their control over the bodies of all black people: "[W]hite men used their ownership of the body of the white female as a terrain on which to lynch the black male."[86] Moreover, Wells argued, though many white women encouraged interracial sexual relationships, white women, protected by the patriarchal idealization of white womanhood, were able to remain silent, unhappily or not, as black men were murdered by mobs.[87] Similarly, Anna Julia Cooper, another nineteenth-century theorist, "saw that the manipulative power of the South was embodied in the southern patriarch, but she describes its concern with 'blood,' inheritance, and heritage in entirely female terms and as a preoccupation that was transmitted from the South to the North and perpetuated by white women."[88]

Nor has this aspect of rape become purely a historical curiosity. Susan Estrich reports that between 1930 and 1967, 89 percent of the men executed for rape in the United States were black;[89] a 1968 study of rape sentencing in Maryland showed that in all 55 cases where the death penalty was imposed the victim had been white, and that between 1960 and 1967, 47 percent of all black men convicted of criminal assaults on black women were immediately released on probation.[90] The case of Joann Little is testimony to the continuing sensitivity of black women to this aspect of rape. As Angela Davis tells the story:

> Brought to trial on murder charges, the young Black woman was accused of killing a white guard in a North Carolina jail where she was the only woman inmate. When Joann Little took the stand, she told how the guard had raped her in her cell and how she had killed him in self-defense with the ice pick he had used to threaten her. Throughout the country, her cause was passionately supported by individuals and organizations in the Black community and within the young women's movement, and her acquittal was hailed as an important victory made possible by this mass campaign. In the immediate aftermath of her acquittal, Ms. Little issued several moving appeals on behalf of a Black man named Delbert Tibbs, who awaited execution in Florida because he had been falsely convicted of raping a white woman.
>
> Many Black women answered Joann Little's appeal to support the cause of Delbert Tibbs. But few white women—and certainly few organized groups within the anti-rape movement—followed her suggestion that they agitate for the freedom of this Black man who had been blatantly victimized by Southern racism.[91]

The rift between white and black women over the issue of rape is highlighted by the contemporary feminist analyses of rape that have explicitly relied on racist ideology to minimize white women's complicity in racial terrorism.[92]

Thus, the experience of rape for black women includes not only a vulnerability to rape and a lack of legal protection radically different from that experienced by white women, but also a unique ambivalence. Black women have simultaneously acknowledged their own victimization and the victimization of black men by a system that has consistently ignored violence against women while perpetrating it against men.[93] The complexity and depth of this experience is not captured, or even acknowledged, by MacKinnon's account.

MacKinnon's essentialist approach recreates the paradigmatic woman in the image of the white woman, in the name of "unmodified feminism." As in the dominant discourse, black women are relegated to the margins, ignored or extolled as "just like us, only more so." But "Black women are not white women with color."[94] Moreover, feminist essentialism represents not just an insult to black women, but a broken promise—the promise to listen to women's stories, the promise of feminist method.

Beyond Essentialism: Black Women and Feminist Theory

> [O]ur future survival is predicated upon our ability to relate within equality. As women, we must root out internalized patterns of oppression within ourselves if we are to move beyond the most superficial aspects of social change. Now we must recognize differences among women who are our equals, neither inferior nor superior, and devise ways to use each others' difference to enrich our visions and our joint struggles.[124]
>
> —Audre Lorde

In this part of the article, I want to talk about what black women can bring to feminist theory to help us move beyond essentialism and toward multiple consciousness as feminist and jurisprudential method. In my view, there are at least three major contributions that black women have to offer post-essentialist feminist theory: the recognition of a self that is multiplicitous, not unitary; the recognition that differences are always relational rather than inherent; and the recognition that wholeness and commonality are acts of will and creativity, rather than passive discovery.

A. The Abandonment of Innocence

Black women experience not a single inner self (much less one that is essentially gendered), but many selves. This sense of a multiplicitous self is not unique to black women, but black women have expressed this sense in ways that are striking, poignant, and potentially useful to feminist theory. bell hooks describes her experience in a creative writing program at a predominantly white college, where she was encouraged to find "her voice," as frustrating to her sense of multiplicity.

> It seemed that many black students found our situations problematic precisely because our sense of self, and by definition our voice, was not unilateral, monologist, or static but rather multi-dimensional. We were as at home in dialect as we were in standard English. Individuals who speak languages other than English, who speak patois as well as standard English, find it a necessary aspect of self-affirmation not to feel compelled to choose one voice over another, not to claim one as more authentic, but rather to construct social realities that celebrate, acknowledge, and affirm differences, variety.[125]

This experience of multiplicity is also a sense of self-contradiction, of containing the oppressor within oneself. In her article *On Being the Object of Property*,[126] Patricia Williams writes about herself writing about her great-great-grandmother, "picking through the ruins for my roots."[127] What she finds is a paradox: She must claim for herself "a heritage the weft of whose genesis is [her] own disinheritance."[128] William's great-great-grandmother, Sophie, was a slave, and at the age of about eleven was impregnated by her owner, a white lawyer named Austin Miller. Their daughter Mary, William's great-grandmother, was taken away from Sophie and raised as a house servant.

When Williams went to law school, her mother told her, "The Millers were lawyers, so you have it in your blood."[129] Williams analyzes this statement as asking her to acknowledge contradictory selves:

> [S]he meant that no one should make me feel inferior because someone else's father was a judge. She wanted me to reclaim that part of my heritage from which I had been disinherited, and she wanted me to use it as a source of strength and self-confidence. At the same time, she was asking me to claim a part of myself that was the dispossessor of another part of myself; she was asking me to deny that disenfranchised little black girl of myself that felt powerless, vulnerable and, moreover, rightly felt so.[130]

The theory of black slavery, Williams notes, was based on the notion that black people are beings without will or personality, defined by "irrationality, lack of control, and ugliness."[131] In contrast, "wisdom, control, and aesthetic beauty signify the whole white personality in slave law."[132] In accepting her white self, her lawyer self, Williams must accept a legacy of not only a disinheritance but a negation of her black self: To the Millers, her forebears, the Williamses, her forebears, did not even have selves as such.

Williams's choice ultimately is not to deny either self, but to recognize them both, and in so doing to acknowledge guilt as well as innocence. She ends the piece by invoking "the presence of polar bears"[133]: bears that mauled a child to death at the Brooklyn Zoo and were subsequently killed themselves, bears judged in public debate as simultaneously "innocent, naturally territorial, unfairly imprisoned, and guilty."[134]

This complex resolution rejects the easy innocence of supposing oneself to be an essential black self with a legacy of oppression by the guilty white Other. With such multilayered analyses, black women can bring to feminist theory stories of how it is to have multiple and contradictory selves, selves that contain the oppressor as well as the oppressed.[135]

B. Strategic Identities and "Difference"

A post-essentialist feminism can benefit not only from the abandonment of the quest for a unitary self, but also from Martha Minow's realization that difference—and therefore identity—is always relational, not inherent.[136] Zora Neale Hurston's work is a good illustration of this notion.

In an essay written for a white audience, *How It Feels to Be Colored Me*,[137] Hurston argues that her color is not an inherent part of her being, but a response to her surroundings. She recalls the day she "became colored"—the day she left her home in an all-black community to go to school: "I left Eatonville, the town of the oleanders, as Zora. When I disembarked from the river-boat at Jacksonville, she was no more. It seemed that I had suffered a sea change. I was not Zora of Orange County any more, I was now a little colored girl."[138] But even as an adult, Hurston insists, her colored self is always situational: "I do not always feel colored. Even now I often achieve the unconscious Zora of Eatonville before the Hegira. I feel most colored when I am thrown against a sharp white background."[139]

Thus, "how it feels to be colored Zora" depends on the answer to these questions: " 'Compared to what? As of when? Who is asking? In what context? For what purpose? With what interests and presuppositions?' What Hurston rigorously shows is that questions of difference and identity are always functions of a specific interlocutory situation—and the answers, matters of strategy rather than truth."[140] Any "essential self" is always an invention; the evil is in denying its artificiality.

To be compatible with this conception of the self, feminist theorizing about "women" must similarly be strategic and contingent, focusing on relationships, not essences. One result will be that men will cease to be a faceless Other and reappear as potential allies in political struggle. Another will be that women will be able to acknowledge their differences without threatening feminism itself. In the process, as feminists begin to attack racism and classism and homophobia, feminism will change from being only about "women as women" (modified women need not apply), to being about all kinds of oppression based on seemingly inherent and unalterable characteristics. We need not wait for a unified theory of oppression; that theory can be feminism.

C. Integrity as Will and Idea

> Because each had discovered years before that they were neither white nor male, and that all freedom and triumph was forbidden to them, they had set about creating something else to be.[131]
>
> —Toni Morrison

Finally, black women can help feminist movement move beyond its fascination with essentialism through the recognition that wholeness of the self and commonality with others are asserted (if never completely achieved) through creative action, not realized in shared victimization. Feminist theory at present, especially feminist legal theory, tends to focus on women as passive victims. For example, for MacKinnon, women have been so objectified by men that the miracle is how they are able to exist at all. Women are the victims, the acted-upon, the helpless, until by radical enlightenment they are somehow empowered to act for themselves.[152]

This story of woman as victim is meant to encourage solidarity by emphasizing women's shared oppression, thus denying or minimizing difference, and to further the notion of an essential woman—she who is victimized. But as bell hooks has succinctly noted, the notion that women's commonality lies in their shared victimization by men "directly reflects male supremacist thinking. Sexist ideology teaches women that to be female is to be a victim."[154] Moreover, the story of woman as passive victim denies the ability of women to shape their own lives, whether for better or worse. It also may thwart their abilities. Like Minnie Bruce Pratt, reluctant to look farther than commonality for fear of jeopardizing the comfort of shared experience, women who rely on their victimization to define themselves may be reluctant to let it go and create their own self-definitions.

At the individual level, black women have had to learn to construct themselves in a society that denied them full selves. Again, Zora Neale Hurston's writings are suggestive. Though Hurston plays with being her "colored self" and again with being "the eternal feminine with its string of beads,"[155] she ends *How It Feels to Be Colored Me* with an image of herself as neither essentially black nor essentially female, but simply

> a brown bag of miscellany propped against a wall. Against a wall in company with other bags, white, red and yellow. Pour out the contents, and there is discovered a jumble of small things priceless and worthless. A first-water diamond, an empty spool, bits of broken glass, lengths of string, a key to a door long since crumbled away, a rusty knife-blade, old shoes saved for a road that never was and never will be, a nail bent under the weight of things too heavy for any nail, a dried flower or two still fragrant. In your hand is the brown bag. On the ground before you is the jumble it held—so much like the jumble in the bags, could they be emptied, that all might be dumped in a single heap

and the bags refilled without altering the content of any greatly. A bit of colored glass more or less would not matter. Perhaps that is how the Great Stuffer of Bags filled them in the first place—who knows?[156]

Hurston thus insists on a conception of identity as a construction, not an essence—something made of fragments of experience, not discovered in one's body or unveiled after male domination is eliminated.

This insistence on the importance of will and creativity seems to threaten feminism at one level, because it gives strength back to the concept of autonomy, making possible the recognition of the element of consent in relations of domination, and attributes to women the power that makes culpable the many ways in which white women have actively used their race privilege against their sisters of color. Although feminists are correct to recognize the powerful force of sheer physical coercion in ensuring compliance with patriarchal hegemony, we must also "come to terms with the ways in which women's culture has served to enlist women's support in perpetuating existing power relations."[160]

However, at another level, the recognition of the role of creativity and will in shaping our lives is liberating, for it allows us to acknowledge and celebrate the creativity and joy with which many women have survived and turned existing relations of domination to their own ends. Works of black literature like *Beloved, The Color Purple,* and *Song of Solomon,* among others, do not linger on black women's victimization and misery; though they recognize our pain, they ultimately celebrate our transcendence.

Finally, on a collective level this emphasis on will and creativity reminds us that bridges between women are built, not found. The discovery of shared suffering is a connection more illusory than real; what will truly bring and keep us together is the use of effort and imagination to root out and examine our differences, for only the recognition of women's differences can ultimately bring feminist movement to strength. This is hard work, and painful work; but it is also radical work, real work. As Barbara Smith has said, "What I really feel is radical is trying to make coalitions with people who are different from you. I feel it is radical to be dealing with race and sex and class and sexual identity all at one time. I think *that* is really radical because it has never been done before."[163]

D. Epilogue: Multiple Consciousness

I have argued in this article that gender essentialism is dangerous to feminist legal theory because in the attempt to extract an essential female self and voice from the diversity of women's experience, the experiences of women perceived as "different" are ignored or treated as variations on the (white) norm. Now I want to return to an earlier point: that legal theory, including feminist legal theory, has been entranced for too long and to too great an extent by the voice of "We the People." In order to energize legal theory, we need to subvert it with narratives and stories, accounts of the particular, the different, and the hitherto silenced.

Whether by chance or not, many of the legal theorists telling stories these days are women of color. Mari Matsuda calls for "multiple consciousness as jurisprudential method";[164] Patricia Williams shows the way with her multilayered stories and meditations.[165] These writings are healthy for feminist legal theory as well as legal theory more generally. In acknowledging "the complexity of messages implied in our being,"[166] they begin the task of energizing legal theory with the creative struggle between Funes and We the People: the creative struggle that reflects a multiple consciousness.

CRITO

PLATO

PERSONS OF THE DIALOGUE:
Socrates, Crito.

SCENE: *The Prison of Socrates.*

SOCRATES: Why have you come at this hour, Crito? it must be quite early?

CRITO: Yes, certainly.

SOCRATES: What is the exact time?

CRITO: The dawn is breaking.

SOCRATES: I wonder that the keeper of the prison would let you in.

CRITO: He knows me, because I often come, Socrates; moreover, I have done him a kindness.

SOCRATES: And are you only just arrived?

CRITO: No, I came some time ago.

SOCRATES: Then why did you sit and say nothing, instead of at once awakening me?

CRITO: I should not have liked myself, Socrates, to be in such great trouble and unrest as you are—indeed I should not: I have been watching with amazement your peaceful slumbers; and for that reason I did not awake you, because I wished to minimize the pain. I have always thought you to be of a happy disposition; but never did I see anything like the easy, tranquil manner in which you bear this calamity.

SOCRATES: Why, Crito, when a man has reached my age he ought not to be repining at the approach of death.

CRITO: And yet other old men find themselves in similar misfortunes, and age does not prevent them from repining.

SOCRATES: That is true. But you have not told me why you come at this early hour.

CRITO: I come to bring you a message which is sad and painful; not, as I believe, to yourself, but to all of us who are your friends, and saddest of all to me.

SOCRATES: What? Has the ship come from Delos, on the arrival of which I am to die?

CRITO: No, the ship has not actually arrived, but she will probably be here to-day, as persons who have come from Sunium tell me that they have left her there; and therefore to-morrow, Socrates, will be the last day of your life.

SOCRATES: Very well, Crito; if such is the will of God, I am willing; but my belief is that there will be a delay of a day.

CRITO: Why do you think so?

SOCRATES: I will tell you. I am to die on the day after the arrival of the ship?

CRITO: Yes; that is what the authorities say.

SOCRATES: But I do not think that the ship will be here until to-morrow; this I infer from a vision which I had last night, or rather only just now, when you fortunately allowed me to sleep.

CRITO: And what was the nature of the vision?

SOCRATES: There appeared to me the likeness of a woman, fair and comely, clothed in bright raiment, who called to me and said: O Socrates,

'The third day hence to fertile Phthia shalt thou go.'[3]

CRITO: What a singular dream, Socrates!

SOCRATES: There can be no doubt about the meaning, Crito, I think.

CRITO: Yes; the meaning is only too clear. But, oh! my beloved Socrates, let me entreat you once more to take my advice and escape. For if you die I shall not only lose a friend who can never be replaced, but there is another evil: people who do not know you and me will believe that I might have saved you if I had been willing to give money, but that I did not care. Now, can there be a worse disgrace than this—that I should be thought to value money more than the life of a friend? For the many will not be persuaded that I wanted you to escape, and that you refused.

SOCRATES: But why, my dear Crito, should we care about the opinion of the many? Good men, and they are the only persons who are worth considering, will think of these things truly as they occurred.

CRITO: But you see, Socrates, that the opinion of the many must be regarded, for what is now happening shows that they can do the greatest evil to anyone who has lost their good opinion.

SOCRATES: I only wish it were so, Crito; and that the many could do the greatest evil; for then they would also be able to do the greatest good—and what a fine thing this would be! But in reality they can do neither; for they cannot make a man either wise or foolish; and whatever they do is the result of chance.

CRITO: Well, I will not dispute with you; but please to tell me, Socrates, whether you are not acting out of regard to me and your other friends: are you not afraid that if you escape from prison we may get into trouble with the informers for having stolen you away, and lose either the whole or a great part of our property; or that even a worse evil may happen to us? Now, if you fear on our account, be at ease; for in order to save you, we ought surely to run this, or even a greater risk; be persuaded, then, and do as I say.

SOCRATES: Yes, Crito, that is one fear which you mention, but by no means the only one.

CRITO: Fear not—there are persons who are willing to get you out of prison at no great cost; and as for the informers, they are far from being exorbitant in their demands—a little money will satisfy them. My means, which are certainly ample, are at your service, and if you have a scruple about spending all mine, here are strangers who will give you the use of theirs; and one of them, Simmias the Theban, has brought a large sum of money for this very purpose; and Cebes and many others are prepared to spend their money in helping you to escape. I say, therefore, do not hesitate on our account, and do not say, as you did in the court[4] that you will have a difficulty in knowing what to do with yourself anywhere else. For men will love you in other places to which you may go, and not in Athens only; there are friends of mine in Thessaly, if you like to go to them, who will value and protect you, and no Thessalian will give you any trouble. Nor can I think that you are at all justified, Socrates, in betraying your own life when you might be saved; in acting thus you are playing into the hands of your enemies, who are hurrying on your destruction. And further I should say that you are deserting your own children; for you might bring them up and educate them; instead of which you go away and leave them, and they will have to take their chance; and if they do not meet with the usual fate of orphans, there will be small thanks to you. No man should bring children into the world who is unwilling to persevere to the end in their nurture and education. But you appear to be choosing the easier part, not the better and manlier, which would have been more becoming in one who professes to care for virtue in all his actions, like yourself. And indeed, I am ashamed not only of you, but of us who are your friends, when I reflect that the whole business will be attributed entirely to our want of courage. The trial need never have come on, or might have been managed differently; and this last act, or crowning folly, will seem to have occurred through our negligence and cowardice, who might have saved you, if we had been good for anything; and you might have saved yourself, for there was no difficulty at all. See now, Socrates, how sad and discreditable are the consequences, both to us and you. Make up your mind then, or rather have your mind already made up, for the time of deliberation is over, and there is only one thing to be done, which must be done this very night, and, if we delay at all, will be no longer practicable or possible; I beseech you therefore, Socrates, be persuaded by me, and do as I say.

SOCRATES: Dear Crito, your zeal is invaluable, if a right one; but if wrong, the greater the zeal the greater the danger; and therefore we ought to consider whether I shall or shall not do as you say. For I am and always have been one of those natures who must be guided by reason, whatever the reason may be which upon reflection appears to me to be the best; and now that this chance has befallen me, I cannot repudiate my own words: the principles which I have hitherto honoured and revered I still honour, and unless we can at once find other and better principles, I am certain not to agree with you; no, not even if the power of the multitude could inflict many more imprisonments, confiscations, deaths, frightening us like children with hobgoblin terrors.[5] What will be the fairest way of considering the question? Shall I return to your old argument about the opinions of men?—we were saying that some of them are to be regarded, and others not. Now were we right in maintaining this before I was condemned? And has the argument which was once good now proved to be talk for the sake of talking—mere childish nonsense? That is what I want to consider with your help, Crito:—whether, under my present circumstances, the argument appears to be in any way different or not; and is to be allowed by me or disallowed. That argument, which, as I believe, is maintained by many persons of authority, was to the effect, as I was saying, that the opinions of some men are to be regarded, and of other men not to be regarded. Now you, Crito, are not going to die to-morrow—at least, there is no human probability of this—and therefore you are disinterested and not liable to be deceived by the circumstances in which you are placed. Tell me then, whether I am right in saying that some opinions, and the opinions of some men only, are to be valued, and that other opinions, and the opinions of other men, are not to be valued. I ask you whether I was right in maintaining this?

CRITO: Certainly.

SOCRATES: The good are to be regarded, and not the bad?

CRITO: Yes.

SOCRATES: And the opinions of the wise are good, and the opinions of the unwise are evil?

CRITO: Certainly.

SOCRATES: And what was said about another matter? Is the pupil who devotes himself to the practice of gymnastics supposed to attend to the praise and blame and opinion of every man, or of one man only—his physician or trainer, whoever he may be?

CRITO: Of one man only.

SOCRATES: And he ought to fear the censure and welcome the praise of that one only, and not of the many?

CRITO: Clearly so.

SOCRATES: And he ought to act and train, and eat and drink in the way which seems good to his single master who has understanding, rather than according to the opinion of all other men put together?

CRITO: True.

SOCRATES: And if he disobeys and disregards the opinion and approval of the one, and regards the opinion of the many who have no understanding, will he not suffer evil?

CRITO: Certainly he will.

SOCRATES: And what will the evil be, whither tending and what affecting, in the disobedient person?

CRITO: Clearly, affecting the body; that is what is destroyed by the evil.

SOCRATES: Very good; and is not this true, Crito, of other things which we need not separately enumerate? In questions of just and unjust, fair and foul, good and evil, which are the subjects of our present consultation, ought we to follow the opinion of the many and to fear them; or the opinion of the one man who has understanding? ought we not to fear and reverence him more than all the rest of the world: and if we desert him shall we not destroy and injure that principle in us which may be assumed to be improved by justice and deteriorated by injustice—there is such a principle?

CRITO: Certainly there is, Socrates.

SOCRATES: Take a parallel instance:—if, acting under the advice of those who have no understanding, we destroy that which is improved by health and is deteriorated by disease, would life be worth having? And that which has been destroyed is—the body?

CRITO: Yes.

SOCRATES: Could we live, having an evil and corrupted body?

CRITO: Certainly not.

SOCRATES: And will life be worth having, if that higher part of man be destroyed, which is improved by justice and depraved by injustice? Do we suppose that principle, whatever it may be in man, which has to do with justice and injustice, to be inferior to the body?

CRITO: Certainly not.

SOCRATES: More honourable than the body?

CRITO: Far more.

SOCRATES: Then, my friend, we must not regard what the many say of us; but what he, the one man who has understanding of just and unjust, will say, and what the truth will say. And therefore you begin in error when you advise that we should regard the opinion of the many about just and unjust, good and evil, honourable and dishonourable.—'Well,' someone will say, 'but the many can kill us.'

CRITO: Yes, Socrates; that will clearly be the answer.

SOCRATES: And it is true; but still I find with surprise that the old argument is unshaken as ever. And I should like to know whether I may say the same of another proposition—that not life, but a good life, is to be chiefly valued?

CRITO: Yes, that also remains unshaken.

SOCRATES: And a good life is equivalent to a just and honourable one—that holds also?

CRITO: Yes, it does.

SOCRATES: From these premises I proceed to argue the question whether I ought or ought not to try and escape without the consent of the Athenians: and if I am clearly right in escaping, then I will make the attempt; but if not, I will abstain. The other considerations which you mention, of money and loss of character and the duty of educating one's children, are, I fear, only the doctrines of the multitude, who would be as ready to restore people to life, if they were able, as they are to put them to death— and with as little reason. But now, since the argument has thus far prevailed, the only question which remains to be considered is whether we shall do rightly either in escaping or in suffering others to aid in our escape and paying them in money and thanks, or whether in reality we shall not do rightly; and if the latter, then death or any other calamity which may ensue on my remaining here must not be allowed to enter into the calculation.

CRITO: I think that you are right, Socrates; how then shall we proceed?

SOCRATES: Let us consider the matter together, and do you either refute me if you can, and I will be convinced; or else cease, my dear friend, from repeating to me that I ought to escape against the wishes of the Athenians: for I highly value your attempts to persuade me to do so, but I may not be persuaded against my own better judgment. And now please to consider my first position, and try how you can best answer me.

CRITO: I will.

SOCRATES: Are we to say that we are never intentionally to do wrong, or that in one way we ought and in another way we ought not to do wrong, or is doing wrong always evil and dishonourable, as I was just now saying, and as has been already acknowledged by us? Are all our former admissions which were made within a few days to be thrown away? And have we, at our age, been earnestly discoursing with one another all our life long only to discover that we are no better than children? Or, in spite of the opinion of the many, and in spite of consequences whether better or worse, shall we insist on the truth of what was then said, that injustice is always an evil and dishonour to him who acts unjustly? Shall we say so or not?

CRITO: Yes.

SOCRATES: Then we must do no wrong?

CRITO: Certainly not.

SOCRATES: Nor, when injured, injure in return, as the many imagine; for we must injure no one at all?[6]

CRITO: Clearly not.

SOCRATES: Again, Crito, may we do evil?

CRITO: Surely not, Socrates.

SOCRATES: And what of doing evil in return for evil, which is the morality of the many—is that just or not?

CRITO: Not just.

SOCRATES: For doing evil to another is the same as injuring him?

CRITO: Very true.

SOCRATES: Then we ought not to retaliate or render evil for evil to anyone, whatever evil we may have suffered from him. But I would have you consider, Crito, whether you really mean what you are saying. For this opinion has never been held, and never will be held, by any considerable number of persons; and those who are agreed and those who are not agreed upon this point have no common ground, and can only despise one another when they see how widely they differ. Tell me, then, whether you agree with and assent to my first principle, that neither injury nor retaliation nor warding off evil by evil is ever right. And shall that be the premise of our argument? Or do you decline and dissent from this? For so I have ever thought, and continue to think; but, if you are of another opinion, let me hear what you have to say. If, however, you remain of the same mind as formerly, I will proceed to the next step.

CRITO: You may proceed, for I have not changed my mind.

SOCRATES: Then I will go on to the next point, which may be put in the form of a question:—Ought a man to do what he admits to be right, or ought he to betray the right?

CRITO: He ought to do what he thinks right.

SOCRATES: But if this is true, what is the application? In leaving the prison against the will of the Athenians, do I wrong any? or rather do I not wrong those whom I ought least to wrong? Do I not desert the principles which were acknowledged by us to be just—what do you say?

CRITO: I cannot tell, Socrates; for I do not know.

SOCRATES: Then consider the matter in this way:—Imagine that I am about to play truant (you may call the proceeding by any name which you like), and the laws and the government come and interrogate me: 'Tell us, Socrates,' they say; 'what are you about? are you not going by an act of yours to overturn us—the laws, and the whole state, as far as in you lies? Do you imagine that a state can subsist and not be overthrown, in which the decisions of law have no power, but are set aside and trampled upon by individuals?' What will be our answer, Crito, to these and the like words? Anyone, and especially a rhetorician, will have a good deal to say on behalf of the law which requires a sentence to be carried out. He will argue that this law should not be set aside; and shall we reply, 'Yes; but the state has injured us and given an unjust sentence.' Suppose I say that?

CRITO: Very good, Socrates.

SOCRATES: 'And was that our agreement with you?' the law would answer; 'or were you to abide by the sentence of the state?' And if I were to express my astonishment at their words, the law would probably add: 'Answer, Socrates, instead of opening your eyes—you are in the habit of asking and answering questions. Tell us,—What complaint have you to make against us which justifies you in attempting to destroy us and the state? In the first place did we not bring you into existence? Your father married your mother by our aid and begat you. Say whether you have any objection to urge against those of us who regulate marriage?' None, I should reply. 'Or against those of us who after birth regulate the nurture and education of children, in which you also were trained? Were not the laws, which have the charge of education, right in commanding your father to train you in music and gymnastic?' Right, I should reply.

'Well then, since you were brought into the world and nurtured and educated by us, can you deny in the first place that you are our child and slave, as your fathers were before you? And if this is true you are not on equal terms with us; nor can you think that you have a right to do to us what we are doing to you. Would you have any right to strike or revile or do any other evil to your father or your master, if you had one, because you have been struck or reviled by him, or received some other evil at his hands? You would not say this. And because we think right to destroy you, do you think that you have any right to destroy us in return, and your country as far as in you lies? Will you, O professor of true virtue, pretend that you are justified in this? Has a philosopher like you failed to discover that our country is more to be valued and higher and holier far than mother or father or any ancestor, and more to be regarded in the eyes of the gods and of men of understanding? also to be soothed, and gently and reverently entreated when angry, even more than a father, and either to be persuaded, or if not persuaded, to be obeyed? And when we are punished by her, whether with imprisonment or stripes, the punishment is to be endured in silence; and if she lead us to wounds or death in battle, thither we follow as is right; neither may any-one yield or retreat or leave his rank, but whether in battle or in a court of law, or in any other place, he must do what his city and his country order him; or he must change their view of what is just: and if he may do no violence to his father or mother, much less may he do violence to his country.' What answer shall we make to this, Crito? Do the laws speak truly, or do they not?

CRITO: I think that they do.

SOCRATES: Then the laws will say: 'Consider, Socrates, if we are speaking truly that in your pres-ent attempt you are going to do us an injury. For, having brought you into the world, and nurtured and educated you, and given you and every other citizen a share in every good which we had to give, we further proclaim to any Athenian by the liberty which we allow him, that if he does not like us when he has become of age and has seen the ways of the city, and made our acquaintance, he may go where he pleases and take his goods with him. None of us laws will forbid him or interfere with him. Anyone who does not like us and the city, and who wants to emigrate to a colony or to any other city, may go where he likes, retaining his property. But he who has experience of the manner in which we order justice and administer the state, and still remains, has entered into an implied contract that he will do as we command him. And he who disobeys us is, as we maintain, thrice wrong; first, because in disobeying us he is disobeying his parents; secondly, because we are the authors of his education; thirdly, because he has made an agreement with us that he will duly obey our commands; and he neither obeys them nor convinces us that our commands are unjust; and we do not rudely impose them, but give him the alternative of obeying or convincing us;—that is what we offer, and he does neither. These are the sort of accusations to which, as we were saying, you, Socrates, will be exposed if you accomplish your inten-tions; you, above all other Athenians.'

Suppose now I ask, why I rather than anybody else? they will justly retort upon me that I above all other men have acknowledged the agreement. 'There is clear proof,' they will say, 'Socrates, that we and the city were not displeasing to you. Of all Athenians you have been the most constant resident in the city, which, as you never leave, you may be supposed to love.[7] For you never went out of the city either to see the games, except once when you went to the Isthmus, or to any other place unless when you were on military service; nor did you travel as other men do. Nor had you any curiosity to know other states or their laws: your affections did not go beyond us and our state; we were your especial favourites, and you acquiesced in our government of you; and here in this city you begat your children, which is a proof of your satisfaction. Moreover, you might in the course of the trial, if you had liked, have fixed the penalty at banishment; the state which refuses to let you go now would have let you go then. But you pretended that you preferred death to exile,[8] and that you were not unwilling to die. And now you have forgotten these fine sentiments, and pay no respect to us the laws, of whom you are the destroyer; and are doing what only a miserable slave would do, running away and turning your back upon the compacts and agreements which you made as a citizen. And first of all answer this very question: Are we right in saying that you agreed to be governed according to us in deed, and not in word only? Is that true or not?' How shall we answer, Crito? Must we not assent?

CRITO: We cannot help it, Socrates.

SOCRATES: Then will they not say: 'You, Socrates, are breaking the covenants and agreements which you made with us at your leisure, not in any haste or under any compulsion or deception, but after you have had seventy years to think of them, during which time you were at liberty to leave the city, if we were not to your mind, or if our covenants appeared to you to be unfair. You had your choice, and might have gone either to Lacedaemon or Crete, both which states are often praised by you for their good government, or to some other Hellenic or foreign state. Whereas you, above all other Athenians, seemed to be so fond of the state, or, in other words, of us, her laws (and who would care about a state which has no laws?), that you never stirred out of her; the halt, the blind, the maimed were not more stationary in her than you were. And now you run away and forsake your agreements. Not so, Socrates, if you will take our advice; do not make yourself ridiculous by escaping out of the city.

'For just consider, if you transgress and err in this sort of way, what good will you do either to yourself or to your friends? That your friends will be driven into exile and deprived of citizenship, or will lose their property, is tolerably certain; and you yourself, if you fly to one of the neighbouring cities, as, for example, Thebes or Megara, both of which are well governed, will come to them as an enemy, Socrates, and their government will be against you, and all patriotic citizens will cast an evil eye upon you as a subverter of the laws, and you will confirm in the minds of the judges the justice of their own condemnation of you. For he who is a corrupter of the laws is more than likely to be a corrupter of the young and foolish portion of mankind. Will you then flee from well-ordered cities and virtuous men? and is existence worth having on these terms? Or will you go to them without shame, and talk to them, Socrates? And what will you say to them? What you say here about virtue and justice and institutions and laws being the best things among men? Would that be decent of you? Surely not. But if you go away from well-governed states to Crito's friends in Thessaly, where there is great disorder and licence, they will be charmed to hear the tale of your escape from prison, set off with ludicrous particulars of the manner in which you were wrapped in a goatskin or some other disguise, and metamorphosed as the manner is of runaways; but will there be no one to remind you that in your old age you were not ashamed to violate the most sacred laws from a miserable desire of a little more life? Perhaps not, if you keep them in a good temper; but if they are out of temper you will hear many degrading things; you will live, but how?—as the flatterer of all men, and the servant of all men; and doing what?—eating and drinking in Thessaly, having gone abroad in order that you may get a dinner. And where will be your fine sentiments about justice and virtue? Say that you wish to live for the sake of your children—you want to bring them up and educate them—will you take them into Thessaly and deprive them of Athenian citizenship? Is this the benefit which you will confer upon them? Or are you under the impression that they will be better cared for and educated here if you are still alive, although absent from them; for your friends will take care of them? Do you fancy that if you are an inhabitant of Thessaly they will take care of them, and if you are an inhabitant of the other world that they will not take care of them? Nay; but if they who call themselves friends are good for anything, they will—to be sure they will.

'Listen, then, Socrates, to us who have brought you up. Think not of life and children first, and of justice afterwards, but of justice first, that you may be justified before the princes of the world below. For neither will you nor any that belong to you be happier or holier or juster in this life, or happier in another, if you do as Crito bids. Now you depart in innocence, a sufferer and not a doer of evil; a victim, not of the laws, but of men. But if you go forth, returning evil for evil, and injury for injury, breaking the covenants and agreements which you have made with us, and wronging those whom you ought least of all to wrong, that is to say, yourself, your friends, your country, and us, we shall be angry with you while you live, and our brethren, the laws in the world below, will receive you as an enemy; for they will know that you have done your best to destroy us. Listen, then, to us and not to Crito.'

This, dear Crito, is the voice which I seem to hear murmuring in my ears, like the sound of the flute in the ears of the mystic; that voice, I say, is humming in my ears, and prevents me from hearing any other. And I know that anything more which you may say will be vain. Yet speak, if you have anything to say.

CRITO: I have nothing to say, Socrates.

SOCRATES: Leave me then, Crito, to fulfil the will of God, and to follow whither he leads.

AN INTRODUCTION

TO THE

PRINCIPLES OF MORALS AND LEGISLATION

JEREMY BENTHAM

Chapter I

Of The Principle Of Utility

1. Nature has placed mankind under the governance of two sovereign masters, *pain* and *pleasure*. It is for them alone to point out what we ought to do, as well as to determine what we shall do. On the one hand the standard of right and wrong, on the other the chain of causes and effects, are fastened to their throne. They govern us in all we do, in all we say, in all we think: every effort we can make to throw off our subjection, will serve but to demonstrate and confirm it. In words a man may pretend to abjure their empire : but in reality he will remain subject to it all the while. The *principle of utility*[1] recognises this subjection, and assumes it for the foundation of that system, the object of which is to rear the fabric of felicity by the hands of reason and of law. Systems which attempt to question it, deal in sounds instead of sense, in caprice instead of reason, in darkness instead of light.

But enough of metaphor and declamation: it is not by such means that moral science is to be improved.

II. The principle of utility is the foundation of the presen work: it will be proper therefore at the outset to give an explicit and determinate account of what is meant by it. By the principle[1] of utility is meant that principle which approves or disapproves of every action whatsoever, according to the tendency which it appears to have to augment or diminish the happiness of the party whose interest is in question: or, what is the same thing in other words, to promote or to oppose that happiness. I say of every action whatsoever; and therefore not only of every action of a private individual, but of every measure of government.

III. By utility is meant that property in any object, whereby it tends to produce benefit, advantage, pleasure, good, or happiness, (all this in the present case comes to the same thing) or (what comes again to the same thing) to prevent the happening of mischief, pain, evil, or unhappiness to the party whose interest is considered: if that party be the community in general, then the happiness of the community: if a particular individual, then the happiness of that individual.

IV. The interest of the community is one of the most general expressions that can occur in the phraseology of morals: no wonder that the meaning of it is often lost. When it has a meaning, it is this. The community is a fictitious *body*, composed of the individual persons who are considered as constituting as it were its *members*. The interest of the community then is, what?—the sum of the interests of the several members who compose it.

V. It is in vain to talk of the interest of the community, without understanding what is the interest of the individual[1]. A thing is said to promote the interest, or to be *for* the interest, of an individual, when it tends to add to the sum total of his pleasures: or, what comes to the same thing, to diminish the sum total of his pains.

VI. An action then may be said to be conformable to the principle of utility, or, for shortness sake, to utility, (meaning with respect to the community at large) when the tendency it has to augment the happiness of the community is greater than any it has to diminish it.

VII. A measure of government (which is but a particular kind of action, performed by a particular person or persons) may be said to be conformable to or dictated by the principle of utility, when in like manner the tendency which it has to augment the happiness of the community is greater than any which it has to diminish it.

VIII. When an action, or in particular a measure of government, is supposed by a man to be conformable to the principle of utility, it may be convenient, for the purposes of discourse, to imagine a kind of law or dictate, called a law or dictate of utility: and to speak of the action in question, as being conformable to such law or dictate.

IX. A man may be said to be a partizan of the principle of utility, when the approbation or disapprobation he annexes to any action, or to any measure, is determined by and proportioned to the tendency which he conceives it to have to augment or to diminish the happiness of the community: or in other words, to its conformity or unconformity to the laws or dictates of utility.

X. Of an action that is conformable to the principle of utility one may always say either that it is one that ought to be done, or at least that it is not one that ought not to be done. One may say also, that it is right it should be done; at least that it is not wrong it should be done: that it is a right action; at least that it is not a wrong action. When thus interpreted, the words *ought*, and *right* and *wrong*, and others of that stamp, have a meaning: when otherwise, they have none.

Chapter XIII

Cases Unmeet For Punishment

§ I. General view of cases unmeet for punishment

I. The general object which all laws have, or ought to have, in common, is to augment the total happiness of the community; and therefore, in the first place, to exclude, as far as may be, every thing that tends to subtract from that happiness: in other words, to exclude mischief.

II. But all punishment is mischief: all punishment in itself is evil. Upon the principle of utility, if it ought at all to be admitted, it ought only to be admitted in as far as it promises to exclude some greater evil[1].

III. It is plain, therefore, that in the following cases punishment ought not to be inflicted.

1. Where it is *groundless:* where there is no mischief for it to prevent; the act not being mischievous upon the whole.
2. Where it must be *inefficacious:* where it cannot act so as to prevent the mischief.
3. Where it is *unprofitable*, or too *expensive:* where the mischief it would produce would be greater than what it prevented.
4. Where it is *needless:* where the mischief may be prevented, or cease of itself, without it: that is, at a cheaper rate.

§ 2. Cases in which punishment is groundless

These are,

IV. I. Where there has never been any mischief: where no mischief has been produced to any body by the act in question. Of this number are those in which the act was such as might, on some occasions, be mischievous or disagreeable, but the person whose interest it concerns gave his *consent* to the performance of it[1]. This consent, provided it be free, and fairly obtained[1], is the best proof that can be produced, that, to the person who gives it, no mischief, at least no immediate mischief, upon the whole, is done. For no man can be so good a judge as the man himself, what it is gives him pleasure or displeasure.

V. 2. Where the mischief was *outweighed:* although a mischief was produced by that act, yet the same act was necessary to the production of a benefit which was of greater value[1] than the mischief. This may be the case with any thing that is done in the way of precaution against instant calamity, as also with any thing that is done in the exercise of the several sorts of powers necessary to be established in every community, to wit, domestic, judicial, military, and supreme[2].

VI. 3. Where there is a certainty of an adequate compensation: and that in all cases where the offence can be committed. This supposes two things: 1. That the offence is such as admits of an adequate compensation: 2. That such a compensation is sure to be forthcoming. Of these suppositions, the latter will be found to be a merely ideal one: a supposition that cannot, in the universality here given to it, be verified by fact. It cannot, therefore, in practice, be numbered amongst the grounds of absolute impunity. It may, however, be admitted as a ground for an abatement of that punishment, which other considerations, standing by themselves, would seem to dictate[3].

§ 3. Cases in which punishment must be inefficacious

These are,

VII. 1. Where the penal provision is *not established* until after the act is done. Such are the cases, 1. Of an *ex-post-facto* law; where the legislator himself appoints not a punishment till after the act is done. 2. Of a sentence beyond the law; where the judge, of his own authority, appoints a punishment which the legislator had not appointed.

VIII. 2. Where the penal provision, though established, is *not conveyed* to the notice of the person on whom it seems intended that it should operate. Such is the case where the law has omitted to employ any of the expedients which are necessary, to make sure that every person whatsoever, who is within the reach of the law, be apprized of all the cases whatsoever, in which (being in the station of life he is in) he can be subjected to the penalties of the law[1].

IX. 3. Where the penal provision, though it were conveyed to a man's notice, *could produce no effect* on him, with respect to the preventing him from engaging in any act of the *sort* in question. Such is the case, 1. In extreme *infancy;* where a man has not yet attained that state or disposition of mind in which the prospect of evils so distant as those which are held forth by the law, has the effect of influencing his conduct. 2. In *insanity;* where the person, if he has attained to that disposition, has since been deprived of it through the influence of some permanent though unseen cause. 3. In *intoxication;* where he has been deprived of it by the transient influence of a visible cause: such as the use of wine, or opium, or other drugs, that act in this manner on the nervous system: which condition is indeed neither more nor less than a temporary insanity produced by an assignable cause[2].

X. 4. Where the penal provision (although, being conveyed to the party's notice, it might very well prevent his engaging in acts of the sort in question, provided he knew that it related to those acts) could not have this effect, with regard to the *individual* act he is about to engage in: to wit, because he knows not that it is of the number of those to which the penal provision relates. This may happen, I. In the case of *unintentionality*; where he intends not to engage, and thereby knows not that he is about to engage, in the *act* in which eventually he is about to engage[1]. 2. In the case of *unconsciousness;* where, although he may know that he is about to engage in the *act* itself, yet, from not knowing all the material *circumstances* attending it, he knows not of the *tendency* it has to produce that mischief, in contemplation of which it has been made penal in most instances. 3. In the case of *missupposal;* where, although he may know of the tendency the act has to produce that degree of mischief, he supposes it, though mistakenly, to be attended with some circumstance, or set of circumstances, which, if it had been attended with, it would either not have been productive of that mischief, or have been productive of such a greater degree of good, as has determined the legislator in such a case not to make it penal[2].

XI. 5. Where, though the penal clause might exercise a full and prevailing influence, were it to act alone, yet by the *predominant* influence of some opposite cause upon the will, it must necessarily be ineffectual; because the evil which he sets himself about to undergo, in the case of his *not* engaging in the act, is so great, that the evil denounced by the penal clause, in case of his engaging in it, cannot appear greater. This may happen, 1. In the case of *physical danger;* where the evil is such as appears likely to be brought about by the unassisted powers of *nature.* 2. In the case of a *threatened mischief;* where it is such as appears likely to be brought about through the intentional and conscious agency of *man*[1].

XII. 6. Where (though the penal clause may exert a full and prevailing influence over the *will* of the party) yet his *physical faculties* (owing to the predominant influence of some physical cause) are not in a condition to follow the determination of the will: insomuch that the act is absolutely *involuntary.* Such is the case of physical *compulsion* or *restraint,* by whatever means brought about; where the man's hand, for instance, is pushed against some object which his will disposes him *not* to touch; or tied down from touching some object which his will disposes him to touch.

§ 4. Cases where punishment is unprofitable

These are,

XIII. 1. Where, on the one hand, the nature of the offence, on the other hand, that of the punishment, are, *in the ordinary state of things,* such, that when compared together, the evil of the latter will turn out to be greater than that of the former.

XIV. Now the evil of the punishment divides itself into four branches, by which so many different sets of persons are affected. 1. The evil of *coercion* or *restraint:* or the pain which it gives a man not to be able to do the act, whatever it be, which by the apprehension of the punishment he is deterred from doing. This is felt by those by whom the law is *observed.* 2. The evil of *apprehension:* or the pain which a man, who has exposed himself to punishment, feels at the thoughts of undergoing it. This is felt by those by whom the law has been *broken*, and who feel themselves in *danger* of its being executed upon them. 3. The evil of *sufferance*[1]: or the pain which a man feels, in virtue of the punishment itself, from the time when he begins to undergo it. This is felt by those by whom the law is broken, and upon whom it comes actually to be executed. 4. The pain of sympathy, and the other *derivative* evils resulting to the persons who are in *connection* with the several classes of original sufferers just mentioned[2]. Now of these four lots of evil, the first will be greater or less, according to the nature of the act from which the party is restrained: the second and third according to the nature of the punishment which stands annexed to that offence.

XV. On the other hand, as to the evil of the offence, this will also, of course, be greater or less, according to the nature of each offence. The proportion between the one evil and the other will therefore be different in the case of each particular offence. The cases, therefore, where punishment is unprofitable on this ground, can by no other means be discovered, than by an examination of each particular offence; which is what will be the business of the body of the work.

XVI. 2. Where, although in the *ordinary state* of things, the evil resulting from the punishment is not greater than the benefit which is likely to result from the force with which it operates, during the same space of time, towards the excluding the evil of the offences, yet it may have been rendered so by the influence of some *occasional circumstances.* In the number of these circumstances may be, 1. The multitude of delinquents at a particular juncture; being such as would increase, beyond the ordinary measure, the *quantum* of the second and third lots, and thereby also of a part of the fourth lot, in the evil of the punishment. 2. The extraordinary value of the services of some one delinquent; in the case where the effect of the punishment would be to deprive the community of the benefit of those services. 3. The displeasure of the *people;* that is, of an indefinite number of the members of the *same* community, in cases where (owing to the influence of some occasional incident) they happen to conceive, that the offence or the offender ought not to be punished at all, or at least ought not to be punished in the way in question. 4. The displeasure of *foreign powers;* that is, of the governing body, or a considerable number of the members of some *foreign* community or communities, with which the community in question is connected.

§ 5. Cases where punishment is needless

These are,

XVII. 1. Where the purpose of putting an end to the practice may be attained as effectually at a cheaper rate: by instruction, for instance, as well as by terror: by informing the understanding, as well as by exercising an immediate influence on the will. This seems to be the case with respect to all those offences which consist in the disseminating pernicious principles in matters of *duty;* of whatever kind the duty be; whether political, or moral, or religious. And this, whether such principles be disseminated *under,* or even *without,* a sincere persuasion of their being beneficial. I say, even *without:* for though in such a case it is not instruction that can prevent the writer from endeavouring to inculcate his principles, yet it may the readers from adopting them: without which, his endeavouring to inculcate them will do no harm. In such a case, the sovereign will commonly have little need to take an active part: if it be the interest of *one* individual to inculcate principles that are pernicious, it will as surely be the interest of *other* individuals to expose them. But if the sovereign must needs take a part in the controversy, the pen is the proper weapon to combat error with, not the sword.

Chapter XIV

Of The Proportion Between Punishments And Offences

I. We have seen that the general object of all laws is to prevent mischief; that is to say, when it is worth while; but that, where there are no other means of doing this than punishment, there are four cases in which it is *not* worth while.

II. When it *is* worth while, there are four subordinate designs or objects, which, in the course of his endeavours to compass, as far as may be, that one general object, a legislator, whose views are governed by the principle of utility, comes naturally to propose to himself.

III. 1. His first, most extensive, and most eligible object, is to prevent, in as far as it is possible, and worth while, all sorts of offences whatsoever[1]: in other words, so to manage, that no offence whatsoever may be committed.

IV. 2. But if a man must needs commit an offence of some kind or other, the next object is to induce him to commit an offence *less* mischievous, *rather* than one *more* mischievous: in other words, to choose always the *least* mischievous, of two offences that will either of them suit his purpose.

V. 3. When a man has resolved upon a particular offence, the next object is to dispose him to do *no more* mischief than is *necessary* to his purpose: in other words, to do as little mischief as is consistent with the benefit he has in view.

VI. 4. The last object is, whatever the mischief be, which it is proposed to prevent, to prevent it at as *cheap* a rate as possible.

VII. Subservient to these four objects, or purposes, must be the rules or canons by which the proportion of punishments[1] to offences is to be governed.

DISCIPLINE AND PUNISH

MICHEL FOUCAULT

1. The body of the condemned

On a March 1757 Damiens the regicide was condemned 'to make the *amende konorable* before the main door of the Church of Paris', where he was to be 'taken and conveyed in a cart, wearing nothing but a shirt, holding a torch of burning wax weighing two pounds'; then, 'in the said cart, to the Place de Grève, where, on a scaffold that will be erected there, the flesh will be torn from his breasts, arms, thighs and calves with red-hot pincers, his right hand, holding the knife with which he committed the said parricide, burnt with sulphur, and, on those places where the flesh will be torn away, poured molten lead, boiling oil, burning resin, wax and sulphur melted together and then his body drawn and quartered by four horses and his limbs and body consumed by fire, reduced to ashes and his ashes thrown to the winds' (*Pieces originales . . .*, 372–4).

'Finally, he was quartered,' recounts the *Gazette & Amsterdam* of 1 April 1757. 'This last operation was very long, because the horses used were not accustomed to drawing; consequently, instead of four, six were needed; and when that did not suffice, they were forced, in order to cut off the wretch's thighs, to sever the sinews and back at the joints. . .

"It is said that, though he was always a great swearer, no blasphemy escaped his lips; but the excessive pain made him utter horrible cries, and he often repeated: "My God, have pity on me! Jesus, help me!" The spectators were all edified by the solicitude of the parish priest of St Paul's who despite his great age did not spare himself in offering consolation to the patient.'

Bouton, an officer of the watch, left us his account: 'The sulphur was lit, but the flame was so poor that only the top skin of the hand was burnt, and that only slightly. Then the executioner, his sleeves rolled up, took the steel pincers, which had been especially made for the occasion, and which were about a foot and a half long, and pulled first at the calf of the right leg, then at the thigh, and from there at the two fleshy parts of the right arm, then at the breasts. Though a strong, sturdy fellow, this executioner found it so difficult to tear away the pieces of flesh that he set about the same spot two or three times, twisting the pincers as he did so, and what he took away formed at each part a wound about the size of a six-pound crown piece.

'After these tearings with the pincers, Damiens, who cried out profusely, though without swearing, raised his head and looked at himself; the same executioner dipped an iron spoon in the pot containing the boiling potion, which he poured liberally over each wound. Then the ropes that were to be harnessed to the horses were attached with cords to the patient's body; the horses were then harnessed and placed alongside the arms and legs, one at each limb.

'Monsieur Le Breton, the clerk of the court, went up to the patient several times and asked him if he had anything to say. He said he had not; at each torment, he cried out, as the damned in bell are supposed to cry out, "Pardon, my God! Pardon, Lord." Despite all this pain, he raised his head from time to time and looked at himself boldly. The cords had been tied so tightly by the men who pulled the ends that they caused him indescribable pain. Monsieur le Breton went up to him again and asked him if he had anything to say; he said no. Several confessors went up to him and spoke to him at length; he willingly kissed the crucifix that was held out to him; he opened his lips and repeated: "Pardon, Lord."

"The horses tugged hard, each pulling straight on a limb, each horse held by an executioner. After a quarter of an hour, the same ceremony was repeated and finally, after several attempts, the direction of the horses had to be changed, thus: those at the arms were made to pull towards the head, those at the thighs towards the arms, which broke the arms at the joints. This was repeated several times without success. He raised his head and looked at himself. Two more horses had to be added to those harnessed to the thighs, which made six horses in all. Without success.

'Finally, the executioner, Samson, said to Montieur Le Breton that there was no way or hope of succeeding, and told him to ask their Lordships if they wished him to have the prisoner cut into pieces. Monsieur Le Breton, who had come down from the town, ordered that renewed efforts be made, and this was done; but the horses gave up and one of those harnessed to the thighs fell to the ground. The confessors returned and spoke to him again. He said to them (I heard him): "Kiss me, gentlemen." The parish priest of St Paul's did not dare to, so Monsieur de Marsilly slipped under the rope holding the left arm and kissed him on the forehead. The executioners gathered round and Damiens told them not to swear, to carry out their task and that he did not think ill of them; he begged them to pray to God for him, and asked the parish priest of St Paul's to pray for him at the first mass.

'After two or three attempts, the executioner Samson and he who had used the pincers each drew out a knife from his pocket and cut the body at the thighs instead of severing the legs at the joints, the four horses gave a tug and carried off the two thighs after them, namely, that of the right side first, the other following; then the same was done to the arms, the shoulders, the arm-pits and the four limbs; the flesh had to be cut almost to the bone, the horses pulling hard carried off the right arm first and the other afterwards.

'When the four limbs had been pulled away, the confessors came to speak to him; but his executioner told them that he was dead, though the truth was that I saw the man move, his lower jaw moving from side to side as if he were talking. One of the executioners even said shortly afterwards that when they had lifted the trunk to throw it on the stake, he was still alive. The four limbs were untied from the ropes and thrown on the stake set up in the enclosure in line with the scaffold, then the trunk and the rest were covered with logs and faggots, and fire was put to the straw mixed with this wood.

'. . . In accordance with the decree, the whole was reduced to ashes. The last piece to be found in the embers was still burning at half-past ten in the evening. The pieces of flesh and the trunk had taken about four hours to burn. The officers of whom I was one, as also was my son, and a detachment of archers remained in the square until nearly eleven o'clock.

'There were those who made something of the fact that a dog had lain the day before on the grass where the fire had been, had been chased away several times, and had always returned. But it is not difficult to understand that an animal found this place warmer than elsewhere' (quoted in Zevaes, 201–14).

Eighty years later, Léon Faucher drew up his rules 'for she House of young prisoners in Paris'.

'Art. 17. The prisoners' day will begin at six in the morning in winter and at five in summer. They will work for nine hours a day throughout the year. Two hours a day will be devoted to instruction. Work and the day will end at nine o'clock in winter and at eight in summer.

Art. 18. *Rising*. At the first drum-roll, the prisoners must rise and dress in silence, as the supervisor opens the cell doors. At the second drum-roll, they must be dressed and make their beds. At the third, they must line up and proceed to the chapel for morning prayer. There is a five-minute interval between each drum-roll.

Art. 19. The prayers are conducted by the chaplain and followed by a moral or religious reading. This exercise must not last more than half an hour.

Art. 20. *Work*. At a quarter to six in the summer, a quarter to seven in winter, the prisoners go down into the courtyard where they must wash their hands and faces, and receive their first ration of bread. Immediately afterwards, they form into work-teams and go off to work, which must begin at six in summer and seven in winter.

Art. 21. *Meal*. At ten o'clock the prisoners leave their work and go to the refectory; they wash their hands in their courtyards and assemble in divisions. After the dinner, there is recreation until twenty minutes to eleven.

Art. 22. *School*. At twenty minutes to eleven, at the drum-roll, the prisoners form into ranks, and proceed in divisions to the school. The class lasts two hours and consists alternately of reading, writing, drawing and arithmetic.

Art. 23. At twenty minutes to one, the prisoners leave the school, in divisions, and return to their courtyards for recreation. At five minutes to one, at the drum-roll, they form into work-teams.

Art. 24. At one o'clock they must be back in the workshops they work until four o'clock.

Art. 25. At four o'clock the prisoners leave their workshops and go into the courtyards where they wash their hands and form into divisions for the refectory.

Art. 26. 'Supper and the recreation that follows it last until five o'clock: the prisoners then return to the workshops.

Art. 27. At seven o'clock in the summer, at eight in winter, work stops; bread is distributed for the last time in the workshops. For a quarter of an hour one of the prisoners or supervisors reads a passage from some instructive or uplifting work. This is followed by evening prayer.

Art. 28. At half-past seven in summer, half-past eight in winter, the prisoners must be back in their cells after the washing of hands and the inspection of clothes in the courtyard; at the first drum-roll, they must undress, and at the second get into bed. The cell doors are closed and the supervisors go the rounds in the corridors, to ensure order and silence' (Faucher, 274–82).

We have, then, a public execution and a time-table. They do not punish the same crimes or the same type of delinquent. But they each define a certain penal style. Less than a century separates them. It was a time when, in Europe and in the United States, the entire economy of punishment was redistributed. It was a time of great 'scandals' for traditional justice, a time of innumerable projects for reform. It saw a new theory of law and crime, a new moral or political justification of the right to punish; old laws were abolished, old customs died out. 'Modern' codes were planned or drawn up: Russia, 1769; Prussia, 1780; Pennsylvania and Tuscany, 1786; Austria, 1788; France, 1791, Year IV, 1808 and 1810. It was a new age for penal justice.

Among so many changes, I shall consider one: the disappearance of torture as a public spectacle. Today we are rather inclined to ignore it; perhaps, in its time, it gave rise to too much inflated rhetoric; perhaps it has been attributed too readily and too emphatically to a process of 'humanization', thus dispensing with the need for further analysis. And, in any case, how important is such a change, when compared with the great institutional transformations, the formulation of explicit, general codes and unified rules of procedure; with the almost universal adoption of the jury system, the definition of the essentially corrective character of the penalty and the tendency, which has become increasingly marked since the nineteenth century, to adapt punishment to the individual offender? Punishment of a less immediately physical kind, a certain discretion in the art of inflicting pain, a combination of more subtle, more subdued sufferings, deprived of their visible display, should not all this be treated as a special case, an incidental effect of deeper changes? And yet the fact remains that a few decades saw the disappearance of the tortured, dismembered, amputated body, symbolically branded on face or shoulder, exposed alive or dead to public view. The body as the major target of penal repression disappeared.

Punishment, then, will tend to become the most hidden part of the penal process. This has several consequences: it leaves the domain of more or less everyday perception and enters that of abstract consciousness; its effectiveness is seen as resulting from its inevitability, not from its visible intensity; it is the certainty of being punished and not the horrifying spectacle of public punishment that must discourage crime; the exemplary mechanics of punishment changes its mechanisms. As a result, justice no longer takes public responsibility for the violence that is bound up with its practice. If it too strikes, if it too kills, it is not as a glorification of its strength, but as an element of itself that it is obliged to tolerate, that it finds difficult to account for. The apportioning of blame is redistributed: in punishment-as-spectacle a confused horror spread from the scaffold; it enveloped both executioner and condemned; and, although it was always ready to invert the shame inflicted on the victim into pity or glory, it often turned the legal violence of the executioner into shame. Now the scandal and the light are to be distributed differently; it is the conviction itself that marks the offender with the unequivocally negative sign: the publicity has shifted to the trial, and to the sentence; the execution itself is like an additional shame that justice is ashamed to impose on the condemned man; so it keeps its distance from the act, tending, always to entrust it to others, under the seal of secrecy. It is ugly to be punishable, but there is no glory in punishing. Hence that double system of protection that justice has set up between itself and the punishment it imposes. Those who carry out the penalty tend to become an autonomous sector; justice is relieved of responsibility for it by a bureaucratic concealment of the penalty itself. It is typical that in France the administration of the prisons should for so long have been the responsibility of the Ministry of the Interior, while responsibility for the *bagnes*, for penal servitude in the convict ships and penal settlements, lay with the Ministry of the Navy or the Ministry of the Colonies. And beyond this distribution of roles operates a theoretical disavowal: do not imagine that the sentences that we judges pass are activated by a desire to punish; they are intended to correct, reclaim, 'cure'; a technique of improvement represses, in the penalty, the strict expiation of evil-doing, and relieves the magistrates of the demeaning task of punishing. In modern justice and on the part of those who dispense it there is a shame in punishing, which does not always preclude zeal. This sense of shame is constantly growing: the psychologists and the minor civil servants of moral orthopaedics proliferate on the wound it leaves.

The modern rituals of execution attest to this double process: the disappearance of the spectacle and the elimination of pain. The same movement has affected the various European legal systems, each at its own rate: the same death for all–the execution no longer bears the specific mark of the crime or the social status of the criminal; a death that lasts only a moment–no torture must be added to it in advance, no further actions performed upon the corpse; an execution that affects life rather than the body. There are no longer any of those long processes in which death was both retarded by calculated interruptions and multiplied by a series of successive attacks. There are no longer any of those combinations of tortures that were organized for the killing of regicides, or of the kind advocated, at the beginning of the eighteenth century, by the anonymous author of *Hanging not Punishment Enough* (1701), by which the condemned man would be broken on the wheel, then flogged until he fainted, then hung up with chains, then finally left to die slowly of hunger. There are no longer any of those executions in which the condemned man was dragged along on a hurdle (to prevent his head smashing against the cobble-stones), in which his belly was opened up, his entrails quickly ripped out, so that he had time to see them, with his own eyes, being thrown on the fire; in which he was finally decapitated and his body quartered.[1] The reduction of these 'thousand deaths' to strict capital punishment defines a whole new morality concerning the act of punishing.

At the beginning of the nineteenth century, then, the great spectacle of physical punishment disappeared; the tortured body was avoided; the theatrical representation of pain was excluded from punishment. The age of sobriety in punishment had begun. By 1830–48, public executions, preceded by torture, had almost entirely disappeared. Of course, this generalization requires some qualification. To begin with, the changes did not come about at once or as part of a single process. There were delays.

It should be added that, although most of the changes had been achieved by 1840, although the mechanisms of punishment had by then assumed their new way of functioning, the process was far from complete. The reduction in the use of torture was a tendency that was rooted in the great transformation of the years 1760–1840, but it did not end there; it can be said that the practice of the public execution haunted our penal system for a long time and still haunts it today.

Similarly, the hold on the body did not entirely disappear in the mid-nineteenth century. Punishment had no doubt ceased to be centred on torture as a technique of pain; it assumed as its principal object loss of wealth or rights. But a punishment like forced labour or even imprisonment–mere loss of liberty–has never functioned without a certain additional element of punishment that certainly concerns the body itself: rationing of food, sexual deprivation, corporal punishment, solitary confinement. Are these the unintentional, but inevitable, consequence of imprisonment? In fact, in its most explicit practices, imprisonment has always involved a certain degree of physical pain. The criticism that was often levelled at the penitentiary system in the early nineteenth century (imprisonment is not a sufficient punishment: prisoners are less hungry, less cold, less deprived in general than many poor people or even workers) suggests a postulate that was never explicitly denied: it is just that a condemned man should suffer physically more than other men. It is difficult to dissociate punishment from additional physical pain. What would a non-corporal punishment be?

There remains, therefore, a trace of 'torture' in the modern mechanisms of criminal justice–a trace that has not been entirely overcome, but which is enveloped, increasingly, by the non-corporal nature of the penal system.

The reduction in penal severity in the last 200 years is a phenomenon with which legal historians are well acquainted. But, for a long time, it has been regarded in an overall way as a quantitative phenomenon: less cruelty, less pain, more kindness, more respect, more 'humanity'. In fact, these changes are accompanied by a displacement in the very object of the punitive operation. Is there a diminution of intensity? Perhaps. There is certainly a change of objective.

If the penality in its most severe forms no longer addresses itself to the body, on what does it lay hold? The answer of the theoreticians–those who, about 1760, opened up a new period that is not yet at an end–is simple, almost obvious. It seems to be contained in the question itself: since it is no longer the body, it must be the soul. The expiation that once rained down upon the body must be replaced by a punishment that acts in depth on the heart, the thoughts, the will, the inclinations. Mably formulated the principle once and for all: 'Punishment, if I may so put it, should strike the soul rather than the body' (Mably, 326).

To begin with, there is a substitution of objects. By this I do not mean that one has suddenly set about punishing other crimes. No doubt the definition of offences, the hierarchy of their seriousness, the margins of indulgence, what was tolerated in fact and what was legally permitted–all this has considerably changed over the last 200 years; many crimes have ceased to be so because they were bound up with a certain exercise of religious authority or a particular type of economic activity; blasphemy has lost its status as a crime; smuggling and domestic larceny some of their seriousness. But these displacements are perhaps not the most important fact: the division between the permitted and the forbidden has preserved a certain constancy from one century to another. On the other hand, 'crime', the object with which penal practice is concerned, has profoundly altered: the quality, the nature, in a sense the substance of which the punishable element is made, rather than its formal definition. Undercover of the relative stability of the law, a mass of subtle and rapid changes has occurred. Certainly the 'crimes' and 'offences' on which judgement is passed are juridical objects defined by the code, but judgement is also passed on the passions, instincts, anomalies, infirmities, maladjustments, effects of environment or heredity; acts of aggression are punished, so also, through them, is aggressivity; rape, but at the same time perversions; murders, but also drives and desires. But, it will be objected, judgement is not actually being passed on them; if they are referred to at all it is to explain the actions in question, and to determine to what extent the subject's will was involved in the crime. This is no answer. For it *is* these shadows lurking behind the case itself that are judged and punished. They are judged indirectly as 'attenuating circumstances' that introduce into the verdict not only 'circumstantial' evidence, but something quite different, which is not juridically codifiable: the knowledge of the criminal, one's estimation of him, what is known about the relations between him, his past and his crime, and what might be expected of him in the future. They are also judged by the interplay of all those notions that have circulated between medicine and jurisprudence since the nineteenth century (the 'monsters' of Georger's times, Chaumié's 'psychical anomalies', the 'perverts' and 'maladjusted' of our own experts) and which, behind the pretext of explaining an action, are ways of defining an individual. They are punished by means of a punishment that has the function of making the offender 'not only desirous, but also capable, of living within the law and of providing for his own needs'; they are punished by the internal economy of a penalty which, while intended to punish the crime, may be altered (shortened or, in certain cases, extended) according to changes in the prisoner's behaviour; and they are punished by the 'security measures' that accompany the penalty (prohibition of entering certain areas, probation, obligatory medical treatment), and which are intended not to punish the offence, but to supervise the individual, to neutralize his dangerous state of mind, to alter his criminal tendencies, and to continue even when this change has been achieved. The criminal's soul is not referred to in the trial merely to explain his crime and as a factor in the juridical apportioning of responsibility; if it is brought before the court, with such pomp and circumstance, such concern to understand and such 'scientific' application, it is because it too, as well as the crime itself, is to be judged and to share in the punishment. Throughout the penal ritual, from the preliminary investigation to the sentence and the final effects of the penalty, a domain has been penetrated by objects that not only duplicate, but also dissociate the juridically defined and coded objects. Psychiatric expertise, but also in a more general way criminal anthropology and the repetitive discourse of criminology, find one of their precise functions here: by solemnly inscribing offences in the field of objects susceptible of scientific knowledge, they provide the mechanisms of legal punishment with a justifiable hold not only on offences, but on individuals; not only on what they do, but also on what they are, will be, may be. The additional factor of the offender's soul, which the legal system has laid hold of, is only apparently explanatory and limitative, and is in fact expansionist. During the 150 or 200 years that Europe has been setting up its new penal systems, the judges have gradually, by means of a process that goes back very far indeed, taken to judging something other than crimes, namely, the 'soul' of the criminal.

And, by that very fact, they have begun to do something other than pass judgement. Or, to be more precise, within the very judicial modality of judgement, other types of assessment have slipped in, profoundly altering its rules of elaboration. Ever since the Middle Ages slowly and painfully built up the great procedure of investigation, to judge was to establish the truth of a crime, it was to determine its author and to apply a legal punishment. Knowledge of the offence, knowledge of the offender, knowledge of the law: these three conditions made it possible to ground a judgement in truth. But now a quite different question of truth is inscribed in the course of the penal judgement. The question is no longer simply: "Has the act been established and is it punishable?' But also: 'What *is* this act, what *is* this act of violence or this murder? To what level or to what field of reality does it belong? Is it a phantasy, a psychotic reaction, a delusional episode, a perverse action?' It is no longer simply: 'Who committed it?' But: 'How can we assign the causal process that produced it? Where did it originate in the author himself? Instinct, unconscious, environment, heredity?' It is no longer simply: 'What law punishes this offence?' But: 'What would be the most appropriate measures to take? How do we see the future development of the offender? What would be the best way of rehabilitating him?' A whole set of assessing, diagnostic, prognostic, normative judgements concerning the criminal have become lodged in the framework of penal judgement. Another truth has penetrated the truth that was required by the legal machinery; a truth which, entangled with the first, has turned the assertion of guilt into a strange scientifico-juridical complex.

And he is not alone in judging. Throughout the penal procedure and the implementation of the sentence there swarms a whole series of subsidiary authorities. Small-scale legal systems and parallel judges have multiplied around the principal judgement: psychiatric or psychological experts, magistrates concerned with the implementation of sentences, educationalists, members of the prison service, all fragment the legal power to punish.

To sum up, ever since the new penal system–that defined by the great codes of the eighteenth and nineteenth centuries–has been in operation, a general process has led judges to judge something other than crimes; they have been led in their sentences to do something other than judge; and the power of judging has been transferred, in part, to other authorities than the judges of the offence. The whole penal operation has taken on extra-juridical elements and personnel. It will be said that there is nothing extraordinary in this, that it is part of the destiny of the law to absorb little by little elements that are alien to it. But what is odd about modern criminal justice is that, although it has taken on so many extra-juridical elements, it has done so not in order to be able to define them juridically and gradually to integrate them into the actual power to punish: on the contrary, it has done so in order to make them function within the penal operation as non-juridical elements; in order to stop this operation being simply a legal punishment; in order to exculpate the judge from being purely and simply he who punishes. 'Of course, we pass sentence, but this sentence is not in direct relation to the crime. It is quite clear that for us it functions as a way of treating a criminal. We punish, but this is a way of saying that we wish to obtain a cure.' Today, criminal justice functions and justifies itself only by this perpetual reference to something other than itself, by this unceasing reinscription in non-juridical systems. Its fate is to be redefined by knowledge.

Beneath the increasing leniency of punishment, then, one may map a displacement of its point of application; and through this displacement, a whole field of recent objects, a whole new system of truth and a mass of roles hitherto unknown in the exercise of criminal justice. A corpus of knowledge, techniques, 'scientific' discourses is formed and becomes entangled with the practice of the power to punish.

In short, try to study the metamorphosis of punitive methods on the basis of a political technology of the body in which might be read a common history of power relations and object relations. Thus, by an analysis of penal leniency as a technique of power, one might understand both how man, the soul, the normal or abnormal individual have come to duplicate crime as objects of penal intervention; and in what way a specific mode of subjection was able to give birth to man as an object of knowledge for a discourse with a 'scientific' status.

JUSTICE HERE AND NOW: A PERSONAL REFLECTION ON THE RESTORATIVE AND COMMUNITY JUSTICE PARADIGMS

LOIS PRESSER

In my first job in criminal justice, I was a caseworker for elderly crime victims in Manhattan. I helped people fill out forms to get government compensation for their losses. I also referred them to psychological therapy as needed. The clients rarely expressed interest in therapy. They preferred to talk to me, as much about their loneliness in the big city as about 'the crime.' Given my considerable caseload, I felt pressed to rush people out of the door.

In my second job in criminal justice, I planned and evaluated treatment programs for prisoners on Rikers Island in New York. The goal was to reduce offender recidivism. I remember that job as very stressful. One summer there was an expectation that the prisoners would riot. All visits to the Island seemed risky. The front line staff were constantly on edge. They had no time or energy for treatment-related questions. That summer the priority we gave to reducing prisoners' future offending—always limited—was preempted even more by the need to control imminent violence.

The focus of the first job was on getting money for people. The focus of the second job was on controlling crime. The jobs felt empty to me. I had no sense that I was promoting justice. When I recall talking with victims and offenders, I have an image of looking past them and not at them. Sometimes I wish I could return to those jobs and connect with people better.

Now I am a criminologist in academia where the focus is again on getting money and controlling crime! This job too could be empty except that I am resisting what I call the *belated orientation* of the work. Difficult as it usually is, I try to focus on the present moment. In teaching, I try to focus on what students are doing with the class material while still in the classroom. In researching offenders, victims, and programs, I am concerned with the humanity—the good and the bad—of the present moment. I listen to people's stories and think about how I am some part of their stories.

So long as restorative justice is directed at what is happening between people right now, it feels humane to me. As restorative justice is called on to promote one or another belated outcome, I feel it strays from its unique potential—to *be* a humane *experience* of justice. Because I have come to think that a belated orientation negates humanity in the here and now, Paul McCold's (2004) argument that process is the heart of restorative justice resonates with me. McCold maintains that dialogic and power-sharing processes are essential to restorative justice but not to community justice.

This is not McCold's only or even his principal claim. He is concerned that restorative justice be distinguished from community justice, which 'relies on the existing criminal justice systems' (p. 21) to implement 'aggregate interventions' (p. 20). Community justice, in his view, does little to shift decision-making power from the state to the individuals who are actually affected by a particular offense. However, to my mind, McCold's most profound claim is that restorative justice should, at least ideally, be defined in terms of specific practices rather than specific outcomes (see also Marshall, 1996; McCold, 2000). McCold (2004) observes: 'The essence of restorative justice is not the end, but the means by which resolution is achieved' (p. 16). Restorative justice offers a vision of *just* living. We live justly by engaging in dialogue, not violence; by taking turns; by engaging everyone; by being sensitive to the needs of all starting now.

At its best, restorative justice process is akin to Habermas's (1970) ideal speech situation. The ideal speech situation is a linguistic representation of a just world. Dorothy Smith (1999, p. 221) describes Habermas's concept very lucidly:

> the ideal speech situation [is one] in which speakers seek to be understood, to tell the truth, in terms of their own feelings as well as what they know of the world beyond their own subjectivity, and to be accepted by the other as speaking in terms of norms and values they share. The relationship is reciprocal. Each party is both speaker and hearer and recognizes the other as such; there is full mutual recognition of each participant as a subject and a symmetry of the presence of subjects for each other; no one participant is privileged in the performance of dialogic roles, with the implication that though one may teach, the other too is recognized as a subject who may argue and question.

In the ideal restorative conference, circle or mediation session, talk is symmetrical. Although victims and community members may teach the offender 'better' ways to act (from their standpoint), the offender is recognized as a person with her own ideas and insights about the world and about her conduct. Of course, the means by which resolution is achieved—through talk—may *not* be symmetrical in practice. Habermas (1970) himself posited honest, free, and just speech as a model. Some offenders, in meeting with victims, may act in ways that are dishonest and uncooperative. Dialogue may then be traumatic for victims, not healing (Presser & Lowenkamp, 1999; Stubbs, 2002). Or power dynamics might keep young offenders from speaking freely (Arrigo & Schehr, 1998).

If dialogue is central to restorative justice, we should exclude from restorative justice practice anything that inhibits dialogue. The primacy of practice implies that scrupulous attention be paid to process. Facilitators must be alert to such dynamics and intervene or encourage others to intervene. Even evaluators of restorative justice might take an 'action approach' (Mika, 2002), speaking up to ensure that processes foster everyone's well-being. Thus we resist objectifying the people we study and evaluation becomes its own valuable process.

For the most part, the criminal justice system does not deal in well-being, peace *or* dialogue. Instead, it does harm (Clear, 1994). The dominant logic of justice is oriented toward the past and the future and not this human moment. That logic is institutionalized in a huge justice apparatus that serves state and corporate interests. How to dismantle it? Apart from system constraints, there are constraints of the heart where certain 'serious' offenses and offenders are concerned. Coercion seems to be the only way to ensure that *some* offenders do not cause harm again (Walgrave, 2000).

I recall people I interviewed who perpetrated violence (Presser, 2002). Some are no longer under formal state supervision. In a few cases, that worries me. I felt particularly threatened by John (a pseudonym), who had attempted to kill a police officer. What bothered me most was how thrilling he seemed to find violence. (Or so he suggested in the *not*-reciprocal talk of the interview.) In speaking with John, my mind wandered from the here and now of his storytelling to the future, when he might harm me. Evans (2001), who collected writings from prisoners, observes that in telling their stories, these men and women 'became meaningful human beings in a society that had branded them as nothing more than worthless criminals' (p. xii). I do not want to be part of that society that castigates and expels. But I fear John and his freedom. Fear keeps us looking forward and backward. So my own heart is not fully into process at this point.

I agree with Braithwaite and Pettit (1990), who conceptualize justice as pursuit of the most civic freedom, for all, that a society can manage. Braithwaite and Pettit stress the importance of orienting to a target (such as freedom) in doing justice. I contend that justice occurs *while* we strive for that target.

The pursuit of freedom is a process, not an outcome. It is a process that we should be grappling with at (inter)personal and concrete levels, with keen attention paid to what freedom means to us emotionally. I grapple with what is gained and what is lost by John's confinement but I do it alone. I am not connecting with anyone else (including John) on this issue.

As Braithwaite and Pettit (1990) note: 'The criminal justice process should always seek to be a communicative process that engages the defendant in moral discourse' (p. 128). A collective grappling about feelings and values—moral dialogue—might occur in the immediate aftermath of a crime, when it is urgently needed. In that case, the dialogue involves the ones injured and the ones who have caused injury. Sentencing panels and meetings that involve citizens concerned about a crime, though not directly affected by that crime, might also instigate moral dialogue. However, McCold (2004) observes that that is not their orientation. Karp's (2001) study exposes the practical difficulties of citizens orienting to concrete harms when victims are not participants. To the extent that community-based sentencing does not center on dialogue about moral trespass and reconciliation, it is not restorative.

In other words, restorative justice is a dialogue *about* repairing conflicts and harms that does not *depend* on the palpable accomplishment of repair. Following that definition, I believe that the truly radical potential of restorative justice is its capacity to change the way people view justice—from a result of practice, to processes that have essential value but are also always unfinished and problematic. That potential is only latent. A distinctive focus on restorative justice *practice* warrants more attention than it has received, especially in the evaluation literature. For example, Latimer, Dowden, and Muise (2001), who 'meta-analyzed' the results of 22 evaluation studies of 35 restorative justice programs, observed that recidivism was the most common measure of program performance across studies. Recidivism measures were followed—not very closely—by increased satisfaction of offenders and victims, and offender compliance with restitution agreements.

I certainly am curious to learn the effects of restorative justice programs and policies. I want to stop (fearing) crime, so I too ask the question: does restorative justice work? Then I catch myself looking past concrete happenings, where people and their needs are; I know nothing with any certainty about tomorrow.

Measuring participants' satisfaction does reflect a focus on practice over outcomes. But satisfaction measures are problematic if they maintain status quo understandings of justice. If participants currently think of justice in terms of restitution payments or an offender being made to feel uncomfortable, then they will indeed be satisfied to the extent that these things occurred. I propose that the extent to which honest and respectful dialogue actually occurred, better captures what justice is and should be. It should be a central measure of performance—at least as common as measures of satisfaction. Of course, it is easy to know honest and respectful dialogue by its absence. It is rather more difficult to measure it, but it can be done (see Presser & Van Voorhis, 2002).

Daly and Immarigeon (1998) are pessimistic about what restorative justice can accomplish. They state: 'Modest aims and strategies may prove more successful for restorative justice programs to achieve than goals such as repairing harms, crime control, and criminal justice reform' (p. 37). They recommend that restorative justice promise *less*. Their recommendation and mine are the same, but for different reasons. I would like to do away with the language of 'aims' and 'success' altogether. Crime fundamentally silences another; justice gives voice. Sullivan and Tifft (2001, p. 35) explain:

> A person who harms another is, in effect, showing a blatant disregard for the needs of that person by defining the nature of their interaction unilaterally. He is essentially denying that person his or her voice and an opportunity to participate in the relationship at any given moment.

A restorative justice intervention is itself the phenomenon we hope to effect in the future—that of relating to one other respectfully and non-hierarchically.

Though I am moving away from Daly and Immarigeon's (1998) concern with results, I agree with the basis of their pessimism. The outcomes of any social encounter are unpredictable. Restorative justice cannot guarantee specific outcomes, even reparative ones like the communication of remorse or forgiveness (Braithwaite, 2002). Yet, with adequate preparation and thoughtful procedures (for example, facilitators asking participants pointed questions about their experiences), restorative justice can, more or less, promise that people will talk. Simply making that promise—and none other—is important and humane.

Questions

1. How do different ideas about human nature relate to different theories about laws and the legal system?

2. How do different views on human relations relate to different theories about laws and the legal system?

3. How would Harris respond to Plato's position on laws?

4. How is power related to the legal system? How does hegemony relate to the legal system?

5. How do you think each of the four mentioned jurisprudence schools within the introduction to this chapter (natural law, legal positivism, legal realism, and critical legal theory) would evaluate laws created by the Nazis that oppressed Jewish citizens in the years leading up to World War II and in the "final solution" that sent Jews, Gypsies, homosexuals, and other 'undesirables' to prison camps?

Suggested Media

Movies

12 Angry Men
Billy Budd
The Exonerated
The Green Mile
Judgment at Nuremburg
To Kill a Mockingbird

Television

The Supreme Court. Public Broadcasting Station (PBS)

Books and articles

J. Austin (1998) *The Providence of Jurisprudence Determined*
S. Bogira (2005) *Courtroom 302*
K. Crenshaw (1989) Demarginalizing the Intersection of Race and Sex: A Black Feminist Critique of
    Antidiscrimination Doctrine, Feminist Theory and Antiracist Politics
A. Davis (2003) *Are prisons obsolete?*
F. Kafka (1925) *The Trial*
I. Kant (2000) "A retributivist theory of punishment" from *The Philosophy of Law*
M.L. King, Jr. (1963) Letter from a Birmingham Jail
H. Lee (1960) *To Kill a Mockingbird*
C. MacKinnon (1991) Feminism, Marxism, method, and the state: toward feminists jurisprudence
H. Melvile (1924) *Billy Budd*
J. Reimen (1998) *The rich get richer and the poor get prison: ideology, class, and criminal justice*
D. Rhode (2004) *Access to justice*
Sophocles *Antigone*

Economy

Economic theories and ideologies are important perspectives on justice, especially since the eighteenth century in Europe, when revolutions and counter-revolutions eventually destroyed feudal economies and their monarchies. Capitalism and socialism emerged as central ideologies from the ashes of these profound social and cultural changes. These revolutions raised the question of the role of justice in society, whether to insure a certain level of economic parity between the social classes (what is called *distributive justice*) or to provide for the peace and security of all persons in society? What is the role of private property, and what should be the rules of its fair exchange? As early as 1690 John Locke argued that private property was a *natural right*, that all persons should be able to buy and sell whatever they had or could produce, and in his classic 1776 work, *The Wealth of Nations,* Adam Smith argued that the system of free markets was superior for both producing the greatest prosperity in society as well as reducing the inequalities between the social classes. A *right* is considered to be a universal claim which any or all individuals may legitimately make upon society. These were important works in the development of *utilitarianism,* initially proposed by various British theorists, which held that justice was that which produced the greatest good for the greatest number (not necessarily all) persons in society. These early British and Scottish thinkers had a very important effect on the U.S. founding fathers who wrote the *U.S. Declaration of Independence* and the *U.S. Constitution*, which give legal force and standing to the ideal of liberty, private property, and the protection of some political rights, for some people.

What we call "capitalism" is a political value or ideology which promotes the relative freedom of persons to do what they wish with their labor, as long as it does not bring harm to others, and to enjoy or invest the "fruits of their labors." If individuals are fortunate enough to produce a relative excess or "profit" from their labors, then they should be free to invest these "profits" in whatever manner they decide. If reinvested, these "profits" become "capital," from which the term *capitalism* is derived, and using profits in such a manner potentially grows and expands the overall economy of society. According to many promoters of capitalism, this freedom or liberty to work as one will, and consume or reinvest the products of one's labor, is not only consistent with the ideal of liberty, but it additionally reduces the potential for conflict between the social classes, and this makes for a more harmonious or peaceful social order.

Socialism is a political value or ideology which places central value on equality or *egalitarianism* among persons, especially concerning issues of income or material wealth. Socialists are generally very critical of capitalist economic systems, because they produce such great inequality among and between the social classes, and this represents a fundamental source of injustice and conflict in society. Karl Marx and his lifelong collaborator Friedrich Engels are commonly seen to be the founding fathers of *communism*, one form of socialism based upon the elimination of private property and thus the supposed material inequalities which stem from that. For Marx and Engels the economic resources of society should be produced in accordance with the skills, abilities, or talents of each individual contributing to their best effort, and then distributed according to what each individual "needs." This is usually captured by the slogan, "From each according to his ability, to each according to his needs." This means that individuals would not work because of self-interest or the incentive to maximize the "profit" from their labor, but would maximize their efforts for the collective good, even if this means that those who work less will receive more, presumably because their "needs" are greater than others. Marx and Engels are even critical of the very existence of the words "justice" or "injustice" in the language, because they say these words have been used historically to justify or legitimize economic inequalities between social classes, and have produced irremediable misery and servitude for lower class working people. Their preferred main principle is *equal right*, which means that economic resources should be distributed only in accordance with the actual labor which workers supply. In the reading "Justice Under Socialism" by Edward Nell and Onora O'Neill, the authors propose several alternatives to the socialist ideal of justice, and several complexities and limitations of these arguments.

It is important to recognize that these highly abstract philosophies about "capitalism" and "socialism" are idealizations about what a society could be or should be. They have become ideologies or political perspectives which have fueled world wars and internal conflicts in societies, but true or pure "capitalism" or "socialism" has never existed in reality. Even the United States has never been a capitalist society, because internal politics have always favored some groups, some industries, and some classes over others. Even today one finds parts of the U.S. economy which come very close to the free market ideal (computer electronics), while other parts come close to extreme socialism (military weapons). Even the former Soviet Union and Communist China, which were extreme in their abolition of private property and the centralization of state power in their promotion of communist or socialist ideals, was never fully successful in controlling all aspects of economic exchange, as their notorious "black" or unofficial markets revealed. The sociologist Peter L. Berger once published a book with the title *Pyramids of Sacrifice (1975)* to communicate how these modern ideologies of capitalism and socialism have brought forth such sacrifices of suffering, misery, human life, and catastrophe. As students, it is important for us to understand the origins and nature of these ideas, and also their real-life costs and consequences for those who suffer under these ideologies.

Today the countries in Western Europe and the United States have mixed economies, where there is a combination of private and state property, a mixture of free and state- or politically-controlled markets, a relatively greater recognition of the rights of women, First Nations people, racial and ethnic minorities, and a range of welfare services or resources allotted to those considered in need of them. We use the term "welfare states" to refer to these mixed economies, because they usually combine private property, some relatively free markets, and regulation of fair trading or business practices along with providing various "welfare rights" or "entitlements" to various groups designated for them by the political process in society. In the reading, "The Nonexistence of Basic Welfare Rights," libertarian Tibor Machan calls into question whether there should be such welfare rights or entitlements, even for those who are poor, mentally or physically disabled, or elderly. Machan says that libertarians agree that such groups deserve their impoverished or disadvantaged condition because they have made significant contributions to their plight by the choices they have made earlier in their life. This position is countered in John Rawls' 1971 book, *A Theory of Justice*, which tries to combine the ideas of capitalism, socialism, libertarianism, utilitarianism, and contract theory into a comprehensive theory of liberty and social justice. Rawls says that, if one stops to think and reflect, it is really in our best interests to support some basic welfare rights or entitlements, because it is entirely possible that we or our beloved family members may find themselves in one of these less fortunate conditions. The views of Machan and other libertarians are commonly taken to advocate a position for a limited or minimal state, that is, they would recognize the legitimacy of state powers only for doing those things which we cannot do for ourselves (such as national security or protecting national/coastal borders). Rawls and other like-minded liberals feel more comfortable with legitimizing state powers for various kinds of welfare rights or entitlements. What these should be, and what should be the relative responsibilities for paying the costs of these services or entitlements is being hotly disputed in the United States as various partisans prepare for the 2012 national elections. The issues raised in these readings are still very much alive in our culture, and current politics are informed by these important ideas of the recent centuries.

We include in this section two readings which are highly critical of the Eurocentric or Western theories of the economy. In "Our Word is Our Weapon," Subcomandante Marcos writes about his local situation in the southeastern Mexican state of Chiapas, which is very rich in natural resources of oil, gas, wood, coffee, beef, corn, tamarind, honey, and many others. These products are extracted and exported, largely to "the Beast" (the United States) according to the "market principles" of corporate globalization, producing considerable ecological destruction and agricultural plunder. Only a small portion of this vast wealth remains in the area where it is extracted, with the sizable profits being taken by the various levels of middlemen and the higher level investors and financiers. Marcos uses the ancient term of prior empires, "tribute," to refer to this newer form of exploitation and impoverishment. These themes are further developed in the subsequent reading by Vandana Shiva (2005), who argues that our current global emphasis on economic growth leads to the disenfranchisement and disposability of local peoples. The power of corporate globalization is the power to command the extraction of natural and human resources outside of its own domain; and this process, imposed on the rest of the world through current political structures and arrangements, creates vast economic injustices and material inequalities. In her discussion of the :"three economies," she puts forth a powerful criticism of both ideologies of socialism and capitalism, which tend to reduce our thinking about human meaning to the dimensions of labor or work.

The economic theories and perspectives included in these readings depend on a view or image of human nature, as we observed in the first section of this book. But it is important to recognize that all of these views of human nature are very oversimplified when compared with what humans are in reality. Humans cannot be reduced to their material interests, incentives, or desires, their lives are actually multifaceted, multilayered, and deeply complex. Just as our Human Genome Project has only managed to raise many more questions about human biological and physical nature, so do these researches and theories of human social and economic nature raise new questions and issues about human complexity. Moreover, only the readings by Marcos and Shiva discuss the many important issues which should be included, such as the consequences of business and economic activity on the environment, global warming, and protecting ourselves from man-made catastrophes such as the BP oil spill near New Orleans, or the recent tsunami and nuclear plant catastrophe in Japan. These readings tend to neglect the many important justice issues about the workplace, about how workers are to be treated, about appropriate limits on supervisors or bosses, about how groups historically discriminated against are to be treated, issues about enforcing an appropriate public morality in our diverse and multicultural world today. Finally, also neglected here are serious concerns about the ill effects of the materialism implied by, or embedded in, most of these theories.

References

Berger, P. (1975). *Pyramids of Sacrifice*. New York: Basic Books.

Smith, A. (2003 [1776]). The Wealth of Nations. New York: Bantam Classics.

THE SOCIALIST IDEAL

KARL MARX AND FRIEDRICH ENGELS

A spectre is haunting Europe—the spectre of Communism. All the Powers of old Europe have entered into a holy alliance to exorcise this spectre: Pope and Czar, Metternich and Guizot, French Radicals and German police-spies.

Where is the party in opposition that has not been decried as Communistic by its opponents in power? Where the Opposition that has not hurled back the branding reproach of Communism, against the more advanced opposition parties, as well as against its reactionary adversaries?

Two things result from this fact.

I. Communism is already acknowledged by all European Powers to be itself a Power.

II. It is high time that Communists should openly, in the face of the whole world, publish their views, their aims, their tendencies, and meet this nursery tale of the Spectre of Communism with a Manifesto of the party itself. . . .

The Communist Program

The Communists do not form a separate party opposed to other working-class parties.

They have no interests separate and apart from those of the proletariat as a whole.

They do not set up any sectarian principles of their own, by which to shape and mould the proletarian movement.

The Communists are distinguished from the other working-class parties by this only: (1) In the national struggles of the proletarians of the different countries, they point out and bring to the front the common interests of the entire proletariat, independently of all nationality. (2) In the various stages of development which the struggle of the working class against the bourgeoisie has to pass through they always and everywhere represent the interests of the movement as a whole.

The Communists, therefore, are on the one hand, practically, the most advanced and resolute section of the working-class parties of every country, that section which pushes forward all others; on the other hand, theoretically, they have over the great mass of the proletariat the advantage of clearly understanding the line of march, the conditions and the ultimate general results of the proletarian movement.

The immediate aim of the Communists is the same as that of all the other proletarian parties: formation of the proletariat into a class, overthrow of the bourgeois supremacy, conquest of political power by the proletariat.

The theoretical conclusions of the Communists are in no way based on ideas or principles that have been invented, or discovered, by this or that would-be universal reformer.

They merely express, in general terms, actual relations springing from an existing class struggle, from a historical movement going on under our very eyes. The abolition of existing property relations is not at all a distinctive feature of Communism.

All property relations in the past have continually been subject to historical change consequent upon the change in historical conditions.

The French Revolution, for example, abolished feudal property in favour of bourgeois property.

The distinguishing feature of Communism is not the abolition of property generally, but the abolition of bourgeois property. But modern bourgeois private property is the final and most complete expression of the system of producing and appropriating products, that is based on class antagonisms, on the exploitation of the many by the few.

In this sense, the theory of the Communists may be summed up in the single sentence: Abolition of private property.

We Communists have been reproached with the desire of abolishing the right of personally acquiring property as the fruit of man's own labour, which property is alleged to be the groundwork of all personal freedom, activity and independence.

Hard-won, self-acquired, self-earned property! Do you mean the property of the petty artisan and of the small peasant, a form of property that preceded the bourgeois form? There is no need to abolish that; the development of industry has to a great extent already destroyed it, and is still destroying it daily.

Or do you mean modern bourgeois private property?

But does wage-labour create any property for the labourer? Not a bit. It creates capital, *i.e.*, that kind of property which exploits wage-labour, and which cannot increase except upon condition of begetting a new supply of wage-labour for fresh exploitation. Property, in its present form, is based on the antagonism of capital and wage-labour. Let us examine both sides of this antagonism.

To be capitalist, is to have not only a purely personal, but a social *status* in production. Capital is a collective product, and only by the united action of many members, nay, in the last resort, only by the united action of all members of society, can it be set in motion.

Capital is, therefore, not a personal, it is a social power.

When, therefore, capital is converted into common property, into the property of all members of society, personal property is not thereby transformed into social property. It is only the social character of the property that is changed. It loses its class-character.

Let us now take wage-labour.

The average price of wage-labour is the minimum wage, *i.e.*, that quantum of the means of subsistence, which is absolutely requisite to keep the labourer in bare existence as a labourer. What, therefore, the wage-labourer appropriates by means of his labour, merely suffices to prolong and reproduce a bare existence. We by no means intend to abolish this personal appropriation of the products of labour, an appropriation that is made for the maintenance and reproduction of human life, and that leaves no surplus wherewith to command the labour of others. All that we want to do away with, is the miserable character of this appropriation, under which the labourer lives merely to increase capital, and is allowed to live only in so far as the interest of the ruling class requires it.

In bourgeois society, living labour is but a means to increase accumulated labour. In Communist society, accumulated labour is but a means to widen, to enrich, to promote the existence of the labourer.

In bourgeois society, therefore, the past dominates the present; in Communist society, the present dominates the past. In bourgeois society capital is independent and has individuality, while the living person is dependent and has no individuality.

And the abolition of this state of things is called by the bourgeois, abolition of individuality and freedom! And rightly so. The abolition of bourgeois individuality, bourgeois independence, and bourgeois freedom is undoubtedly aimed at.

By freedom is meant, under the present bourgeois conditions of production, free trade, free selling and buying.

But if selling and buying disappears, free selling and buying disappears also. This talk about free selling and buying, and all the other "brave words" of our bourgeoisie about freedom in general, have a meaning, if any, only in contrast with restricted selling and buying, with the fettered traders of the

Middle Ages, but have no meaning when opposed to the Communistic abolition of buying and selling, of the bourgeois conditions of production, and of the bourgeoisie itself.

You are horrified at our intending to do away with private property. But in your existing society, private property is already done away with for nine-tenths of the population; its existence for the few is solely due to its non-existence in the hands of those nine-tenths. You reproach us, therefore, with intending to do away with a form of property, the necessary condition for whose existence is the non-existence of any property for the immense majority of society.

In one word, you reproach us with intending to do away with your property. Precisely so; that is just what we intend.

From the moment when labour can no longer be converted into capital, money, or rent, into a social power capable of being monopolised, *i.e.*, from the moment when individual property can no longer be transformed into bourgeois property, into capital, from that moment, you say, individuality vanishes.

You must, therefore, confess that by "individual" you mean no other person than the bourgeois, than the middle-class owner of property. This person must, indeed, be swept out of the way, and made impossible.

Communism deprives no man of the power to appropriate the products of society; all that it does is to deprive him of the power to subjugate the labour of others by means of such appropriation.

It has been objected that upon the abolition of private property all work will cease, and universal laziness will overtake us.

According to this, bourgeois society ought long ago to have gone to the dogs through sheer idleness; for those of its members who work, acquire nothing, and those who acquire anything, do not work. The whole of this objection is but another expression of the tautology: that there can no longer be any wage-labour when there is no longer any capital.

All objections urged against the Communistic mode of producing and appropriating material products, have, in the same way, been urged against the Communistic modes of producing and appropriating intellectual products. Just as, to the bourgeois, the disappearance of class property is the disappearance of production itself, so the disappearance of class culture is to him identical with the disappearance of all culture.

That culture, the loss of which he laments, is, for the enormous majority, a mere training to act as a machine.

But don't wrangle with us so long as you apply, to our intended abolition of bourgeois property, the standard of your bourgeois notions of freedom, culture, law, [and so on]. Your very ideas are but the outgrowth of the conditions of your bourgeois production and bourgeois property, just as your jurisprudence is but the will of your class made into a law for all, a will, whose essential character and direction are determined by the economical conditions of existence of your class.

The selfish misconception that induces you to transform into eternal laws of nature and reason, the social forms springing from your present mode of production and form of property—historical relations that rise and disappear in the progress of production—this misconception you share with every ruling class that has preceded you. What you see clearly in the case of ancient property, what you admit in the case of feudal property, you are of course forbidden to admit in the case of your own bourgeois form of property.

Abolition of the family! Even the most radical flare up at this infamous proposal of the Communists.

On what foundation is the present family, the bourgeois family, based? On capital, on private gain. In its completely developed form this family exists only among the bourgeoisie. But this state of things finds its complement in the practical absence of the family among the proletarians, and in public prostitution.

The bourgeois family will vanish as a matter of course when its complement vanishes, and both will vanish with the vanishing of capital.

Do you charge us with wanting to stop the exploitation of children by their parents? To this crime we plead guilty.

But, you will say, we destroy the most hallowed of relations, when we replace home education by social.

And your education! Is not that also social, and determined by the social conditions under which you educate, by the intervention, direct or indirect, of society, by means of schools, [and so on]? The Communists have not invented the intervention of society in education; they do but seek to alter the character of that intervention, and to rescue education from the influence of the ruling class.

The bourgeois clap-trap about the family and education, about the hallowed co-relation of parent and child, becomes all the more disgusting, the more, by the action of Modern Industry, all family ties among the proletarians are torn asunder, and their children transformed into simple articles of commerce and instruments of labour.

But you Communists would introduce community of women, screams the whole bourgeoisie in chorus.

The bourgeois sees in his wife a mere instrument of production. He hears that the instruments of production are to be exploited in common, and, naturally, can come to no other conclusion than that the lot of being common to all will likewise fall to the women.

He has not even a suspicion that the real point aimed at is to do away with the status of women as mere instruments of production.

For the rest, nothing is more ridiculous than the virtuous indignation of our bourgeois at the community of women which, they pretend, is to be openly and officially established by the Communists. The Communists have no need to introduce community of women; it has existed almost from time immemorial.

Our bourgeois, not content with having the wives and daughters of their proletarians at their disposal, not to speak of common prostitutes, take the greatest pleasure in seducing each other's wives.

Bourgeois marriage is in reality a system of wives in common and thus, at the most, what the Communists might possibly be reproached with, is that they desire to introduce, in substitution for a hypocritically concealed, an openly legalised community of women. For the rest, it is self-evident that the abolition of the present system of production must bring with it the abolition of the community of women springing from that system, *i.e.*, of prostitution both public and private.

The Communists are further reproached with desiring to abolish countries and nationality.

The working men have no country. We cannot take from them what they have not got. Since the proletariat must first of all acquire political supremacy, must rise to be the leading class of the nation, must constitute itself *the* nation, it is, so far, itself national, though not in the bourgeois sense of the word.

National differences and antagonisms between peoples are daily more and more vanishing, owing to the development of the bourgeoisie, to freedom of commerce, to the world-market, to uniformity in the mode of production and in the conditions of life corresponding thereto.

The supremacy of the proletariat will cause them to vanish still faster. United action, of the leading civilised countries at least, is one of the first conditions for the emancipation of the proletariat.

In proportion as the exploitation of one individual by another is put an end to, the exploitation of one nation by another will also be put an end to. In proportion as the antagonism between classes within the nation vanished, the hostility of one nation to another will come to an end.

The charges against Communism made from a religious, a philosophical, and, generally, from an ideological standpoint, are not deserving of serious examination.

Does it require deep intuition to comprehend that man's ideas, views and conceptions, in one word, man's consciousness, changes with every change in the conditions of his material existence, in his social relations and in his social life?

What else does the history of ideas prove, than that intellectual production changes its character in proportion as material production is changed? The ruling ideas of each age have ever been the ideas of its ruling class.

When people speak of ideas that revolutionise society, they do but express the fact, that within the old society, the elements of a new one have been created, and that the dissolution of the old ideas keeps even pace with the dissolution of the old conditions of existence.

When the ancient world was in its last throes, the ancient religions were overcome by Christianity. When Christian ideas succumbed in the 18th century to rationalist ideas, feudal society fought its death battle with the then revolutionary bourgeoisie. The ideas of religious liberty and freedom of conscience merely gave expression to the sway of free competition within the domain of knowledge.

"Undoubtedly," it will be said, "religious, moral, philosophical and juridical ideas have been modified in the course of historical development. But religion, morality, philosophy, political science, and law, constantly survived this change."

"There are, besides, eternal truths, such as Freedom, Justice, etc., that are common to all states of society. But Communism abolishes eternal truths, it abolishes all religion, and all morality, instead of constituting them on a new basis; it therefore acts in contradiction to all past historical experience."

What does this accusation reduce itself to? The history of all past society has consisted in the development of class antagonisms, antagonisms that assumed different forms at different epochs.

But whatever form they may have taken, one fact is common to all past ages, *viz.*, the exploitation of one part of society by the other. No wonder, then, that the social consciousness of past ages, despite all the multiplicity and variety it displays, moves within certain common forms, or general ideas, which cannot completely vanish except with the total disappearance of class antagonisms.

The Communist revolution is the most radical rupture with traditional property relations; no wonder that its development involves the most radical rupture with traditional ideas.

But let us have done with the bourgeois objections to Communism.

We have seen above, that the first step in the revolution by the working class, is to raise the proletariat to the position of ruling class, to win the battle of democracy.

The proletariat will use its political supremacy to wrest, by degrees, all capital from the bourgeoisie, to centralise all instruments of production in the hands of the State, *i.e.*, of the proletariat organised as the ruling class; and to increase the total of productive forces as rapidly as possible.

Of course, in the beginning, this cannot be effected except by means of despotic inroads on the rights of property, and on the conditions of bourgeois production; by means of measures, therefore, which appear economically insufficient and untenable, but which, in the course of the movement, outstrip themselves, necessitate further inroads upon the old social order, and are unavoidable as a means of entirely revolutionising the mode of production.

These measures will of course be different in different countries.

Nevertheless in the most advanced countries, the following will be pretty generally applicable.

1. Abolition of property in land and application of all rents of land to public purposes.
2. A heavy progressive or graduated income tax.
3. Abolition of all right of inheritance.
4. Confiscation of the property of all emigrants and rebels.
5. Centralisation of credit in the hands of the State, by means of a national bank with State capital and an exclusive monopoly.

6. Centralisation of the means of communication and transport in the hands of the State.
7. Extension of factories and instruments of production owned by the State; the bringing into cultivation of waste-lands, and the improvement of the soil generally in accordance with a common plan.
8. Equal liability of all to labour. Establishment of industrial armies, especially for agriculture.
9. Combination of agriculture with manufacturing industries; gradual abolition of the distinction between town and country, by a more equable distribution of the population over the country.
10. Free education for all children in public schools. Abolition of children's factory labour in its present form. Combination of education with industrial production [and so on].

When, in the course of development, class distinctions have disappeared, and all production has been concentrated in the hands of a vast association of the whole nation, the public power will lose its political character. Political power, properly so called, is merely the organized power of one class for oppressing another. If the proletariat during its contest with the bourgeoisie is compelled, by the force of circumstances, to organise itself as a class, if, by means of a revolution, it makes itself the ruling class, and, as such, sweeps away by force the old conditions of production, then it will, along with these conditions, have swept away the conditions for the existence of class antagonisms and of class generally, and will thereby have abolished its own supremacy as a class.

In place of the old bourgeois society, with its classes and class antagonisms, we shall have an association, in which the free development of each is the condition for the free development of all. . . .

Critique of Social Democracy

> In present-day society, the instruments of labour are the monopoly of the capitalist class; the resulting dependence of the working class is the cause of misery and servitude in all its forms.

This sentence, borrowed from the Statutes of the International, is incorrect in this "improved" edition.
In present-day society the instruments of labour are the monopoly of the landowners (the monopoly of property in land is even the basis of the monopoly of capital) *and* the capitalists. In the passage in question, the Statutes of the International do not mention by name either the one or the other class of monopolists. They speak of the "*monopoly of the means of labour, that is the sources of life.*" The addition, "*sources of life*" makes it sufficiently clear that land is included in the instruments of labour.
The correction was introduced because Lassalle, for reasons now generally known, attacked *only* the capitalist class and not the landowners. In England, the capitalist is usually not even the owner of the land on which his factory stands.

> The emancipation of labour demands the promotion of the instruments of labour to the common property of society, and the co-operative regulation of the total labour with equitable distribution of the proceeds of labour.

"Promotion of the instruments of labour to the common property" ought obviously to read, their "conversion into the common property," but this only in passing.
What are the "proceeds of labour"? The product of labour or its value? And in the latter case, is it the total value of the product or only that part of the value which labour has newly added to the value of the means of production consumed?
The "proceeds of labour" is a loose notion which Lassalle has put in the place of definite economic conceptions.

What is "equitable distribution"?

Do not the bourgeois assert that the present-day distribution is "equitable"? And is it not, in fact, the only "equitable" distribution on the basis of the present-day mode of production? Are economic relations regulated by legal conceptions or do not, on the contrary, legal relations arise from economic ones? Have not also the socialist sectarians the most varied notions about "equitable" distribution?

To understand what idea is meant in this connection by the phrase "equitable distribution," we must take the first paragraph and this one together. The latter implies a society wherein "the instruments of labour are common property, and the total labour is co-operatively regulated," and from the first paragraph we learn that "the proceeds of labour belong undiminished with equal right to all members of society."

"To all members of society"? To those who do not work as well? What remains then of the "undiminished proceeds of labour"? Only to those members of society who work? What remains then of the "equal right" of all members of society?

But "all members of society" and "equal right" are obviously mere phrases. The kernel consists in this, that in this communist society every worker must receive the "undiminished" Lassallean "proceeds of labour."

Let us take first of all the words "proceeds of labour" in the sense of the product of labour, then the co-operative proceeds of labour are the *total social product.*

From this is then to be deducted:

First, cover for replacement of the means of production used up.

Secondly, additional portion for expansion of production.

Thirdly, reserve or insurance fund to provide against mis-adventures, disturbances through natural events, etc.

These deductions from the "undiminished proceeds of labour" are an economic necessity and their magnitude is to be determined by available means and forces, and partly by calculation of probabilities, but they are in no way calculable by equity.

There remains the other part of the total product, destined to serve as means of consumption.

Before this is divided among the individuals, there has to be deducted from it:

First, the general costs of administration not belonging to production.

This part will, from the outset, be very considerably restricted in comparison with present-day society and it diminishes in proportion as the new society develops.

Secondly, that which is destined for the communal satisfaction of needs, such as schools, health services, etc.

From the outset this part is considerably increased in comparison with present-day society and it increases in proportion as the new society develops.

Thirdly, funds for those unable to work, etc., in short, what is included under so-called official poor relief today.

Only now do we come to the "distribution" which the programme, under Lassallean influence, alone has in view in its narrow fashion, namely that part of the means of consumption which is divided among the individual producers of the co-operative society.

The "undiminished proceeds of labour" have already quietly become converted into the "diminished" proceeds, although what the producer is deprived of in his capacity as a private individual benefits him directly or indirectly in his capacity as a member of society.

Just as the phrase "undiminished proceeds of labour" has disappeared, so now does the phrase "proceeds of labour" disappear altogether.

Within the co-operative society based on common ownership of the means of production, the producers do not exchange their products; just as little does the labour employed on the products appear here *as the value* of these products, as a material quality possessed by them, since now, in contrast to capitalist society, individual labour no longer exists in an indirect fashion but directly as a component part of the total labour. The phrase "proceeds of labour," objectionable even today on account of its ambiguity, thus loses all meaning.

What we have to deal with here is a communist society, not as it has *developed* on its own foundations, but, on the contrary, as it *emerges* from capitalist society; which is thus in every respect, economically, morally and intellectually, still stamped with the birthmarks of the old society from whose womb it emerges. Accordingly the individual producer receives back from society—after the deductions have been made—exactly what he gives to it. What he has given to it is his individual amount of labour. For example, the social working day consists of the sum of the individual labour hours; the individual labour time of the individual producer is the part of the social labour day contributed by him, his share in it. He receives a certificate from society that he has furnished such and such an amount of labour (after deducting his labour for the common fund), and with this certificate he draws from the social stock of means of consumption as much as the same amount of labour costs. The same amount of labour which he has given to society in one form, he receives back in another.

Here obviously the same principle prevails as that which regulates the exchange of commodities, as far as this is exchange of equal values. Content and form are changed, because under the altered circumstances no one can give anything except his labour, and because, on the other hand, nothing can pass into the ownership of individuals except individual means of consumption. But, as far as the distribution of the latter among the individual producers is concerned, the same principle prevails as in the exchange of commodity-equivalents, so much labour in one form is exchanged for an equal amount of labour in another form.

Hence, *equal right* here is still in principle—*bourgeois right*, although principle and practice are no longer in conflict, while the exchange of equivalents in commodity exchange only exists on the *average* and not in the individual case.

In spite of this advance, this *equal right* is still stigmatised by a bourgeois limitation. The right of the producers is *proportional* to the labour they supply; the equality consists in the fact that measurement is made with an *equal standard*, labour.

But one man is superior to another physically or mentally and so supplies more labour in the same time, or can labour for a longer time; and labour, to serve as a measure, must be defined by its duration or intensity, otherwise it ceases to be a standard of measurement. This *equal* right is an unequal right for unequal labour. It recognises no class differences, because everyone is only a worker like everyone else; but it tacitly recognises unequal individual endowment and thus productive capacity as natural privileges. *It is therefore a right of inequality in its content, like every right.* Right by its very nature can only consist in the application of an equal standard; but unequal individuals (and they would not be different individuals if they were not unequal) are only measurable by an equal standard in so far as they are brought under an equal point of view, are taken from one *definite* side only, *e.g.*, in the present case are regarded *only as workers*, and nothing more seen in them, everything else being ignored. Further, one worker is married, another not; one has more children than another and so on and so forth. Thus with an equal output, and hence an equal share in the social consumption fund, one will in fact receive more than another, one will be richer than another, and so on. To avoid all these defects, right, instead of being equal, would have to be unequal.

But these defects are inevitable in the first phase of communist society as it is when it has just emerged after prolonged birth pangs from capitalist society. Right can never be higher than the economic structure of society and the cultural development thereby determined.

In a higher phase of communist society, after the enslaving subordination of individuals under division of labour, and therewith also the antithesis between mental and physical labour, has vanished; after labour, from a mere means of life, has itself become the prime necessity of life; after the productive forces have also increased with the all-round development of the individual, and all the springs of co-operative wealth flow more abundantly—only then can the narrow horizon of bourgeois right be fully left behind and society inscribe on its banners: from each according to his ability, to each according to his needs!

I have dealt more at length with the "undiminished proceeds of labour" on the one hand, and with "equal right" and "equitable distribution" on the other, in order to show what a crime it is to attempt, on the one hand, to force on our party again, as dogmas, ideas which in a certain period had some meaning but have now become obsolete rubbishy phrases, while on the other, perverting the realistic outlook, which has cost so much effort to instill into the party, but which has now taken root in it, by means of ideological nonsense about "right" and other trash common among the democrats and French Socialists.

Quite apart from the analysis so far given, it was in general incorrect to make a fuss about so-called "*distribution*" and put the principal stress on it.

The distribution of the means of consumption at any time is only a consequence of the distribution of the conditions of production themselves. The latter distribution, however, is a feature of the mode of production itself. The capitalist mode of production, for example, rests on the fact that the material conditions of production are in the hands of non-workers in the form of property in capital and land, while the masses are only owners of the personal condition of production, *viz.*, labour power. Once the elements of production are so distributed, then the present-day distribution of the means of consumption results automatically. If the material conditions of production are the co-operative property of the workers themselves, then this likewise results in a different distribution of the means of consumption from the present one. Vulgar socialism (and from it in turn a section of democracy) has taken over from the bourgeois economists the consideration and treatment of distribution as independent of the mode of production and hence the presentation of socialism as turning principally on distribution. After the real position has long been made clear, why go back again?

JUSTICE UNDER SOCIALISM

EDWARD NELL AND ONORA O'NEILL

"From each according to his ability, to each according to his need."

The stirring slogan that ends *The Critique of the Gotha Program* is generally taken as a capsule summary of the socialist approach to distributing the burdens and benefits of life. It can be seen as the statement of a noble ideal and yet be found wanting on three separate scores. First, there is no guarantee that, even if all contribute according to their abilities, all needs can be met: the principle gives us no guidance for distributing goods when some needs must go unmet. Second, if all contribute according to their abilities, there may be a material surplus after all needs are met: again, the principle gives us no guidance for distributing such a surplus. Third, the principle incorporates no suggestion as to why each man would contribute according to his ability: no incentive structure is evident.

These apparent shortcomings can be compared with those of other principles a society might follow in distributing burdens and benefits. Let us call

1. "From each according to his ability, to each according to his need," the *Socialist Principle of Justice.*

Its Capitalist counterpart would be

2. From each according to his choice, given his assets, to each according to his contribution. We shall call this the *Laissez-Faire Principle.*

These two principles will require a good deal of interpretation, but at the outset we can say that in the Socialist Principle of Justice "abilities" and "needs" refer to persons, whereas the "choices" and "contributions" in the Laissez-Faire Principle refer also to the management of impersonal property, the given assets. It goes without saying that some of the "choices," particularly those of the propertyless, are normally made under considerable duress. As "choice" is the ideologically favored term, we shall retain it.

In a society where the Socialist Principle of Justice regulates distribution, the requirement is that everyone use such talents as have been developed in him (though this need not entail any allocation of workers to jobs), and the payment of workers is contingent not upon their contributions but upon their needs. In a laissez-faire society, where individuals may be endowed with more or less capital or with bare labor power, they choose in the light of these assets how and how much to work (they may be dropouts or moonlighters), and/or how to invest their capital, and they are paid in proportion.

None of the three objections raised against the Socialist Principle of Justice holds for the Laissez-Faire Principle. Whatever the level of contribution individuals choose, their aggregate product can be distributed in proportion to the contribution—whether of capital or of labor—each individual chooses to make. The Laissez-Faire Principle is applicable under situations both of scarcity and of abundance, and it incorporates a theory of incentives: people choose their level of contribution in order to get a given level of material reward.

Principles 1 and 2 can be crossfertilized, yielding two further principles:

---

3. From each according to his ability, to each according to his contribution.
4. From each according to his choice, to each according to his need.

Principle 3 could be called an *Incentive Socialist Principle* of distribution. Like the Socialist Principle of Justice, it pictures a society in which all are required to work in proportion to the talents that have been developed in them. Since unearned income is not available and rewards are hinged to contribution rather than need, all work is easily enforced in an economy based on the Incentive Socialist Principle. This principle, however, covers a considerable range of systems. It holds for a Stalinist economy with an authoritarian job allocation. It also holds for a more liberal, market socialist economy in which there is a more or less free labor market, though without an option to drop out or live on unearned income, or the freedom to choose the level and type of qualification one is prepared to acquire. The Incentive Socialist Principle rewards workers according to their contribution: it is a principle of distribution in which an incentive system—reliance on material rewards—is explicit. Marx believed this principle would have to be followed in the early stages of socialism, in a society "still stamped with the birthmarks of the old society."

Under the Incentive Socialist Principle, each worker receives back the value of the amount of work he contributes to society in one form or another. According to Marx, this is a form of bourgeois right that "tacitly recognizes unequal individual endowments, and thus natural privileges in respect of productive capacity." So this principle holds for a still deficient society where the needs of particular workers, which depend on many things other than their productive capacity, may not be met. Although it may be less desirable than the Socialist Principle of Justice, the Incentive Socialist Principle clearly meets certain criteria the Socialist Principle of Justice cannot meet. It provides a principle of allocation that can be applied equally well to the various situations of scarcity, sufficiency, and abundance. Its material incentive structure explains how under market socialism, given a capital structure and a skill structure, workers will choose jobs and work hard at them—and also why under a Stalinist economy workers will work hard at jobs to which they have been allocated.

Under the Incentive Socialist Principle, workers—whether assigned to menial work or to specific jobs—respond to incentives of the same sort as do workers under the Laissez-Faire Principle. The difference is that, while the Laissez-Faire Principle leaves the measurement of the contribution of a worker to be determined by the level of wage he is offered, the Incentive Socialist Principle relies on a bureaucratically determined weighting that takes into account such factors as the difficulty, duration, qualification level, and risk involved in a given job.

There is another difference between societies living under the Laissez-Faire Principle and those following the Incentive Socialist Principle. Under the Laissez-Faire Principle, there is no central coordination of decisions, for assets are managed according to the choices of their owners. This gives rise to the well-known problems of instability and unemployment. Under the Incentive Socialist Principle, assets are managed by the central government; hence one would expect instability to be eliminated and full employment guaranteed. However, we do not regard this difference as a matter of principle on the same level with others we are discussing. Moreover, in practice some recognizable capitalist societies have managed to control fluctuations without undermining the Laissez-Faire Principle as the principle of distribution.

Let us call Principle 4 the *Utopian Principle of Justice*. It postulates a society without any requirement of contribution or material incentives, but with guaranteed minimal consumption. This principle suffers from the same defect as the Socialist Principle of Justice: it does not determine distributions of benefits under conditions either of scarcity or of abundance, and it suggests no incentive structure to explain why enough should be contributed to its economy to make it possible to satisfy needs. Whether labor is contributed according to choice or according to ability, it is conceivable that the aggregate social product should be such that either some needs cannot be met or that, when all needs are met, a surplus remains that cannot be divided on the basis of needs.

On the surface, this Utopian Principle of Justice exudes the aroma of laissez-faire: though needs will not go unmet in utopia, contributions will be made for no more basic reason than individual whim. They are tied neither to the reliable effects of the incentive of material reward for oneself, nor to those of the noble ideal of filling the needs of others, nor to a conception of duty or self-sacrifice. Instead, contributions will come forth, if they do, according to the free and unconstrained choices of individual economic agents, on the basis of their given preferences. Preferences, however, are not "given"; they develop and change, are learned and unlearned, and follow fashions and fads. Whim, fancy, pleasure, desire, wish are all words suggesting this aspect of consumer choice. By tying the demand for products to needs and the supply of work to choice, the Utopian Principle of Justice ensures stability in the former but does not legislate against fluctuations and unpredictable variability in the latter.

So the Socialist Principle of Justice and the Utopian Principle of Justice suffer from a common defect. There is no reason to suppose these systems will operate at precisely the level at which aggregate output is sufficient to meet all the needs without surplus. And since people do not need an income in money terms but rather an actual and quite precisely defined list of food, clothing, housing, etc. (bearing in mind the various alternatives that might be substituted), the *aggregate* measured in value terms could be right, yet the *composition* might still be unable to meet all the people's needs. People might choose or have the ability to do the right amount of work, but on the wrong projects. One could even imagine the economy growing from a situation of scarcity to one of abundance without ever passing through any point at which its aggregate output could be distributed to meet precisely the needs of its population.

So far, we have been considering not the justification or desirability of alternative principles of distribution, but their practicality. It appears that, in this respect, principles hinging reward on contribution rather than on need have a great advantage. They can both provide a general principle of distribution and indicate the pattern of incentives to which workers will respond.

It might be held that these advantages are restricted to the Incentive Socialist Principle in its various versions, since under the Laissez-Faire Principle there is some income—property income—which is not being paid in virtue of any contribution. This problem can be dealt with either, as we indicated above, by interpreting the notion of contribution to cover the contribution of one's assets to the capital market, or by restricting the scope of the Laissez-Faire Principle to cover workers only, or by interpreting the notion of property income so as to regard wages as a return to property, i.e., property in one's labor power. One can say that under capitalism part of the aggregate product is set aside for the owners of capital (and another part, as under market socialism, for government expenditure) and the remainder is distributed according to the Laissez-Faire Principle. Or one may say that property income is paid in virtue of past contributions, whose reward was not consumed at the time it was earned but was stored. Apologists tend to favor interpretations that make the worker a sort of capitalist or the capitalist a sort of slow-consuming worker. Whichever line is taken, it is clear that the Laissez-Faire Principle—however undesirable we may find it—is a principle of distribution that can be of general use in two senses. Appropriately interpreted, it covers the distribution of earned and of unearned income, and it applies in situations both of scarcity and of abundance.

So we seem to have reached the paradoxical conclusion that the principle of distribution requiring that workers' needs be met is of no use in situations of need, since it does not assign priorities among needs, and that the principle demanding that each contribute according to his ability is unable to explain what incentives will lead him to do so. In this view, the Socialist Principle of Justice would have to be regarded as possibly noble but certainly unworkable.

The Socialist Principle Defended

But this view should not be accepted. Marx formulated the Socialist Principle of Justice on the basis of a conception of human abilities and needs that will yield some guidance to its interpretation. We shall now try to see whether the difficulties discussed above can be alleviated when we consider this principle in the light of Marxian theory.

Marx clearly thought that the Socialist Principle of Justice was peculiarly relevant to situations of abundance. In the last section we argued that, on the contrary, it was an adequate principle of distribution only when aggregate output exactly covered total needs. The source of this discrepancy lies in differing analyses of human needs.

By fulfillment of needs we understand at least a subsistence income. Needs are not met when a person lacks sufficient food, clothing, shelter, medical care, or socially necessary training/education. But beyond this biological and social minimum we can point to another set of needs, which men do not have qua men but acquire qua producers. Workers need not merely a biological and social minimum, but whatever other goods—be they holidays or contacts with others whose work bears on theirs or guaranteed leisure, which they need to perform their jobs as well as possible. So a principle of distribution according to needs will not be of use only to a subsistence-level economy. Very considerable goods over and above those necessary for biological subsistence can be distributed according to a principle of need.

But despite this extension of the concept of need the Socialist Principle of Justice still seems to face the three problems listed [earlier]:

1. What guarantees are there that even under abundance the *composition* of the output with all contributing according to their abilities, will suffice to fill all needs? (There may still be scarcities of goods needed to fill either biological or job-related needs.)
2. What principle can serve to distribute goods that are surplus both to biological and to job-related needs?
3. What system of incentives explains why each will contribute to the full measure of his abilities, though he is not materially rewarded for increments of effort? Whether or not there is authoritative job allocation, job performance cannot be guaranteed.

Marx's solution to these problems does not seem too explicit. But much is suggested by the passage at the end of the *Critique of the Gotha Program* where he describes the higher phase of communist society as one in which "labor is no longer merely a means of life but has become life's principal need."

To most people it sounds almost comic to claim that labor could become life's principal need: it suggests a society of compulsive workers. Labor in the common view is intrinsically undesirable, but undertaken as a means to some further, typically material, end. For Marx this popular view would have been confirmation of his own view of the degree to which most labor under capitalism is alienating. He thought that under capitalism laborers experienced a threefold alienation: alienation from the *product* of their labor, which is for them merely a means to material reward; alienation from the *process* of labor, which is experienced as forced labor rather than as desirable activity; and alienation from *others*, since activities undertaken with others are undertaken as a means to achieving further ends, which are normally scarce and allocated competitively. Laborers cooperate in production but, under capitalism, compete for job and income, and the competition overrides the cooperation. Hence Marx claims (in the *Economic and Philosophical Manuscripts*) that "life itself appears only as a means to life." Though the horror of that situation is apparent in the very words, many people accept that labor should be only a means to life—whose real ends lie elsewhere; whether in religion, consumption, personal relations, or leisure.

Marx, on the other hand, held that labor could be more than a means; it could also be an end of life, for labor in itself—*the activity*—can, like other activities, be something for whose sake one does other things. We would be loath to think that activity itself should appear only as a means to life—on the contrary, life's worth for most people lies in the activities undertaken. Those we call labor do not differ intrinsically from the rest, only in relation to the system of production. In Marx's view a system was possible in which all activities undertaken would be nonalienating. Nobody would have to compete to engage in an activity he found unpleasant for the sake of a material reward. Instead, workers would cooperate in creative and fulfilling activities that provide occasions for the experience of talents, for taking responsibilities, and that result in useful or beautiful products. In such a situation one can see why labor would be regarded as life's greatest need, rather than as its scourge. Nonalienated labor is humanly fulfilling activity.

In the course of switching from the conception of alienating labor to that of nonalienating labor, it might seem that we have moved into a realm for which principles of distribution may be irrelevant. What can the Socialist Principle of Justice tell us about the distribution of burdens and benefits in "the higher phase of Communist society?"

In such a society each is to contribute according to his abilities. In the light of the discussion of nonalienated labor, it is clear that there is no problem of incentives. Each man works at what he wants to work at. He works because that is his need. (This is not a situation in which "moral incentives" have replaced material ones, for both moral and material incentives are based on alienating labor. The situation Marx envisages is one for which incentives of *all* sorts are irrelevant.)

Though this disposes of the problem of incentives under the Socialist Principle of Justice, it is much less clear whether this principle can work for a reasonable range of situations. Can it cope with both the situation of abundance and that of scarcity?

In the case of abundance, a surplus of goods over and above those needed is provided. But if all activities are need-fulfilling, then no work is done that does not fulfill some need. In a sense there is no surplus to be distributed, for nothing needless is being done. Nevertheless, there may be a surplus of material goods that are the by-product of need-fulfilling activity. In a society where everybody fulfills himself by painting pictures, there may be a vast surplus of pictures. If so, the Socialist Principle of Justice gives no indication of the right method for their distribution; they are not the goal for which the task was undertaken. Since they do not fulfill an objective need, the method for their distribution is not important. In this the higher phase of communist society is, as one might expect, the very antithesis of consumerism; rather than fabricate reasons for desiring and so acquiring what is not needed, it disregards anything that is not needed in decisions of distribution.

There, nevertheless, is a problem of distribution the Socialist Principle of Justice does not attempt to solve. Some of the products of need-fulfilling activity may be things other people either desire or detest. When need-fulfilling activity yields works of art or noisy block parties, its distribution cannot be disregarded. Not all planning problems can be solved by the Socialist Principle of Justice. We shall not discuss the merits of various principles that could serve to handle these cases, but shall only try to delimit the scope of the Socialist Principle of Justice.

This brings us to the problem of scarcity. Can the Socialist Principle of Justice explain why, when all contribute to the extent of their abilities, all needs can be met? Isn't it conceivable that everyone should find fulfillment in painting, but nobody find fulfillment in producing either biological necessities or the canvases, brushes, and paints everybody wants to use? Might not incentive payments be needed, even in this higher phase of communist society, to guarantee the production of subsistence goods and job-related necessities? In short, will not any viable system involve some alienating labor?

Marx at any rate guarantees that communism need not involve much alienating labor. He insists that the Socialist Principle of Justice is applicable only in a context of abundance. For only when man's needs can be met is it relevant to insist that they ought to be met. The Socialist Principle of Justice comes into its own only with the development of the forces of production. But, of course, higher productivity does not by itself guarantee the right composition of output. Subsistence goods and job-related services and products might not be provided as the population fulfills itself in painting, poetry, and sculpture. Man cannot live by works of art alone.

This socialist version of the story of Midas should not alarm us too much. The possibility of starvation amidst abundant art works seemed plausible only because we abstracted it from other features of an abundant socialist society. Such a society is a planned society, and part of its planning concerns the ability structure of the population. Such a society would include people able to perform all tasks necessary to maintain a high level of material well-being.

Nevertheless, there may be certain essential tasks in such a society whose performance is not need-fulfilling for anybody. Their allocation presents another planning problem for which the Socialist Principle of Justice, by hypothesis, is not a solution. But the degree of coercion need not be very great. In a highly productive society the amount of labor expended on nonfulfilling tasks is a diminishing proportion of total labor time. Hence, given equitable allocation of this burden (and it is here that the planning decisions are really made), nobody would be prevented from engaging principally in need-fulfilling activities. In the limiting case of abundance, where automation of the production of material needs is complete, nobody would have to do any task he did not find intrinsically worthwhile. To the extent that this abundance is not reached, the Socialist Principle of Justice cannot be fully implemented.

However, the degree of coercion experienced by those who are allocated to necessary but nonfulfilling chores may be reducible if the planning procedure is of a certain sort. To the extent that people participate in planning and that they realize the necessity of the nonfulfilling chores in order for everyone to be able to do also what he finds need-fulfilling, they may find the performance of these chores less burdensome. As they want to achieve the ends, so—once they are informed—they cannot rationally resent the means, provided they perceive the distribution of chores as just.

The point can be taken a step further. Under the Socialist Principle of Justice, households do not put forth productive effort to be rewarded with an aliquot portion of time and means for self-fulfillment. It is precisely this market mentality from which we wish to escape. The miserable toil of society should be

> performed gratis for the benefit of society . . . performed not as a definite duty, not for the purpose of obtaining a right to certain products, not according to previously established and legally fixed quotas, but voluntary labor . . . performed because it has become a habit to work for the common good, and because of a conscious realization (that has become a habit) of the necessity of working for the common good.[1]

Creative work should be done for its own sake, not for any reward. Drudgery should be done for the common good, not to be rewarded with opportunity and means for creative work. Of course, the better and more efficient the performance of drudgery, the more will be the opportunities for creative work. To realize this, however, is to understand the necessity of working for the common good, not to be animated by private material incentives. For the possibilities of creative work are opened by the simultaneous and parallel development of large numbers of people. To take the arts, poets need a public, authors readers, performers audiences, and all need (though few want) critics. One cannot sensibly wish, under the Socialist Principle of Justice, to be rewarded *privately* with opportunities and means for nonalienated work.

There is a question regarding the distribution of educational opportunities. Before men can contribute according to their abilities, their abilities must be developed. But in whom should society develop which abilities? If we regard education as consumption, then according to the Socialist Principle of Justice, each should receive it according to his need.

It is clear that all men require some early training to make them viable social beings; further, all men require certain general skills necessary for performing work. But we could hardly claim that some men need to be doctors or economists or lawyers, or need to receive any other specialized or expensive training. If, on the other hand, we regard education as production of those skills necessary for maintaining society and providing the possibility of fulfillment, then the Socialist Principle of Justice can determine a lower bound to the production of certain skills: so-and-so many farmers/doctors/mechanics must be produced to satisfy future subsistence and job-related needs. But the Socialist Principle of Justice cannot determine who shall get which of these educational opportunities. One traditional answer might be that each person should specialize at whatever he is relatively best suited to do. Yet this only makes sense in terms of tasks done as onerous means to desirable ends. Specialization on the basis of comparative advantage minimizes the effort in achieving given ends; but if work is itself fulfilling, it is not an "effort" that must be minimized.

In conditions of abundance, it is unlikely that anyone will be denied training they want and can absorb, though they may have to acquire skills they do not particularly want, since some onerous tasks may still have to be done. For even in conditions of abundance, it may be necessary to compel some or all to undertake certain unwanted training in the interests of the whole. But it is not necessary to supplement the Socialist Principle of Justice with an incentive scheme, whether material or moral. The principle already contains the Kantian maxim: develop your talents to the utmost, for only in this way can a person contribute to the limits of his ability. And if a society wills the end of self-fulfillment, it must will sufficient means. If the members of society take part in planning to maintain and expand the opportunities for everyone's nonalienated activity, they must understand the necessity of allocating the onerous tasks, and so the training for them.

Perhaps we can make our point clearer by looking briefly at Marx's schematic conception of the stages of modern history—feudalism, capitalism, socialism, communism—where each stage is characterized by a higher productivity of labor than the preceding stage. In feudalism, the principle of distribution would be:

5. From each according to his status, to each according to his status—the *Feudal Principles of Justice.*

There is no connection between work and reward. There are no market incentives in the "ideal" feudal system. Peasants grow the stuff for their own subsistence and perform traditional labor services for their lord on domain land. He in turn provides protection and government in traditional fashion. Yet, though labor is not performed as a means to a distant or abstract end, as when it is done for money, it still is done for survival, not for its own sake, and those who do it are powerless to control their conditions of work or their own destinies. Man lives on the edge of famine and is subject to the vagaries of the weather and the dominion of tradition. Only a massive increase in productive powers frees him. But to engender this increase men must come to connect work directly with reward. This provides the incentive to labor, both to take those jobs most needed (moving from the farm to the factory) and to work sufficiently hard once on the job.

But more than work is needed; the surplus of output over that needed to maintain the work force (including materials) and replace and repair the means of production (machines, raw materials) must be put to productive use; it must be reinvested, not consumed. In capitalism, station at birth determines whether one works or owns capital; workers are rewarded for their contribution of work, capitalists for theirs of reinvestment. There is a stick as well as a carrot. Those workers who do not work, starve; those capitalists who fail to reinvest, fail to grow and will eventually be crushed by their larger rivals. Socialism rationalizes this by eliminating the two-class dichotomy and by making reinvestment a function of the institutions of the state, so that the capital structure of the society is the collective property of the citizenry, all of whom must work for reward. In this system the connection between work and reward reaches its fullest development, and labor in one sense is most fully alienated. The transition to communism then breaks this link altogether.

The link between work and rewards serves a historical purpose; namely, to encourage the development of the productive forces. But as the productive forces continue to develop, the demand for additional rewards will tend to decline, while the difficulty of stimulating still further growth in productivity may increase. This at least, seems to be implied by the principles of conventional economics—diminishing marginal utility and diminishing marginal productivity. Even if one rejects most of the conventional wisdom of economics, a good case can be made for the diminishing efficacy of material incentives as prosperity increases. For as labor productivity rises, private consumption needs will be met, and the most urgent needs remaining will be those requiring *collective* consumption—and, indeed, some of these needs will be generated by the process of growth and technical progress. These last needs, if left unmet, may hinder further attempts to raise the productive power of labor. So the system of material incentives could in principle come to a point where the weakened encouragements to extra productivity offered as private reward for contribution might be offset by the accumulated hindrances generated by the failures to meet collective needs and by the wastes involved in competition. At this point, it becomes appropriate to break the link between work and reward. Breaking the link, however, is not enough. Both the Socialist Principle of Justice and the Utopian Principle of Justice break the link between work and reward. But the Utopian Principle of Justice leaves the distinction between them. Work is a means, the products of work are the ends. Given a high productivity of labor, workers would in principle choose their occupations and work-leisure patterns, yet still producing enough to satisfy everyone's needs. This would be a society devoted to minimizing effort, a sort of high-technology Polynesia. Since it neither makes consumption dependent upon work nor regards work as other than a regrettable means to consumption, it fails to explain why sufficient work to supply basic needs should ever be done. The alienation of labor cannot be overcome by eliminating labor rather than alienation.

Breaking the link, between work and reward, while leaving the distinction itself intact, may also lead to the loss of the productive powers of labor. For without reward, and when the object is to work as little as possible, why expend the effort to acquire highly complex skills? What is the motive to education, self-improvement, self-development? A high-technology Polynesia contains an inner contradiction.

By contrast, the Socialist Principle of Justice not only does not make reward depend upon work but denies that there is a distinction between the two. Because man needs fulfilling activity—work that he chooses and wants—men who get it contribute according to their ability.

Yet there still may remain routine and menial, unfulfilling jobs. But who wills the end wills the means. The society must plan to have such jobs done. No doubt many will be mechanized or automated, but the remaining ones will form a burden that must be allocated.

The Socialist Principle of Justice cannot solve this problem of allocation. But everyone has some interest in getting uncoveted but essential work done. Hence it should not be difficult to find an acceptable supplementary principle of distribution for allocating these chores. For instance, the Principle of Comparative Advantage might be introduced to assign each the drudgery at which he is relatively best. There can be no quarrel with this so long as such alienating work is only a small fraction of a man's total activity, conferring no special status. It is only when alienating work takes up the bulk of one's waking hours, and determines status, that specialization inevitably entails some form of class structure.

The Socialist Principle of Justice cannot solve all allocation problems. But once one understands that it is based on a denial of a distinction between work, need, and reward, it is clear that it can solve an enormous range of such problems. In a highly productive society the only allocation problems the Socialist Principle of Justice cannot solve are the distribution of unmechanized and uncoveted chores and of the material by-products of creative endeavor.

THE NONEXISTENCE OF BASIC WELFARE RIGHTS

TIBOR R. MACHAN

James Sterba and others maintain that we all have the right to "receive the goods and resources necessary for preserving" ourselves. This is not what I have argued human beings have a right to. They have the right, rather, not to be killed, attacked, and deprived of their property—by persons in or outside of government. As Abraham Lincoln put it, "no man is good enough to govern another man, without that other's consent."[1]

Sterba claims that various political outlooks would have to endorse these "rights." He sets out to show, in particular, that welfare rights follow from libertarian theory itself.[2] Sterba wishes to show that *if* Lockean libertarianism is correct, then we all have rights to welfare and equal (economic) opportunity. What I wish to show is that since Lockean libertarianism—as developed in this work—is true, and since the rights to welfare and equal opportunity require their violation, no one has these latter rights. The reason some people, including Sterba, believe otherwise is that they have found some very rare instances in which some citizens could find themselves in circumstances that would require disregarding rights altogether. This would be in situations that cannot be characterized to be "where peace is possible."[3] And every major libertarian thinker from Locke to the present has treated these kinds of cases.[4]

Let us be clear about what Sterba sets out to show. It is that libertarians are philosophically unable to escape the welfare-statist implications of their commitment to negative liberty. This means that despite their belief that they are only supporting the enforceable right of every person not to be coerced by other persons, libertarians must accept, by the logic of their own position, that individuals also possess basic enforceable rights to being provided with various services from others. He holds, then, that basic negative rights imply basic positive rights.

To Lockean libertarians the ideal of liberty means that we all, individually, have the right not to be constrained against our consent within our realm of authority—ourselves and our belongings. Sterba states that for such libertarians "Liberty is being unconstrained by persons from doing what one has a right to do."[5] Sterba adds, somewhat misleadingly, that for Lockean libertarians "a right to life [is] a right not to be killed unjustly and a right to property [is] a right to acquire goods and resources either by initial acquisition or voluntary agreement."[6] Sterba does realize that these rights do not entitle one to receive from others the goods and resources necessary for preserving one's life.

A problem with this foundation of the Lockean libertarian view is that political justice—not the justice of Plato, which is best designated in our time as "perfect virtue"—for natural-rights theorists presupposes individual rights. One cannot then explain rights in terms of justice but must explain justice in terms of rights.

For a Lockean libertarian, to possess any basic right to receive the goods and resources necessary for preserving one's life conflicts with possessing the right not to be killed, assaulted, or stolen from. The latter are rights Lockean libertarians consider to be held by all individual human beings. Regularly to protect and maintain—that is, enforce—the former right would often require the violation of the latter. A's right to the food she has is incompatible with B's right to take this same food. Both the rights could not be fundamental in an integrated legal system. The situation of one's having rights to welfare, and so forth, and another's having rights to life, liberty, and property is thus theoretically intolerable and practically unfeasible. The point of a system of rights is the securing of mutually peaceful and consistent moral conduct on the part of human beings. As Rand observes,

> "Rights" are . . . the link between the moral code of a man and the legal code of a society, between ethics and politics. *Individual rights are the means of subordinating society to moral law.*[7]

Sterba asks us—in another discussion of his views—to consider what he calls "a *typical* conflict situation between the rich and the poor." He says that in his situation "the rich, of course, have more than enough resources to satisfy their basic needs. By contrast, the poor lack the resources to meet their most basic needs even though *they have tried all the means available to them that libertarians regard as legitimate for acquiring such resources*"[8] (my emphasis).

The goal of a theory of rights would be defeated if rights were typically in conflict. Some bureaucratic group would have to keep applying its moral intuitions on numerous occasions when rights claims would *typically* conflict. A constitution is workable if it helps remove at least the largest proportion of such decisions from the realm of arbitrary (intuitive) choice and avail a society of men and women of objective guidelines that are reasonably integrated, not in relentless discord.

Most critics of libertarianism assume some doctrine of basic needs that they invoke to show that whatever basic needs are not satisfied for some people, while others have "resources" that are not basic needs for them, the former have just claims against the latter. (The language of resources of course loads the argument in the critic's favor since it suggests that these goods simply come into being and happen to be in the possession of some people, quite without rhyme or reason, arbitrarily [as John Rawls claims].)[9]

This doctrine is full of difficulties. It lacks any foundation for why the needs of some persons must be claims upon the lives of others. And why are there such needs anyway—to what end are they needs, and whose ends are these and why are not the persons whose needs they are held responsible for supplying the needs? (Needs, as I have already observed, lack any force in moral argument without the prior justification of the purposes they serve, or the goals they help to fulfill. A thief has a basic need of skills and powers that are clearly not justified if theft is morally unjustified. If, however, the justification of basic needs, such as food and other resources, presupposes the value of human life, and if the value of human life justifies, as I have argued earlier, the principle of the natural rights to life, liberty and property, then the attainment or fulfillment of the basic need for food may not involve the violation of these rights.)

Sterba claims that without guaranteeing welfare and equal-opportunity rights, Lockean libertarianism violates the most basic tenets of any morality, namely, that "ought" implies "can." The thrust of "'ought' implies 'can'" is that one ought to do that which one is free to do, that one is morally responsible only for those acts that one had the power either to choose to engage in or not to engage in. (There is debate on just how this point must be phrased—in terms of the will being free or the person being free to will something. For our purposes, however, all that counts is that the person must have [had] a genuine option to do X or not to do X before it can be true that he or she ought to do X or ought to have done X.) If an innocent person is forced by the actions of another to forgo significant moral choices, then that innocent person is not free to act morally and thus his or her human dignity is violated.

This is not so different from the common-sense legal precept that if one is not sound of mind one cannot be criminally culpable. Only free agents, capable of choosing between right and wrong, are open to moral evaluation. This indeed is the reason that many so-called moral theories fail to be anything more than value theories. They omit from consideration the issue of self-determination. If either hard or soft determinism is true, morality is impossible, although values need not disappear.[10]

If Sterba were correct about Lockean libertarianism typically contradicting "'ought' implies 'can,'" his argument would be decisive. (There are few arguments against this principle that I know of and they have not convinced me. They trade on rare circumstances when persons feel guilt for taking actions that had bad consequences even though they could not have avoided them.)[11] It is because Karl Marx's and Herbert Spencer's systems typically, normally, indeed in every case, violate this principle that they are not bona fide moral systems. And quite a few others may be open to a similar charge.[12]

Sterba offers his strongest argument when he observes that "'ought' implies 'can'" is violated "when the rich prevent the poor from taking what they require to satisfy their basic needs even though they have tried all the means available to them that libertarians regard as legitimate for acquiring such resources."[13]

Is Sterba right that such are—indeed, must be—typical conflict cases in a libertarian society? Are the rich and poor, even admitting that there is some simple division of people into such economic groups, in such hopeless conflict all the time? Even in the case of homeless people, many find help without having to resort to theft. The political factors contributing to the presence of helpless people in the United States and other Western liberal democracies are a hotly debated issue, even among utilitarians and welfare-state supporters. Sterba cannot make his argument for the typicality of such cases by reference to history alone. (Arguably, there are fewer helpless poor in near-libertarian, capitalist systems than anywhere else—why else would virtually everyone wish to live in these societies rather than those where welfare is guaranteed, indeed enforced? Not, at least originally, for their welfare-statist features. Arguably, too, the disturbing numbers of such people in these societies could be due, in part, to the lack of consistent protection of all the libertarian natural rights.)

Nonetheless, in a system that legally protects and preserves property rights there will be cases where a rich person prevents a poor person from taking what belongs to her (the rich person)—for example, a chicken that the poor person might use to feed herself. Since after such prevention the poor person might starve, Sterba asks the rhetorical question, "Have the rich, then, in contributing to this result, killed the poor, or simply let them die; and if they have killed the poor, have they done so unjustly?"[14] His answer is that they have. Sterba holds that a system that accords with the Lockean libertarian's idea that the rich person's preventive action is just "imposes an unreasonable sacrifice upon" the poor, one "that we could not blame them for trying to evade." Not permitting the poor to act to satisfy their basic needs is to undermine the precept that "'ought' implies 'can,'" since, as Sterba claims, that precept means, for the poor, that they ought to satisfy their basic needs. This they must have the option to do if they ought to do it.

When people defend their property, what are they doing? They are protecting themselves against the intrusive acts of some other person, acts that would normally deprive them of something to which they have a right, and the other has no right. As such, these acts of protectiveness make it possible for men and women in society to retain their own sphere of jurisdiction intact, protect their own "moral space."[15] They refuse to have their human dignity violated. They want to be sovereigns and govern their own lives, including their own productive decisions and actions. Those who mount the attack, in turn, fail or refuse to refrain from encroaching upon the moral space of their victims. They are treating the victim's life and its productive results as though these were unowned resources for them to do with as they choose.

Now the argument that cuts against the above account is that on some occasions there can be people who, with no responsibility for their situation, are highly unlikely to survive without disregarding the rights of others and taking from them what they need. This is indeed possible. It is no less possible that there be cases in which someone is highly unlikely to survive without obtaining the services of a doctor who is at that moment spending time healing someone else, or in which there is a person who is highly unlikely to survive without obtaining one of the lungs of another person, who wants to keep both lungs so as to be able to run the New York City marathon effectively. And such cases could be multiplied indefinitely.

But are such cases typical? The argument that starts with this assumption about a society is already not comparable to the libertarianism that has emerged in the footsteps of Lockean natural-rights doctrine, including the version advanced in this book. That system is developed for a human community in which "peace is possible." Libertarian individual rights, which guide men and women in such an adequately hospitable environment to act without thwarting the flourishing of others, are thus suitable bases for the legal foundations of a human society. It is possible for people in the world to pursue their proper goals without thwarting a similar pursuit by others.

The underlying notion of society in such a theory rejects the description of human communities implicit in Sterba's picture. Sterba sees conflict as typically arising from some people producing and owning goods, while others having no alternative but to take these goods from the former in order to survive. But these are not the typical conflict situations even in what we today consider reasonably free human communities—most thieves and robbers are not destitute, nor are they incapable of doing something aside from taking other people's property in order to obtain their livelihood.

The typical conflict situation in society involves people who wish to take shortcuts to earning their living (and a lot more) by attacking others, not those who lack any other alternative to attacking others so as to reach that same goal. This may not be evident from all societies that teem with human conflict—in the Middle East, or Central and South America, for example. But it must be remembered that these societies are far from being even near-libertarian. Even if the typical conflicts there involved the kind Sterba describes, that would not suffice to make his point. Only if it were true that in comparatively free countries the typical conflict involved the utterly destitute and helpless arrayed against the well-to-do, could his argument carry any conviction.

The Lockean libertarian has confidence in the willingness and capacity of *virtually all persons* to make headway in life in a free society. The very small minority of exceptional cases must be taken care of by voluntary social institutions, not by the government, which guards self-consistent individual rights.

The integrity of law would be seriously endangered if the government entered areas that required it to make very particular judgments and depart from serving the interest of the public as such. We have already noted that the idea of "satisfying basic needs" can involve the difficulty of distinguishing those whose actions are properly to be so characterized. Rich persons are indeed satisfying their basic needs as they protect and preserve their property rights. . . . Private property rights are necessary for a morally decent society.

The Lockean libertarian argues that private property rights are morally justified in part because they are concrete requirements for delineating the sphere of jurisdiction of each person's moral authority, where her own judgment is decisive.[16] This is a crucial basis for the right to property. And so is the contention that we live in a metaphysically hospitable universe wherein people normally need not suffer innocent misery and deprivation—so that such a condition is usually the result of negligence or the violation of Lockean rights, a violation that has made self-development and commerce impossible. If exceptional emergencies set the agenda for the law, the law itself will disintegrate. (A just legal system makes provision for coping with emergencies that are brought to the attention of the authorities, for example, by way of judicial discretion, without allowing such cases to determine the direction of the system. If legislators and judges don't uphold the integrity of the system, disintegration ensues. This can itself encourage the emergence of strong leaders, demagogues, who promise to do what the law has not been permitted to do, namely, satisfy people's sense of justice. Experience with them bodes ill for such a prospect.)

Normally persons do not "lack the opportunities and resources to satisfy their own basic needs." Even if we grant that some helpless, crippled, retarded, or destitute persons could offer nothing to anyone that would merit wages enabling them to carry on their lives and perhaps even flourish, there is still the other possibility for most actual, known hard cases, namely seeking help. I am not speaking here of the cases we know: people who drop out of school, get an unskilled job, marry and have kids, only to find that their personal choice of inadequate preparation for life leaves them relatively poorly off. "'Ought' implies 'can'" must not be treated ahistorically—some people's lack of current options results from their failure to exercise previous options prudently. I refer here to the "truly needy," to use a shop-worn but still useful phrase—those who have never been able to help themselves and are not now help-less from their own neglect. Are such people being treated *unjustly*, rather than at most uncharitably, ungenerously, indecently, pitilessly, or in some other respect immorally—by those who, knowing of the plight of such persons, resist forcibly efforts to take from them enough to provide the ill-fated with what they truly need? Actually, if we tried to pry the needed goods or money from the well-to-do, we would not even learn if they would act generously. Charity, generosity, kindness, and acts of compassion pre-suppose that those well enough off are not coerced to provide help. These virtues cannot flourish, nor can the corresponding vices, of course, without a clearly identified and well-protected right to private property for all.

If we consider the situation as we are more likely to find it, namely, that desperate cases not caused by previous injustices (in the libertarian sense) are rare, then, contrary to what Sterba suggests, there is much that unfortunate persons can and should do in those plausible, non-emergency situations that can be considered typical. They need not resort to violating the private-property rights of those who are better off. The destitute can appeal for assistance both from the rich and from the many voluntary social service agencies that emerge from the widespread compassion of people who know about the mishaps that can at times strike perfectly decent people.

Consider, as a prototype of this situation on which we might model what concerns Sterba, that if one's car breaks down on a remote road, it would be unreasonable to expect one not to seek a phone or some other way of escaping one's unfortunate situation. So one ought to at least try to obtain the use of a phone.

But should one break into the home of a perfect stranger living nearby? Or ought one instead to request the use of the phone as a favor? "'Ought' implies 'can'" is surely fully satisfied here. Actual prac-tice makes this quite evident. When someone is suffering from misfortune and there are plenty of others who are not, and the unfortunate person has no other avenue for obtaining help than to obtain it from others, it would not be unreasonable to expect, morally, that the poor seek such help as surely might be forthcoming. We have no justification for assuming that the rich are all callous, though this caricature is regularly painted by communists and in folklore. Supporting and gaining advantage from the insti-tution of private property by no means implies that one lacks the virtue of generosity. The rich are no more immune to virtue than the poor are to vice. The contrary view is probably a legacy of the idea that only those concerned with spiritual or intellectual matters can be trusted to know virtue— those concerned with seeking material prosperity are too base.

The destitute typically have options other than to violate the rights of the well-off. "'Ought' implies 'can'" is satisfiable by the moral imperative that the poor ought to seek help, not loot. There is then no injustice in the rich preventing the poor from seeking such loot by violating the right to private prop-erty. "'Ought' implies 'can'" is fully satisfied if the poor can take the kind of action that could gain them the satisfaction of their basic needs, and this action could well be asking for help.

All along here I have been considering only the helplessly poor, who through no fault of their own, nor again through any rights violation by others, are destitute. I am taking the hard cases seriously, where violation of "'ought' implies 'can'" would appear to be most probable. But such cases are by no means typical. They are extremely rare. And even rarer are those cases in which all avenues regarded as legitimate from the libertarian point of view have been exhausted, including appealing for help.

The bulk of poverty in the world is not the result of natural disaster or disease. Rather it is political oppression, whereby people throughout many of the world's countries are not legally permitted to look out for themselves in production and trade. The famines in Africa and India, the poverty in the same countries and in Central and Latin America, as well as in China, the Soviet Union, Poland, Rumania, and so forth, are not the result of lack of charity but of oppression. It is the kind that those who have the protection of even a seriously compromised document and system protecting individual negative human rights, such as the U.S. Constitution, do not experience. The first requirement for men and women to ameliorate their hardship is to be free of other people's oppression, not to be free to take others people's belongings.

Of course, it would be immoral if people failed to help out when this was clearly no sacrifice for them. But charity or generosity is not a categorical imperative, even for the rich. There are more basic moral principles that might require the rich to refuse to be charitable—for example, if they are using most of their wealth for the protection of freedom or a just society. Courage can be more important than charity or benevolence or compassion. But a discussion of the ranking of moral virtues would take us far afield. One reason that many critics of libertarians find their own cases persuasive is that they think the libertarian can only subscribe to *political* principles or values. But this is mistaken.[17]

There can be emergency cases in which there is no alternative available to disregarding the rights of others. But these are extremely rare, and not at all the sort invoked by critics such as Sterba. I have in mind the desert-island case found in ethics books where instantaneous action, with only one violent alternative, faces persons—the sort we know from the law books in which the issue is one of immediate life and death. These are not cases, to repeat the phrase quoted from Locke by H. L. A. Hart, "where peace is possible." They are discussed in the libertarian literature and considerable progress has been made in integrating them with the concerns of law and politics. Since we are here discussing law and politics, which are general systematic approaches to how we normally ought to live with one another in human communities, these emergency situations do not help us except as limiting cases. And not surprisingly many famous court cases illustrate just this point as they now and then confront these kinds of instances after they have come to light within the framework of civilized society.

Since the time of the original publication of the above discussion—as part of my book *Individuals and Their Rights*—James Sterba has made several attempts to counter the arguments advanced here. The central claim on which he attempts to rest the argument that within a libertarian system many people would have no chance for self-directed flourishing goes as follows:

> [W]ho could deny that most of 1.2 billion people who are currently living in conditions of absolute poverty "lack the opportunities and necessities to satisfy their basic needs"? And even within our country [USA], it is estimated that some 32 million Americans live below the official poverty index [$14,000 per annum for a family, $7,000 per annum for an individual], and that one fifth of American children are growing up in poverty. Surely, it is impossible to deny that many of these Americans also "lack the opportunities and resources to satisfy their basic needs."[18]

There is little discussion in Sterba's work of why people are poor or otherwise experience circumstances that afford them little or no opportunity for flourishing. Among libertarians, however, there is considerable agreement on the position that many who face such circumstances make significant contribution to their own plight. Many others suffer such circumstances because their negative rights to liberty (to produce and to keep what they produce) are violated.

Certainly, libertarians draw a sharp distinction between those who are in dire straits because they are unfortunate, through no fault of their own, and those who fail to act in ways that would probably extricate them from their adverse living conditions. In the philosophical literature that draws on the legacy of Marx, Engels, and their followers, this distinction is not easy to make, since in this tradition human behavior is taken to be determined by a person's economic circumstances, so one is bound by one's situation and cannot make choices that would overcome them. More generally, in modern political philosophy there has been a strong tendency to view human beings as passive, unable to initiate their own conduct and moved by innate drives or environmental stimuli. Thus, those who are well-off could not have achieved this through their own initiative, nor could those who are badly off have failed in significant ways. Accordingly, all the poor or badly off, be they victims of others' oppression, casualties of misfortune, or products of their own misconduct are regarded alike. It is not clear how much Sterba's reasoning may be influenced by these considerations. In the absence of significant discussion of the matter, it is understandable why Sterba appears to view life as largely a zero sum game.[19]

Sterba claims, then, that poverty is typical, including, we must assume, of libertarian societies. Without that assumption, the story about poverty would have no bearing on libertarian politics. Sterba, therefore, needs to argue, as he does, that in a fully libertarian system, which respects and protects only negative individual rights (to life, liberty, and property), massive poverty would ensue—it would be the typical situation for there to be great masses of poor people.

Libertarians, as suggested above, seriously dispute this point. Indeed, they are not pure deontologists regarding negative individual liberty or the right to it, for they believe that respect for and protection of it would produce a better life for most people, in all relevant respects (moral, economic, intellectual, psychological, and cultural), provided they make an effort to improve themselves. They argue, in the main, that the most prosperous and otherwise beneficial societies are also those that give greatest respect and protection to negative individual rights. In turn, they hold, that where poverty is widespread, negative individual liberty is, in the main, left unrespected and unprotected.

This part of their argument is, for most libertarians, a fairly reasonable analytical and historical stance. They would argue, analytically, that it is the protection of negative individual liberty—the right to free association, freedom of trade, freedom of wealth accumulation, freedom of contract, freedom of entrepreneurship, freedom of speech, freedom of thought—that provides the most hospitable social climate for the creation of wealth. While no libertarian claims that this guarantees that no one will be destitute, those who are poor would either have failed of their own accord or would have been the few unfortunate people who are innocently incapacitated and do not enjoy the benefit of others' generosity, charity, compassion, and similar support. According to libertarians, there is no reason to think that there would be many such persons, at least compared to the numbers one can expect in societies lacking respect and protection for negative individual rights. Thus, even the most well known opponent of capitalism (the economic system of libertarianism), Karl Marx, was aware that unless human nature itself changes and the "new man" develops, socialism can do no more than to socialize poverty, i.e., make everyone poor.

As to the historical evidence, it is hard to argue that other than substantially capitalist economic systems, which tend in the direction of libertarianism (at least as far as the legal respect for and protection of private property or the right to it are concerned) have fared much better in reducing poverty than have others, without also causing massive political and other social failures (such as abolition of civil liberties, institution for forced labor and involuntary servitude, regimentation of the bulk of social relations, arresting scientific and technological progress, or censorship of the arts and other intellectual endeavors). Thus, America is still the freest of societies, with many of its legal principles giving expression to classical liberal, near-libertarian ideas, and it is, at the same time, the most generally productive (creative and culturally rich) of all societies, with its wealth aiding in the support of hundreds of other societies across the globe. Barring the impossible-to-conduct controlled sociopolitical-economic experiment, such historical evidence is all we can adduce to examine which political economic system produces more poverty. No one can seriously dispute that the near-libertarian systems have fared much better than those going in the opposite direction, including the welfare state. Even though some people wish for more in the way of empirical backing, it is difficult to know what they could wish for apart from the relatively plain fact of history that societies in which negative liberty flourishes produce far more (tangible) wealth than do ones in which such freedom is systematically denied. It is no secret that the Western liberal nations in general and the United States of America in particular contribute the most to the rescue of casualties of famines and other natural disasters across the globe. The US supports the United Nations' treasury far more than do other nations. While factors other than the political-economic conditions of a country contribute to these circumstances, barring some kind of controlled experiment in which those factors can be isolated, this will have to do for present purposes.

There is another point to be stressed, though, that Sterba has not taken into consideration. This is that there can be people in a libertarian society—indeed, in any society—for whom a lack of wealth, even extreme poverty relative to the mean, may not be a great liability. Not everyone wants to, or even ought to, live prosperously. For some individuals a life of ostensible poverty could be of substantial benefit. Contenders would be monks, hobos, starving artists, and the like who, despite the protection of their negative liberty or the right to it, do not elect to seek economic prosperity, at least in preference to other important objectives. Among the citizens of a libertarian society, then, we could find some who are poor but who are not, therefore, worse off than the rich, provided we do not confine ourselves to counting economic prosperity as the prime source of well-being.

At one point, Sterba suggests that libertarians, because they do not see the need to affirm as a principle of justice the right to welfare, may not care sufficiently for the poor. As he puts it:

> Machan seems reluctant to take the steps required to secure the basic needs of the poor. Why then does he balk at taking any further steps? Could it be that he does not see the oppression of the poor as truly oppressive after all?[20]

There is perhaps something to this, although not in the way Sterba's rhetorical question suggests, namely, that libertarians are callous or uncaring where the cultivation of care is warranted. But it is true enough that just being poor does not necessarily warrant being cared for, just as simply being sick does not place upon another the obligation to help, if the sickness is the result of self-abuse or gross negligence, or affects a thoroughly evil person.

Furthermore, some artists who are poor are happier than some merchants who are rich. There is no justification for feeling compassion for such artists, despite their poverty. In short, being poor in and of itself does not justify special consideration.[21] Being in need of what it takes to attain one's well-being warrants, if the need is a matter of natural misfortune or injury from others, feelings and conduct amounting to care, generosity, and charity. Poverty does not always constitute such neediness.

Nevertheless, Sterba may also underestimate what Marxists might call the objective generosity or charity of libertarians. One must consider just how much greater the long range prospects for economic well-being are for everyone within a libertarian political economy, and how benevolent it is for people not to be cuddled and treated as if they were inept in attaining prosperity; this system fosters institutional conditions within which they will probably be much better off than they would be in any welfare state (which seems clearly to encourage long-range economic ineptitude and dependence) the libertarian could well be regarded as the political theory with the greatest concern for the poor.[22]

It seems, therefore, that Sterba hasn't supported his main contention: that libertarianism implies the welfare state. The reason is that he has failed to appreciate the analytical and historical context within which libertarianism is argued. But there is more.

Sterba has also failed to appreciate that, although in some cases a person might not be required to respect the negative individual rights all citizens have—e.g., in some rare case of helpless destitution—nothing follows from this regarding the rights that everyone in society has by virtue of being a human individual living in a community of other human individuals. As Rasmussen and Den Uyl so carefully argue, the system of negative individual rights is a metanormative system or, in other words, a political framework within which human beings normally would and should pursue their highly varied flourishing. Focusing on exceptional, rare cases, wherein "peace is not possible," and, thus, it is justified to disregard consideration of basic (political) rights, does not justify the abrogation of the system of justice based on such rights that does, in fact, best befit human beings in their communities. On rare occasions, for particular persons, exceptions might be made, just as courts in extraordinary circumstances make such exceptions in the criminal law by pardoning someone who has violated a law but could not be expected to abide by it; these pardons do not abolish the law in question.

The point is, one ought not to abandon political principles to accommodate what can only be deemed extraordinary circumstances, Sterba's advice to the contrary notwithstanding.

JUSTICE AS FAIRNESS[1]

JOHN RAWLS

1. It might seem at first sight that the concepts of justice and fairness are the same, and that there is no reason to distinguish them, or to say that one is more fundamental than the other. I think that this impression is mistaken. I wish to show that the fundamental idea in the concept of justice is fairness; and I wish to offer an analysis of the concept of justice from this point of view. To bring out the force of this claim, and the analysis based upon it, I shall then argue that it is this aspect of justice for which utilitarianism, in its classical form, is unable to account, but which is expressed, even if misleadingly, by the idea of the social contract.

To start with I shall develop a particular conception of justice by stating and commenting upon two principles which specify it, and by considering the circumstances and conditions under which they may be thought to arise. The principles defining this conception, and the conception itself, are, of course, familiar. It may be possible, however, by using the notion of fairness as a framework, to assemble and to look at them in a new way. Before stating this conception, however, the following preliminary matters should be kept in mind.

Throughout I consider justice only as a virtue of social institutions, or what I shall call practices.[2] The principles of justice are regarded as formulating restrictions as to how practices may define positions and offices, and assign thereto powers and liabilities, rights and duties. Justice as a virtue of particular actions or of persons I do not take up at all. It is important to distinguish these various subjects of justice, since the meaning of the concept varies according to whether it is applied to practices, particular actions, or persons. These meanings are, indeed, connected, but they are not identical. I shall confine my discussion to the sense of justice as applied to practices, since this sense is the basic one. Once it is understood, the other senses should go quite easily.

Justice is to be understood in its customary sense as representing but *one* of the many virtues of social institutions, for these may be antiquated, inefficient, degrading, or any number of other things, without being unjust. Justice is not to be confused with an all-inclusive vision of a good society; it is only one part of any such conception. It is important, for example, to distinguish that sense of equality which is an aspect of the concept of justice from that sense of equality which belongs to a more comprehensive social ideal. There may well be inequalities which one concedes are just, or at least not unjust, but which, nevertheless, one wishes, on other grounds, to do away with. I shall focus attention, then, on the usual sense of justice in which it is essentially the elimination of arbitrary distinctions and the establishment, within the structure of a practice, of a proper balance between competing claims.

Finally, there is no need to consider the principles discussed below as *the* principles of justice. For the moment it is sufficient that they are typical of a family of principles normally associated with the concept of justice. The way in which the principles of this family resemble one another, as shown by the background against which they may be thought to arise, will be made clear by the whole of the subsequent argument.

2. The conception of justice which I want to develop may be stated in the form of two principles as follows: first, each person participating in a practice, or affected by it, has an equal right to the most

From "Justice as Fairness" by John Rawls in *The Philosophical Review*, Vol. 67(2), April 1958, published by Duke University Press.

extensive liberty compatible with a like liberty for all; and second, inequalities are arbitrary unless it is reasonable to expect that they will work out for everyone's advantage, and provided the positions and offices to which they attach, or from which they may be gained, are open to all. These principles express justice as a complex of three ideas: liberty, equality, and reward for services contributing to the common good.[3]

The first principle holds, of course, only if other things are equal: that is, while there must always be a justification for departing from the initial position of equal liberty (which is defined by the pattern of rights and duties, powers and liabilities, established by a practice), and the burden of proof is placed on him who would depart from it, nevertheless, there can be, and often there is, a justification for doing so. Now, that similar particular cases, as defined by a practice, should be treated similarly as they arise, is part of the very concept of a practice; it is involved in the notion of an activity in accordance with rules.[4] The first principle expresses an analogous conception, but as applied to the structure of practices themselves. It holds, for example, that there is a presumption against the distinctions and classifications made by legal systems and other practices to the extent that they infringe on the original and equal liberty of the persons participating in them. The second principle defines how this presumption may be rebutted.

It might be argued at this point that justice requires only an equal liberty. If, however, a greater liberty were possible for all without loss or conflict, then it would be irrational to settle on a lesser liberty. There is no reason for circumscribing rights unless their exercise would be incompatible, or would render the practice defining them less effective. Therefore no serious distortion of the concept of justice is likely to follow from including within it the concept of the greatest equal liberty.

The second principle defines what sorts of inequalities are permissible; it specifies how the presumption laid down by the first principle may be put aside. Now by inequalities it is best to understand not *any* differences between offices and positions, but differences in the benefits and burdens attached to them either directly or indirectly, such as prestige and wealth, or liability to taxation and compulsory services. Players in a game do not protest against there being different positions, such as batter, pitcher, catcher, and the like, nor to there being various privileges and powers as specified by the rules; nor do the citizens of a country object to there being the different offices of government such as president, senator, governor, judge, and so on, each with their special rights and duties. It is not differences of this kind that are normally thought of as inequalities, but differences in the resulting distribution established by a practice, or made possible by it, of the things men strive to attain or avoid. Thus they may complain about the pattern of honors and rewards set up by a practice (e.g., the privileges and salaries of government officials) or they may object to the distribution of power and wealth which results from the various ways in which men avail themselves of the opportunities allowed by it (e.g., the concentration of wealth which may develop in a free price system allowing large entrepreneurial or speculative gains).

It should be noted that the second principle holds that an inequality is allowed only if there is reason to believe that the practice with the inequality, or resulting in it, will work for the advantage of *every* party engaging in it. Here it is important to stress that *every* party must gain from the inequality. Since the principle applies to practices, it implies that the representative man in every office or position defined by a practice, when he views it as a going concern, must find it reasonable to prefer his condition and prospects with the inequality to what they would be under the practice without it. The principle excludes, therefore, the justification of inequalities on the grounds that the disadvantages of those in one position are outweighed by the greater advantages of those in another position. This rather simple restriction is the main modification I wish to make in the utilitarian principle as usually understood. When coupled with the notion of a practice, it is a restriction of consequence[5], and one which some utilitarians, e.g., Hume and Mill, have used in their discussions of justice without realizing apparently its significance, or at least without calling attention to it.[6] Why it is a significant modification of principle, changing one's conception of justice entirely, the whole of my argument will show.

Further, it is also necessary that the various offices to which special benefits or burdens attach are open to all. It may be, for example, to the common advantage, as just defined, to attach special benefits to certain offices. Perhaps by doing so the requisite talent can be attracted to them and encouraged to give its best efforts. But any offices having special benefits must be won in a fair competition in which contestants are judged on their merits. If some offices were not open, those excluded would normally be justified in feeling unjustly treated, even if they benefited from the greater efforts of those who were allowed to compete for them. Now if one can assume that offices are open, it is necessary only to consider the design of practices themselves and how they jointly, as a system, work together. It will be a mistake to focus attention on the varying relative positions of particular persons, who may be known to us by their proper names, and to require that each such change, as a once for all transaction viewed in isolation, must be in itself just. It is the system of practices which is to be judged, and judged from a general point of view: unless one is prepared to criticize it from the standpoint of a representative man holding some particular office, one has no complaint against it.

3. Given these principles one might try to derive them from a priori principles of reason, or claim that they were known by intuition. These are familiar enough steps and, at least in the case of the first principle, might be made with some success. Usually, however, such arguments, made at this point, are unconvincing. They are not likely to lead to an understanding of the basis of the principles of justice, not at least as principles of justice. I wish, therefore, to look at the principles in a different way.

Imagine a society of persons amongst whom a certain system of practices is *already* well established. Now suppose that by and large they are mutually self-interested; their allegiance to their established practices is normally founded on the prospect of self-advantage. One need not assume that, in all senses of the term "person," the persons in this society are mutually self-interested. If the characterization as mutually self-interested applies when the line of division is the family, it may still be true that members of families are bound by ties of sentiment and affection and willingly acknowledge duties in contradiction to self-interest. Mutual self-interestedness in the relations between families, nations, churches, and the like, is commonly associated with intense loyalty and devotion on the part of individual members. Therefore, one can form a more realistic conception of this society if one thinks of it as consisting of mutually self-interested families, or some other association. Further, it is not necessary to suppose that these persons are mutually self-interested under all circumstances, but only in the usual situations in which they participate in their common practices.

Now suppose also that these persons are rational: they know their own interests more or less accurately; they are capable of tracing out the likely consequences of adopting one practice rather than another; they are capable of adhering to a course of action once they have decided upon it; they can resist present temptations and the enticements of immediate gain; and the bare knowledge or perception of the difference between their condition and that of others is not, within certain limits and in itself, a source of great dissatisfaction. Only the last point adds anything to the usual definition of rationality. This definition should allow, I think, for the idea that a rational man would not be greatly downcast from knowing, or seeing, that others are in a better position than himself, unless he thought their being so was the result of injustice, or the consequence of letting chance work itself out for no useful common purpose, and so on. So if these persons strike us as unpleasantly egoistic, they are at least free in some degree from the fault of envy.[7]

Finally, assume that these persons have roughly similar needs and interests, or needs and interests in various ways complementary, so that fruitful cooperation amongst them is possible; and suppose that they are sufficiently equal in power and ability to guarantee that in normal circumstances none is able to dominate the others. This condition (as well as the others) may seem excessively vague; but in view of the conception of justice to which the argument leads, there seems no reason for making it more exact here.

Since these persons are conceived as engaging in their common practices, which are already established, there is no question of our supposing them to come together to deliberate as to how they will set these practices up for the first time. Yet we can imagine that from time to time they discuss with one another whether any of them has a legitimate complaint against their established institutions. Such discussions are perfectly natural in any normal society. Now suppose that they have settled on doing this in the following way. They first try to arrive at the principles by which complaints, and so practices themselves, are to be judged. Their procedure for this is to let each person propose the principles upon which he wishes his complaints to be tried with the understanding that, if acknowledged, the complaints of others will be similarly tried, and that no complaints will be heard at all until everyone is roughly of one mind as to how complaints are to be judged. They each understand further that the principles proposed and acknowledged on this occasion are binding on future occasions. Thus each will be wary of proposing a principle which would give him a peculiar advantage, in his present circumstances, supposing it to be accepted. Each person knows that he will be bound by it in future circumstances the peculiarities of which cannot be known, and which might well be such that the principle is then to his disadvantage. The idea is that everyone should be required to make in *advance* a firm commitment, which others also may reasonably be expected to make, and that no one be given the opportunity to tailor the canons of a legitimate complaint to fit his own special condition, and then to discard them when they no longer suit his purpose. Hence each person will propose principles of a general kind which will, to a large degree, gain their sense from the various applications to be made of them, the particular circumstances of which being as yet unknown. These principles will express the conditions in accordance with which each is the least unwilling to have his interests limited in the design of practices, given the competing interests of the others, on the supposition that the interests of others will be limited likewise. The restrictions which would so arise might be thought of as those a person would keep in mind if he were designing a practice in which his enemy were to assign him his place.

The two main parts of this conjectural account have a definite significance. The character and respective situations of the parties reflect the typical circumstances in which questions of justice arise. The procedure whereby principles are proposed and acknowledged represents constraints, analogous to those of having a morality, whereby rational and mutually self-interested persons are brought to act reasonably. Thus the first part reflects the fact that questions of justice arise when conflicting claims are made upon the design of a practice and where it is taken for granted that each person will insist, as far as possible, on what he considers his rights. It is typical of cases of justice to involve persons who are pressing on one another their claims, between which a fair balance or equilibrium must be found. On the other hand, as expressed by the second part, having a morality must at least imply the acknowledgment of principles as impartially applying to one's own conduct as well as to another's, and moreover principles which may constitute a constraint, or limitation, upon the pursuit of one's own interests. There are, of course, other aspects of having a morality: the acknowledgment of moral principles must show itself in accepting a reference to them as reasons for limiting one's claims, in acknowledging the burden of providing a special explanation, or excuse, when one acts contrary to them, or else in showing shame and remorse and a desire to make amends, and so on. It is sufficient to remark here that having a morality is analogous to having made a firm commitment in advance; for one must acknowledge the principles of morality even when to one's disadvantage.[8] A man whose moral judgments always coincided with his interests could be suspected of having no morality at all.

Thus the two parts of the foregoing account are intended to mirror the kinds of circumstances in which questions of justice arise and the constraints which having a morality would impose upon persons so situated. In this way one can see how the acceptance of the principles of justice might come about, for given all these conditions as described, it would be natural if the two principles of justice were to be acknowledged. Since there is no way for anyone to win special advantages for himself, each might consider it reasonable to acknowledge equality as an initial principle. There is, however, no reason why they should regard this position as final; for if there are inequalities which satisfy the second principle, the immediate gain which equality would allow can be considered as intelligently invested in view of its future return. If, as is quite likely, these inequalities work as incentives to draw out better efforts, the members of this society may look upon them as concessions to human nature: they, like us, may think that people ideally should want to serve one another. But as they are mutually self-interested, their acceptance of these inequalities is merely the acceptance of the relations in which they actually stand, and a recognition of the motives which lead them to engage in their common practices. *They* have no title to complain of one another. And so provided that the conditions of the principle are met, there is no reason why they should not allow such inequalities. Indeed, it would be short-sighted of them to do so, and could result, in most cases, only from their being dejected by the bare knowledge, or perception, that others are better situated. Each person will, however, insist on an advantage to himself, and so on a common advantage, for none is willing to sacrifice anything for the others.

These remarks are not offered as a proof that persons so conceived and circumstanced would settle on the two principles, but only to show that these principles could have such a background, and so can be viewed as those principles which mutually self-interested and rational persons, when similarly situated and required to make in advance a firm commitment, could acknowledge as restrictions governing the assignment of rights and duties in their common practices, and thereby accept as limiting their rights against one another. The principles of justice may, then, be regarded as those principles which arise when the constraints of having a morality are imposed upon parties in the typical circumstances of justice.

OUR WORD IS OUR WEAPON

SUBCOMANDANTE MARCOS

Written in August 1992, this essay by Marcos was not released publicly until January 27, 1994

Suppose that you live in the north, center, or west of this country. Suppose that you heed the old Department of Tourism slogan: "Get to know Mexico first." Suppose that you decide to visit the southeast of your country and that in the southeast you choose to visit the state of Chiapas.

[. . .]

Good, suppose you have. You have now entered by one of the three existing roads into Chiapas: the road into the northern part of the state, the road along the Pacific coast, and the road by which you entered are the three ways to get to this southeastern corner of the country by land. But the state's natural wealth doesn't leave just by way of these three roads. Chiapas loses blood through many veins: through oil and gas ducts, electric lines, railways; through bank accounts, trucks, vans, boats, and planes; through clandestine paths, gaps, and forest trails. This land continues to pay tribute to the imperialists: petroleum, electricity, cattle, money, coffee, banana, honey, corn, cacao, tobacco, sugar, soy, melon, sorghum, mamey, mango, tamarind, avocado, and Chiapaneco blood all flow as a result of the thousand teeth sunk into the throat of the Mexican Southeast. These raw materials, thousands of millions of tons of them, flow to Mexican ports, railroads, air and truck transportation centers. From there they are sent to different parts of the world—the United States, Canada, Holland, Germany, Italy, Japan—but all to fulfill one same destiny: to feed imperialism. Since the beginning, the fee that capitalism imposes on the southeastern part of this country makes Chiapas ooze blood and mud.

A handful of businesses, one of which is the Mexican state, take all the wealth out of Chiapas and in exchange leave behind their mortal and pestilent mark: in 1989 these businesses took 1,222,669,000,000 pesos from Chiapas and only left behind 616,340,000,000 pesos worth of credit and public works.[1] More than 600,000,000,000 pesos went to the belly of the beast.

In Chiapas, Pemex[2] has eighty-six teeth sunk into the townships of Estación Juárez, Reforma, Ostuacán, Pichucalco, and Ocosingo. Every day they suck out 92,000 barrels of petroleum and 517,000,000,000 cubic feet of gas. They take away the petroleum and gas and, in exchange, leave behind the mark of capitalism: ecological destruction, agricultural plunder, hyperinflation, alcoholism, prostitution, and poverty. The beast is still not satisfied and has extended its tentacles to the Lacandon Jungle: eight petroleum deposits are under exploration. The paths are made with machetes by the same campesinos who are left without land by the insatiable beast. The trees fall and dynamite explodes on land where campesinos are not allowed to cut down trees to cultivate. Every tree that is cut down costs them a fine that is ten times the minimum wage, and a jail sentence. The poor cannot cut down trees, but the petroleum beast can, a beast that every day fells more and more into foreign hands. The campesinos cut them down to survive, the beast cuts them down to plunder.

From "Our Word is Our Weapon" written August 1992 by Subcomandante Marcos in *Our Word is Our Weapon: Selected Writings of Subcomandante Marcos*, Juana Ponce de Leon, Seven Stories Press, 1994.

Chiapas also bleeds coffee. Thirty-five percent of the coffee produced in Mexico comes from this area. The industry employs 87,000 people. Forty-seven percent of the coffee is for national consumption, and 53 percent is exported abroad, mainly to the United States and Europe. More than 100,000 tons of coffee are taken from this state to fatten the beast's bank accounts: in 1988 a kilo of pergamino coffee was sold abroad for 8,000 pesos. The Chiapaneco producers were paid 2,500 pesos or less.

After coffee, the second most important plunder is beef. Three million head of cattle wait for middlemen and a small group of businessmen to take them away to fill refrigerators in Arriaga, Villahermosa, and Mexico City. The cattle are sold for 400 pesos per kilo by the poor farmers and resold by the middlemen and businessmen for up to ten times the price they paid for them.

The tribute that capitalism demands from Chiapas has no historical parallel. Fifty-five percent of national hydroelectric energy comes from this state, along with 20 percent of Mexico's total electricity. However, only a third of the homes in Chiapas have electricity. Where do the 12,907 kilowatts produced annually by hydroelectric plants in Chiapas go?

In spite of the current trend toward ecological awareness, the plunder of wood continues in Chiapas' forests. Between 1981 and 1989, 2,444,777 cubic meters of precious woods, conifers, and tropical trees were taken from Chiapas to Mexico City, Puebla, Veracruz, and Quintana Roo. In 1988, wood exports brought a revenue of 23,900,000,000 pesos, 6,000 percent more than in 1980.

The honey that is produced in 79,000 beehives in Chiapas goes entirely to the United States and European markets. The 2,756 tons of honey produced annually in the Chiapaneco countryside is converted into dollars that the people of Chiapas never see.

Of the corn produced in Chiapas, more than half goes to the domestic market. Chiapas is one of the largest corn producers in the country. Sorghum grown in Chiapas goes to Tabasco. Ninety percent of the tamarind goes to Mexico City and other states. Two-thirds of the avocados and all the mameys are sold outside of the state. Sixty-nine percent of the cacao goes to the national market, and 31 percent is exported to the United States, Holland, Japan, and Italy. The majority of the bananas produced are exported.

[. . .]

March 17, 1995

[. . .]

We, the first inhabitants of these lands, the indigenous, were left forgotten in a corner, while the rest began to grow and become stronger. We only had our history with which to defend ourselves, and we held it tightly so we would not die. And that's how this part of history arrived, and it seems like a joke because a single country, the country of money, put itself above all flags. When they uttered, "Globalization," we knew that this was how the absurd order was going to be called, an order in which money is the only country served and the borders are erased, not out of brotherhood but because of the bleeding that fattens the powerful without nationality. The lie became the universal coin, and for a few in our country it wove a dream of prosperity above everyone else's nightmare.

Corruption and falsehoods were our motherland's principal exports. Being poor, we dressed in the wealth of our scarcities, and because the lie was so deep and so broad, we ended up mistaking it for truth. We prepared for the great international forums and, by the will of the government, poverty was declared an illusion that faded before the development proclaimed by economic statistics. Us? We became even more forgotten, and until our history wasn't enough to keep us from dying just like that, forgotten and humiliated. Because death does not hurt; what hurts is to be forgotten. We discovered then that we no longer existed, and those who govern had forgotten about us in their euphoria of statistics and growth rates.

A country that forgets itself is a sad country. A country that forgets its past cannot have a future. And so we took up arms and went into the cities, where we were considered animals. We went and told the powerful, "We are here!" And to the whole country we shouted: "We are here!" And to all of the world we yelled, "We are here!" And they saw how things were because, in order for them to see us, we covered our faces; so that they would call us by name, we gave up our names; we bet the present to have a future; and to live . . . we died. And then came the planes and the bombs and bullets and death. And we went back to our mountains, and even there death pursued us. And many people from many places said, "Talk." And the powerful said: "Let's talk." And we said, "Okay, let's talk." And we talked. And we told them what we wanted, and they did not understand very well, and we repeated that we wanted democracy, liberty, and justice. And they made a face like they didn't understand. And they reviewed their macroeconomic plans and all their neoliberal points, and they could not find these words anywhere. And they said to us, "We don't understand." And they offered us a prettier corner in history's museum, and a long-term death, and a chain of gold with which to tie our dignity. And we, so that they would understand our demands, began to organize ourselves according to the wishes of the majority, and so that we too could see what it was like to live with democracy, with liberty, and with justice. And this is what happened:

For a year the law of the Zapatistas governed the mountains of Southeastern Mexico. We the Zapatistas, who have no face, no name, no past, governed ourselves. (For the most part we are indigenous, although lately more brothers and sisters of other lands and races have joined us.) All of us are Mexicans. When we governed these lands, we did the following:

We lowered to zero the rate of alcoholism. The women here became very angry and said that alcohol was only good to make the men beat their women and children; therefore, they gave the order that no drinking was allowed. The people who most benefited were the children and women, and the ones most suffered were the businessmen and the government. With support of nongovernmental organizations, both national and international, health campaigns were carried out, lifting the hope of life for the civilian population, even though the challenge from the government reduced the hope for life for us combatants. The women are a full third of our fighting force. They are fierce and they are armed. And so they "convinced" us to accept their laws, and that they participate in the civilian and military direction of our struggle. We say nothing, what can we say?

The cutting down of trees also was prohibited, and laws were made to protect the forests. It was forbidden to hunt wild animals, even if they belonged to the government. The cultivation, consumption, and trafficking of drugs were also prohibited. These laws were all upheld. The rate of infant mortality became very small, as small as the children. And the Zapatista laws were applied uniformly, without regard for social position or income level. And we made all of the major decisions, the "strategic" ones, of our struggle, by means of a method called "referendum" and "plebiscite." We got rid of prostitution. Unemployment disappeared and with it ended begging. The children came to know sweets and toys. We made many errors and had many failures, but we also accomplished what no other government in the world, regardless of its political affiliation, is capable of doing honestly, recognizing its errors and taking steps to remedy them.

We were doing this, learning, when the tanks and the helicopters and the planes and the thousands of soldiers arrived, and they said that they came to defend the national sovereignty. We told them that where sovereignty was being violated was at the IUESAY[3] and not in Chiapas, that the national sovereignty cannot be defended by trampling the rebel dignity of indigenous Chiapas. They did not listen because the noise of their war machines made them deaf, and they came in the name of the government. As for the government, betrayal is the ladder by which one climbs to power, and for us loyalty is the level playing field that we desire for everyone. The legality of the government came mounted on bayonets, and our legality was based on consensus and reason. We wanted to convince, the government wanted to conquer. We said that no law that had to resort to arms to be carried out could be called a law, that it is arbitrary regardless of its legalese trappings. He who orders that a law be carried out and enforced with weapons is a dictator, even if he says that the majority elected him. And we were run out of our lands. With the war-tanks came the law of the government, and the law of the Zapatistas left. And once again, prostitution, drinking, theft, drugs, destruction, death, corruption, sickness, poverty, came following the government's war tanks.

People from the government came and said that they had now restored law in Chiapas, and they came with bulletproof vests and with war tanks, and they stayed there just long enough to make their statements in front of the chickens and roosters and pigs and dogs and cows and horses and a cat that had gotten lost. And that's what the government did, and maybe you all know this because it's true that many reporters saw this and publicized it. This is the "legality" that rules in our lands now. And this is how the government conducted its war for "legality" and for "national sovereignty" against the indigenous people of Chiapas. The government also waged war against all other Mexicans, but instead of tanks and planes, they launched an economic program that is also going to kill them, just more slowly . . .

[. . .]

December 1994

Months later, the indigenous of southeastern Mexico again reiterated their rebellion, their unwilling-ness to disappear, to die . . . The reason? The supreme government decides to carry out the organized crime—essential to neoliberalism—that the god of modernity has planned: money. Many thousands of soldiers, hundreds of tons of war materials, millions of lies. The objective? The destruction of libraries and hospitals, of homes and fields seeded with corn and beans, the annihilation of every sign of rebel-lion. The indigenous Zapatistas resisted, they retreated to the mountains, and they began an exodus that today, even as I write these lines, has not ended. Neoliberalism disguises itself as the defense of a sovereignty that has been sold in dollars on the international market.

Neoliberalism, the doctrine that makes it possible for stupidity and cynicism to govern in diverse parts of the earth, does not allow participation other than to hold on by disappearing. "Die as a social group, as a culture, and above all as a resistance. Then you can be part of modernity," say the great capitalists, from their seats of government, to the indigenous campesinos. These indigenous people with their rebellion, their defiance, and their resistance irritate the modernizing logic of neomercan-tilism. It's irritated by the anachronism of their existence within the economic and political project of globalization, a project that soon discovers that poor people, that people in opposition—which is to say, the majority of the population—are obstacles. The Zapatista indigenous people's character, armed with, "We are here!" does not matter much to them; they lose no sleep over them. (A little fire and lead will be enough to end such "imprudent" defiance.) What matters to them, what both-ers them, is their mere existence, and that the moment they speak out and are heard it becomes a reminder of an embarrassing omission by the "neoliberal modernity": "These Indians should not exist today; we should have put an end to them BEFORE. Now, annihilating them will be more dif-ficult, which is to say, more expensive." This is the burden that weighs upon the born again neoliberal government in Mexico.

"Let's resolve the causes of the uprising," say the government's negotiators (the leftists of yesterday, the shamed of today), as if they were saying, "All of you should not exist; all of this is an unfortunate error of modern history." "Let's solve the problems" is an elegant synonym for "we will eliminate them." The campesinos, the indigenous, do not fit in the plans and projects of this system, which concentrates wealth and power and distributes death and poverty. They have to be gotten rid of, just like we have to get rid of the herons . . . and the eagles.

Notes

1. The exchange of pesos to dollars in 1989 was 3,000 pesos for one U.S. dollar.
2. Pemex stands for Petroleum of Mexico, a government-owned company.
3. IUESAY is a phonetic play on U.S.A.

LIVING ECONOMIES

The earth provides enough resources for everyone's need, but not for some people's greed.

—Mahatma Gandhi[1]

The word *economics* is derived from the Greek word *oikos*, meaning home. Home is where one is born, grows up, and is looked after. Mathew Fox wrote, "Our true home is the universe itself."[2] Robert Frost observes, "Home is the place where when you go there, they have to take you in."[3] Home is where there is always a place for you at the table and where you can count on sharing what is at the table. To be part of a home, a household, is to have access to life. How is it that economic systems today are such unwelcoming spaces? How have they become places that, rather than take us in, often bar our entry, and, in the process, refuse us not only a home, but a right to sustenance, stability, and ultimately life?

The dominant economy goes by many names—the market economy, the globalized economy, corporate globalization, and capitalism, to name a few—but all these names fail to acknowledge that this economy is but one of the three major economies at work in the world today. In Earth Democracy every being has equal access to the earth's resources that make life possible; this access is assured by recognizing the importance of the other two economies: nature's economy and the sustenance economy.

The globalized free market economy, which dominates our lives, is based on rules that extinguish and deny access to life and livelihoods by generating scarcity. This scarcity is created by the destruction of nature's economy and the sustenance economy, where life is nourished, maintained, and renewed. Globalization and free trade decimate the conditions for productive, creative employment by enclosing the commons, which are necessary for the sustenance of life. The anti-life dimensions of economic globalization are rooted in the fact that capital exchange is taking the place of living processes and the rights of corporations are displacing those of living people.

The economic conflict of our times is not just a North-South divide, though the inequalities created by colonialism, the mal-development model of debt-slavery imposed by the IMF and the World Bank, and the rules of the WTO—have that dimension. The contest is between a global economy of death and destruction and diverse economies for life and creation. In our age, "have or have not" has mutated into "live or live not."

THE THREE ECONOMIES

Why does the dominant economic model fail to meet the needs of so many societies and communities? Why is success, measured by economic growth, so intimately related to increased poverty, hunger, and thirst? There are two reasons why ecological disasters and the number of displaced, destitute, and disposable people increase in direct proportion to economic growth. First is the reduction of the visible economy to the market and activities controlled by capital. Second, the legal rights of corporations have increased at the cost of the rights of real people.

As the dominant economy myopically focuses on the working of the market, it ignores both nature's economy and the sustenance economy, on which it depends. In a focus on the financial bottom line, the market makes invisible nature's economy and people's sustenance economies.

While the exchange of goods and services has always been a characteristic of human societies, the elevation of the market to the highest organizing principle of society has led to the neglect of the other two vital economies. When exclusive attention is given to the growth of the market, living processes become invisible externalities. The requirements of nature, not backed up by suitable purchasing power, cannot be registered or fulfilled by the the market economy. Not only does this focus on the market hide the existence of nature's economy and the sustenance economy, it hides the harm that market growth causes. As a result, especially in the context of Third World countries, nature's need for resources gets ignored. So too are the requirements of the sustenance economy that provides for the biological survival of the marginalized poor and the reproduction of society. The hidden damage caused by market-based development and globalization processes have created new forms of poverty and underdevelopment. The political economy of Earth Democracy movements cannot be understood without a clear comprehension of the place of natural resources in the three distinct economies.

Furthermore, economic growth is leading to disenfranchisement and disposability of people as hard-won rights designed to protect people are increasingly transferred to corporations. Free-market rules for corporate freedom are increasingly rules which exclude real people from the economic and political affairs of society and disenfranchise them from nature. The legal status of corporations serves to hold the people running the corporations free from responsibility for the harm the corporations cause. And just as the corporation gained the legal standing of a person, the market, too, has become personified. More pages in the media are devoted to the "health of the market" than to the health of the planet or well-being of people.

NATURE'S ECONOMY

Like the word *economy, ecology* also comes from the Greek word for home or household. Yet in the context of market-oriented development, economy and ecology have been pitted against each other. The market economy separates nature from people and ecology from economy. Nature is defined as free of humans. Conservation is reduced to "wilderness" management. Development is viewed as the exclusive domain of production. Nature and people's self-provisioning economies have no productive role according to the market.

However nature's economy is the first economy, the primary economy on which all other economies rest. Nature's economy consists of the production of goods and services by nature—the water recycled and distributed through the hydrologic cycle, the soil fertility produced by microorganisms, the plants fertilized by pollinators. Human production, human creativity shrinks to insignificance in comparison with nature.

Natural resources are produced and reproduced through a complex network of ecological processes. Nature is the world's dominant producer, but its products are not, and cannot be, acknowledged as such in the market economy. Only production and productivity in the context of market economics has been considered production. Organic productivity in forestry or agriculture has also been viewed narrowly with the marketable products as the total productive output. This has resulted in vast areas of productive work—the production of humus by forests, the regeneration of water resources, the natural evolution of genetic products, the creation of fertile soil from eroding rock—remaining beyond the scope of economics. Many of these productive processes are dependent on a number of other ecological processes and are not fully understood even within the natural sciences.

The ecological destruction associated with uncontrolled exploitation of natural resources for commercial gains is symptomatic of the conflict over how wealth is generated in the market and in nature.

THE SUSTENANCE ECONOMY: BRINGING PEOPLE BACK INTO THE PICTURE

In the sustenance economy, people work to directly provide the conditions necessary to maintain their lives. This is the economy through which human production and reproduction is primarily possible. It is the women's economy where, because of the patriarchal division of labor, societal reproduction takes place. Women's work provides sustenance and support to all human activities—including the visible activities of the market dominated economy. The sustenance economy is the economy of the two-thirds of humanity engaged in craft production, peasant agriculture, artisanal fishing, and indigenous forest economies. The sustenance economy includes all spheres in which humans produce in balance with nature and reproduce society through partnerships, mutuality, and reciprocity.

Without the sustenance economy, there would be no market economy. Sustenance economies exist even where capital markets do not. Yet capital's markets cannot exist without the sustenance economy, nor can the market fully internalize the sustenance economy because externalizing the social burden is the very basis of profits and capital accumulation. As structural adjustments and globalization destroy livelihoods, women work longer hours, at multiple part-time jobs to feed their families. As privatization of health care dismantles public health systems, families take on the burden of looking after the ill. The more markets depend on work outside the market, the more the sustenance economy is rendered invisible, and left without resources.

The poverty of the Third World has resulted from centuries of the drain of resources from the sustenance economy. Globalization has accelerated and expanded the methods used to deplete the sustenance economy—the privatization of water, the patenting of seeds and biodiversity, and the corporatization of agriculture. This deliberate starving of the sustenance economy is at the root of the violence of globalization

Modern economics, the concept of development and progress, and now the paradigm of globalization cover but a minuscule portion of the history of human economic production. The sustenance economy has given human societies the material means of survival by deriving livelihoods directly from nature. Within the context of a limited resource base, diverting natural resources from directly sustaining human existence to generating growth in the marker economy destroys the sustenance economy. In the sustenance economy, satisfying basic needs and ensuring long-term sustainability are the organizing principles for natural resource use, whereas the exploitation of resources for profits and capital accumulation are the organizing principles for the market.

MARKETS AND THE MARKET

Markets are places of exchange. The bazaar, thriving even today in India, is a place where people exchange products they have grown and produced. The concrete, embedded market grows out of society. Based on direct relationships and face-to-face transactions, it is in fact an extension of society. When markets are replaced by *the market*, society is replaced by capital and the market becomes the anonymous face of corporations. Real people, exchanging what they create and what they need, are replaced by the abstract and invisible hand of the market.

There are two kinds of markets. Markets embedded in nature and society are places of exchange, of meeting, of culture. Some are simultaneously cultural festivals and spaces for economic transactions, with real people buying and selling real things they have produced or directly need. Such markets are diverse and direct. They serve people, and are shaped by people.

The market shaped by capital, excludes people as producers. Cultural spaces of exchange are replaced by invisible processes. People's needs are substituted for by greed, profit, and consumerism. The market becomes the mystification of processes of crude capital accumulation, the mask behind which those wielding corporate power hide.

It is this disembodied, decontextualized market which destroys the environment and peoples' lives.

THE DOMINATION OF THE MARKET

A key to the domination of the market economy is its ability to claim resources from outside of its scope. The transformation of land from public to private ownership was essential for the market economy to become the dominant economy. The transformation, known as the enclosure of the commons, was usually triggered by the greed and power of the privateers. The word *enclosure* describes the physical exclusion of the community from their commons by "surrounding a piece of land with hedges, ditches, or other barriers to the free passage of men and animals."

The land called the commons was formally owned by the landlord, but the rights to use it belonged to the commoners. It was the removal of these rights to common property which enabled enclosure. In England, where the movement began in the sixteenth century, the enclosures were driven by the hunger of machines, by the increased demand for wool by the textile industry. The landlords, supported by industrialists, merchants, and bankers, pushed peasants off the land and replaced them with sheep. "Sheep eat men" is how Sir Thomas More described the phenomena of the enclosures of the commons.

> Your sheep, that were wont to be so meek and tame and so small eaters, now, and I had hear say become so great devourers and so wild, that they eat up and swallow down the very man themselves. They consume, destroy and devour whole fields, houses and cities.

The economics of enclosure worked for the landlords, but against the peasants. While one acre of arable land on the commons could produce 670 pounds of bread, it could only maintain a few sheep. In terms of the food and the sustenance economy this was a loss, since the sheep could only produce 176 pounds of mutton. However, in monetary terms, the landlords gained. A single shepherd tending the sheep produced much higher returns for the landlord than the rents paid by dozens of peasants. That the peasants were growing the food, fodder, fuel, and other essentials for their survival on the commons was, for the landlord, not a matter of consideration. The profits provided the necessary justification for the privateers to expand the market economy, despite the cost to nature's economy and the sustenance economy.

Five processes constitute enclosing the commons.

1. The exclusion of people from access to resources that had been their common property or held in common.
2. The creation of "surplus" or "disposable" people by denying rights of access to the commons that sustained them.
3. The creation of private property by the enclosure of common property.
4. The replacement of diversity that provides for multiple needs and performs multiple functions with monocultures that provide raw material and commodities for the marker.
5. The enclosure of minds and imagination, with the result that enclosures are defined and perceived as universal human progress, not as growth of privilege and exclusive rights for a few and dispossession and impoverishment for the many.

Enclosures were exalted as allowing "an unparallel expansion of productive possibilities." Productivity was defined from the perspective of the rich and the powerful, not from that of the commoner, and valued only profits and the benefit to the marker, not nature's sustainability or people's sustenance. The rich "deplored the insubordination of commoners, the unimprovability of their pastures, and the brake on production represented by shared property." Despite the opinion of the landlords, the commons were not wasted land; they were a rich resource providing the community with a degree of self-reliance and self-governance.

The market created its own multiplier effect which pushed the sustenance economy further from view. The more the powerful gained economic and political power from the growing market economy, the more they dispossessed the poor and enclosed their common property. And the more the poor were dispossessed of their means to provide their own sustenance, the more they had to turn to the market to buy what they had formerly produced themselves.

> When the cottager was cut off from his resources . . . there was little else that he could do in the old way. It was out of the question to obtain most of his supplies by his own handiwork: they had to be procured, ready made from another source. That source, I need hardly say, was a shop.

As it was with the land commons, so it is today with the bio-diversity and seed commons through intellectual property rights and the water commons through privatization. Now the seeds, the medicine, the water that historically have been the common property of communities need to be bought at high cost from gene giants like Monsanto, who own the patents, and water giants like Suez, Bechtel, and Vivendi, who own the concessions. The transformation of common property rights into private property rights implicitly denies the right to survival for large sections of society.

ECONOMIC GLOBALIZATION/CORPORATE GLOBALIZATION

In the early stages of industrialization, the enclosures movement in England declared the peasantry dispensable and pushed them off the land. Industrialization was brought as "development" to countries of the South. Corporate rule through globalization continues to build upon the foundation that colonialism created and continues to leave behind it a trail of devastation and destruction.

The market economy inevitably produces a major shift in the way rights to resources are perceived. The transformation of commons into commodities has two implications. It deprives the politically weaker groups of their right to survival, which they had through access to commons, and it robs from nature its right to self-renewal and sustainability, by eliminating the social constaints on resource use that are the basis of common property management.

In Third World countries the transformation of natural resources into commodities has been largely mediated by the state. Though couched in the language of advancing the collective public interest, the state is often a powerful instrument for the privatization of resources. The transformation of forests from village commons to state-reserved forests serves the interests of the private pulp and paper industry by ensuring cheap and regular supply of raw material. Similarly, dams are built with public funds, but they aim to satisfy the energy and water needs of private industry or the irrigation needs of cash-crop cultivation. Credit from public-sector banks is used to finance the private wells or private trawlers of economically powerful groups. Conflicts over natural resources are conflicts over rights.

Corporate globalization has been imposed on us. It represents itself as the ocean everyone needs to be swimming in, an inevitable process to be part of. Corporate globalization, commonly associated with international trade, is something that many people think they can ignore. But corporate globalization is not about goods crossing national boundaries. We've had international trade forever. Goods were traded across borders before colonialism. In fact, colonialism was caused by the desire to control that trade. Spices were traded long before European colonizers sought control over the spice trade. Corporate globalization now crosses borders with far more serious consequences for the planet and for humanity than those artificial borders that define nations. Compared to the ethical borders being crossed, international trade is very easy to deal with. These ethical boundaries have been created over centuries by faiths, cultures, and societies which declared certain things are not part of commerce. Certain things are not tradable and will be governed by values other than commodity values.

Globalization is, in fact, the ultimate enclosure—of our minds, our hearts, our imaginations, and our resources. Until corporate globalization claimed the resources of this planet—especially water and biodiversity—to be tradable commodities, it was recognized that water couldn't belong to anyone. Rain falls, flows through river basins and underground aquifers, meets the ocean, and evaporates in an amazing hydrological cyde that brings us water. Sometimes the cycle is slow and gives us drought, but we can deal with the drought that the water cycle gives. We cannot deal with engineered drought that says water will only flow one way—uphill to money.

We were promised that globalization would bring us peace by constructing a global village in which everyone will be connected. But the number of wars that have occurred since 1995, when corporate globalization became, literally, the legal constitution of the world, gives lie to this claim. Look at the misunderstandings between cultures that have resulted. I talk more about the connections between corporate globalization and the rise of terrorism, the rise of extremism, and the rise of the right wing. A second promise was prosperity: "'When the waters rise, all boats will rise." The waters haven't risen. They have fallen. They have been depleted by the very processes of giving control over these resources to corporations.

While unbridled capitalist greed has been referred to as "compassionate capitalism" in the US, compassionate economics of sustenance and nature are precisely what is destroyed by corporate rule and the rule of capital. Protection of nature and people's rights are defined as protectionism, as trade barriers, and as barriers to investment. Trade rules and neoliberal reform institutionalize laws which render compassion itself illegal, Thus, cultures of compassion which treat all life as sacred are made illegal through patents on life. Cultures of compassion and social justice which share social wealth and nature's wealth are rendered illegal through privatization of essential public services like water, health, education. Economies that aim to guarantee and protect livelihoods, jobs, and social security are dismantled, leaving people with no place in society or the economy. These are not examples of compassionate economies, they are examples of a violent economy which looks more and more like warfare, both in its methods and its results.

A typical example of the neoliberal paradigm that dominates current economic and social policy can be found in a book published by the IMF entitled *Who Will Pay? Coping with Aging Societies, Climate Change, and Other Long-Term Fiscal Challenges.* In one fell swoop the book's title redefines the challenges of social and ecological reproduction and renewal as fiscal challenges. Humans and nature have disappeared only to be substituted for money. Market economists who see only markets and money are blind to nature and society. They are unable to see that the wealthy's riches are accumulated by exploitation of nature and society. These economists fail to value what nature and people have already contributed. Their contribution is an ecological and social loan greater than any given by the IMF.

Native American and Indian cultures both uphold a seventh-generation logic that states that the impact on the seventh generation should be taken into account before acting. The neo-liberal recipe to dismantle Social Security in the present for future generation's security is not really based on the consideration of the welfare of future generations. It is a means of diverting finances from the sustenance economy to the market economy, leaving both present and future generations without security.

GROWTH AND EFFICIENCY IN THE MARKET

Another myth about the market economy is that it is the most efficient method of production. But the "efficient" market economy becomes highly inefficient when the destruction of nature's economy is taken into account. The efficiency and productivity of industrial agriculture hides the costs of depletion of soils, exploitation of groundwater, erosion, and extinction of biodiversity. Industrial agriculture uses 10 times more energy than it produces. It uses 10 times more water than biodiverse farming with water-prudent crops and organic practices use. In fact, when assessed from nature's economy, biodiverse, ecological farms have much higher productivity than large-scale, industrial, monoculture farms. The illusion of efficiency is produced by externalizing the ecological costs.

Frequently, growth is generated by converting resources from nature's economy into market commodities. Economic growth takes place through the exploitation of natural resources. Deforestation creates growth. Mining of groundwater creates growth. Overfishing creates growth. Further economic growth cannot help regenerate the very spheres which must be destroyed for economic growth to occur. Nature shrinks as capital grows. The growth of the market cannot solve the very crisis it creates. Furthermore, while natural resources can be converted into cash, cash cannot be converted into nature's wealth. Market economists trying to address the ecological crisis limit themselves to the market, and look for substitutes for the commercial function of natural resources as commodities and raw material. The increased availability of financial resources cannot regenerate the life lost in nature through ecological destruction. An African peasant captured this essence: "You cannot turn a calf into a cow by plastering it with mud." In nature's economy and the sustenance economy the currency is not money, it is life.

JUSTICE & STABILITY

Gandhi's economic constitution reads:

> According to me, the economic constitution of India and, for the matter of that, the world should be such that no one under it should suffer from want of food and clothing. In other words everybody should be able to get sufficient work to enable him to make the two ends meet. And this ideal can be universally realized only if the means of production of the elementary necessaries of life remain in the control of the masses. These should be freely available to all as God's air and water are or ought to be; they should not be made a vehicle of traffic for the exploitation of others. Their monopolization by any country, nation or groups of persons would be unjust. The neglect of this simple principle is the cause of the destitution that we witness today not only in this unhappy land but in other parts of the world, too.

The suicidal market economy destroys nature's economy and the people's sustenance economy, creating ecologic crisis and economic crisis, while making growth nonsustainable and inequitable. Living economies rejuvenate ecological processes while reactivating people's creativity, solidarity, and interdependence. Robust living economies are people-centered, decentralized, sustainable, and `hood-generating. They are based on co-ownership and coproduction, on sharing and participation. Living economies are not mere concepts; they exist and continue to emerge in our times. Living economies are being shaped by ordinary people in their everyday lives.

Living economies are based on the vibrant, resilient, and renewable nature's economies and rich, diverse, and sustainable people's economies. Living economies are sustainable and just. They respect the renewable limits of natural resources and share those resources to ensure everyone's needs are met. This is why biodiversity and water must stay in the commons. And why the defense of the commons is the basis of many movements that fall within the constellation of Earth Democracy.

LOCALIZATION

What happens in Iraq doesn't matter to most people in the US. Except for the families of the soldiers who have been sent there, it's not a pain that most people feel on a daily basis. The distance isolates them. This isolation is why localization, the elevating of local concerns and regulation, is a key tenet of Earth Democracy. Localization provides a test for justice. Localization is a test of sustainability. This is not to say all decisions will be made on a local level. There will of course be decisions and policies made on the national level and the global level; but to reach these other levels they have to constantly pass the screen of living democracy. Authority is delegated to more distant levels of government on the principle of subsidiarity: things are most effectively done at the level closest to where the impact is felt. This principle is an ecological imperative.

Devaluing the role of natural resources—in ecological processes and in people's sustenance economy—and the diverting and destroying of these resources for commodity production and capital accumulation are the main reasons for the ecological crisis and the crisis of survival in the Third World. The solution lies in giving local communities control over local resources so that they have the right, responsibility, and ability to rebuild nature's economy, and through it their own sustainability. This is what living economies are undertaking.

Living economies are based on people's creativity and self-organization. Living economies grow outward, from the individual to the community to the region to the country to the global level. The most intense relationships are at the local level and the thinnest interactions at the international level. That is why living economies are primarily local and decentralized, in contrast to the dominant model, which is global and centralized. Localization and decentralization do not imply isolation or the inability to coordinate with a high level of organization. In living economies small self-organizing systems can network to an extremely complex level of organization. In India, the women of Lijjat Papad and the Tiffin carriers of Mumbai who inspire even the global market giants powerfully demonstrate this.

REGULATING THE MARKET

Living economies are grounded by two ecological principles necessary to protect and restore nature and society that free market economists have resisted implementing. These principles are the "precautionary principle" and the "polluter pays principle" as enshrined in Agenda 21 of the UN Conference on Environment and Development (1992), known as the Earth Summit. The precautionary principle calls for not undertaking activities that could cause ecological harm. The polluter pays principle requires that the polluter must pay for any harm done to nature and society and for the costs of the cleanup.

Under the polluter pays principle, those engaged in selling fossil fuels and fossil-fuel-based energy and transportation systems must pay for the impacts of climate change, for processes which reduce CO_2 emissions, and to develop sustainable, renewable energy alternatives. It is now recognized that over the next century the climate will change because of fossil fuel use and greenhouse-gas emissions—especially CO_2. The concentration of greenhouse gases already present in the atmosphere will cause the earth's atmosphere to warm in the range of 1.9 to 5.8 degrees Celsius over the next century. And while the industrialized world accounts for the major share of CO_2 emissions—because changes in temperature and precipitation will have greater impact on the viability of agriculture in the tropics; because people in the South are more dependent on local agriculture; and because sea-level rise will have higher impact on coastal communities and small island states—the South will feel the major impact.

Attempts have been made to draft a climate-change agreement addressing the common problems—but with different responsibilities—stemming from atmospheric pollution. The Kyoto Protocol attempts to put the responsibility for reducing greenhouse gasses on countries. In Earth Democracy the responsibility of resolving the climate change problems would be on the companies—and their CEOs. The responsibility of governments and intergovernmental agreements would be to ensure that production and consumption patterns operate within sustainable cycles.

LIVING ECONOMIES FOR REJUVENATION OF LIVELIHOODS

Livelihoods are the human source of sustenance, meaning, and purpose; they provide a sense of self and of community. Livelihoods are ways of living and means of life. Livelihoods are not "jobs," where one sells labor power to someone else who pays wages. A peasant cultivating food does not have a job, but does have a livelihood. Livelihoods are self-generated. Creative production through "self-employment" needs access to resources and this is what commons ensure. Fishing communities need access to the seas as commons for their livelihoods, forest communities need access to the forest commons for their livelihoods, and farming communities need access to biological and hydrological commons for their livelihoods. The enclosures of the commons rob people not just of their resources, but also of their self-sustainability and livelihoods.

In India, 5 million peasants are displaced annually. Seventy-five percent of India's 1 billion people base their livelihoods on agriculture. In spite of 6 percent annual growth of GNP over the past decade, India's employment in agriculture and manufacturing has declined. Even the services sector is witnessing jobless growth. The much heralded outsourcing of information technology jobs to India currently contributes less than 1 percent of the GDP and employs less than 1 million people—a mere .01 percent of the population. Furthermore, these jobs are restricted to the less than 5 percent of Indians who receive a college education. Thus, agriculture and manufacturing will remain the source of livelihood for most Indians.[64]

While globalization is leading to jobless growth and creating disposable people, living economies ensure work for all. Living economies are based on working for sustenance. They put human beings and nature at the center. In living economies, economics and ecology are not in conflict. They are mutually supportive.

Questions

1. Who should "own" property?

2. What should be the limitations on the state for controlling the economy?

3. What is the best way for economic activities to take into consideration the environmental impact?

4. Which form of economy is consistent with which view of human nature?

Suggested Media

Movies:

Inside Job
Wall Street: Money Never Sleeps
Wal-Mart: The High Cost of Low Price
Capitalism: A Love Story
The Corporation (available online at no cost)
Collapse
The Social network
Blood Diamond

Blogs

The Independent Institute
The Nation

Conclusion

> I care about life, but, too, I care about Justice. If I cannot have both, then I choose Justice. I care about life, but then there are things that I care about more than life. For that reason, I will not seek life improperly.
>
> Mencius, 1990 p.58

This book has provided an elaboration on some of the many ways of interpreting and understanding justice. We have engaged in multiple visions of justice, including historical and contemporary, visions that stem from different geographical locations and visions that pay homage to political, social, legal, and economic theorists who have provided the voices that bring to light struggles for justice. In the words of bell hooks, we are "grateful to the many women and men who dare to create theory from the location of pain and struggle, who courageously expose wounds to give us their experience to teach and guide, as a means to chart new theoretical journeys. Their work is liberatory. It not only enables us to remember and recover ourselves, it charges and challenges us to renew our commitment to an active, inclusive" vision of justice (1994, pp.74-75).

We have presented various ideas about the many ways that we can understand the nature of human beings. Throughout history, human nature has frequently been characterized through the dichotomies of good vs. evil, right vs. wrong, selfish vs. altruistic. We have attempted to provide a more nuanced understanding of human nature and personhood as complicated. Further, individuals cannot be understood outside of their relations to each other. Theorists within this text have interrogated ideas about relations, power, institutions, and intersections and have provided a complex understanding of how individuals interact and engage with one another, frequently in unjust ways.

Social and structural institutions including Law, economy, government/state, family, communities and community organizations, and social groups, among others, provide the space in which we institute popular, secular, religious, and personal notions of justice. Governance and Law are often bureaucracies and institutions that are formed to represent and uphold particular notions on justice. It is, therefore, not coincidental that much civil disobedience is aimed at these state institutions. Often, these institutions support, constrict, and conflict with personal ideologies about justice. Just as with ideas about political and social institutions, theorists of justice have grappled with the many ways that economies both reinforce oppression and domination, as well as liberation. Each of the sections within this reader provides a working knowledge of justice both inside and outside of dominant Western concepts of justice. Justice is not just the province of states or institutions or structures, but rather a feature of our everyday lives. We live with justice, and grapple with the questions of justice. With each act of kindness, compassion, love, caring, and empathy, we create and regenerate these in our everyday lives with others.

The study of justice is misleading because rather than focusing on justice we frequently are forced to engage with the study of injustice instead. Justice is not so much a problem to be "solved" as it is a set of questions or issues that we live and struggle with. By providing you with a vision of the world that has many intersecting, overlapping forms of domination and oppression, these readings have raised more questions than they answer, but we encourage further grappling with the many visions of justice. As can be seen in the final readings, justice and theory are intimately linked.

As can be seen the final readings, justice and theory are intimately linked. You also have your own views on justice, even before ever opening this book. While some may be new, some of the ideas and theories discussed in this text may have seemed familiar to you, despite their language. This is in part because we encounter these ideas everyday. As students of justice theory, we have the privilege to ponder through these ideas and discuss them amongst others committed to the same pursuit; however, theories are not just things we talk about within the academic classroom. They are very much a part of our everyday existence and our decisions on how to treat one another and how we interact, inside and outside the classroom. In their piece, Sullivan, Tifft and Cordell comment on justice theory and education. They discuss what it means to be justice literate and their comments will remind you of the readings throughout this book: justice literacy requires examining how structure and process, ideologies and concepts, and systems of power impact our society, our relationships with one another, and justice.

In a speech she gave to Justice Studies' students in 1994, Avery Gordon (1994/2004) pointed out that social justice and social theory are intertwined. One cannot have social justice without theory, but, in the end, social justice must have the last word. As a student of justice, you must develop your own theoretical claim to justice, which will develop over time, will continually change with your experiences with our world, and will be challenged and reinforced as you engage in your pursuit for justice. Just as Mencius would hold, we must choose justice. Because you are a scholar of Justice Studies, your task is to: reveal intersecting forms of injustice; engage in multiple visions of justice; and transform pathways to justice.

References

Gordon, A. (1994). "Theory and Justice" in *Keeping Good Time: Reflections on Knowledge, Power, and People*. A. Gordon 2004. London: Paradigm Publishers.

hooks, b. (1994). *Teaching to Transgress: Education as the Practice of Freedom*. New York: Routledge.

Mencius "On the Mind". In *What is Justice*. R. Solomon and M. Murphy. 1990. Oxford: Oxford University Press.

EDITORS' INTRODUCTORY REMARKS: A CONTEXT FOR UNDERSTANDING JUSTICE LITERACY

DENNIS SULLIVAN, LARRY TIFFT AND PETER CORDELLA

For many teachers and students of criminology, criminal justice, and related fields of study that deal with issues of justice, the concept of "justice literacy," that is, what every student needs to know about justice before graduating from college, is a cut-and-dry subject. It is a matter of providing a list of essential books and related resource materials for students to familiarize themselves with in order to have the tools to enter graduate school or the marketplace fully equipped (Thornberry, 1990; Siegel and Zalman, 1991). When debate over justice literacy has arisen, it has centered around whether there is or should be a "canon" of works that ought to be read and, if so, how inclusive that canon should be with respect to issues such as gender and diversity (Lynch, Huey, Santiago Nunez, Close, Johnston, 1992; Barak, 1991; Denby, 1996: 376–379).

That questions about literacy are being revisited at this time by teachers of criminology and criminal justice is not surprising because the question of what literature today's students should be familiar with or what body of knowledge they should possess is being asked in other disciplines as well; in English, the Humanities, and Political Science to name only a few (Denby, 1996; Bloom, 1994; Kernan, 1997; Aronowitz and Grioux, 1988). We even see the notion of literacy being addressed in the spiritual realm, what holy works people need to be familiar with in order to have a solid spiritual foundation for life (Brussat and Brussat, 1997). And although the subject matter is spoken of in terms of moral development rather than literacy, the moral literacy of children has also come to the fore (Coles, 1997). Indeed, some writers have put together volumes of materials they believe kids should be familiar with (Bennett, 1993; 1995; Greer and Kohl, 1995) if they are to grow up with, as William Bennett urges, "good habits."

If we look back for a moment in an attempt to pinpoint the genesis of the recent concerns over literacy in its various forms, we see that they grow out of a sense that young people either are not being taught or are not learning the essentials for a moral or "educated" life. One result of this failure in the United States, according to Alan Bloom at least, is a phenomenon he describes as "the closing of the American mind," the title of his book on cultural literacy (1988). The subtitle of the work, *How Higher Education has Failed Democracy and Impoverished the Souls of Today's Students*, tells us the extent of Bloom's concerns. In part, he was responding to the social consciousness that held sway on many university campuses in the 1980s, what was pejoratively referred to as "political correctness." Among some scholars, Bloom included, there was a sense that college students (and the general population of the United States) were not learning the common language that enables people to communicate with each other, to speak with each other civilly, all of which has implications for how we carry ourselves as a nation. And, of course, with such concerns, there is the only feebly hidden concern that a poorly-educated populace will inhibit a nation from competing successfully in the world market. So with respect to cultural literacy, there are ultimately economic and political concerns as well.

In an effort to pry open the strictures in our cultural mind's funnel, if you will, some creative antidotes have been offered (Levine, 1996). Some writers have gone so far as to suggest that, if young people were introduced to the basics of culture and became culturally literate, it would be possible to transform the economic opportunity structure of the United States. Indeed, Hirsch (1987: xiii) claims that "cultural literacy constitutes the only sure avenue of opportunity for disadvantaged children, the only reliable way for combating the social determinism that now condemns them to remain in the same social and educational condition as their parents." For Hirsch and others who share this view, cultural literacy is the *sine qua non* for a leg up, the great social and economic equalizer. But, on the face of it, such sentiments smack of an extraordinary political naiveté (or perhaps a masked foxiness) that fails to recognize the enormous power of the cultural, economic, political, and social structural conditions that dismiss the needs of large segments of the population in our society and cause ever-solidifying forms of marginalization. (Sklar, 1994). So, when we hear statements such as that made by Hirsch, we have to adjust our reasoning abilities for a moment and wonder whether the demands for cultural literacy are not masked proposals for greater doses of discipline and control of those segments of the population which are seen as a threat to economic security, domestically and internationally. Certainly this is the agenda of some who call for moral literacy, for the more intensified development of "good habits" and character development (Bennett, 1993), but who fail to take into account the larger social context in which children grow up and in which terms such as discipline and character derive their definition and purpose (Tifft, Sullivan, and Sullivan, 1997; Schumacher and Wieck, 1983).

When we turn our attention to defining the body of knowledge "every American needs to know" to be culturally literate, Hirsch suggests that it is not necessary for the average person to go beyond "a northerly border, above which lies specialized knowledge" (1987: 138). That is, at a certain point, there is knowledge or information that only the professional "expert" is expected to know, information that the average person does not need to be culturally literate. Agreeing with this assessment, some criminal justice scholars, who are interested in the applicability of cultural literacy to the fields of criminology and criminal justice, have noted that these too are specialized fields of knowledge which the average person does not need to master. They argue that in these fields the body of knowledge "consists of highly focused, arcane information and specific methodologies that allow graduates to go forth and practice their profession or profess their academic specialities" (Siegel and Zalman, 1991: 16). It is knowledge suited to the professional and not the ordinary person. With this we would agree but for very different reasons. Indeed, we would go a step further and suggest that much of it is information that is so specialized that it is detrimental to the justice literacy quotient of all persons, not only the ordinary student or person but also those who major in or focus on this body of knowledge right up to the level of Ph.D.

We are suggesting that the way criminology and criminal justice curricula are currently structured and presented in course-form, they offer very little to enhance or expand the justice literacy of students, because in nearly every form they represent the interests of the state and of those who benefit from the prevailing market economy, not the needs of the ordinary person and the human community as a whole. By and large, these disciplines do not reflect an interest in exploring the personal bases and anthropological fundamentals of justice, demonstrating where criminal justice fits into the larger context of justice-done, nor do they teach how crime fits into the larger category of personal and social harms. Hence, students of criminology and criminal justice develop little working knowledge of how the definition of harms and the administration of justice by the state are related to the definition and resolution of disputes by other means, legal and otherwise (Nader and Todd, 1978). They rarely get to see that discipline and punishment as external modes of social control reflect only one kind of response among many to the harms we do to each other daily and that these modes of control grow out of the needs of a particular cultural and political economic framework. Indeed, we are suggesting that part of the hidden agenda of criminology and criminal justice programs is to diminish the value of cultural and social structural alternatives to powerbased strategies of social interaction and conflict resolution.

In a very real sense, then, what we see today across the United States are criminal justice and criminology programs that reflect an inversion of justice studies, taking a part (criminal justice) for the whole (social justice) and dismissing the importance of situating criminology and criminal justice in the larger context of social harms and social justice (Sullivan and Bennett, 1996). While administrators and faculty of criminology and criminal justice programs assiduously measure themselves against their past performance and competing programs to assess their achieved degree of professionalization, these programs, regardless of how far they have come, remain within the same category as their judged inferior counterparts on the central categories of justice literacy. The central issues of justice literacy do not revolve around the level of demonstrated professionalization of a given program or the credentials of its faculty, but with the fact that justice programs are professionalized in the first place and that teachers for the most part exclude all not-credentialized or not accredited voices from serious participation in the justice dialogue. Or, at least, they do not take these voices and the needs they represent seriously.

Of course, many teachers and administrators will assert adamantly that this is not the case. But the way curricula are structured and courses are taught belies such protestation. The reality of the matter is that, currently, criminology and criminal justice programs at all levels have become essentially training divisions and personnel offices for government agencies serving to reinforce ideological perspectives that manufacture consent for market strategists who promote the needs of some at the expense of others. Such programs might be fruitful in professionalizing the thinking of students in preparation for the job market, but they have little to do with facilitating literacy on the subject of justice. For example, in multitudinous programs across the United States, almost invariably the first courses taught to entering students are the Administration of Criminal Justice and Theories of Crime. These courses establish a framework that defines the kinds of questions which will be allowed and the kinds of inquiries that will be taken seriously. During class discussions and examinations, students are often asked to assume the role of a police chief and render decisions as such under certain hypothetical circumstances. Or they are asked to confront the dilemmas faced by a probation administrator or render parole revocation decisions in hypothetical cases, or learn the details of court cases as if they were preparing to practice law or become a prison/corrections administrator. And, in criminology courses, these same students study "crime causation" theories derived from state-focused, non-needs-based political economies without ever examining the moral foundations of or alternatives to such political economies. If such courses must be offered to cater to those interested in a professional career in criminal justice, they might be better positioned at the end of a series of courses students can take as electives. But examined in the light of what such courses offer for enhancing justice literacy, we would have to conclude that they are better treated as exercises or components of on-the-job training.

And with respect to the teaching qualifications of those working in justice-related programs, justice literacy cannot concern itself with whether a retired police lieutenant or a parole administrator with twenty years of work experience is better or worse qualified to teach a course than a Ph.D in the subject, but rather, that the course content and learning method are geared toward "the professionalization of the mind" and that only the certified professional is deemed to have the knowledge and authority to teach about such matters. Although the content of criminology and criminal justice curricula are out in the open for study and review, we have to describe these curricula as *hidden* because built into their very structure are assumptions about knowledge development that are rarely examined. And this issue transcends the content of a particular course or canon of works because it makes no difference whether the *curriculum* "is designed to teach the principles of fascism, liberalism, Catholicism, socialism, or liberation, so long as the institution claims the authority to define which activities are legitimate 'education'" (Illich, 1977: 70). The important element to take note of with respect to hidden curriculum is that students "learn that education is valuable when it is acquired in the school through a graded process of consumption, that the degree of success the individual will enjoy in society depends on the amount of learning he consumes, and that learning about the world is more valuable than learning *from* the world" (Illich, 1977: 70–71).

For those who disagree with such an assessment, again, all we have to do is point to the core curricula of criminology and criminal justice programs around the United States. In most such programs, law and the state are treated as the only viable means for fostering a sense of safety and meeting human needs. Indeed, these institutions are treated as beneficent and effective in reconciling those in conflict and for developing communities of human concern. Not only does anthropology of justice generally remain absent, but law and the state are treated ahistorically and outside the social and economic context in which these institutions derive their legitimacy and purpose.

In effect, we are saying that to discuss issues of justice literacy in the context of criminal justice and criminology as professionalized agencies of knowledge is a contradiction in terms. Moreover, it is an approach to justice that masks the more fundamental questions of justice literacy; that is, the nature of the "texts" to be used, and the derivation of those texts. What, for example, is the basis or source of our knowledge about justice (criminal, social, and restorative) and who has the authority to teach about such issues? Does the authority reside within everyone or does it reside within a caste of institutional professionals who pontificate over the development of curricula and course syllabi (Schillebeeckx, 1995: 232)?

Here then is the crux of the matter of justice literacy. When we talk about justice literacy, what we need to begin with and keep in mind at every step of the way is that every student who walks into a university classroom, indeed every person, (and from a very early age), knows all he or she needs to know about justice (Coles, 1997). That is, each person has already experienced hurts, injustices, and harms in some way, has developed his or her own view of what constitutes a harm or injustice-done, and knows what constitutes a suitable response to such harms and injustices in the form of justice-done. In this respect, each student can be considered to be quite learned regarding his or her own "theory of crime" and system for administering justice, having used both on multitudinous occasions for defining and resolving harm situations in which he or she (or another) was involved. Even the most fledgling of justice students can speak with an authority about what needs to be done in harm-based situations that is every bit as valid and authoritative as that of the professional justicians who are their assigned teachers (Sullivan, in press). The problem, of course, is that relatively few students (and teachers) are aware of the political economic foundations on which their sense of justice is based and, therefore, remain unaware of the effect their system of justice has on others when put into practice.

Nevertheless, each person can claim to know about justice and to have as much right or authority to speak about such matters as professionally-certified teachers because the justice perspective of each of us is derived from our experience with needs. Each person's perspective on justice is developed and shaped by how his or her needs are attended to and have been attended to throughout his or her lifetime, particularly how they have been given or denied consideration in comparison to the needs of others (Sullivan and Tifft, in press, a). It is through the expression of our unique needs and the response of others to them that each of us defines who we are and develops an identity. Our sense of being treated justly or unjustly develops in accordance with how much we have been encouraged to express our needs and how attentive others are to sharing in their satisfaction. If our needs are not permitted expression or respected or given the kind of consideration that says we are important in and of ourselves, we grow up with a very different sense of self, of equality, well-being, justice, and community than if our needs are deemed to be valid and are paid attention to.

At its core then, justice literacy is first and foremost integrally connected with an understanding of how our perspective on justice develops in relation to needs, how we are enabled to define them, how they are responded to, and the kind of misery and suffering we experience when our needs are denied expression and satisfaction (Quinney, 1991). Justice literacy is also integrally connected with our understanding of the way we develop a social ethic through which we define some as worthy of needs attention and others not, and why we eventually define those in the latter category as belonging to a whole other category of being (Herman and Chomsky, 1988). Hence, justice literacy must include an understanding of this divisive process that we might describe as structural violence (Gil, 1996); that is a process that sanctions acts that deny voice, that marginalize, that denigrate the needs of some for the benefit of others, and that define as troublemakers those who seek a voice for all (Sullivan and Tifft, in press, b).

Justice literacy must also include an examination of the responses to such structural violence, to structured needs denial. We are aware of how many of those who become marginalized develop counter-responses to such violence which are sometimes violent (Gil, 1996; Tifft, 1993). While such responses are intended to insure that needs are met, they too reflect a perspective on justice that says equality is achieved through acts of power, exclusion, and denigration, not mutual consideration (Cordella, forthcoming). But when faced with the opportunity to examine both forms of violence, personal and structural, in the development of their theories of crime, punishment, and justice, professional justicians tend to focus only on interpersonal acts of violence, especially counterviolence, thereby allowing forms of structural violence to escape the attention of students. It is in this sense that criminologists and criminal justicians have become standard bearers for law, the state, and the market economy and dismissive of a whole range of questions that are conducive to literacy. While the professional justician might assert that he or she is an expert in knowing what individuals and communities need, such a perspective reflects an arrogation of the right, indeed need, for each member of a community to bespeak his or her own needs and thereby develop a sense of justice that is satisfying (Sullivan, 1980). How the latter process is facilitated or denied is a determinant of how justice literate a person will become.

Therefore, what needs to be addressed in any curriculum of justice studies with respect to fostering literacy, long before issues related to the development of a "required reading" list can be addressed, is how to facilitate an archeology of each student's perspective on justice coupled with a thorough exploration of the assumptions on which that perspective is based. As indicated, this entails examining the political economic framework from which these perspectives derive their meaning and purpose; that is, how needs are defined, expressed, and responded to. This means that each student must examine his or her view of justice against the specifications of deserts-based, rights-based, and needs-based economies and assess how his or her view manifests itself in relationships in all areas of our lives: in the family, the school, and the workplace (Miller, 1976; Tifft, 1978). Of course, when engaging in such analysis, there is no way of escaping an exploration of issues of power, authority, control, discipline, privilege, prestige, scarcity and surplus, and related issues to see to what extent they promote injustice and for whom.

Looked at from this perspective, clearly justice literacy has much to do with moral choice. The purpose of examining the various dimensions of one's perspective on justice in light of the specifications of deserts-based, rights-based, and needs-based economies is to allow each person to situate him- or herself on a spectrum of values that these economies reflect, from values based in power (deserts-based) to those based in mutual care (needs-based). This kind of examination serves as a mirror in which a person can see him- or herself as he or she truly is and explore in honesty the consequences of one's acts for others. And the teacher who considers him-or herself a just person cannot force or threaten any student to assume a particular ideological position for the sake of a grade or any other assessment, only help each student situate him- or herself on the spectrum of political economic values and open up to making the moral choice that such self-defining involves.

Finally, once a person has situated him- or herself along the spectrum of political economic values, he or she can then examine all the relevant aspects of his or her view of justice within an anthropology of justice, to see how his or her personal view is similar to or different from those held by people living in other cultural contexts. This is not an option for achieving cultural literacy but a *sine qua non* for developing a larger cultural framework in which to understand issues of law and the state, crime and harm, discipline and control, punishment and reconciliation as political economic means to ends. It also enables each person to read what happens in the world with a critical eye and to grasp the political economic assumptions of justice that underlie not only literary texts but social situations. By going through this intensive process, wherever one eventually comes out, each person at the very least comes to see that he or she does indeed have the authority to talk about all aspects of justice.

Many people regard the late Donald Newman's (1967) *Conviction: The Determination of Guilt or Innocence Without Trial* as a kind of criminal justice classic and, on one level, it might well be. But, while this book might enlighten us as to the way criminal "cases" were handled in the courts of the United States at a particular time, it was written in such a way that it did not explore the political and economic function of the plea bargaining process. Therefore, many who read the work might decry the callous conditions that plea bargaining creates and in response call or work for organizational reform. But a critical reading of the book in the context of political economy tells us that a system of justice that is based on power and dedicated to meet the needs of some at the expense of others (Reiman, 1995; Pepinsky, 1991) will cut deals ("plea bargain") to maintain its own identity even when those deals cheat people of a chance to engage in a reconciliation process and hopefully regain, or develop for the first time, a feeling of worth. But these remarks ought not to be construed that Donald Newman lacked understanding of the political economic implications of the study of criminal justice for he was known to have said at the beginning of his introductory course in the Administration of Justice, "This is not a program to get involved in if you are not willing to get blood on your shoes."

Regardless of how aware students and teachers might be of their assumptions regarding justice going into the classroom, it is easy to see how the beginning of each course is a potential source of conflict. Whose curriculum is going to be examined? Whose curriculum is going to prevail as the text, the text derived from the injustice/justice experiences of all or that based in an arcane, professionalized body of knowledge? Clearly power will play a central role in such a determination which means that in most situations the teacher will enforce the learning of the professional texts, the law, and the state over texts and social institutions based in personal experience and community. But, when this occurs, students hide who they really are and deny expression to their true self in the interest of short-term rewards such as a grade or the avoidance of an unwinable conflict.

In a very real sense, then, for someone to approach teaching about justice through a social ethic that promotes hierarchy and power-based modes of relationship is to set one's self in opposition to the requirements of personal growth and community (Rogers, 1961; 1980). From the very earliest time, when specialists or experts, whether priests, artists, or magicians, were created to aid the faltering community, they were given authority by the community to specify what action it needed to take to alleviate its suffering, to get beyond its current traumatic situation, which could be as basic as learning how to "ensure the food-supply, to promote the multiplication of the hunted game and secure success in the chase" (Childe, 1942; 40). By performing the magic rites and reading the sacred texts that the specialist set forth, the individual and the community as a whole sought to restore confidence in their competencies to face the struggles of life. If a community was willing to submit to the requirements of this hierarchical arrangement and temporarily give up participation in ceremonies or rites that all traditionally shared in (Gaster, 1961: 48), it was because its members believed there would be a greater restoration for all, that the needs of all would be taken into account. Each was willing to give up his or her own voice to a representative in order to once again speak with greater confidence, to become the self one truly was (Kierkegaard, 1941).

We can trace the lineage of this hierarchical relationship between the specialist and the community from the magic leader of simpler societies to the priest-king or god-king of the first civilization (Brown, 1959: 252; Frazer, 1922; 83–106) to today's secular priests, the professional expert We see that in each edition of the relationship the specialist was assigned the task of helping the community develop an alternative vision of justice, alternative social arrangements for satisfying the needs of all (Illich, 1977; Sullivan, 1980). A major part of becoming justice literate entails becoming aware of how this task was carried out, understanding how and to what extent those charged with restoring individual and communal competencies often became treasonous to the community by telling its members they lacked the competency to fend for themselves and then exercising power over them. Justice literacy is an education in the nuances of dependency production and confinement as well those of freedom and liberation.

But the history of the specialist's refusal to enable the community to regain a sense of itself and his usurpation of personal and communal resources in the process cannot be fully grasped until one begins to excavate the foundations of justice within one's self and to contrast them point by point with the perspectives peddled by the specialist. As we have said throughout, this archaeological process resides at the heart of the development of justice literacy. Through it, we learn how to become a moral person, we learn how to act and speak in behalf of what fosters and sustains just community; that is, a community organized to take into account the needs of all. We also learn how to act and speak in behalf of reconciliation, a process that heals this community when someone, in the process of meeting his or her needs, harms another.

As editors of *The Contemporary Justice Review*, we believe that one of the most important aspects of human development is literacy in the basics of justice in all areas of our lives. It is for this reason that we have invited some of the most resourceful scholars writing about justice today to contribute to this special issue of *CJR*. As you will see, each of the articles demonstrates that there are many ways to approach issues related to learning about justice but the questions asked and answered here also show a common thread. They point to the ill-effects of power-based social institutions and forms of justice and to the ever-present need for the voice of each to be heard in all areas of life. That is, if the relationships in question are expected to promote not only justice literacy but justice as well.

THEORY AND JUSTICE

AVERY GORDON

It's wonderful to be here today to talk to you about theory and justice. Because your conversations about theory take place under the rubric of Justice Studies, you have already placed the theoretical enterprise in relation to a demand, justice, that it must meet at least halfway, and which I am taking for granted here with you. Recently, I have been talking and teaching social theory in relation to sociology which involves, by contrast, spending an enormous amount of time simply establishing the relevance of justice. To be in Justice Studies, then, is to already know a lot about what knowledge and theory is for. Whereas in sociology, they are always repeating the famous question Robert Lynd demanded of his professional colleagues in 1938, when fascism in Europe had created what he felt was a "critical time for social science": knowledge for what?

I have one simple point to make today, and then I will entertain any questions you want to raise for discussion. My one simple point is that social justice needs theory, and good social theory will, of necessity, be oriented towards social justice. In my opinion, social justice and social theory are intertwined. But I also believe that social justice must always have the last word. We must end and end up with social justice, not theory per se. This is my view and what I strive to accomplish as a social theorist. I am using the word justice here in two ways. First, I'm using it as a way of calling you by your work-name, a name, as I've suggested, that confers a certain speaking position within the university. But I'm also using the word deliberately vaguely because justice is not some thing determined in advance but a name for the calculus by which we judge the rightness of the way things are. That judgment is never objective once and for all—it is not an object or a scale. Rather, it is both the subject of the something to be done right, and it is also a living, breathing measure of the humanity and the human potential of what we call, always in effect mistakenly, the political subject.

Let me approach the question of why justice and theory are intertwined in a less philosophical and cryptic way. I'll give you three reasons.

The first reason is because, to paraphrase Patricia Williams, *it is a fact of great analytic importance that life is complicated.*[1] That life is complicated may seem a banal formulation of the obvious, but I think it's actually a significant theory. There are at least two dimensions to such a theory. The first dimension is that the power relations that characterize any society are never as transparently clear as the names we give to them suggest. Power can be invisible, it can be fantastic, it can be dull and routine, it can be grand and obvious. It can reach you by the baton of the police, it can speak in the language of your own thoughts and desires. It can feel like remote control, it can exhilarate like liberation. It can travel through time and it can drown you in the present. It is dense and superficial, it can cause bodily injury, and it can injure you without seemingly ever touching you. It causes dreams to live and dreams to die. It is systematic and it is particularistic. We can and must call it by names like racism, for example, but also we need to understand that power arrives in forms that can range from blatant white supremacy to "furniture without memories."

In an exercise with my students, I asked them to make a thorough list of every possible explanation Toni Morrison gives for why dreams die in her novel *The Bluest Eye*. It was a long list ranging from explicit externally imposed and internalized white supremacist standards of beauty and ugliness, the *nature of white man's work*, and the dialectics of violence and hatred, to *disappointment*, to *folding up inside*, to the *fear of being put outdoors*, to *the weather*, to *deformed feet and lost teeth*, to *nobody pays attention*, to *it's too late*, to *total damage*, to *furniture without memories*, to the *unyielding soil*, and to what she sometimes just calls *the thing*, the sedimented conditions that constitute what's in place in the first place. These turn out to be not a random or simply surreal list, but a way of conceptualizing the complicated workings of those social structures we call race, class, gender. Such a conception requires that we constantly move within and between *deformed feet and lost teeth* and words with capital letters like Slavery or Capitalism. We must move analytically within and between them because that is the nature of their movement.

But what this list also reminds us is that even those living in the most dire circumstances possess a complex and oftentimes contradictory humanity and subjectivity that is never covered by viewing them as victims, or as superhuman agents. And this is the second aspect of the theory that life is complicated. It has never made sense to me why those most committed to understanding and changing domination too often withhold from the very people they are seemingly most concerned about the right to complex personhood. Complex personhood means that all people, albeit in specific forms, are beset by contradiction, remember and forget, and recognize and misrecognize themselves and others. Complex personhood means that people suffer graciously and selfishly too, get stuck in what symptomizes their troubles and also transform themselves. Complex personhood means that even those the society names "other" are never that. Complex personhood means that even those who haunt the dominant society are haunted too by things they sometimes have names for and sometimes do not. Complex personhood means that the stories people tell about themselves, about their problems, about their society and about their society's problems are entangled and weave between what's immediately available as a story and what their imaginations are reaching toward. Complex personhood means that groups of people will act together, that they will vehemently disagree with and sometimes harm each other, and that they will do both at the same time and expect the rest of us to figure it out for ourselves, intervening and withdrawing as the situation requires. At the very least, complex personhood is about conferring the respect on others that comes from presuming that life and people's lives are straightforward and full of enormously complex meanings.

That life is complicated is a philosophy or theory which is necessary for guiding the attempt to treat gender, race, or class dynamics and consciousness as much broader, much deeper, much more significant than the flat terms *discrimination* or *prejudice* often imply. It is a theory that can guide a critique of privately purchased rights, of various forms of blindness and neutrality; that can guide an attempt to drive a wedge into our market-based notions of freedom. It is a theory that might allow us to see deep into the heart and soul of American life and culture, to track events, stories, anonymous and history-making actions to their density, to the point where we might catch a glimpse of the "vast networking of society" and imagine otherwise. This is folk theory. We need to know where we live in order to imagine living elsewhere. We need to imagine living elsewhere before we can live there.

Patricia Williams is a contract lawyer. Her great-great-grandmother was property. Her great-great-grandmother's owner and the father of her children was Austin Miller, a well-known Tennessee lawyer and jurist. In *The Alchemy of Race and Rights* where Williams works out this theory that life is complicated, what is she looking for?

> I track meticulously the dimension of meaning in my great-great-grandmother as chattel: the meaning of money, the power of a consumerist world view, the deaths of those we label the unassertive and the inefficient. I try to imagine where and who she would be today. I am engaged in a long-term project of tracking his [Austin Miller's] words—through his letters and opinions—and those of his sons, who were also lawyers and judges, of finding the shape described by her absence in all this.

> I see her shape and his hand in the vast networking of our society, and in the evils and oversights that plague our lives and laws. The control he had over her body. The force he was in her life, in the shape of my life today. The power he exercised in the choice to breed her or not. The choice to breed slaves in his image, to choose her mate and be that mate. In his attempt to own what no man can own, the habit of his power and the absence of her choice.
>
> I look for her shape and his hand.[2]

This is a massive project, very difficult and very fragile. In Williams's case, this is a project that requires listening to four-year-olds, rather than their inattentive parents, to understand "the semiotics of power relations, of dominance and submission, of assertion and deference, of big and little." Understanding the "semiotics of power relations" involves crashing through "norms that refuse to allow for difference," requires keeping subjugated subjectivities in view, requires paying attention to what people say they see. What are you looking for and where?

Second, justice and theory need each other because anti-intellectualism has almost always been a form of conservatism, with a particularly long and honored tradition in the United States, most ably described by Richard Hofstadter in his 1962 book, *Anti-Intellectualism in American Life*. Anti-intellectualism is never, as Hofstadter says, a "single proposition" or a "constant thread," but is a "force fluctuating in strength from time to time and drawing its power from varying sources." It is a "complex" whose form is never pure, but "ambivalent."[3] Indeed, not outright rejection but ambivalence towards expert, "book," or "cultured" knowledge is its most common form. There are many dimensions to anti-intellectualism and the dismissal of theory is one of them. And like many forms of anti-intellectualism, the dismissal of theory is often underwritten by a genuinely populist mistrust of elites, of the rule of elite knowledge, and of the often disembodied and inaccessible nature of intellectual work and theory in particular. In my view, there is certainly good evidence and a long historical warrant to question and challenge elite knowledge, its institutional authority, and its social and human consequences. However, populism becomes complicit with elitism itself when it cedes the very activity of theorizing, by abandoning it, to those very same elites. To replace elite with popular knowledge, and to replace the social order we have now with a better, more just one, we certainly need a richer, more precise and complex understanding of power and people. Giving over that task to those to whom it cannot be trusted is foolish and tragic.

Whatever its specific form, anti-intellectualism ultimately involves refusing to theorize. It involves refusing to reflect critically, refusing to see the operating general assumptions, either "limited domain assumptions" or "world-hypotheses," in both large-scale social organizations and in everyday actions, thoughts or inactions.[4] Theorizing can indeed involve rejecting that disembodied, abstract thought that is Theory with a capital T, *but only to take it over, to claim for theory some other ways of seeing and knowing*. It is the job of the activist scholar to encourage and effect such a rebellion and seizure of the power of knowledge. The heart may be leading the head, but both must be working together. Let me give you another example from Patricia Williams, one that demonstrates the ways in which refusing to engage in critical thinking, in theorizing, leads not just to conservatism as an ideology, but to the conservation of what Williams calls a sacrificial society.

> I am sitting in the library preparing a class on homelessness and the law. A student of mine, B, interrupts my writing. She is angry at me because she says my class is 'out of control.' She has been made to feel guilty, by the readings and the discussion, that her uncle is, as she describes him, 'a slumlord.' She says that the rich can't help who they are. I resent this interruption and snap at her. . . . I am very angry and it shows.

> [But] I think about B's uncle the slumlord and the tax I seem to have extorted in her life's bargain not to think about him with guilt. I wonder at the price her uncle must have charged to begin with, in the agreement not to think of him in unheroic terms. And if the consideration in such an exchange is more than just money and material gain—if the real transaction is not for 'salary' but for survival itself, for love and family and connection, then this becomes a contract of primal dimensions.
>
> If both rich and poor are giving up life itself and yet both are deeply dissatisfied, even suffering, they will never feel paid enough for their lot in life: what has gone on is not a trade or exchange, but a sacrifice.[5]

For my purposes here, these passages and the longer story they tell are important for three reasons. First, Williams locates anti-intellectualism where it usually resides: in those who have a vested and organized interest in not knowing. Second, she recognizes that the kind of thinking she is asking this obviously very capable student to do is very difficult. Third, Williams understands that the difficulty does not really lie in her demand that B think abstractly or conceptually about property, family, value, and equity by reading "hard" books. Rather, the difficulty lies in a prior agreement B's uncle has extracted, *without her even knowing it,* "not to think of him in unheroic terms." Here, the theoretical enterprise, as represented by the kinds of "unacceptable" and "inappropriate" questions and readings Williams is asking her law students to entertain, is what gives us insight into the "formulas" that structure a racialized and gendered class system and into the very nature of our experiential access to them. To the extent that anti-intellectualism is an "agreement not to think," it will always benefit those who can get away without it. However, as Williams suggests, that benefit is, even for the powerful, a terrible sacrifice that causes real pain and a damaging corollary: the confusion of powerlessness with powerfulness. B feels personally powerless as many of us do in a variety of settings. Because she is unwilling to think through the source of those feelings, she confuses a personal experience, which she no doubt describes honestly, with her obvious social power, her status, authority, privilege, and financial wealth. That compounds the confusion, it doesn't clarify it. B can get away without theory because in fact her very powerfulness requires it. The activist scholar—the Justice or Justice Studies scholar—is a person who can never get away without theory, ever, and whose obligation is to act precisely with knowledge of that confusion and towards a less sacrificial resolution of its forfeitures.

Finally, justice and theory are intertwined because disempowered people have a right to do theory, to do the kind of intellectual work that is often signaled by the word theory, and to do so for its own sake. The pursuit of knowledge not driven by functional aims or institutional prerogatives, even if these are for progressive social change and for justice, is particularly crucial in a capitalist society, which tries to reduce all values to exchange value. In and of itself, such a pursuit represents an important drag or brake (not a revolution or any such monumental outcome) on this reductive process of exchange. Real social change requires the gestation, production, and refinement of an imagination well beyond what is usual or socially acceptable, and that requires generous time and space. Most significantly, from my point of view, theoretical thinking and intellectual largesse are the activities most denied to those who are powerless. Denied because the powerless are not presumed to possess the "mind" that could produce generalizable imaginations for all of us; denied because the division between mental and manual labor takes all kinds of forms, including this one; denied because this privilege belongs to those to whom the institutions of higher learning belong. The denial, in itself, would be reason enough for me to agree that, at the very least, it is an act of historical reparation to invite some folks to spend a lot of time doing what is often considered "useless" intellectual work. Of course, you see I don't think it is useless, but its economy of use is different and not necessarily tied to immediate service work for others. One of the goals of the society I would rather live in consists in making available to all the pleasures (and the challenges and the range of other emotions and outcomes) of thinking, of learning, of reading aimlessly, of "wasting" your time by filling your head with "useless stuff," as it was always described to me as a kid. Why? Because knowledge in its own right, of all kinds, is a great gift of culture and something too long hoarded and manipulated and forcibly withheld from people. Giving it all away without having to earn it seems like a good idea to me. Mind you, I'm not saying that in our current society scholars or anybody else should turn a sanctioned blind eye to the implications or presumptions of their work or their thought. But I am suggesting that we can most certainly afford to redistribute the "luxury," if you think of it that way, of intellectual work. This is a particularly urgent issue as our schools are being readied for another onslaught of corporatization, in which too many educational problems are attributed to the failure of educators to produce citizens fine-tuned for the competitive and utilitarian corporate world.

I don't want to leave you with the impression that I think good theorizing of social life simply produces a will to justice or justice itself. However, perhaps this is an appropriate note to end on and to begin our discussions so that your experiences and concerns are part of the picture. Since I was asked to talk also about my own research and I'm going to read you an example of it later from the book I'm writing about haunting, let me just say this by way of conclusion. Basically, I'm a trained "professional" social theorist, even if I have defined the job in a somewhat unconventional way: as a grounded theorist, a participant observer of radical thought in action. In general, in my writing and teaching, I try to provide theoretical justification for critical and liberatory ideas and practices, which have been marginalized or ghosted. One of my goals is to expand what counts as radical social thought and to open the official archive to people and ideas excluded from it or included in utterly unacceptable ways. The human dimension—the ethical and emotional complexity and that which exceeds rational explanatory models and the visual empiricum—is what I tend to see and so what I try to write about. No doubt, this way of seeing what's there and what's not there is my strength and also my weakness as a thinker.

I encourage you to find your theoretical tools, mediums, and voices where and how you can. I found mine by starting with what was experientially accessible to me. I knew something was missing. I knew something was wrong. I knew I had lost something I never had. I was told, everything is out there for you. Nothing is missing. Little fundamental is wrong. I heard voices, I saw ghosts, and I followed them—in the name of Justice, for them, for me, and for you. You'll have to find your own tools and voices where and how you can. You need them for advanced work in Justice Studies. And if I may, I'd like to ask that you consider carefully before you give away the right to think or sign on to any binding agreements on this matter. Selfishly, I need you to help me do my work (and so do the others who are similarly engaged). And I'm hoping that you all, as representatives of Justice, will be in charge of those official archives one day, and that consequently I'll spend a little less time with ghosts.

1994

Glossary

4 conditions "unmet for punishment"—expressing a utilitarian view of punishment, Jeremy Bentham argues that there are cases were punishment for a criminal act would not be desirable. The conditions where the punishment would be considered not desirable: when punishment would be groundless, inefficacious, unprofitable, or needless.

Anarchy—a system that promotes the idea that humankind should have the individual liberty to act in accordance to their own will and absent of constraint.

Aristocracy—is a governance system that is ruled by the elite, privileged upper class and hereditary nobility.

Asymmetric Ignorance—idea that while non-Westerners must read the "great" Western histories in order to produce good histories, Western scholars are not expected to know the non-Western works.

Autonomy—independence of one's will and action. Used by Prakash to describe the impossibility, by definition, of the subaltern's autonomy.

Big "L" Law—an ideal that is based in the values, structure, process, procedures and purpose of a legal system; for example, the value of equality expressed within the U.S. ("Equal justice under the law").

Body politic—a group of people considered to be a collective unit, such as a nation, state, society or corporation.

Capitalism—a value or ideology which advocates the relative freedom of market forces from state control and/or regulation, which produces an economic system where business owners or operators contract for human labor by paying less then its full value in order to produce a "profit," which is then reinvested for greater business growth or development. Capitalists generally see market institutions and forces as more efficient than state-controlled enterprises.

Colonialism—a practice of domination, subjugation of one people to another.

Colorblind approach—an approach/ideology that favors the absence of race and race consciousness and is frequently associated with post-racialism. This approach is critiqued by Angela Harris, who argues that Catherine MacKinnon's theory takes the colorblind approach. Critics of this approach maintain that it fails to recognize multiple consciousness and race as an existing issue.

Commonwealth—a community that is founded and organized with the intent to uphold the common good.

Communism—an extreme form of Socialism which involves the attempted abolition of private property in favor of state ownership of the means of production, and state control of the economic and productive processes. Soviet Communism, Chinese Communism under Mao Zedong, and Cambodian Communism under Pol Pot are examples of attempts to create communist states.

Corporeal substance—is something that is tangible and material, such as having a body. This is the opposite of a spirit/soul.

Counter-hegemony—attempts to critique and/or dismantle hegemonic power and structure. Gramsci sets forth the notion of counter-hegemony as a revolutionary ideology created by intellectuals from the exploited class in order to overturn the standing capitalist order and replace it with democratic socialism. He argues that these ideologues have to create a counter-hegemonic vision through anti-ruling class institutions and lead the masses in staging a universal revolution through cultural subversion as opposed to violence (Boggs 1968, p.164).

Critical Legal Theory—Critical legal studies, the newest of these schools, began to develop in the 1970s (Fitzpatrick & Hunt, 1987, p.1). An early formative statement adopted by the Critical Legal Conference states: "The central focus of the critical legal approach is to explore the manner in which legal doctrine and legal education and the practices of legal institutions work to buttress and support a pervasive system of oppressive, inegalitarian relations" (as cited in Fitzpatrick & Hunt, 1987, p.1–2). The statement continues: "Critical theory works to develop radical alternatives, and to explore and debate the role of law in the creation of social, economic and political relations that will advance human emancipation" (as cited in Fitzpatrick & Hunt, 1987, p.2). This multi-faceted field is critical of traditional understandings of law. Scholars in this field argue that legal doctrines are hegemonic. They propose that legal doctrines reflect the ideas of the dominant, most powerful social groups, and so they rationalize and support existing inequality (see Murphy & Coleman, 1990, p.51–52).

Critical Theory (and **critical theory**)—are descriptive and normative theories that seek a practical purpose: to increase human freedom / emancipation and decrease oppression and domination.

Decolonized system of difference—to liberate, free and gain independence from a tyrannical power that systemically looks to oppress.

Deliberative model of democracy—is the idea that through deliberation, consensus building and equal representation (more than just voting) a more legitimate democracy will exist.

Democracy—is a governance system that emphasizes the "rule by the people" and citizenship, participation, and communication.

Desert—a justice concept related to the allocation of goods, including punishment, according to merit. An example of the theorist expressing this concept is Immanuel Kant.

Distributive justice—values or principles which advocate a just or fair distribution of the material (such as property or material resources) and non-material (prestige, status, respect) aspects of human labor. Capitalism and Socialism are theories of distributive justice.

Dominance Theory—a theory offered by Catherine MacKinnon; this theory documents how law is utilized as a mechanism to support gender norms in favor of male dominance and the subordination of women.

Egalitarian reciprocity—all members of the minority groups must have an equal political, economic, social, and civil right as the majority members.

Egalitarianism—the theory that commits to fairness in political relations, economic relations, social relations and civil rights by removing the inequities, which hinder action towards equality. This is the belief that all people are equal in their fundamental worth and moral state. Christian theology has used this philosophy to best describe the teachings of and example set by Jesus.

Feminism—a collection of intellectual and political movements that advocate for social, political and economic equality (broadly defined) for women. There have been several waves of feminism (1st, 2nd, 3rd, post) and many different kinds of feminists. Overall, feminism is motivated by the quest for social justice and provides a range of perspectives on social, cultural, economic, and political phenomena. Feminists have interrogated notions of the body, class, word, sexuality, globalization, the family, popular culture, race and racism, reproduction, disability, to name only a few.

Gender Ambiguous terms—the idea that theorists either try to use generic male terms of reference or attempt to use gender neutral language. For example, either always using Men, mankind, he, and his or attempting to be gender neutral by using individual, moral person or head of household. Okin argues that there is a blindness to sexism inherent in using these terms.

Habermas' ideal speech situation—the conditions for "Ideal speech situation" are that no individual who is capable of making a relevant contribution has been excluded; the included individuals have equal voice; the included individuals are free to speak their honest opinion (without any form of deception); and there are no sources of coercion.

Hegemony (and hegemony proper)—Hegemony is a means by which those with power in a society maintain dominance by normalizing and naturalizing their values, interests, and norms so that the majority of the people take these values, interests, and norms as their own. Hegemonic ideologies are expressed as commonsensical and utilized to judge others.

Heterogeneity—the existence of difference and differential relationships within a bounded category; diversity w/in "racial groups".

Historiograhy—the history of history. Instead of looking at specific historical events, historiography is the history of the history of the event (the way that history has been written, the conflicting objectives of those who have written about it over time, and the way this influences our understanding of the actual event).

Human nature—a concept that suggests all humans share general traits such as behavior, affect, and mental development.

Hybridity—multiraciality, which disrupts fixed notions about race and opens up new possibilities for dialogue and engagement across color lines.

Institution—structures or practices, their rules and norms, and their language and symbols that mediate social interactions within them (ex. family, state, workplace, education, the university, media, etc.).

Intersectionality—term coined by Kimberle Crenshaw to recognize that we all have various social identities (gender, race, class, ability, sexual orientation, religion, citizenship, etc.) that overlap and impact that impact how we understand ourselves and others. This concept deessentializes difference and rejects racial and gender essentialism.

Jurisprudence—the theory/philosophy of law; there are various schools of jurisprudence, including natural law theory, legal positivism, legal realism, critical legal theory, feminist legal theory, and critical race feminism.

legal positivism—Largely reacting to natural law theories, legal positivists believe that there is not necessarily a connection between morality and law. Law is a practical endeavor that varies over time and space. Legal positivists believe that law is a human construct. Both John Austin and H.L.A Hart were legal positivists. (see Murphy & Coleman, 1990, p.19)

Legal realism—Legal realists include Justice Oliver Wendall Holmes, who said "Law is a prediction of what the courts will decide." (as cited in Murphy & Coleman, 1990, p.34). Holmes critiqued legal positivism, arguing that law is not a system of rules that the judge mechanically applies and instead claimed that judges make law. The "rules" allow free play and, consequently, other factors (such as class, temperament, etc.) help determine judicial decisions. Legal realists believe that it is the real world practice of law that determines what law is. (see Murphy & Coleman, 1990, p.33)

Libertarianism—the theory that all individuals fully own themselves and have a moral right to their own individual liberty to act as they see fit without infringing on someone else's liberty and to acquire private property without coercion. Free-market capitalism and anarchist though tend to be associated to libertarianism.

little "l" law—specific rules that we have to restrict, regulate and/or promote behavior; for example, civil rights laws, criminal laws, and the like.

Locke's law of nature—is the idea that there are certain moral truths, applicable to all regardless of their place and experience in the world.

Marxism—a political position or ideology which has experienced great changes over the last 150 years. Karl Marx (1818–1883) advocated a form of socialism based on dialectical materialism, the labor theory of value, and the dictatorship of the proletariat, presumably to eventually achieve a society where there would be no social classes. There have always been great disputes among Marxists themselves, and in recent year elements of Marxist ideology have been incorporated into other (economic and non-economic) ideologies.

Mischief—in utilitarianism, as expressed by Jeremy Bentham, the least amount of mischief (unhappiness) is sought. In other words, mischief/unhappiness is seen as undesirable.

Multiplicity—the interaction patterns between and among a multiplicity of groups.

Multiple consciousness—concept expressed by Angela Harris that highlights the multiple voices, multiple selves—that sometimes conflict and are not fixed—people are composed of. This concept calls into question essentialism. In her piece, Harris highlights the multiple consciousness that Black women have.

Natural law theory—Natural law theories connect morality and law. Natural law is different than "man-made law." Existing outside any state structure or society, natural law is seen as natural to human-beings and thus consistent with human nature. Any law that is not consistent with human nature is not a true law; as St. Augustine famously said "an unjust law is no law at all" (as cited in Murphy & Coleman, 1990, p.11) This position should remind you of Lon Fuller's argument about the morality of law and of claims that human nature can be a test of a valid law. (see Murphy & Coleman, 1990, p.11)

Negritude—part of francophone, was literary movement, for example, "I am black and proud of it".

Neoliberalism—a contemporary ideology which advocates free markets and open economic markets, which includes advocating the transformation of former state-controlled markets to private markets (e.g., advocating the state-owned petroleum company of Mexcio, PEMEX, into a privately owned and controlled company). Neoliberalism generally advocates greater roles for private as opposed to state sectors of the economy.

Orientalism—Edward Said's (1978) idea that there is a "regularized (or Orientalized) writing, vision, and study, dominated by imperatives, perspectives, and ideological biases ostensibly suited to the Orient". It is the image of the Orient expressed as an entire system of thought and scholarship.

"Ought implies can"—This principle started with Immanuel Kant and is the idea that if we "ought" to morally do something, then we "can" or are able to do it.

Phantasm—this is a religious belief in abstract imagery, such as dreams, imagination and visions that are meant to inspire.

Political and civil society—offered by Gramsci; political society is a domain of force, domination, and coercive state; civil society is the domain of consent; referred to as "hegemony" proper; Power of ruling class exerted in political and civil society.

Post-racialism—color-blind viewpoint maintaining society is beyond race.

Post-structuralism, post-modernism—theories that seek to reveal how "scientific truths" are outcomes of contingent historical forces. They maintain that various aspects of social life – discourse, institutions, power relations, space and time, and the like – come together to impact the development of social knowledge. Michel Foucault has been associated with these theories.

Practical rationality—is the idea that through deliberation, rational choice and reasoning, one can act in a more appropriate way.

Privilege—a range of advantages people receive because of their skin color, or gender, or class, or citizenship status, etc. In addition to specific advantages enjoyed by the privileged, it is also the exemption from certain burdens and liabilities. For example, White Privilege is the advantages, immunity, rights attached to someone solely based on their being white.

Public Good—is a commodity or service that is collective consumed and benefits all.

Race—not a "scientific" concept rooted in discernibly biological difference, but rather socially constructed difference. Race is a dominant organizing principle of individual identity and collective consciousness.

Race Project—the active efforts to interpret, represent, explain, and (re)distribute resources along racial lines; these projects express meanings/theories of race.

Racial Formation—a sociohistorical process whereby racial categories are created, inhabited, transformed, and/or destroyed.

Racial Formation Theory—offered by Omi and Winant (1994), this theory maintains that race is socially constructed; discusses the processes that form and challenge ideas on race; and explains how ideas on race relate to individual, political, and state action.

Racialization—the process whereby meaning is given to racial categories.

Racialized Power—the racialized distribution of power. Shifts in what "race" means are indicative of reconfigurations in the nature of "racialized power" and emphasize the need to interrogate specific concepts of racism.

Racism—has relationship with power; social, political, and economic restructuring provide new contexts for race and racism. "Lawrence Blum (2002) examines both the concept of race and the problem of racism. He argues that "racism" be restricted to two referents: *inferiorization*, or the denigration of a group due to its putative biological inferiority; and *antipathy*, or the bigotry, hostility, and hatred towards another group defined by its putatively inherited physical traits (2002, p. 8)."

Republic—is a governance system in which the constitution is seen as an essential document organizing the collective will and rule of law.

Restorative justice—in Western criminal justice, a theory of justice that emphasizing repairing relations amongst victims, offenders, and community after a criminal act. The indigenous model of restorative justice not only highlights reparative measures, it also emphasizes preventative ones.

Retribution—a theory of justice that promotes punishment when it is considered morally right and fully deserved. This theory of punishment is associated with the concept of desert. An example of a retributivist theorist is Immanuel Kant.

Social Compact—this is an agreement accepted by individuals to abandon their sovereignty to a governing authority so that they may receive order through the set of rules, which govern them. The U.S. Constitution is a prime example of a social compact that we accept to live by and is applicable to all.

Social contract theory (Contractarianism)—the theory that maintain any political authority and/ or moral norms have derived legitimacy from social consent, mutual agreement. The United States Constitution is an example of this theory in practice.

Sovereign—an entity that is fully independent and is self-determined.

State of nature – is the hypothetical view of how humankind behaved, felt, and thought before being organized by a collective order.

Subaltern—draws from Gramsci and refers to the subordination in terms of class, caste, gender, race, language, and culture and is used to specific the centrality of dominant/dominated relationships in history.

Theocracy—is a governance system like communism, but emphasizes that "absolute" rule and regulation comes from God and those appointed to speak for God.

Utilitarianism—this theory upholds that just action is the one that produces the greatest utility, the "most good," the "greatest happiness." Utility (happiness) (+) is described as a desired good, while "mischief" (unhappiness) (−) is seen as undesirable. This theory invokes mathematical calculations attempting to determine the highest net happiness/utility by the consequences of an action on everyone's happiness. This theory maintains that moral actions should be determined by evaluation of the consequences and have been exemplified by the phrase the "Greatest amount of good for greatest number of people." Pres. Harry Truman would argue that dropping the atomic bomb on Hiroshima, Japan in 1945 was an example of utilitarianism.

Utility—in utilitarianism, as expressed by Jeremy Bentham, the greatest amount of utility (happiness) is sought. In other words, utility/happiness is seen as desirable. Utility is measured by examining the potential "happiness" (+) and unhappiness (i.e. "mischief") (−) created by an act.

Veil of Ignorance—a concept described by Rawls in *A Theory of Justice*. The Veil of Ignorance is the idea that those people making decisions about just societies are veiled in ignorance of what their social position will be in the world they are creating (i.e. they do not know their race, class standing, citizenship status, etc.) and therefore are more likely to create a more just environment because since no one knows what their social position will be, all think identically and the standpoint of any one party represents all parties.

Welfare State—a "mixed economy" which tries to combine free markets with some forms of state control or regulation of markets, usually to benefit vulnerable populations, such as children and he elderly. All Western democracies today are "mixed economies."

Young's communicative model of democracy—procedures for communicative exchanges in relationships wherein others are recognized and acknowledged on their own terms. Because power enters the form of speech, more marginalized groups often tend to be excluded and silenced. Communicative model of democracy involves speaking and listening across wide differences of social position, culture, and recognizing particularity.